Here are some basic map concepts tl
the most out of the maps in this textbook.

- Always look at the scale, which allows you to determine the distance in miles or kilometers between locations on the map.

- Examine the legend carefully. It explains the colors and symbols used on the map.

- Note the locations of mountains, rivers, oceans, and other geographic features, and consider how these would affect such human activities as agriculture, commerce, travel, and warfare.

- Read the map caption thoroughly. It provides important information, sometimes not covered in the text itself, and poses a thought question to encourage you to think beyond the mere appearance of the map and make connections across chapters, regions, and concepts.

- Several "spot maps" appear in each chapter, to allow you to view in detail smaller areas that may not be apparent in larger maps.

- Many of the text's maps also carry a globe icon alongside the title, which indicates that the map appears in interactive form on the text's website.

# www.wadsworth.com

*www.wadsworth.com* is the website for
Thomson Wadsworth and is your direct source
to dozens of online resources.

At *www.wadsworth.com* you can find out about
supplements, demonstration software, and
student resources. You can also send email to
many of our authors and preview new
publications and exciting new technologies.

**www.wadsworth.com**
Changing the way the world learns®

THE WORLD SINCE

# WORLD WAR II

## WILLIAM J. DUIKER
### THE PENNSYLVANIA STATE UNIVERSITY

Australia • Canada • Mexico • Singapore • Spain
United Kingdom • United States

## THOMSON
### WADSWORTH

*Publisher:* Clark Baxter
*Senior Development Editor:* Sue Gleason
*Assistant Editor:* Paul Massicotte
*Editorial Assistant:* Richard Yoder
*Senior Technology Project Manager:* Melinda Newfarmer
*Marketing Manager:* Caroline Croley and Lori Grebe Cook
*Marketing Assistant:* Mary Ho
*Advertising Project Manager:* Stacey Purviance and Brian Chaffee
*Project Manager, Editorial Production:* Kimberly Adams
*Print/Media Buyer:* Doreen Suruki

*Permissions Editor:* Joohee Lee
*Production Service:* Orr Book Services
*Text Designer:* Diane Beasley
*Photo Researcher:* Image Quest
*Copy Editor:* Bruce Emmer
*Illustrator:* Maps.com and G & S Typesetters
*Cover Designer:* Liz Harasymczuk
*Cover Image:* Hong Kong. ©David Bell/CORBIS.
*Printer:* R.R. Donnelley/Willard
*Compositor:* G & S Typesetters

For more information about our products, contact us at:
**Thomson Learning Academic Resource Center**
**1-800-423-0563**
For permission to use material from this text or product, submit a request online at http://www.thomsonrights.com.
Any additional questions about permissions can be submitted by email to thomsonrights@thomson.com.

Library of Congress Control Number: 2004106588
Student Edition: ISBN 0-534-62812-5

**Thomson Wadsworth**
**10 Davis Drive**
**Belmont, CA 94002-3098**
**USA**

**Asia**
Thomson Learning
5 Shenton Way #01-01
UIC Building
Singapore 068808

**Australia/New Zealand**
Thomson Learning
102 Dodds Street
Southbank, Victoria 3006
Australia

**Canada**
Nelson
1120 Birchmount Road
Toronto, Ontario M1K 5G4
Canada

**Europe/Middle East/Africa**
Thomson Learning
High Holborn House
50/51 Bedford Row
London WC1R 4LR
United Kingdom

**Latin America**
Thomson Learning
Seneca, 53
Colonia Polanco
11560 Mexico D.F.
Mexico

**Spain/Portugal**
Paraninfo
Calle Magallanes, 25
28015 Madrid, Spain

# ABOUT THE AUTHOR

WILLIAM J. DUIKER is liberal arts professor emeritus of East Asian studies at The Pennsylvania State University. A former U.S. diplomat with service in Taiwan, South Vietnam, and Washington, D.C., he received his doctorate in Far Eastern history from Georgetown University in 1968, where his dissertation dealt with the Chinese educator and reformer Cai Yuanpei. At Penn State, he has written extensively on the history of Vietnam and modern China, including the widely acclaimed *The Communist Road to Power in Vietnam* (revised edition, Westview Press, 1996), which was selected for a Choice Outstanding Academic Book Award in 1982–1983 and 1996–1997. Other recent books are *China and Vietnam: The Roots of Conflict* (Berkley, 1987), *Sacred War: Nationalism and Revolution in a Divided Vietnam* (McGraw-Hill, 1995), and *Ho Chi Minh* (Hyperion, 2000). While his research specialization is in the field of nationalism and Asian revolutions, his intellectual interests are considerably more diverse. He has traveled widely and has taught courses on the History of Communism and Non-Western Civilizations at Penn State, where he was awarded a Faculty Scholar Medal for Outstanding Achievement in the spring of 1996.

To Kirsten and Zachary,
as you face the challenges of the new century
W. J. D.

# BRIEF CONTENTS

# DETAILED CONTENTS

## *Prologue* THE OUTBREAK OF WORLD WAR II 1

## *Part* I ACROSS THE IDEOLOGICAL DIVIDE 25

# Part II THIRD WORLD RISING 123

# Part III BEGINNING A NEW MILLENNIUM 203

# Documents

# MAPS

# PREFACE

The twentieth century was an era of paradox. When it began, Western civilization was a patchwork of squabbling states that bestrode the world like a colossus. As the century came to an end, the West was prosperous and increasingly united, yet there were signs that despite the recent financial crisis in Asia, global economic and political hegemony were beginning to shift to the East. The era of Western dominance had come to an end. It had been an era marked by war and revolution but also by rapid industrial growth and widespread economic prosperity, a time of growing interdependence but also of burgeoning ethnic and national consciousness, a period that witnessed the rising power of science but also fervent religiosity and growing doubts about the impact of technology on the human experience.

*The World Since World War II* attempts to chronicle the key events in this revolutionary century since World War II, while seeking to throw light on some of the underlying issues that shaped the times. Did the beginning of a new millennium mark the end of the long period of Western dominance? If so, will recent decades of European and American superiority be followed by a "Pacific century" with economic and political power shifting to the nations of eastern Asia? Will the end of the Cold War lead to a "new world order" marked by global cooperation, or are we on the verge of an unstable era of ethnic and national conflict? Why was a time of unparalleled prosperity and technological advancement accompanied by deep pockets of poverty and widespread doubts about the role of government and the capabilities of human reason? Although this book does not promise final answers to such questions, it can provide a framework for analysis and a better understanding of some of the salient issues of modern times.

A number of decisions must be made by any author sufficiently foolhardy to seek to encompass a single volume history of the world since the Second World War. First in importance is whether to present the topic as an integrated whole or to focus on individual cultures and societies. The world that we live in today is in many respects an interdependent one in terms of economics as well as culture and communications, a reality that is often expressed by the familiar phrase "global village." At the same time, the process of globalization is by no means complete, as ethnic, religious, and regional differences continue to exist and to shape the course of our times. The tenacity of these differences is reflected not only in the rise of internecine conflicts in such divergent areas as Africa, South Asia, and Eastern Europe but also in the emergence in recent years of such regional organizations as the Organization of African Unity, the Association for the Southeast Asian Nations, and the European Economic Community. Political leaders in various parts of the world speak routinely (if sometimes wistfully) of "Arab unity," the "African road to socialism," and the "Confucian path to economic development."

A second problem is a practical one. College students today are all too often not well informed about the distinctive character of civilizations such as China, India, and sub-Saharan Africa. Without sufficient exposure to the historical evolution of such societies, students will assume all too readily that the peoples in these countries have had historical experiences similar to their own and respond to various stimuli in a similar fashion to those living in Western Europe or the United States. If it is a mistake to ignore the forces that link us together, it is equally erroneous to underestimate the factors that continue to divide us and to differentiate us into a world of diverse peoples.

My response to this challenge has been to adopt an overall global approach to the history of the twentieth century since World War II, while at the same time attempting to do justice to the distinctive character and recent development of individual civilizations and regions in the world. The Prologue focuses on the global impact of World War II. Subsequent chapters center on individual regions of the world, although one chapter is devoted to the international implications of the Cold War and its aftermath. The book is divided into three parts. The first two parts are each followed by a short section labeled "Reflection," which attempts to link events in a broad comparative and global framework. The chapter in the third and final part examines some of the common problems of our time—including environmental pollution, the population explosion, and spiritual malaise—and takes a cautious look into the future to explore how such issues will evolve in the twenty-first century.

Another issue that requires attention is the balance of the treatment of Western civilization and its counterparts in Asia and Africa. The modern world is often viewed essentially as the history of Europe and the Western Hemisphere, with other regions treated as appendages of the industrial countries. It is certainly true that much of the twentieth century was dominated by events in Europe and North America, and in recognition of this fact, the Prologue focuses primarily on issues related to the crisis in Europe. In recent decades, however, other parts of the world have assumed greater importance, thus restoring a global balance that had existed prior to the scientific and technological revolution that transformed the West in the eighteenth and nineteenth centuries. Later chapters examine this phenomenon, according to regions such as Africa, Asia, and Latin America the importance that they merit today.

This book seeks balance in another area as well. Many textbooks tend to simplify the content of history courses by emphasizing an intellectual or political perspective or, most recently, a social perspective, often at the expense of providing sufficient details in a chronological framework. This approach is confusing to students whose high school social studies programs have often neglected a systematic study of world history. I have attempted to write a well-balanced work in which political, economic, social, and cultural history have been integrated into a chronologically ordered synthesis. A strong narrative, linking key issues in a broad interpretive framework, is still the most effective way to present the story of the past to young minds.

To enliven the text, I have included a number of boxed essays that explore key issues within each chapter, citing important works in the field, and boxed primary source documents in each chapter. Extensive maps and illustrations, each positioned at the appropriate place in the chapter, serve to deepen the reader's understanding of the text. "Spot maps," which provide details not visible in the larger maps, have been added to this edition. Redesigned timelines appear at the ends of the chapters, comparing chronological developments in parallel regions of the world. An annotated bibliography at the end of the book reviews the most recent literature on each period while referring also to some of the older "classical" works in the field.

The following supplements are available for instructors' use:

- **Transparency Acetates for World History**—includes over one hundred full-color maps from the text and other sources.
- **Book Companion Web Site** (http://history.wadsworth. com/duiker_wwii/)—provides chapter-by-chapter resources for this textbook for both instructors and students, as well as access to the Wadsworth World His-

tory Resource Center. Text-specific content for students includes interactive maps, interactive timelines, tutorial quizzes, glossary, hyperlinks, InfoTrac® exercises, and Internet activities. Instructors also have access to the Instructor's Manual, lesson plans, and PowerPoint slides (access code required). From the home page, instructors and students can access many selections, such as an Internet Guide for History, a career center, simulations, movie activities, the World History image bank, and links to a wealth of primary-source documents.

I would like to express my appreciation to the reviewers who have read individual chapters and provided me with useful suggestions for improvement: George Esenwein, University of Florida; Richard Follett, Covenant College; James Harrison, Siena College; George Kosar, Bentley College/Tufts University; Arlene Lazarowitz, California State University—Long Beach; Steven Leibo, SUNY Albany; Constance McGovern, Frostburg State University; Marco Rimanelli, St. Leo University; Mark Rosenberg, Bentley College; Todd Shepard, Oklahoma University; and Dmitry Shlapentokh, Indiana University, South Bend. Jackson Spielvogel, who is coauthor of our textbook *World History* (now in its fourth edition), has been kind enough to permit me to use some of his sections in that book for the purposes of writing this one. Several of my other colleagues at Penn State—including Kumkum Chatterjee, On-cho Ng, and Arthur F. Goldschmidt —have provided me with valuable assistance in understanding parts of the world that are beyond my own area of concentration. To Clark Baxter, whose unfailing good humor, patience, and sage advice have so often eased the trauma of textbook publishing, I offer my heartfelt thanks. I am also grateful to Sue Gleason and Kim Adams of Wadsworth Publishing, and to Amy Guastello, for their assistance in bringing this project to fruition, and to John Orr of Orr Book Services for production. For this edition, ImageQuest has been helpful in obtaining images for the book.

Finally, I am eternally grateful to my wife, Yvonne V. Duiker, Ph.D. Her research and her written contributions on art, architecture, literature, and music have added sparkle to this book. Her presence at my side has added immeasurable sparkle to my life.

*William J. Duiker*
The Pennsylvania State University

# THE OUTBREAK OF WORLD WAR II

In September 1931, acting on the pretext that Chinese troops had attacked a Japanese railway near the northern Chinese city of Mukden, Japanese military units stationed in the area seized control throughout Manchuria. Although Japanese military authorities in Manchuria announced that China had provoked the action, the "Mukden incident," as it was called, had actually been carried out by Japanese saboteurs. Eventually, worldwide protests against the Japanese action led the League of Nations to send an investigative commission to Manchuria. When the commission issued a report condemning the seizure, Japan withdrew from the League. Over the next several years, the Japanese consolidated their hold on Manchuria, renaming it Manchukuo and placing it under the titular authority of former Chinese emperor and now Japanese puppet, Pu Yi.

Although no one knew it at the time, the Manchurian incident would later be singled out by some observers as the opening shot of World War II. The failure of the League of Nations to take decisive action sent a strong signal to Japan and other potentially aggressive states that they might seek their objectives without the risk of united opposition by the major world powers. Despite its agonizing efforts to build a system of peace and stability that would prevent future wars, the League had failed dismally, and the world was once again about to slide inexorably into a new global conflict.

# RETREAT FROM DEMOCRACY: THE RISE OF DICTATORIAL REGIMES

In Europe, the first clear step to war took place two years later. On February 3, 1933, only four days after he had been appointed chancellor of Germany, Adolf Hitler met secretly with Germany's leading generals. He revealed to them his desire to remove the "cancer of democracy," create a new authoritarian leadership, and forge a new domestic unity. His foreign policy objectives were equally striking. Since Germany's living space was too small for its people, Hitler said, Germany must rearm and prepare for "the conquest of new living space in the east and its ruthless Germanization." From the outset, Adolf Hitler had a clear vision of his goals, and their implementation meant another war.

There was thus a close relationship between the rise of dictatorial regimes in the 1930s and the coming of World War II. The apparent triumph of liberal democracy in 1919 proved extremely short-lived. By 1939, only two major states in Europe, France and Great Britain, remained democratic. Italy and Germany had installed fascist regimes, and the Soviet Union under Joseph Stalin was a repressive totalitarian state. A host of other European states, and Latin American countries as well, adopted authoritarian systems, while a militarist regime in Japan moved that country down the path to war.

Dictatorship was by no means a new phenomenon, but the modern totalitarian state was. The totalitarian regime extended the functions and powers of the central state far beyond what they had been in the past. If the immediate origins of totalitarianism can be found in the total warfare of World War I, when governments exercised controls over economic, political, and personal freedom to achieve victory, a more long-tem cause stemmed from the growth of the state as the primary focus of human action at a time when traditional sources of identity, such as religion and the local community, were in a state of decline. Under such conditions, as the philosopher Hannah Arendt noted in *The Origins of Totalitarianism* (1951), alienated intellectuals found fertile ground for their radical ideas among rootless peoples deprived of their communal instincts by the corrosive effects of the Industrial Age.

The modern totalitarian state transcended the ideal of passive obedience expected in a traditional dictatorship or authoritarian monarchy. It expected the active loyalty and commitment of its citizens to the regime and its goals and used modern mass propaganda techniques and high-speed communications to conquer citizens' minds and hearts. That control had a purpose: the active involvement of the masses in the achievement of the regime's goals, whether they be war, a classless utopia, or a thousand-year Reich.

The modern totalitarian state was to be led by a single leader and single party. It ruthlessly rejected the liberal ideal of limited government power and constitutional guarantees of individual freedoms. Indeed, individual freedom was to be subordinated to the collective will of the masses, organized and determined for them by a leader or leaders. Modern technology also gave totalitarian states the ability to use unprecedented police powers to impose their wishes on their subjects.

Totalitarianism is an abstract concept that transcended traditional political labels. Fascism in Italy and Nazism in Germany grew out of extreme rightist preoccupations with nationalism and, in the case of Germany, racism. Communism in the Soviet Union emerged out of Marxism and the concept of the dictatorship of the proletariat. Thus totalitarianism could and did exist in what were perceived as extreme right-wing and extreme left-wing regimes. This fact helped bring about a new concept of the political spectrum in which the extremes were no longer seen as opposites on a linear scale but came to be viewed as similar to each other in key respects.

## The Birth of Fascism

In the early 1920s, in the wake of economic turmoil, political disorder, and the general insecurity and fear stemming from World War I, Mussolini (1883–1945) burst upon the Italian scene with the first Fascist movement in Europe. Mussolini began his political career as a socialist but was expelled from the Socialist Party after supporting Italy's entry into World War I, a position contrary to the socialist principle of ardent neutrality in imperialist wars. In 1919, Mussolini established a new political group, the *Fascio di Combattimento*, or League of Combat. It received little attention in the parliamentary elections of 1919, but Italy's three major political parties were unable to form an effective governmental coalition. When socialists began to speak of the need for revolution, provoking worker strikes and a general climate of class violence, alarmed conservatives turned to the Fascists, who formed armed squads to attack socialist offices and newspapers. By 1922, Mussolini's nationalist rhetoric and ability to play to middle-class fears of radicalism, revolution, and disorder were attracting ever more adherents. On October 29, 1922, after Mussolini and the Fascists threatened to march on Rome if they were not given power, King Victor Emmanuel III (1900–1946) capitulated and made Mussolini prime minister of Italy.

By 1926, Mussolini had established the institutional framework for his Fascist dictatorship. Press laws gave the government the right to suspend any publication that fostered disrespect for the Catholic church, the monarchy, or the state. The prime minister was made "head of government" with the power to legislate by decree. A police law empowered the police to arrest and confine anybody for both nonpolitical and political crimes without due process of law. In 1926, all anti-Fascist parties were outlawed. By the end of 1926, Mussolini ruled Italy as *Il Duce*, the leader.

Mussolini left no doubt of his intentions. Fascism, he said, "is totalitarian, and the Fascist State, the synthesis and unity of all values, interprets, develops and gives strength to the whole life of the people."[1] His regime attempted to mold Italians into a single-minded community by developing Fascist organizations. By 1939, about two-thirds of the population between eight and eighteen had been enrolled in some kind of Fascist youth group. Activities for these groups included Saturday afternoon marching drills and calisthenics, seaside and mountain summer camps, and youth contests. Beginning in the 1930s, all young men were given some kind of premilitary exercises to develop discipline and provide training for war.

Mussolini hoped to create a new Italian: hardworking, physically fit, disciplined, intellectually sharp, and martially inclined. In practice, the Fascists largely reinforced traditional social attitudes, as is evident in their policies toward women. The Fascists portrayed the family as the pillar of the state and women as the foundation of the family. "Woman into the home" became the Fascist slogan. Women were to be homemakers and baby producers, "their natural and fundamental mission in life," according to Mussolini, who viewed population growth as an indicator of national strength. A practical consideration also underlay the Fascist attitude toward women: working women would compete with males for jobs in the depression economy of the 1930s. Eliminating women from the market reduced male unemployment.

## Hitler and Nazi Germany

As Mussolini began to lay the foundations of his fascist state in Italy, a young admirer was harboring similar dreams in Germany. Born on April 20, 1889, Adolf Hitler was the son of an Austrian customs official. He had done poorly in secondary school and eventually made his way to Vienna to become an artist. Through careful observation of the political scene, Hitler became an avid German nationalist who learned from his experience in mass politics in Austria how political parties could use propaganda and terror effectively. But it was only after World War I, during which he had served as a soldier on the Western Front, that Hitler became actively involved in politics. By then, he had become convinced that the cause of German defeat had been the Jews, for whom he now developed a fervent hatred.

Anti-Semitism, of course, was not new to European civilization. Since the Middle Ages, Jews had been portrayed as the murderers of Christ and were often subjected to mob violence and official persecution. Their rights were restricted, and they were physically separated from Christians in residential quarters known as ghettos. By the nineteenth century, as a result of the ideals of the Enlightenment and the French Revolution, Jews were increasingly granted legal equality in many European countries. Nevertheless, Jews were not completely accepted, and this ambivalence was apparent throughout Europe.

Nowhere in Europe were Jews more visible than in Germany and the German-speaking areas of Austria-Hungary. During the nineteenth century, many Jews in both countries had left the ghetto and become assimilated into the surrounding Christian population. Some entered what had previously been the closed world of politics and the professions. Many Jews became successful as bankers, lawyers, scientists, scholars, journalists, and stage performers. In 1880, for example, Jews made up 10 percent of the population of Vienna but accounted for 39 percent of its medical students and 23 percent of its law students.

All too often, such achievements provoked envy and distrust. During the last two decades of the century, conservatives in Germany and Austria founded right-wing parties that used dislike of Jews to win the votes of traditional lower-middle-class groups who felt threatened by changing times. Such parties also played on the rising sentiment of racism in German society. Spurred by social Darwinist ideas that nations, like the human species, were engaged in a brutal struggle for survival, rabid German nationalists promoted the concept of the *Volk* (nation, people, or race) as an underlying idea in German history since the medieval era. Portraying the German people as the successors of the pure "Aryan" race, the true and original creators of Western culture, nationalist groups called for Germany to take the lead in a desperate struggle to fight for European civilization and save it from the destructive assaults of such allegedly lower races as Jews, blacks, and Asians.

## HITLER'S RISE TO POWER, 1919-1933

At the end of World War I, Hitler joined the obscure German Workers' Party, one of a number of right-wing nationalist parties in Munich. By the summer of 1921, he had assumed total control over the party, which he renamed the National Socialist German Workers' Party (NSDAP), or Nazi for short. Hitler worked assiduously to develop the party into a mass political movement with flags, party badges, uniforms, its own newspaper, and its own police force or party militia known as the SA—the *Sturmabteilung,* or Storm Troops. The SA added an element of force and terror to the growing Nazi movement. Hitler's own oratorical skills were largely responsible for attracting an increasing number of followers.

In November 1923, Hitler staged an armed uprising against the government in Munich, but the so-called Beer Hall Putsch was quickly crushed, and Hitler was sentenced to prison. During his brief stay in jail, he wrote *Mein Kampf* (My Struggle), an autobiographical account of his movement and its underlying ideology. Virulent German nationalism, anti-Semitism, and anticommunism were linked together by a social Darwinian theory of struggle that stressed the right of superior nations to *Lebensraum* ("living space") through expansion and the right of superior individuals to secure authoritarian leadership over the masses.

After his release from prison, Hitler worked assiduously to reorganize the Nazi Party on a regional basis and expand it to all parts of Germany, growing in size from 27,000 members in 1925 to 178,000 by the end of 1929. Especially noticeable was the youthfulness of the regional, district, and branch leaders of the Nazi organization. Many young Germans were fiercely committed to Hitler because he gave them the promise of a new life.

By 1932, the Nazi Party had 800,000 members and had become the largest party in the Reichstag. No doubt, Germany's economic difficulties were a crucial factor in the Nazi rise to power. Unemployment rose dramatically, from 4.35 million in 1931 to 6 million by the winter of 1932. The economic and psychological impact of the Great Depression made extremist parties more attractive. But Hitler claimed to stand above politics and promised to create a new Germany free of class differences and party infighting. His appeal to national pride, national honor, and traditional militarism struck chords of emotion in his listeners.

Increasingly, the right-wing elites of Germany—the industrial magnates, landed aristocrats, military establishment, and higher bureaucrats—came to see Hitler as the man who had the mass support to establish a right-wing, authoritarian regime that would save Germany from a Communist takeover. Under pressure, President Paul von Hindenburg agreed to allow Hitler to become chancellor on January 30, 1933, and form a new government.

Within two months, Hitler had laid the foundations for the Nazis' complete control over Germany. On February 27, he convinced Hindenburg to issue a decree suspending all basic rights for the full duration of the emergency, thus enabling the Nazis to arrest and imprison anyone without redress. The crowning step in Hitler's "legal" seizure of power came on March 23, when the Reichstag passed the Enabling Act by a two-thirds vote. This legislation, which empowered the government to dispense with constitutional forms for four years while it issued laws that dealt with the country's problems, provided the legal basis for Hitler's subsequent acts. In effect, Hitler became a dictator appointed by the parliamentary body itself.

With their new source of power, the Nazis acted quickly to consolidate their control. The civil service was purged of Jews and democratic elements, concentration camps were established for opponents of the new regime, trade unions were dissolved, and all political parties except the Nazis were abolished. When Hindenburg died on August 2, 1934, the office of Reich president was abolished, and Hitler became sole ruler of Germany. Public officials and soldiers were all required to take a personal oath of loyalty to Hitler as the "Führer (leader) of the German Reich and people."

## THE NAZI STATE, 1933-1939

Having smashed the Weimar Republic, Hitler now turned to his larger objective, the creation of an Aryan racial state that would dominate Europe and possibly the world for generations to come. The Nazis pursued the vision of this totalitarian state in a variety of ways. Most dramatic were the mass demonstrations and spectacles employed to integrate the German nation into a collective fellowship and to mobilize it as an instrument for Hitler's policies. In the economic sphere, the Nazis pursued the use of public works projects and "pump-priming" grants to private construction firms to foster employment and end the depression. But there is little doubt that rearmament contributed far more to solving the unemployment problem. Unemployment, which had stood at 6 million in 1932, dropped to 2.6 million in 1934 and less than 500,000 in 1937. The regime claimed full credit for solving Germany's economic woes, although much of the success must be ascribed to decisions made at the initiative of local officials. Hitler himself had little interest in either economics or administration, and his prestige undoubtedly benefited enormously from spontaneous efforts undertaken throughout the country by his followers.

For its enemies, the Nazi totalitarian state had its instruments of terror and repression. Especially important was the SS (*Schutzstaffel*, or "protection echelon"). Originally created as Hitler's personal bodyguard, the SS, under the direction of Heinrich Himmler (1900–1945), came to control all of the regular and secret police forces. Himmler and the SS functioned on the basis of two principles, ideology and terror, and would eventually play a major role in the execution squads and death camps for the extermination of the Jews.

Other institutions, including the Catholic and Protestant churches, primary and secondary schools, and universities, were also brought under the control of the state. Nazi professional organizations and leagues were formed for civil servants, teachers, women, farmers, doctors, and lawyers, and youth organizations—the *Hitler Jugend* (Hitler Youth) and its female counterpart, the *Bund Deutscher Mädel* (League of German Maidens)—were given special attention.

The Nazi attitude toward women was largely determined by ideological considerations. Women played a crucial role in the Aryan racial state as bearers of the children who would ensure the triumph of the Aryan race. To the Nazis, the differences between men and women were quite natural. Men were warriors and political leaders, while women were destined to be wives and mothers. Certain professions, including university teaching, medicine, and law, were considered inappropriate for women, especially married women. Instead, the Nazis encouraged women to pursue professional occupations that had direct practical application, such as social work and nursing. In addition to restrictive legislation against females, the Nazi regime pushed its campaign against working women with such poster slogans as "Get hold of pots and pans and broom and you'll sooner find a groom!"

From the beginning, the Nazi Party reflected the strong anti-Semitic beliefs of Adolf Hitler. Many of the early attacks on Jews, however, were essentially spontaneous in character. The regime quickly took note, and in September 1935, the Nazis announced new racial laws at the annual party rally in Nuremberg. These Nuremberg laws excluded German Jews from German citizenship and forbade marriages and extramarital relations between Jews and German citizens. But a more violent phase of anti-Jewish activity was initiated on November 9–10, 1938, the infamous *Kristallnacht,* or night of shattered glass. The assassination of a German diplomat in Paris became the excuse for a Nazi-led destructive rampage against the Jews, in which synagogues were burned, seven thousand Jewish businesses were destroyed, and at least one hundred Jews were killed. Moreover, twenty thousand Jewish males were rounded up and sent to concentration camps. Jews were now barred from all public buildings and prohibited from owning, managing, or working in any retail store. Finally, under the direction of the SS, Jews were encouraged to "emigrate from Germany." After the outbreak of World War II, the policy of emigration was replaced by a more gruesome one.

## Authoritarian States in Europe

Nowhere had the map of Europe been more drastically altered by World War I than in eastern Europe. The new states of Austria, Poland, Czechoslovakia, and Yugoslavia adopted parliamentary systems, and the preexisting kingdoms of Romania and Bulgaria gained new parliamentary constitutions in 1920. Greece became a republic in 1924. Hungary's government was parliamentary in form but controlled by its landed aristocrats. Thus at the beginning of the 1920s, political democracy seemed well established. Yet almost everywhere in eastern Europe, parliamentary governments soon gave way to authoritarian regimes.

Several problems helped create this situation. Eastern European states had little tradition of liberalism or parliamentary politics and no substantial middle class to support them. Then, too, these states were largely rural and agrarian. Many of the peasants were largely illiterate, and much of the land was still dominated by large landowners who feared the growth of agrarian peasant parties with their schemes for land redistribution. Ethnic conflicts also threatened to tear these countries apart. Fearful of land reform, Communist agrarian upheaval, and ethnic conflict, powerful landowners, the churches, and even some members of the small middle class looked to authoritarian governments to maintain the old system. Only Czechoslovakia, with its substantial middle class, liberal tradition, and strong industrial base, maintained its political democracy.

In Spain, democracy also failed to survive. Fearful of the rising influence of left-wing elements in the government, Spanish military forces led by General Francisco Franco (1892–1995) launched a brutal and bloody civil war that lasted three years. Foreign intervention complicated the situation. Franco's forces were aided by arms, money, and men from Italy and Germany, while the government was assisted by forty thousand foreign volunteers and trucks, planes, tanks, and military advisers from the Soviet Union. After Franco's forces captured Madrid on March 28, 1939, the Spanish Civil War finally came to an end. General Franco soon established a dictatorship that favored large landowners, businessmen, and the Catholic clergy.

## The Soviet Union

During the mid-1920s, Soviet society gradually recovered from the enormous damage caused by the Great War. As he consolidated his power at the expense of rivals within the party, Joseph Stalin followed a centrist policy that avoided confrontation with his capitalist enemies abroad while encouraging capitalist forces at home under the careful guidance of the state. But Stalin—fearful that the rising influence of the small Russian bourgeoisie could undermine the foundations of party rule—had no intention of permitting the New Economic Policy to continue indefinitely. In the late 1920s, he used the issue to bring the power struggle to a head.

Stalin had previously joined with the moderate Bukharin and other members of the party to defend the NEP against Leon Trotsky, whose "left opposition" wanted a more rapid advance toward socialism. Then, in 1928, Stalin reversed course: he now claimed that the NEP had achieved its purpose and called for a rapid advance to socialist forms of ownership. Beginning in 1929, a series of new programs changed the face of Soviet society. Private capitalism in manufacturing and trade was virtually abolished, and party and state control over the economy was extended. The first of a series of five-year plans was launched to promote rapid "socialist industrialization," and in a massive effort to strengthen the state's hold over the agricultural economy, all private farmers were herded onto collective farms.

The bitter campaign to collectivize the countryside aroused the antagonism of many peasants and led to a decline in food production and in some areas to mass starvation. It also further divided the Communist Party and led to a massive purge of party members at all levels who opposed Stalin's effort to achieve rapid economic growth and the socialization of Russian society. A series of brutal purge trials eliminated thousands of "Old Bolsheviks" (people who had joined the party before the 1917 Revolution) and resulted in the conviction and death of many of Stalin's chief rivals. Trotsky, driven into exile, was dispatched by Stalin's assassin in 1940. Of the delegates who had attended the National Congress of the CPSU (Communist Party of the Soviet Union) in 1934, fully 70 percent had been executed by the time of the National Congress in 1939.

By the late 1930s, as the last of the great purge trials came to an end, the Russian Revolution had been in existence for more than two decades. It had achieved some successes. Stalin's policy of forced industrialization had led to rapid growth in the industrial sector, surpassing in

PICASSO'S *GUERNICA* (1937). In 1937, Picasso painted *Guernica*, his diatribe against the violence of war, inspired by the bombing of a Basque town during the Spanish Civil War. It screams with pain and suffering and stands as one of the most expressive paintings in Western art. *Guernica* was to be the last great painting portraying the horrors of war, soon to be followed by war photography. How could painting compete any longer with those black-and-white frozen images of Auschwitz, with the quiet mountains of discarded eyeglasses, false teeth, and shoes?

many respects what had been achieved in the capitalist years prior to World War I. Between 1918 and 1937, steel production increased from 4 to 18 million tons per year, and hard coal output went from 36 to 128 million tons. New industrial cities sprang up overnight in the Urals and Siberia. The Russian people in general were probably better clothed, better fed, and better educated than they had ever been before. The cost had been enormous, however. Millions had died by bullet or starvation. Thousands, perhaps millions, languished in Stalin's concentration camps. The remainder of the population lived in a society now officially described as socialist, under the watchful eye of a man who had risen almost to the rank of a deity, the great leader of the Soviet Union, Joseph Stalin.

The impact of Joseph Stalin on Soviet society in one decade had been enormous. If Lenin had brought the party to power and nursed it through the difficult years of the civil war, it was Stalin, above all, who had mapped out the path to economic modernization and socialist transformation. To many foreign critics of the regime, the Stalinist terror and autocracy were an inevitable consequence of the concept of the vanguard party and the centralized state built by Lenin. Others traced Stalinism back to Marx. It was he, after all, who had formulated the idea of the dictatorship of the proletariat, which now provided ideological justification for the Stalinist autocracy. Still others found the ultimate cause in the Russian political culture, which had been characterized by autocracy since the emergence of Russian society from Mongol control in the fifteenth century.

Was Stalinism an inevitable outcome of Marxist-Leninist doctrine and practice? Or as Mikhail Gorbachev later claimed, were Stalin's crimes "alien to the nature of socialism" and a departure from the course charted by Lenin before his death? Certainly, Lenin had not envisaged a party dominated by a figure who became even larger than the organization itself and who, in the 1930s, almost destroyed the party. On the other hand, recent evidence shows that Lenin was capable of the brutal suppression of perceived enemies of the revolution in a way that is reminiscent in manner, if not in scope, of that of his successor, Stalin.

It is clear from the decade of the 1920s that there were other models for development in Soviet society than that adopted by Stalin; the NEP program, so ardently supported by Bukharin, is testimony to that fact. But it is also true that the state created by Lenin provided the conditions for a single-minded leader like Stalin to rise to absolute power. The great danger that neither Marx nor Lenin had foreseen had come to pass: the party itself, the

vanguard organization leading the way into the utopian future, had become corrupted.

## The Rise of Militarism in Japan

The rise of militant forces in Japan resulted not from a seizure of power by a new political party but from the growing influence of such elements at the top of the political hierarchy. During the 1920s, a multiparty system based on democratic practices appeared to be emerging. Two relatively moderate political parties, the Minseito and the Seiyukai, dominated the Diet and took turns providing executive leadership in the cabinet. Radical elements existed at each end of the political spectrum, but neither militant nationalists nor violent revolutionaries appeared to present a threat to the stability of the system.

In fact, the political system was probably weaker than it seemed at the time. Both of the major parties were deeply dependent on campaign contributions from powerful corporations (the *zaibatsu*), and conservative forces connected to the military or the old landed aristocracy were still highly influential behind the scenes. As in the Weimar Republic in Germany during the same period, the actual power base of moderate political forces was weak, and politicians unwittingly undermined the fragility of the system by engaging in bitter attacks on each other.

The road to war in Asia began in 1928 when Zhang Xueliang, son and successor of the Japanese puppet Marshall Zhang Zuolin decided to integrate Manchuria into the Nanjing republic. Appeals from Tokyo to Washington for a U.S. effort to restrain Chiang Kai-shek were rebuffed.

Already suffering from the decline of its business interests on the mainland, after 1929 Japan began to feel the impact of the Great Depression when the United States and major European nations raised their tariff rates against Japanese imports in a desperate effort to protect local businesses and jobs. The value of Japanese exports dropped by 50 percent from 1929 to 1931, and wages dropped nearly as much. Hardest hit were the farmers as the price of rice and other staple food crops plummeted. At the same time, militant nationalists, outraged at Japan's loss of influence in Manchuria, began to argue that the Shidehara policy of peaceful cooperation with other nations in maintaining the existing international economic order had been a failure. It was undoubtedly that vision that had motivated the military coup d'état launched in Mukden in the early fall of 1931.

During the early 1930s, civilian cabinets managed to cope with the economic challenges presented by the

Great Depression. By abandoning the gold standard, Prime Minister Inukai Tsuyoshi was able to lower the price of Japanese goods on the world market, and exports climbed back to earlier levels. But the political parties were no longer able to stem the growing influence of militant nationalist elements. Despite its doubts about the wisdom of the Mukden incident, the cabinet was too divided to disavow it, and military officers in Manchuria increasingly acted on their own initiative.

In May 1932, Inukai Tsuyoshi was assassinated by right-wing extremists. He was succeeded by a moderate, Admiral Saito Makoto, but ultranationalist patriotic societies began to terrorize opponents, assassinating businessmen and public figures identified with the policy of conciliation toward the outside world. Some, like the publicist Kita Ikki, were convinced that the parliamentary system had been corrupted by materialism and Western values and should be replaced by a system that would return to traditional Japanese values and imperial authority. His message, "Asia for the Asians," had not won widespread support during the relatively prosperous 1920s but increased in popularity after the Great Depression, which convinced many Japanese that capitalism was unsuitable for Japan.

During the mid-1930s, the influence of the military and extreme nationalists over the government steadily increased. Minorities and left-wing elements were persecuted, and moderates were intimidated into silence. Terrorists tried for their part in assassination attempts portrayed themselves as selfless patriots and received light sentences. Japan continued to hold national elections, and moderate candidates continued to receive substantial popular support, but the cabinets were dominated by the military or advocates of Japanese expansionism. In February 1936, junior officers in the army led a coup in the capital city of Tokyo, briefly occupying the Diet building and other key government installations and assassinating several members of the cabinet. The ringleaders were quickly tried and convicted of treason, but under conditions that strengthened even further the influence of the military in the halls of power.

# THE PATH TO WAR

Only twenty years after the war to end war, the world plunged back into a new era of heightened international tension. The efforts at collective security in the 1920s — the League of Nations, the attempts at disarmament, the pacts and treaties — all proved ineffective in coping with the growth of Nazi Germany and the rise of Japan.

## The Path to War in Europe

When Hitler became chancellor on January 30, 1933, Germany's situation in Europe seemed weak. The Versailles Treaty had created a demilitarized zone on Germany's western border that would allow the French to move into the heavily industrialized parts of Germany in the event of war. To Germany's east, the smaller states, such as Poland and Czechoslovakia, had defensive treaties with France. The Versailles Treaty had also limited Germany's army to 100,000 troops with no air force and only a small navy.

Posing as a man of peace in his public speeches, Hitler emphasized that Germany wished only to revise the unfair provisions of Versailles by peaceful means and occupy Germany's rightful place among the European states. On March 9, 1935, he announced the creation of a new air force and, one week later, the introduction of a military draft that would expand Germany's army from 100,000 to 550,000 troops. France, Great Britain, and Italy condemned Germany's unilateral repudiation of the Versailles Treaty but took no concrete action.

On March 7, 1936, buoyed by his conviction that the Western democracies had no intention of using force to maintain the Treaty of Versailles, Hitler sent German troops into the demilitarized Rhineland. According to the Versailles Treaty, the French had the right to use force against any violation of the demilitarized Rhineland. But France would not act without British support, and the British viewed the occupation of German territory by German troops as reasonable action by a dissatisfied power. The London *Times* noted that the Germans were only "going into their own back garden."

Meanwhile, Hitler gained new allies. In October 1935, Benito Mussolini committed Fascist Italy to imperial expansion by invading Ethiopia. Angered by French and British opposition to his invasion, Mussolini welcomed Hitler's support and began to draw closer to the German dictator he had once called a buffoon. The joint intervention of Germany and Italy on behalf of General Francisco Franco in the Spanish Civil War in 1936 also drew the two nations closer together. In October 1936, Mussolini and Hitler concluded an agreement that recognized their common political and economic interests. One month later, Germany and Japan concluded the Anti-Comintern Pact and agreed to maintain a common front against communism.

### STALIN SEEKS A UNITED FRONT

From behind the walls of the Kremlin in Moscow, Joseph Stalin undoubtedly observed the effects of the Great Depression with a measure of satisfaction. During the early 1920s, once it became clear that the capitalist states in Europe had managed to survive without socialist revolutions, Stalin decided to improve relations with the outside world as a means of obtaining capital and technological assistance in promoting economic growth in the Soviet Union. But Lenin had predicted that after a brief period of stability in Europe, a new crisis brought on by overproduction and intense competition was likely to occur in the capitalist world. That, he added, would mark the beginning of the next wave of revolution. In the meantime, he declared, "We will give the capitalists the shovels with which to bury themselves."

To Stalin, the onset of the Great Depression was a signal that the next era of turbulence in the capitalist world was at hand, and during the early 1930s, Soviet foreign policy returned to the themes of class struggle and social revolution. When the influence of the Nazi Party reached significant proportions in the early 1930s, Stalin viewed it as a pathological form of capitalism and ordered the Communist Party in Germany not to support the fragile Weimar Republic. Hitler would quickly fall, he reasoned, leading to a Communist takeover.

By 1935, Stalin became uneasily aware that Hitler was not only securely in power in Berlin but also represented a serious threat to the Soviet Union. That summer, at a major meeting of the Communist International held in Moscow, Soviet officials announced a shift in policy. The Soviet Union would now seek to form a united front with capitalist democratic nations throughout the world against the common danger of Naziism and fascism. Communist parties in capitalist countries and in colonial areas were instructed to cooperate with "peace-loving democratic forces" in forming coalition governments called Popular Fronts.

In most capitalist countries, Stalin's move was greeted with suspicion, but in France, a coalition of leftist parties—Communists, Socialists, and Radicals—fearful that rightists intended to seize power, formed a Popular Front government in June 1936. The new government succeeded in launching a program for workers that some called the French New Deal. It included the right of collective bargaining, a forty-hour workweek, two-week paid vacations, and minimum wages. But such policies failed to solve the problems of the depression, and although it survived until 1938, the Front was for all intents and purposes dead before then. Moscow signed a defensive treaty with France and reached an agreement with three noncommunist states in eastern Europe (Czechoslovakia, Romania, and Yugoslavia), but talks with Great Britain achieved little result. The Soviet Union, rebuffed by London and disappointed by Paris,

feared that it might be forced to face the might of Hitler's *Wehrmacht* alone.

## DECISION AT MUNICH

By the end of 1936, the Treaty of Versailles had been virtually scrapped, and Germany had erased much of the stigma of defeat. Hitler, whose foreign policy successes had earned him much public acclaim, was convinced that neither the French nor the British would provide much opposition to his plans and decided in 1938 to move on Austria. By threatening Austria with invasion, Hitler coerced the Austrian chancellor into putting Austrian Nazis in charge of the government. The new government promptly invited German troops to enter Austria and assist in maintaining law and order. One day later, on March 13, 1938, Hitler formally annexed Austria to Germany.

The annexation of Austria, which had not raised objections in other European capitals, put Germany in position for Hitler's next objective—the destruction of Czechoslovakia. Although the latter was quite prepared to defend itself and was well supported by pacts with France and the Soviet Union, Hitler believed that its allies would not use force to defend it against a German attack.

He was right again. On September 15, 1938, Hitler demanded the cession to Germany of the Sudetenland (an area in western Czechoslovakia that was inhabited largely by ethnic Germans) and expressed his willingness to risk "world war" to achieve his objective. Instead of objecting, the British, French, Germans, and Italians—at a hastily arranged conference at Munich—reached an agreement that essentially met all of Hitler's demands. German troops were allowed to occupy the Sudetenland as the Czechs, abandoned by their Western allies, as well as by the Soviet Union, stood by helplessly. The Munich Conference was the high point of Western appeasement of Hitler. British Prime Minister Neville Chamberlain returned to England from Munich boasting that the agreement meant "peace in our time." Hitler had promised Chamberlain that he had made his last demand (see the box on p. 10).

In fact, Munich confirmed Hitler's perception that the Western democracies were weak and would not fight. Increasingly, he was convinced of his own infallibility and had by no means been satisfied at Munich. In March 1939, Hitler occupied the Czech lands (Bohemia and Moravia), and the Slovaks, with his encouragement, declared their independence of the Czechs and set up the German puppet state of Slovakia. On the evening of March 15, 1939, Hitler triumphantly declared in Prague

# THE MUNICH CONFERENCE

*At the Munich Conference, the leaders of France and Great Britain capitulated to Hitler's demands on Czechoslovakia. When the British Prime Minister, Neville Chamberlain, defended his actions at Munich as necessary for peace, another British statesman, Winston Churchill, characterized the settlement at Munich as "a disaster of the first magnitude." After World War II, political figures in Western Europe and the United States would cite the example of appeasement at Munich to encourage vigorous resistance to expansionism in the Soviet Union.*

## WINSTON CHURCHILL, SPEECH TO THE HOUSE OF COMMONS (OCTOBER 5, 1938)

I will begin by saying what everybody would like to ignore or forget but which must nevertheless be stated, namely, that we have sustained a total and unmitigated defeat, and that France has suffered even more than we have. . . . The utmost my right honorable Friend the Prime Minister . . . has been able to gain for Czechoslovakia and in the matters which were in dispute has been that the German dictator, instead of snatching his victuals from the table, has been content to have them served to him course by course. . . . And I will say this, that I believe the Czechs, left to themselves and told they were going to get no help from the Western Powers, would have been able to make better terms than they have got. . . .

We are in the presence of a disaster of the first magnitude which has befallen Great Britain and France. Do not let us blind ourselves to that. . . .

And do not suppose that this is the end. This is only the beginning of the reckoning. This is only the first sip, the first foretaste of a bitter cup which will be proffered to us year by year unless by a supreme recovery of moral health and martial vigor, we arise again and take our stand for freedom as in the olden time.

## NEVILLE CHAMBERLAIN, SPEECH TO THE HOUSE OF COMMONS (OCTOBER 6, 1938)

That is my answer to those who say that we should have told Germany weeks ago that, if her army crossed the border of Czechoslovakia, we should be at war with her. We had no treaty obligations and no legal obligations to Czechoslovakia. . . . When we were convinced, as we became convinced, that nothing any longer would keep the Sudetenland within the Czechoslovakian State, we urged the Czech Government as strongly as we could to agree to the cession of territory, and to agree promptly. . . . It was a hard decision for anyone who loved his country to take, but to accuse us of having by that advice betrayed the Czechoslovakian State is simply preposterous. What we did was save her from annihilation and give her a chance of new life as a new State, which involves the loss of territory and fortifications, but may perhaps enable her to enjoy in the future and develop a national existence under a neutrality and security comparable to that which we see in Switzerland today. Therefore, I think the Government deserves the approval of this House for their conduct of affairs in this recent crisis, which has saved Czechoslovakia from destruction and Europe from Armageddon.

Sources: *Parliamentary Debates, House of Commons* (London: His Majesty's Stationery Office, 1938), vol. 339, pp. 361–369; Neville Chamberlain, *In Search of Peace* (New York: Putnam, 1939), pp. 215, 217.

---

that he would be known as the greatest German of them all.

At last, the Western states reacted vigorously to the Nazi threat. Hitler's naked aggression had made it clear that his promises were utterly worthless. When he began to demand the return to Germany of Danzig (which had been made a free city by the Treaty of Versailles to serve as a seaport for Poland), Britain recognized the danger and offered to protect Poland in the event of war. Both France and Britain realized that they needed Soviet help to contain Nazi aggression and began political and military negotiations with Stalin. Their distrust of Soviet communism, however, made an alliance unlikely.

Meanwhile, Hitler pressed on in the belief that Britain and France would not go to war over Poland. To preclude an alliance between the western European states and the Soviet Union, which would create the danger of a two-front war, Hitler, ever the opportunist, approached Stalin, who had given up hope of any alliance with Britain and France. The announcement on August 23, 1939, of the Nazi-Soviet Nonaggression Pact shocked the world. The treaty with the Soviet Union gave Hitler the freedom he sought, and on September 1, German forces invaded Poland. Two days later, Britain and France declared war on Germany. Europe was again at war.

## The Path to War in Asia

In the years immediately following the Japanese seizure of Manchuria in the fall of 1931, Japanese military forces

# JAPAN'S JUSTIFICATION FOR EXPANSION

*dvocates of Japanese expansion in the 1920s and 1930s justified their proposals by claiming both economic necessity and moral imperatives. Note the familiar combination of motives, so often cited by advocates of colonial expansion, in the passage written by an extremist military leader in the late 1930s.*

## HASHIMOTO KINGORO, "THE NEED FOR EMIGRATION AND EXPANSION"

We have already said that there are only three ways left to Japan to escape from pressure of surplus population. We are like a great crowd of people packed into a small and narrow room, and there are only three doors through which we might escape, namely emigration, advance into world markets, and expansion of territory. The first door, emigration, has been barred to us by the anti-Japanese immigration policies of other countries. The second door, advance into world markets, is being pushed shut by tariff barriers and the abrogation of commercial treaties. What should Japan do when two of the three doors have been closed against her?

It is quite natural that Japan should rush upon the last remaining door.

It may sound dangerous when we speak of territorial expansion, but the territorial expansion of which we speak does not in any sense of the word involve the occupation of the possessions of other countries, the planting of the Japanese flag thereon, and the declaration of the annexation to Japan. It is just that since the Powers have suppressed the circulation of Japanese materials and merchandise abroad, we are looking for some place overseas where Japanese capital, Japanese skills and Japanese labor can have free play, free from the oppression of the white race.

We would be satisfied with just this much. What moral right do the world powers who have themselves closed to us the two doors of emigration and advance into world markets have to criticize Japan's attempt to rush out of the third and last door?

If they do not approve of this, they should open the door which they have closed against us and permit the free movement overseas of Japanese emigrants and merchandise. . . .

At the time of the Manchurian incident, the entire world joined in criticism of Japan. They said that Japan was an untrustworthy nation. The said that she had recklessly brought cannon and machine guns into Manchuria, which was the territory of another country, flown airplanes over it, and finally occupied it. But the military action taken by Japan was not in the least a selfish one. Moreover, we do not recall ever having taken so much as an inch of territory belonging to another nation. The result of this incident was the establishment of the splendid new nation of Manchuria. The Powers are still discussing whether or not to recognize this new nation, but regardless of whether or not other nations recognize her, the Manchurian empire has already been established, and now, seven years after its creation, the empire is further consolidating its foundations with the aid of its friend, Japan.

And if it is still protested that our actions in Manchuria were excessively violent, we may wish to ask the white race just which country it was that sent warships and troops to India, South Africa, and Australia and slaughtered innocent natives, bound their hands and feet with iron chains, lashed their backs with iron whips, proclaimed these territories as their own, and still continues to hold them to this very day.

Source: *Sources of Japanese Tradition* by William Theodore de Bary. Copyright © 1958 by Columbia University Press, New York. Reprinted with permission of the publisher.

began to expand gradually into North China. Using the tactics of military intimidation and diplomatic bullying rather than all-out attack, Japanese military authorities began to carve out a new "sphere of influence" south of the Great Wall.

Not all politicians in Tokyo agreed with this aggressive policy—the young Emperor Hirohito, who had succeeded to the throne in 1926, was himself nervous about possible international repercussions—but right-wing terrorists assassinated some of its key critics and intimidated others into silence. The United States refused to recognize the Japanese takeover of Manchuria, which Secretary of State Henry L. Stimson declared an act of "international outlawry," but was unwilling to threaten the use of force. Instead, the Americans attempted to appease Japan in the hope of encouraging moderate forces in Japanese society. As one senior U.S. diplomat with long experience in Asia warned in a memorandum to the president:

> Utter defeat of Japan would be no blessing to the Far East or to the world. It would merely create a new set of stresses, and substitute for Japan the USSR—as the successor to Imperial Russia—as a contestant (and at least an equally unscrupulous and dangerous one) for the mastery of the East. Nobody except perhaps Russia would gain from our victory in such a war.[2]

For the moment, the prime victim of Japanese aggression was China. Chiang Kai-shek attempted to avoid a confrontation with Japan so that he could deal with what he considered the greater threat from the Communists. When clashes between Chinese and Japanese troops broke out, he sought to appease the Japanese by granting them the authority to administer areas in North China. But as Japan moved steadily southward, popular protests in Chinese cities against Japanese aggression intensified. In December 1936, Chiang was briefly kidnapped by military forces commanded by General Zhang Xueliang, who compelled him to end his military efforts against the Communists in Yan'an and form a new united front against the Japanese. After Chinese and Japanese forces clashed at Marco Polo Bridge, south of Beijing, in July 1937, China refused to apologize, and hostilities spread.

Japan had not planned to declare war on China, but neither side would compromise, and the 1937 incident eventually turned into a major conflict. The Japanese advanced up the Yangtze valley and seized the Chinese capital of Nanjing, raping and killing thousands of innocent civilians in the process. But Chiang Kai-shek refused to capitulate and moved his government upriver to Hankou. When the Japanese seized that city, he moved on to Chongqing, in remote Sichuan Province. Japanese strategists had hoped to force Chiang to join a Japanese-dominated New Order in East Asia, comprising Japan, Manchuria, and China. Now they established a puppet regime in Nanjing that would cooperate with Japan in driving western influence out of East Asia. Tokyo hoped eventually to seize Soviet Siberia, rich in resources, and create a new "Monroe Doctrine for Asia" under which Japan would guide its Asian neighbors on the path to development and prosperity (see the box on p. 11). After all, who better to instruct Asian societies on modernization than the one Asian country that had already achieved it?

During the late 1930s, Japan began to cooperate with Nazi Germany on a plan to launch a joint attack on the Soviet Union and divide up its resources between them. But when Germany surprised Tokyo by signing a nonaggression pact with the Soviets in August 1939, Japanese strategists were compelled to reevaluate their long-term objectives. Japan was not strong enough to defeat the Soviet Union alone, as a small but bitter border war along the Siberian frontier near Manchukuo had amply demonstrated. So the Japanese began to shift their gaze southward to the vast resources of Southeast Asia—the oil of the Dutch East Indies, the rubber and tin of Malaya, and the rice of Burma and Indochina.

A move southward, of course, would risk war with the European colonial powers and the United States. Japan's attack on China in the summer of 1937 had already aroused strong criticism abroad, particularly from the United States, where President Franklin D. Roosevelt threatened to "quarantine" the aggressors after Japanese military units bombed an American naval ship operating in China. Public fear of involvement forced the president to draw back, but when Japan suddenly demanded the right to occupy airfields and exploit economic resources in French Indochina in the summer of 1940, the United States warned the Japanese that it would impose economic sanctions unless Japan withdrew from the area and returned to its borders of 1931.

Tokyo viewed the U.S. threat of retaliation as an obstacle to its long-term objectives. Japan badly needed liquid fuel and scrap iron from the United States. Should they be cut off, Japan would have to find them elsewhere. The Japanese were thus caught in a vise. To obtain guaranteed access to the natural resources that were necessary to fuel the Japanese military machine, Japan must risk being cut off from its current source of the raw materials that would be needed in case of a conflict. After much debate, the Japanese decided to launch a surprise attack on U.S. and European colonies in Southeast Asia in the hope of a quick victory that would evict the United States from the region.

## THE COURSE OF WORLD WAR II

Using *Blitzkrieg*, or "lightning war," Hitler stunned Europe with the speed and efficiency of the German attack. Panzer divisions (a panzer division was a strike force of about three hundred tanks and accompanying forces and supplies), supported by airplanes, broke quickly through Polish lines and encircled the bewildered Polish troops, whose courageous cavalry units were no match for the mechanized forces of their adversary. Conventional infantry units then moved in to hold the newly conquered territory. Within four weeks, Poland had surrendered. On September 28, 1939, Germany and the Soviet Union officially divided Poland between them.

### Europe at War

Although Hitler was apparently surprised when France and Britain declared war on September 3, he was confident of ultimate victory. After a winter of waiting (called the "phony war"), on April 9, 1940, Germany launched a *Blitzkrieg* against Denmark and Norway. One month later, the Germans attacked the Netherlands,

Belgium, and France. German panzer divisions broke through the weak French defensive positions in the Ardennes forest and raced across northern France, splitting the Allied armies and trapping French troops and the entire British army on the beaches of Dunkirk. Only by heroic efforts did the British succeed in a gigantic evacuation of 330,000 Allied (mostly British) troops. The French capitulated on June 22. German armies occupied about three-fifths of France while the French hero of World War I, Marshal Philippe Pétain (1856–1951), established a puppet regime (known as Vichy France) over the remainder. Germany was now in control of western and central Europe (see Map P.1). Britain had still not been defeated, but it was reeling, and the wartime cabinet under Prime Minister Winston Churchill debated whether to seek a negotiated peace settlement.

As Hitler realized, an amphibious invasion of Britain could succeed only if Germany gained control of the air. In early August 1940, the *Luftwaffe* (German air force) launched a major offensive against British air and naval bases, harbors, communication centers, and war industries. The British fought back doggedly, supported by an effective radar system that gave them early warning of German attacks. Nevertheless, the British air force suffered critical losses and was probably saved by Hitler's change in strategy. In September, in retaliation for a British attack on Berlin, Hitler ordered a shift from military targets to massive bombing of cities to break British morale. The British rebuilt their air strength quickly and were soon inflicting major losses on *Luftwaffe* bombers. By the end of September, Germany had lost the Battle of Britain, and the invasion of the British Isles had to be abandoned.

At this point, Hitler pursued a new strategy, which would involve the use of Italian troops to capture Egypt and the Suez Canal, thus closing the Mediterranean to British ships and thereby shutting off Britain's supply of oil. This strategy failed when the British routed the Ital-

⟫ DAY OF HUMILIATION. On June 23, 1940, France was forced to surrender after a brief six-week war with Nazi Germany. German Chancellor Adolf Hitler, shown in the middle of this photograph, attended the armistice ceremony, which took place in a railway car in the Compiègne Forest in northern France. Immediately to Hitler's left is Field Marshal Hermann Goering, chief of the German air force.

Courtesy of William J. Duiker

**MAP P.1** World War II in Europe and North Africa. With its fast and effective military, Germany quickly overwhelmed much of western Europe. However, Hitler overestimated his country's capabilities and underestimated those of his foes. By late 1942, his invasion of the Soviet Union was failing, and the United States had become a major factor in the war. The Allies successfully invaded Italy in 1943 and France in 1944. ➢ *Which countries were neutral, and how did geography help make their neutrality an option?*

World War II: Europe and Africa

- German-Italian Axis, 1939
- Axis satellites and allies, 1941
- Axis conquests, 1939–1942
- Allied Powers and areas under Allied control
- Neutral nations
- Axis offensives, 1939–1942
- Farthest Axis advance, 1941–1942
- Allied offensives, 1942–1945
- Soviet annexations, 1939–1940

ian army. Although Hitler then sent German troops to the North African theater of war, his primary concern lay elsewhere; he had already reached the decision to fulfill his long-time obsession with the acquisition of territory in the east. In *Mein Kampf*, Hitler had declared that future German expansion must lie in the east, in the vast plains of southern Russia.

Hitler was now convinced that Britain was remaining in the war only because it expected Soviet support. If the Soviet Union were smashed, Britain's last hope would be eliminated. Moreover, the German general staff was convinced that the Soviet Union, whose military leadership had been decimated by Stalin's purge trials, could be defeated quickly and decisively. The invasion of the Soviet

Union was scheduled for spring 1941 but was delayed because of problems in the Balkans. Mussolini's disastrous invasion of Greece in October 1940 exposed Italian forces to attack from British air bases in that country. To secure their Balkan flank, German troops seized both Yugoslavia and Greece in April 1941. Hitler had already obtained the political cooperation of Hungary, Bulgaria, and Romania. Now reassured, Hitler ordered an invasion of the Soviet Union on June 22, 1941, in the belief that the Soviets could still be decisively defeated before winter set in. It was a fateful miscalculation.

The massive attack stretched out along an 1,800-mile front. German troops, supported by powerful panzer units, advanced rapidly, capturing two million Russian soldiers. By November, one German army group had swept through Ukraine and a second was besieging Leningrad; a third approached within 25 miles of Moscow, the Russian capital. An early winter and unexpected Soviet resistance, however, brought a halt to the German advance. For the first time in the war, German armies had been stopped. A counterattack in December 1941 by Soviet army units newly supplied with U.S. weapons came as an ominous ending to the year for the Germans.

## Asia at War

On December 7, 1941, Japanese carrier-based aircraft attacked the U.S. naval base at Pearl Harbor in the Hawaiian Islands. The same day, other units launched assaults on the Philippines and began advancing toward the British colony of Malaya. Shortly thereafter, Japanese forces invaded the Dutch East Indies and occupied a number of islands in the Pacific Ocean. In some cases, as on the Bataan peninsula and the island of Corregidor in the Philippines, resistance was fierce, but by the spring of 1942, almost all of Southeast Asia and much of the western Pacific had fallen into Japanese hands. Japan formed the entire region into the Great East Asia Co-Prosperity Sphere and announced its intention to liberate Southeast Asia from Western rule. For the moment, however, Japan needed the resources of the region for its war machine and placed its conquests under its rule on a wartime footing.

Japanese leaders had hoped that their strike at American bases would destroy the U.S. Pacific Fleet and persuade the Roosevelt administration to accept Japanese domination of the Pacific. The American people, in the eyes of Japanese leaders, had been made soft by material indulgence. But the Japanese had miscalculated. The attack on Pearl Harbor galvanized American opinion and won broad support for Roosevelt's war policy. The United States now joined with European nations and Nationalist China in a combined effort to defeat Japan's plan to achieve hegemony in the Pacific. Believing that U.S. involvement in the Pacific would render its forces ineffective in the European theater, Hitler declared war on the United States four days after Pearl Harbor.

## The Turning Point of the War, 1942–1943

The entry of the United States into the war created a coalition, called the Grand Alliance, that ultimately defeated the Axis Powers (Germany, Italy, and Japan). Nevertheless, the three major Allies—Britain, the United States, and the Soviet Union—had to overcome mutual suspicions before they could operate as an effective alliance. In a bid to allay Stalin's suspicion of U.S. intentions, President Roosevelt declared that the defeat of Germany should be the first priority of the alliance. The United States, under its Lend-Lease program, also sent large amounts of military aid, including $50 billion worth of trucks, planes, and other arms, to the Soviet Union. In 1943, the Allies agreed to fight until the Axis Powers surrendered unconditionally. This had the effect of making it nearly impossible for Hitler to divide his foes. On the other hand, it likely discouraged dissident Germans and Japanese from overthrowing their governments to arrange a negotiated peace.

Victory, however, was only a vision for the distant future in the minds of Allied leaders at the beginning of 1942. As Japanese forces advanced into Southeast Asia and the Pacific after crippling the American naval fleet at Pearl Harbor, Axis forces continued the war in Europe against Britain and the Soviet Union. Reinforcements in North Africa enabled the Afrika Korps under General Erwin Rommel to break through the British defenses in Egypt and advance toward Alexandria. In the spring of 1942, a renewed German offensive in the Soviet Union led to the capture of the entire Crimea, causing Hitler to boast that in two years, German divisions would be on the Indian border. By that fall, however, the war had begun to turn against the Germans. In North Africa, British forces stopped Rommel's troops at El Alamein in the summer of 1942 and then forced them back across the desert. In November, U.S. forces landed in French North Africa and forced the German and Italian troops to surrender in May 1943. On the Eastern Front, the turning point of the war occurred at Stalingrad. After capturing the Crimea, Hitler's generals wanted him to concentrate on the Caucasus and its oil fields, but Hitler decided that Stalingrad, a major industrial center on the Volga, should be taken first. After three months of bitter fighting, German troops were stopped, then encircled, and finally

MAP P.2 World War II in Asia and the Pacific. In 1937, Japan invaded northern China, beginning its effort to create the "Great East Asia Co-Prosperity Sphere." Further expansion induced America to end iron and oil sales to Japan. Deciding that war with the United States was inevitable, Japan engineered a surprise attack on Pearl Harbor. ➢ *Why was control of the islands in the western Pacific of great importance both to the Japanese and to the Allies?*

forced to surrender on February 2, 1943. The entire German Sixth Army of 300,000 men was lost, but Soviet casualties were estimated at nearly one million, more than the United States lost in the entire war. By spring, long before Allied troops returned to the European continent, even Hitler knew that the Germans would not defeat the Soviet Union.

The tide of battle in the Pacific also turned dramatically in 1942 (see Map P.2). In the Battle of the Coral Sea in early May, U.S. naval forces stopped the Japanese advance and temporarily relieved Australia of the threat of invasion. On June 4, near Midway Island, American carrier planes destroyed all four of the attacking Japanese aircraft carriers and established U.S. naval superiority in the Pacific, even though almost all the American planes were shot down in the encounter. By the fall of 1942, Allied forces were beginning to gather for offensive operations into South China from Burma, through the Indonesian islands by a process of "island hopping" by troops commanded by U.S. General Douglas MacArthur, and across the Pacific with a combination of army, marine, and navy attacks on Japanese-held islands. After a series of bitter engagements in the waters off the Solomon Islands from August to November 1942, Japanese fortunes began to fade.

## The Last Years of the War

By the beginning of 1943, the tide of battle had begun to turn against the Axis. On July 10, the Allies crossed the Mediterranean and carried the war to Italy. After taking Sicily, Allied troops began the invasion of mainland Italy in September. Following the ouster and arrest of Benito Mussolini, a new Italian government offered to surrender to Allied forces. But the Germans, in a daring raid, liberated Mussolini and set him up as the head of a puppet German state in northern Italy while German troops occupied much of Italy. The new defensive lines established by the Germans in the hills south of Rome were so effective that the Allied advance up the Italian peninsula was slow and marked by heavy casualties. Rome finally fell on June 4, 1944. By that time, the Italian war had assumed a secondary role as the Allies opened their long-awaited second front in western Europe.

Since the autumn of 1943, under considerable pressure from Stalin, the Allies had been planning a cross-channel invasion of France from Britain. Under the direction of U.S. General Dwight D. Eisenhower (1890–1969), five assault divisions landed on the Normandy beaches on June 6, 1944, in history's greatest naval invasion. An initially indecisive German response enabled the Allied forces to establish a beachhead. Within three months, they had landed two million men and a half-million vehicles that pushed inland and broke through the German defensive lines.

After the breakout, Allied troops moved south and east, liberating Paris by the end of August. By March 1945, they had crossed the Rhine and advanced farther into Germany. In late April, they finally linked up with Soviet units at the Elbe River. The Soviets had come a long way since the Battle of Stalingrad in 1943. In the summer of 1943, Hitler gambled on taking the offensive by making use of newly developed "Tiger" tanks. At the Battle of Kursk (July 5–12), the greatest tank battle of World War II, the Soviets soundly defeated the German forces. Soviet forces now supplied with their own "T-34" heavy tanks, began a relentless advance westward. The Soviets reoccupied the Ukraine by the end of 1943, lifted the siege of Leningrad, and moved into the Baltic states by the beginning of 1944. Advancing along a northern front, Soviet troops occupied Warsaw in January 1945 and entered Berlin in April. Meanwhile, Soviet troops along a southern front swept through Hungary, Romania, and Bulgaria.

In January 1945, Hitler moved into a bunker 55 feet under Berlin to direct the final stages of the war. He committed suicide on April 30, two days after Mussolini was shot by partisan Italian forces. On May 7, German commanders surrendered. The war in Europe was over.

The war in Asia continued, although with a significant change in approach. Allied war planners had initially hoped to focus their main effort on an advance through China with the aid of Chinese Nationalist forces trained and equipped by the United States. But Roosevelt became disappointed with Chiang Kai-shek's failure to take the offensive against Japanese forces in China and eventually approved a new strategy to strike toward the Japanese home islands directly across the Pacific. This island-hopping approach took an increasing toll on enemy resources, especially at sea and in the air.

As Allied forces drew inexorably closer to the main Japanese islands in the summer of 1945, President Harry Truman, who had succeeded to the presidency on the death of Franklin Roosevelt in April, had an excruciatingly difficult decision to make. Should he use atomic weapons (at the time, only two bombs were available, and their effectiveness had not been demonstrated) to bring the war to an end without the necessity of an Allied invasion of the Japanese homeland? The invasion of the island of Okinawa in April had resulted in thousands of casualties on both sides, with many Japanese troops committing suicide rather than surrendering to enemy forces.

After an intensive debate, Truman approved use of America's new superweapon. The first bomb was dropped on the city of Hiroshima on August 6. Truman then called on Japan to surrender or expect a "rain of ruin from the air." When the Japanese did not respond, a second bomb was dropped on Nagasaki. Japan surrendered unconditionally on August 14. World War II, in which seventeen million combatants died in battle and perhaps eighteen million civilians perished as well (some estimate total losses at fifty million), was finally over.

## ⤫ THE NEW ORDER

What did the Germans and Japanese do with the opportunity to create a new order in Europe and Asia? Although both countries presented positive images of the new order for publicity purposes, in practice both followed policies of ruthless domination of their subject peoples.

## The New Order in Europe

After the German victories in Europe, Nazi propagandists created glowing images of a new European order based on the equality of all nations in an integrated economic community. The reality was rather different. Hitler saw the Europe he had conquered simply as subject to German domination. Only the Germans, he once said, "can really organize Europe."

The Nazi empire, which at its greatest extent stretched across continental Europe from the English Channel in the west to the outskirts of Moscow in the east, was organized in two different ways. Some areas, such as western Poland, were annexed and transformed into German provinces. Most of occupied Europe, however, was administered indirectly by German officials with the assistance of collaborationist regimes.

Racial considerations played an important role in how conquered peoples were treated. German civil administrations were established in Norway, Denmark, and the Netherlands because the Nazis considered their peoples to be Aryan, or racially akin to the Germans, and hence worthy of more lenient treatment. Latin peoples, such as the occupied French, were given military administrations. All the occupied territories were ruthlessly exploited for material goods and manpower for Germany's labor needs.

Because the conquered lands in the east contained the living space for German expansion and were populated in Nazi eyes by racially inferior Slavic peoples, Nazi administration there was considerably more ruthless. Heinrich Himmler, the leader of the SS, was put in charge of German resettlement plans in the region. His task was to replace the indigenous population with Germans, a policy first applied to the new German provinces created in western Poland. One million Poles were uprooted and dumped in southern Poland. Hundreds of thousands of ethnic Germans (descendants of Germans who had migrated years earlier from Germany to different parts of southern and eastern Europe) were encouraged to colonize designated areas in Poland. By 1942, two million ethnic Germans had been settled in Poland.

The invasion of the Soviet Union inflated Nazi visions of German colonization in the east. Hitler spoke to his intimate circle of a colossal project of social engineering after the war, in which Poles, Ukrainians, and Russians would become slave labor while German peasants settled on the abandoned lands and Germanized them. Nazis involved in this kind of planning were well aware of the human costs. Himmler told a gathering of SS officers that the destruction of thirty million Slavs was a prerequisite for German plans in the east. "Whether nations live in prosperity or starve to death interests me only insofar as we need them as slaves for our culture. Otherwise it is of no interest."[3]

Labor shortages in Germany led to a policy of ruthless mobilization of foreign labor. After the invasion of the Soviet Union, the four million Russian prisoners of war captured by the Germans, along with more than two million workers conscripted in France, became a major source of heavy labor. In 1942, a special office was created to recruit labor for German farms and industries. By the summer of 1944, seven million foreign workers were laboring in Germany, constituting 20 percent of Germany's labor force. At the same time, another seven million workers were supplying forced labor in their own countries on farms, in industries, and even in military camps. The brutal character of Germany's recruitment policies often led more and more people to resist the Nazi occupation forces.

## The Holocaust

No aspect of the Nazi new order was more tragic than the deliberate attempt to exterminate the Jewish people of Europe. By the beginning of 1939, Nazi policy focused on promoting the "emigration" of German Jews from Germany. Once the war began in September 1939, the so-called Jewish problem took on new dimensions. For a while, there was discussion of the Madagascar Plan—a mass shipment of Jews to the African island of Madagascar. When war contingencies made this plan impracticable, an even more drastic policy was conceived.

The SS was given responsibility for what the Nazis called the Final Solution to the Jewish problem—the annihilation of the Jewish people. Reinhard Heydrich (1904–1942), head of the SS's Security Service, was given administrative responsibility for the Final Solution. After the defeat of Poland, Heydrich ordered his special strike forces (*Einsatzgruppen*) to round up all Polish Jews and concentrate them in ghettos established in a number of Polish cities.

In June 1941, the *Einsatzgruppen* were given new responsibilities as mobile killing units. These death squads followed the regular army's advance into the Soviet Union. Their job was to round up Jews in the villages and execute and bury them in mass graves, often giant pits dug by the victims themselves before they were shot. Such constant killing produced morale problems among the SS executioners. During a visit to Minsk in the Soviet Union, Himmler tried to build morale by pointing out that

> he would not like it if Germans did such a thing gladly. But their conscience was in no way impaired, for they were sol-

diers who had to carry out every order unconditionally. He alone had responsibility before God and Hitler for everything that was happening, . . . and he was acting from a deep understanding of the necessity for this operation.[4]

Although it has been estimated that as many as one million Jews were killed by the *Einsatzgruppen*, this approach to solving the Jewish problem was soon perceived as inadequate. Instead, the Nazis opted for the systematic annihilation of the European Jewish population in specially built death camps. Jews from occupied countries would be rounded up, packed like cattle into freight trains, and shipped to Poland, where six extermination centers were built for this purpose. The largest and most famous was Auschwitz-Birkenau. Zyklon B (the commercial name for hydrogen cyanide) was selected as the most effective gas for quickly killing large numbers of people in gas chambers designed to look like shower rooms to facilitate the cooperation of the victims.

By the spring of 1942, the death camps were in operation. Although initial priority was given to the elimination of the ghettos in Poland, Jews were soon also being shipped from France, Belgium, and the Netherlands and eventually from Greece and Hungary. Despite desperate military needs, the Final Solution had priority in using railroad cars to transport Jews to the death camps.

About 30 percent of the arrivals at Auschwitz were sent to a labor camp, and the remainder went to the gas chambers. After they had been gassed, the bodies were burned in crematoria. The victims' goods and even their bodies were used for economic gain. Women's hair was cut off, collected, and turned into mattresses or cloth. Some inmates were also subjected to cruel and painful "medical" experiments. The Germans killed between five and six million Jews, more than three million of them in the death camps. Virtually 90 percent of the Jewish populations of Poland, the Baltic countries, and Germany were exterminated. Overall, the Holocaust was responsible for the death of nearly two of every three European Jews.

The Nazis were also responsible for the death by shooting, starvation, or overwork of at least another nine to ten million people. Because the Nazis considered the Gypsies (like the Jews) an alien race, they were systematically rounded up for extermination. About 40 percent of Europe's one million Gypsies were killed in the death camps. The leading elements of the Slavic peoples—the clergy, intelligentsia, civil leaders, judges, and lawyers—were also arrested and executed. Probably an additional four million Poles, Ukrainians, and Belorussians lost their lives as slave laborers for Nazi Germany, and at least three to four million Soviet prisoners of war were killed in captivity. The Nazis also singled out homosexuals for perse-cution, and thousands lost their lives in concentration camps.

## The New Order in Asia

Once the Japanese takeover was completed, Japanese policy in the occupied areas of Asia became essentially defensive as Japan hoped to use its new possessions to meet its burgeoning needs for raw materials, such as tin, oil, and rubber, as well as an outlet for Japanese manufactured goods. To provide an organizational structure for the new Great East Asia Co-Prosperity Sphere, a Ministry for Great East Asia, staffed by civilians, was established in Tokyo in October 1942 to handle relations between Japan and the conquered territories.

The Japanese conquest of Southeast Asia had been accomplished under the slogan "Asia for the Asiatics," and many Japanese sincerely believed that their government was bringing about the liberation of the Southeast Asian peoples from European colonial rule. Japanese officials in the occupied territories made contact with nationalist elements and promised that independent governments would be established under Japanese tutelage. Such governments were eventually set up in Burma, the Dutch East Indies, Vietnam, and the Philippines.

In fact, however, real power rested with the Japanese military authorities in each territory, and the local Japanese military command was directly subordinated to the Army General Staff in Tokyo. The economic resources of the colonies were exploited for the benefit of the Japanese war machine, while natives were recruited to serve in local military units or conscripted to work on public works projects. In some cases, the people living in the occupied areas were subjected to severe hardships. In Indochina, for example, forced requisitions of rice by the local Japanese authorities for shipment abroad created a food shortage that caused the starvation of more than a million Vietnamese in 1944 and 1945.

The Japanese planned to implant a new moral and social order as well as a new political and economic order in the occupied areas. Occupation policy stressed traditional values such as obedience, community spirit, filial piety, and discipline that reflected the prevailing political and cultural bias in Japan, while supposedly Western values such as materialism, liberalism, and individualism were strongly discouraged. To promote the creation of this new order, occupation authorities gave particular support to local religious organizations but discouraged the formation of formal political parties.

At first, many Southeast Asian nationalists took Japanese promises at face value and agreed to cooperate with their new masters. In Burma, an independent government was established in 1943 and subsequently declared war on the Allies. But as the exploitative nature of Japanese occupation policies became increasingly clear, sentiment turned against the new order. Japanese officials sometimes unwittingly provoked resentment by their arrogance and contempt for local customs. In the Dutch East Indies, for example, Indonesians were required to bow in the direction of Tokyo and recognize the divinity of the Japanese emperor, practices that were repugnant to Muslims. In Burma, Buddhist pagodas were sometimes used as military latrines.

Like German soldiers in occupied Europe, Japanese military forces often had little respect for the lives of their subject peoples. In their conquest of Nanjing, China, in 1937, Japanese soldiers had spent several days in killing, raping, and looting. Almost 800,000 Koreans were sent overseas, most of them as forced laborers, to Japan. Tens of thousands of Korean women were forced to be "comfort women" (prostitutes) for Japanese troops. In construction projects to help their war effort, the Japanese also made extensive use of labor forces composed of both prisoners of war and local peoples. In building the Burma-Thailand railway in 1943, for example, the Japanese used 61,000 Australian, British, and Dutch prisoners of war and almost 300,000 workers from Burma, Malaya, Thailand, and the Dutch East Indies. An inadequate diet and appalling work conditions in an unhealthy climate led to the death of 12,000 Allied prisoners of war and 90,000 native workers by the time the railway was completed.

Such Japanese behavior created a dilemma for many nationalists, who had no desire to see the return of the colonial powers. Some turned against the Japanese, and others lapsed into inactivity. Indonesian patriots tried to have it both ways, feigning support for Japan while attempting to sabotage the Japanese administration. In Indochina, Ho Chi Minh's Indochinese Communist Party established contacts with American military units in South China and agreed to provide information on Japanese troop movements and rescue downed American fliers in the area. In Malaya, where Japanese treatment of ethnic Chinese residents was especially harsh, many joined a guerrilla movement against the occupying forces. By the end of the war, little support remained in the region for the erstwhile "liberators."

## THE HOME FRONT: THREE EXAMPLES

World War II was even more of a global war than World War I. Fighting was much more widespread, economic mobilization was more extensive, and so was the mobilization of women. And the number of civilians killed was far higher: almost twenty million were killed by bombing raids, mass extermination policies, and attacks by invading armies.

The home fronts of the major belligerents varied with the local circumstances. World War II had an enormous impact on the Soviet Union. Two of every five persons killed in World War II were Soviet citizens. Leningrad experienced nine hundred days of siege, during which its inhabitants became so desperate for food that they ate dogs, cats, and mice. As the German army made its rapid advance into Soviet territory, the factories in the western part of the Soviet Union were dismantled and shipped to the interior—to the Urals, western Siberia, and the Volga region.

Soviet women played a major role in the war effort. Women and girls worked in industries, mines, and railroads. Overall, the number of women working in industry increased by almost 60 percent. Soviet women were also expected to dig antitank ditches and work as air-raid wardens. Finally, the Soviet Union was the only country to use women as combatants in World War II. Soviet women functioned as snipers and also as air crews in bomber squadrons. The female pilots who helped defeat the Germans at Stalingrad were known as the "Night Witches."

The home front in the United States was quite different from those of its chief wartime allies, largely because the United States faced no threat of war on its own territory. Although the economy and labor force were slow to mobilize, the United States eventually became the arsenal of the Allied Powers, producing the military equipment they needed. At the height of war production in 1943, the nation was constructing six ships a day and $6 billion worth of war-related goods a month. Much of this industrial labor was done by American women, who, despite some public opposition, willingly took jobs in factories to replace husbands and brothers who had gone off to war.

The mobilization of the U.S. economy caused social problems. The construction of new factories created boomtowns where thousands came to work but then faced shortages of housing, health facilities, and schools. More than one million African Americans migrated from the rural South to the industrial cities of the North and West, looking for jobs in industry. The presence of African Americans in areas where they had not been present before led to racial tensions and sometimes even race riots.

Japanese Americans were treated especially shabbily. On the West Coast, 110,000 Japanese Americans, 65 percent of them born in the United States, were removed to camps encircled by barbed wire and made to take loyalty oaths. Although public officials claimed that this policy was necessary for security reasons, no similar treatment of German Americans or Italian Americans ever took place. Eventually, President Roosevelt agreed to alleviate the situation for Japanese Americans, and by 1943, one-third of those interned had been released from the camps to work in factories or enter military service.

In Japan, society had been put on a wartime footing even before the attack on Pearl Harbor. A conscription law was passed in 1938, and economic resources were placed under strict government control. Two years later, all political parties were merged into the so-called Imperial Rule Assistance Association. Labor unions were dissolved, and education and culture were purged of all "corrupt" Western ideas in favor of traditional values emphasizing the divinity of the emperor and the higher spirituality of Japanese civilization. During the war, individual rights were severely curtailed as the entire population was harnessed to the needs of the war effort.

Japan was reluctant, however, to mobilize women on behalf of the war effort. General Hideki Tojo, prime minister from 1941 to 1944, opposed female employment, arguing that "the weakening of the family system would be the weakening of the nation. . . . We are able to do our duties only because we have wives and mothers at home."[5] Female employment increased during the war, but only in areas, such as the textile industry and farming, where women traditionally worked. Instead of using women to meet labor shortages, the Japanese government brought in Korean and Chinese laborers.

# AFTERMATH OF THE WAR

In November 1943, Stalin, Roosevelt, and Churchill, the leaders of the Grand Alliance, met at Tehran (the capital of Iran) to decide the future course of the war. Their major strategic decision involved approval for an American-British invasion of the Continent through France, which they scheduled for the spring of 1944. The acceptance of this plan had important consequences. It meant that Soviet and British-American forces would meet in defeated Germany along a north-south dividing line and that eastern Europe would most likely be liberated by Soviet forces. The Allies also agreed to a partition of postwar Germany until denazification could take place. Roosevelt privately assured Stalin that Soviet borders in Europe would be moved westward to compensate for the loss of territories belonging to the old Russian Empire after World War I. Poland would receive lands in eastern Germany to make up for territory lost in the east to the Soviet Union.

In February 1945, the three Allied leaders met once more at Yalta, on the Crimean peninsula of the Soviet Union. Since the defeat of Germany was a foregone conclusion, much of the attention focused on the war in the Pacific. Roosevelt sought Soviet military help against Japan. Development of the atomic bomb was not yet assured, and U.S. military planners feared the possibility of heavy casualties in amphibious assaults on the Japanese home islands. Roosevelt therefore agreed to Stalin's price for military assistance against Japan: possession of Sakhalin and the Kurile Islands, as well as two warm-water ports and railroad rights in Manchuria.

The creation of the United Nations was a major U.S. concern at Yalta. Roosevelt hoped to ensure the participation of the Big Three Powers in a postwar international organization before difficult issues divided them into hostile camps. After a number of compromises, both Churchill and Stalin accepted Roosevelt's plans for the United Nations organization and set the first meeting for San Francisco in April 1945.

The issues of Germany and eastern Europe were treated less decisively. The Big Three reaffirmed that Germany must surrender unconditionally and created four occupation zones. German reparations were set at $20 billion. A compromise was also worked out in regard to Poland. Stalin agreed to free elections in the future to determine a new government. But the issue of free elections in eastern Europe would ultimately cause a serious rift between the Soviets and the Americans. The Allied leaders agreed on an ambiguous statement that eastern European governments would be freely elected but were also supposed to be friendly to the Soviet Union. This attempt to reconcile the irreconcilable was doomed to failure.

Even before the next conference at Potsdam, Germany, took place in July 1945, Western relations with the Soviets had begun to deteriorate rapidly. The Grand Alliance had been one of necessity in which ideological incompatibility had been subordinated to the pragmatic concerns of the war. The Allied Powers' only common aim was the defeat of Nazism. Once this aim had been all but accomplished, the many differences that antagonized East-West relations came to the surface.

The Potsdam conference of July 1945, the last Allied conference of World War II, consequently began under a cloud of mistrust. Roosevelt had died on April 12 and had been succeeded as president by Harry Truman. During the conference, Truman received word that the atomic bomb had been successfully tested. Some historians have argued that this knowledge stiffened Truman's resolve against the Soviets. Whatever the reasons, there was a new coldness in the relations between the Soviets and

⤜ **THE VICTORIOUS ALLIED LEADERS AT YALTA.** Even before World War II ended, the leaders of the Big Three of the Grand Alliance— Churchill, Roosevelt, and Stalin (shown seated from left to right)—met in wartime conferences to plan the final assault on Germany and negotiate the outlines of the postwar settlement. At the Yalta meeting (February 5–11, 1945), the three leaders concentrated on postwar issues. The American president, visibly weary at Yalta, died two months later.

the Americans. At Potsdam, Truman demanded free elections throughout eastern Europe. Stalin responded: "A freely elected government in any of these East European countries would be anti-Soviet, and that we cannot allow."[6] After a bitterly fought and devastating war, Stalin sought absolute military security, which in his view could be ensured only by the presence of Communist states in eastern Europe. Free elections might result in governments hostile to the Soviet Union. By the middle of 1945, only an invasion by Western forces could undo developments in eastern Europe, and in the immediate aftermath of the world's most destructive conflict, few people favored such a policy. But the stage was set for a new confrontation, this time between the two major victors of World War II.

## CONCLUSION

World War II was the most devastating total war in human history. Germany, Italy, and Japan had been utterly defeated. Perhaps as many as forty million people—soldiers and civilians—had been killed in only six years. In Asia and Europe, cities had been reduced to rubble, and

millions of people faced starvation as once fertile lands stood neglected or wasted. Untold millions of people had become refugees.

What were the underlying causes of the war? One direct cause was the effort by two rising capitalist powers, Germany and Japan, to make up for their relatively late arrival on the scene to carve out their own global empires. Key elements in both countries had resented the agreements reached after the end of World War I that divided the world in a manner favorable to their rivals and hoped to overturn them at the earliest opportunity. Neither Germany nor Japan possessed a strong tradition of political pluralism; to the contrary, in both countries, the legacy of a feudal past marked by a strong military tradition still wielded strong influence over the political system and the mind-set of the entire population. It is no surprise that under the impact of the Great Depression, the effects of which were severe in both countries, fragile democratic institutions were soon overwhelmed by militant forces determined to enhance national wealth and power.

Unlike World War I, which has often been blamed on the entire system of balance of power politics, the consensus is that responsibility for World War II falls squarely on the shoulders of leaders in Berlin and Tokyo who were willfully determined to reverse the verdict of Versailles and divide the world between them. The bitterest controversy to come out of World War II was thus less how it began than how it ended. Truman's decision to approve the use of nuclear weapons to compel Japan to surrender has often been criticized, not only for causing thousands of civilian casualties but also for introducing a frightening new weapon that could threaten the future survival of the human race. Some analysts have even charged that Truman's real purpose in ordering the nuclear strikes was to intimidate the Soviet Union. Defenders of his decision argue that the human costs of invading the Japanese home islands would have been infinitely higher had the bombs not been dropped, and the Soviet Union would have had ample time to consolidate its control over Manchuria. More than half a century later, that debate has not yet come to an end.

Whatever the causes of World War II and its controversial conclusion, the consequences were soon to be evident. European hegemony over the world was at an end, and two new superpowers on the fringes of Western civilization had emerged to take its place. Even before the last battles had been fought, the United States and the Soviet Union had arrived at different visions of the postwar world. No sooner had the war ended than their differences gave rise to a new and potentially even more devastating conflict: the Cold War. Though Europeans seemed merely pawns in the struggle between the two superpowers, they managed to stage a remarkable recovery of their own civilization. In Asia, defeated Japan made a miraculous economic recovery, and the era of European domination finally came to an end.

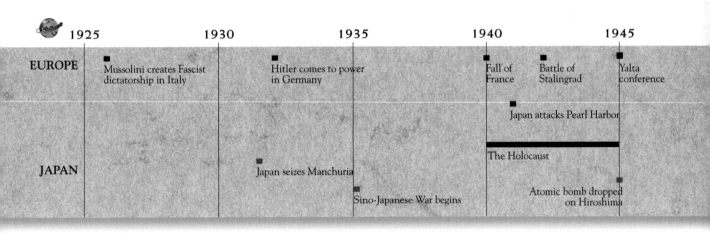

| | 1925 | 1930 | 1935 | 1940 | 1945 |
|---|---|---|---|---|---|
| EUROPE | ■ Mussolini creates Fascist dictatorship in Italy | | ■ Hitler comes to power in Germany | ■ Fall of France    ■ Battle of Stalingrad | ■ Yalta conference |
| | | | | ■ Japan attacks Pearl Harbor | |
| | | | | ▬▬▬▬▬▬▬ The Holocaust | |
| JAPAN | | | ■ Japan seizes Manchuria | | |
| | | | ■ Sino-Japanese War begins | | ■ Atomic bomb dropped on Hiroshima |

# INFOTRAC COLLEGE EDITION

Visit source collections at **http://infotrac.thomsonlearning.com**, and use the Search function with the following key terms:

Hitler or Nazi or Nazism
Holocaust
Totalitarianism
Weimar Republic
World War, 1939–1945

# WORLD HISTORY RESOURCES

Visit the *The World Since World War II* Companion Web site for resources specific to this textbook:

**http://history.wadsworth.com/duiker_wwii/**

The Wadsworth World History Resource Center at **http://history.wadsworth.com/world/** offers a variety of tools to help you succeed in this course, including access to quizzes; images; documents; interactive simulations, maps, and timelines; movie explorations; and a wealth of other sources.

# CHAPTER NOTES

1. Benito Mussolini, "The Doctrine of Fascism," in *Italian Fascisms from Pareto to Gentile,* ed. Adrian Lyttleton (London, 1973), p. 42.
2. John Van Antwerp MacMurray, quoted in Arthur Waldron, *How the Peace Was Lost: The 1935 Memorandum* (Stanford, Calif., 1992), p. 5.
3. International Military Tribunal, *Trial of the Major War Criminals* (Nuremberg, 1947–1949), vol. 22, p. 480.
4. Quoted in Raul Hilberg, *The Destruction of the European Jews,* rev. ed. (New York, 1985), vol. 1, pp. 332–333.
5. Quoted in John Campbell, *The Experience of World War II,* (New York, 1989), p. 143.
6. Quoted in Norman Graebner, *Cold War Diplomacy, 1945–1960* (Princeton, N.J., 1962), p. 117.

# ACROSS THE
# IDEOLOGICAL
# DIVIDE

AP/Wide World Photos

# IN THE GRIP OF THE COLD WAR: THE BREAKDOWN OF THE YALTA SYSTEM

*O*ur meeting here in the Crimea has reaffirmed our common determination to maintain and strengthen in the peace to come that unity of purpose and of action which has made victory possible and certain for the United Nations in this war. We believe that this is a sacred obligation which our Governments owe to our peoples and to all the peoples of the world.[1]

With these ringing words, drafted at the Yalta Conference in February 1945, President Franklin D. Roosevelt, Generalissimo Joseph Stalin, and Prime Minister Winston Churchill affirmed their common hope that the Grand Alliance, which had brought their countries to victory in World War II, could be sustained in the postwar era. Only through the continuing and growing cooperation and understanding among the three victorious allies, the statement asserted, could a secure and lasting peace be realized that, in the words of the Atlantic Charter, would "afford assurance that all the men in all the lands may live out their lives in freedom from fear and want."

Roosevelt hoped that the decisions reached at Yalta would provide the basis for a stable peace in the postwar era. Allied occupation forces—American, British, and French in the west and Soviet in the east—were to bring about the end of Axis administration and the holding of free elections to form democratic governments throughout Europe. To foster an attitude of mutual trust and an end to the suspicions that had marked relations between the capitalist world and the Soviet Union prior to World War II, Roosevelt tried to reassure Stalin that Moscow's legitimate territorial aspirations and genuine security needs would be adequately met in a durable peace settlement.

It was not to be. Within months after the German surrender, the attitude of mutual trust among the victorious allies—if it had ever existed—rapidly disintegrated, and the dream of a stable peace was replaced by the specter of a nuclear holocaust. As the Cold War conflict between Moscow and Washington intensified, Europe was divided into two armed camps, and the two superpowers, glaring at each other across a deep ideological divide, held the survival of the entire world in their hands. •

## THE COLLAPSE OF THE GRAND ALLIANCE

The problem started in Europe. At the end of the war, Soviet military forces occupied all of Eastern Europe and the Balkans (except for Greece, Albania, and Yugoslavia), while U.S. and other allied forces completed their occupation of the western part of the continent. Roosevelt had assumed that free elections administered by "democratic and peace-loving forces" would lead to the creation of democratic governments responsive to the aspirations of the local population. But it soon became clear that Moscow and Washington differed in their interpretations of the Yalta agreement. When Soviet occupation authorities turned their attention to forming a new Polish government in Warsaw, Stalin refused to accept the legitimacy of the Polish government in exile —headquartered in London during the war, it was composed primarily of representatives of the landed aristocracy who harbored a deep distrust of the Soviets—and instead installed a government composed of Communists who had spent the war in Moscow. Roosevelt complained to Stalin but was preoccupied with other problems and eventually agreed to a compromise solution whereby two members of the exile government in London were included in a new regime dominated by the Communists. A week later, Roosevelt was dead of a cerebral hemorrhage.

Similar developments took place elsewhere in Eastern Europe as all of the states occupied by Soviet troops became part of Moscow's sphere of influence. Coalitions of all political parties (except Fascist or right-wing parties) were formed to run the government, but within a year or two, the Communist parties in these coalitions had assumed the lion's share of power. The next step was the creation of one-party Communist governments. The timetables for these takeovers varied from country to country, but between 1945 and 1947, Communist governments became firmly entrenched in East Germany, Bulgaria, Romania, Poland, and Hungary. In Czechoslovakia, with its strong tradition of democratic institutions, the Communists did not achieve their goals until 1948. In the elections of 1946, the Communist Party became the largest party but was forced to share control of the government with non-Communist rivals. When it appeared that the latter might win new elections early in 1948, the Communists seized control of the government on February 25. All other parties were dissolved, and Communist leader Klement Gottwald became the new president of Czechoslovakia.

Yugoslavia was a notable exception to the pattern of growing Soviet dominance in Eastern Europe. The Communist Party there had led resistance to the Nazis during the war and easily took over power when the war ended. Josip Broz, known as Tito (1892–1980), the leader of the Communist resistance movement, appeared to be a loyal Stalinist. After the war, however, he moved toward the establishment of an independent Communist state in Yugoslavia. Stalin hoped to take control of Yugoslavia, just as he had done in other Eastern European countries. But Tito refused to capitulate to Stalin's demands and gained the support of the people (and some sympathy in the West) by portraying the struggle as one of Yugoslav national freedom. In 1958, the Yugoslav party congress asserted that Yugoslav Communists did not see themselves as deviating from communism, only from Stalinism. They considered their more decentralized economic and political system, in which workers could manage themselves and local communes could exercise some political power, closer to the Marxist-Leninist ideal.

To Stalin (who had once boasted, "I will shake my little finger, and there will be no more Tito"), the creation of pliant pro-Soviet regimes throughout Eastern Europe may simply have represented his interpretation of the Yalta peace agreement and a reward for sacrifices suffered during the war while satisfying Moscow's aspirations for a buffer zone against the capitalist West. Recent evidence suggests that Stalin did not decide to tighten communist control over the new Eastern European governments until U.S. actions—notably the promulgation of the Marshall Plan (see below)—threatened to undermine Soviet authority in the region. If the Soviet leader had any intention of promoting future Communist revolutions in Western Europe—and there is some indication that he did—in his mind such developments would have to await the appearance of a new capitalist crisis a decade or more into the future. As Stalin undoubtedly recalled, Lenin had always maintained that revolutions come in waves.

# THE TRUMAN DOCTRINE

*By 1947, the battle lines had been clearly drawn in the Cold War. This excerpt is taken from a speech by President Harry Truman to the U.S. Congress in which he justified his request for aid to Greece and Turkey. Truman expressed the urgent need to contain the expansion of communism. Truman presented the emerging dispute with Moscow in a melodramatic manner on the advice of subordinates, who argued that only by so doing would the American people turn their full attention to the problem. Future presidents would frequently rely on this tactic to promote their foreign policy initiatives.*

## TRUMAN'S SPEECH TO CONGRESS, MARCH 12, 1947

The peoples of a number of countries of the world have recently had totalitarian regimes forced upon them against their will. The Government of the United States has made frequent protests against coercion and intimidation, in violation of the Yalta agreement, in Poland, Romania, and Bulgaria. I must also state that in a number of other countries there have been similar developments.

At the present moment in world history nearly every nation must choose between alternative ways of life. The choice is too often not a free one.

One way of life is based upon the will of the majority, and is distinguished by free institutions, representative government, free elections, guarantees of individual liberty, freedom of speech and religion, and freedom from political oppression.

The second way of life is based upon the will of a minority forcibly imposed upon the majority. It relies upon terror and oppression, a controlled press and radio, fixed elections, and the suppression of personal freedoms.

I believe that it must be the policy of the United States to support free peoples who are resisting attempted subjugation by armed minorities or by outside pressures.

I believe that we must assist free people to work out their own destinies in their own way.

I believe that our help should be primarily through economic and financial aid, which is essential to economic stability and orderly political processes. . . . I therefore ask the Congress for assistance to Greece and Turkey in the amount of $400,000,000.

Source: U.S. Congress, *Congressional Record*, 80th Congress, 1st Session (Washington, D.C.: U.S. Government Printing Office, 1947), vol. 93, p. 1981.

## The Truman Doctrine and the Beginnings of Containment

In the United States, the Soviet takeover of Eastern Europe represented an ominous development that threatened Roosevelt's vision of a durable peace. Public suspicion of Soviet intentions grew rapidly, especially among the millions of Americans who still had relatives living in Eastern Europe. Winston Churchill was quick to put such fears into words. In a highly publicized speech given to an American audience at Westminster College in Fulton, Missouri, in March 1946, the former British prime minister declared that an "Iron Curtain" had "descended across the continent," dividing Germany and Europe itself into two hostile camps. Stalin responded by branding Churchill's speech a "call to war with the Soviet Union." But he need not have worried. Although public opinion in the United States placed increasing pressure on Washington to devise an effective strategy to counter Soviet advances abroad, the American people were in no mood for another war.

A civil war in Greece created another potential arena for confrontation between the superpowers and an opportunity for the Truman administration to take a stand. Communist guerrilla forces supported by Tito's Yugoslavia had taken up arms against the pro-Western government in Athens. Great Britain had initially assumed primary responsibility for promoting postwar reconstruction in the eastern Mediterranean, but in 1947, continued postwar economic problems caused the British to withdraw from the active role they had been playing in both Greece and Turkey. U.S. President Harry S Truman (1884–1972), alarmed by British weakness and the possibility of Soviet expansion into the eastern Mediterranean, responded with the Truman Doctrine (see the box above), which said in essence that the United States would provide money to countries that claimed they were threatened by Communist expansion. If the Soviets were not stopped in Greece, the Truman argument ran, then the United States would have to face the spread of communism throughout the free world. As Dean Acheson, the American secretary of state, explained, "Like apples in a barrel infected by disease, the corruption of Greece would infect Iran and all the East . . . likewise Africa . . . Italy . . . France. . . . Not since Rome and Carthage has there been such a polarization of power on this earth."[2]

The U.S. suspicion that Moscow was actively supporting the insurgent movement in Greece was inaccurate. Stalin was apparently unhappy with Tito's promoting of the conflict, not only because it suggested that the latter was attempting to create his own sphere of influence in the Balkans but also because it risked provoking a direct confrontation between the Soviet Union and the United States. The proclamation of the Truman Doctrine was soon followed in June 1947 by the European Recovery Program, better known as the Marshall Plan. Intended to rebuild prosperity and stability, this program included $13 billion for the economic recovery of war-torn Europe. Underlying the program was the belief that Communist aggression fed off economic turmoil. General George C. Marshall noted in a speech at Harvard, "Our policy is not directed against any country or doctrine but against hunger, poverty, desperation and chaos."[3]

From the Soviet perspective, the Marshall Plan was nothing less than capitalist imperialism, a thinly veiled attempt to buy the support of the smaller European countries, which in return would be expected to submit to economic exploitation by the United States. The White House indicated that the Marshall Plan was open to the Soviet Union and its Eastern European satellite states, but they refused to participate. The Soviets, however, were in no position to compete financially with the United States and could do little to counter the Marshall Plan except to tighten their control in Eastern Europe.

## Europe Divided

By 1947, the split in Europe between East and West had become a fact of life. At the end of World War II, the United States had favored a quick end to its commitments in Europe. But U.S. fears of Soviet aims caused the United States to play an increasingly important role in European affairs. In an article in *Foreign Affairs* in July 1947, George Kennan, a well-known U.S. diplomat with much knowledge of Soviet affairs, advocated a policy of containment against further aggressive Soviet moves. Kennan favored the "adroit and vigilant application of counter-force at a series of constantly shifting geographical and political points, corresponding to the shifts and maneuvers of Soviet policy." After the Soviet blockade of Berlin in 1948, containment of the Soviet Union became formal U.S. policy.

The fate of Germany had become a source of heated contention between East and West. Besides denazification and the partitioning of Germany (and Berlin) into four occupied zones, the Allied Powers had agreed on little with regard to the conquered nation. Even denazification proceeded differently in the various zones of occupation. The Americans and British proceeded methodically—the British had tried two million cases by 1948—while the Soviets went after major criminals and allowed lesser officials to go free. The Soviet Union, hardest hit by the war, took reparations from Germany in the form of booty. The technology-starved Soviets dismantled and removed to Russia 380 factories from the western zones of Berlin before transferring their control to the Western powers. By the summer of 1946, two hundred chemical, paper, and textile factories in the East German zone had likewise been shipped to the Soviet Union. At the same time, the German Communist Party was reestablished under the control of Walter Ulbricht (1893–1973) and was soon in charge of the political reconstruction of the Soviet zone in eastern Germany.

Although the foreign ministers of the four occupying powers (the United States, the Soviet Union, Great Britain, and France) kept meeting in an attempt to arrive at a final peace treaty with Germany, they grew further and further apart. At the same time, the British, French, and Americans gradually began to merge their zones economically and by February 1948 were making plans for unification of these sectors and the formation of a national government. The Soviet Union responded with a blockade of West Berlin that prevented all traffic from entering the city's three western zones through Soviet-controlled territory in East Germany. The Soviets hoped to force the Western powers to stop the creation of a separate West German state, which threatened Stalin's plan to create a reunified Germany that could eventually be placed under Soviet domination.

The Western powers faced a dilemma. Direct military confrontation seemed dangerous, and no one wished to risk World War III. Therefore, an attempt to break through the blockade with tanks and trucks was ruled out. The solution was the Berlin Airlift: supplies for the city's inhabitants were brought in by plane. At its peak, the airlift flew 13,000 tons of supplies daily into Berlin. The Soviets, also not wanting war, did not interfere and finally lifted the blockade in May 1949. The blockade of Berlin had severely increased tensions between the United States and the Soviet Union and confirmed the separation of Germany into two states. The Federal Republic of Germany (FRG) was formally created from the three Western zones in September 1949, and a month later, the separate German Democratic Republic (GDR) was established in East Germany. Berlin remained a divided city and the source of much contention between East and West.

The search for security in the new world of the Cold War also led to the formation of military alliances. The North Atlantic Treaty Organization (NATO) was formed in April 1949 when Belgium, Luxembourg, the Netherlands, France, Britain, Italy, Denmark, Norway, Portugal, and Iceland signed a treaty with the United States and Canada (see Map 1.1). All the powers agreed to provide mutual assistance if any one of them was attacked. A few years later, West Germany and Turkey joined NATO.

The Eastern European states soon followed suit. In 1949, they formed the Council for Mutual Economic Assistance (COMECON) for economic cooperation. Then, in 1955, Albania, Bulgaria, Czechoslovakia, East Germany, Hungary, Poland, Romania, and the Soviet Union organized a formal military alliance, the Warsaw Pact. Once again, Europe was tragically divided into hostile alliance systems.

By the end of the 1950s, then, the dream of a stable peace in Europe had been obliterated. There has been considerable historical debate over who bears the most responsibility for starting what would henceforth be called the Cold War. In the 1950s, most scholars in the West assumed that the bulk of the blame must fall on the shoulders of Joseph Stalin, whose determination to impose Soviet rule on the countries of Eastern Europe

➤ **A CITY DIVIDED.**   In 1948, U.S. planes airlifted supplies into Berlin to break the blockade that Soviet troops had imposed to isolate the city. Shown here is "Checkpoint Charlie," located at the boundary between the U.S. and Soviet zones of Berlin, just as Soviet roadblocks are about to be removed. The banner at the entry to the Soviet sector reads: "The sector of freedom greets the fighters for freedom and right of the Western sector."

| United States and NATO | Soviet Union and Warsaw Pact | |
|---|---|---|
| Missile bases: NATO | Missile bases: Warsaw Pact | NATO member |
| Troops: U.S. | Troops: Soviet | Non-NATO ally |
| Nuclear bombers: U.S. | Nuclear bombers: Soviet | NATO member until 1969 |
| Naval port: U.S. | Naval port: Soviet | Warsaw Pact member |
| Fleet: U.S. | Fleet: Soviet | Unrest or revolt in Eastern Europe |
| Nuclear missile submarine: U.S. | Nuclear missile submarine: Soviet | |

snuffed out hopes for freedom and self-determination there and aroused justifiable fears of Communist expansion in the Western democracies. During the next decade, however, a new school of revisionist historians—influenced in part by aggressive U.S. policies to prevent a Communist victory in Southeast Asia—began to argue that the fault lay primarily in Washington, where President Truman and his anti-Communist advisers aban-

doned the precepts of Yalta and sought to encircle the Soviet Union with a tier of pliant U.S. client states.

Both the United States and the Soviet Union took steps at the end of World War II that were unwise or might have been avoided. Both nations, however, were working within a framework conditioned by the past. Ultimately, the rivalry between the two superpowers stemmed from their different historical perspectives and their irreconcilable political ambitions. Intense competition for political and military supremacy had long been a regular feature of Western civilization. The United States and the Soviet Union were the heirs of that European tradition of power politics, and it should not come as a surprise that two such different systems would seek to extend their way of life to the rest of the world. Because of its need to feel secure on its western border, the Soviet Union was not prepared to give up the advantages it had gained in Eastern Europe from Germany's defeat. But neither were Western leaders prepared to accept without protest the establishment of a system of Soviet satellites that not only threatened the security of Western Europe but also deeply offended Western sensibilities because of its blatant disregard of the Western concept of human rights.

This does not necessarily mean that both sides bear equal responsibility for starting the Cold War. Some revisionist historians have claimed that the U.S. doctrine of containment was a provocative action that aroused Stalin's suspicions and drove Moscow into a position of hostility to the West. This charge lacks credibility. As information from the Soviet archives and other sources has become available, it is increasingly clear that Stalin's suspicions of the West were rooted in his Marxist-Leninist worldview and long predated Washington's enunciation of the doctrine of containment. As his foreign minister, Vyacheslav Molotov, once remarked, Soviet policy was inherently aggressive and would be triggered whenever the opportunity offered. Although Stalin apparently had no master plan to advance Soviet power into Western Europe, he was probably prepared to make every effort to do so once the next revolutionary wave appeared on the horizon. Western leaders were fully justified in reacting to this possibility by strengthening their own lines of defense. On the other hand, it has been argued—by no less than George Kennan himself—that in deciding to respond to the Soviet challenge in a primarily military manner, Western leaders overreacted to the situation and virtually guaranteed that the Cold War would be transformed into an arms race that could quite conceivably result in a new and uniquely destructive war.

# COLD WAR IN ASIA

The Cold War was somewhat slower to make its appearance in Asia. At Yalta, Stalin formally agreed to enter the Pacific war against Japan three months after the close of the conflict with Germany. As a reward for Soviet participation in the struggle against Japan, Roosevelt promised that Moscow would be granted "preeminent interests" in Manchuria (interests reminiscent of those possessed by imperial Russia prior to its defeat by Japan in 1904–1905) and the establishment of a Soviet naval base at Port Arthur. In return, Stalin promised to sign a treaty of alliance with the Republic of China, thus implicitly committing the Soviet Union not to provide the Chinese Communists with support in a possible future civil war. Although many observers would later question Stalin's sincerity in making such a commitment to the vocally anti-Communist Chiang Kai-shek, in Moscow the decision probably had a logic of its own. Stalin had no particular liking for the independent-minded Mao Zedong and did not anticipate a victory by the Chinese Communist Party (CCP) in the eventuality of a civil war in China. Only an agreement with Chiang Kai-shek could provide the Soviet Union with a strategically vital economic and political presence in North China.

Despite these commitments, Allied agreements soon broke down, and the region was sucked into the vortex of the Cold War by the end of the decade. The root of the problem lay in the underlying weakness of the Chiang Kai-shek regime, which threatened to create a political vacuum in East Asia that both Moscow and Washington would be tempted to fill.

## The Chinese Civil War

As World War II came to an end in the Pacific, relations between the government of Chiang Kai-shek in China and its powerful U.S. ally had become frayed. Although Roosevelt had hoped that republican China would be the keystone of his plan for peace and stability in Asia after the war, U.S. officials eventually became disillusioned with the corruption of Chiang's government and his unwillingness to risk his forces against the Japanese (he hoped to save them for use against the Communists after the war in the Pacific ended), and China became a backwater as the war came to a close. Nevertheless, U.S. military and economic aid to China had been substantial, and at war's end, the Truman administration still hoped that it could rely on Chiang to support U.S. postwar goals in the region.

While Chiang Kai-shek wrestled with Japanese aggression and problems of postwar reconstruction, the Communists were building up their liberated base in North China. An alliance with Chiang in December 1936 had relieved them from the threat of immediate attack from the south, although Chiang was chronically suspicious of the Communists and stationed troops near Xian to prevent them from infiltrating areas under his control.

He had good reason to fear for the future. During the war, the Communists patiently penetrated Japanese lines and built up their strength in North China. To enlarge their political base, they carried out a "mass line" policy (from the masses to the masses), reducing land rents and confiscating the lands of wealthy landlords. By the end of World War II, according to Communist estimates, twenty to thirty million Chinese were living under their administration, and their People's Liberation Army (PLA) included nearly one million troops.

As the war came to an end, world attention began to focus on the prospects for renewed civil strife in China. Members of a U.S. liaison team stationed in Yan'an during the last months of the war were impressed by the performance of the Communists, and some recommended that the United States should support them or at least remain neutral in a possible conflict between Communists and Nationalists for control of China. The Truman administration, though skeptical of Chiang's ability to forge a strong and prosperous country, was increasingly concerned over the spread of communism in Europe and tried to find a peaceful solution through the formation of a coalition government of all parties in China.

The effort failed. By 1946, full-scale war between the Nationalist government, now reinstalled in Nanjing, and the Communists resumed. The Communists, having taken advantage of the Soviet occupation of Manchuria in the last days of the war, occupied rural areas in the region and laid siege to Nationalist garrisons hastily established there. Now Chiang Kai-shek's errors came home to roost. In the countryside, millions of peasants, attracted to the Communists by promises of land and social justice, flocked to serve in the PLA. In the cities, middle-class Chinese, who were normally hostile to communism, were alienated by Chiang's brutal suppression of all dissent and his government's inability to slow the ruinous rate of inflation or solve the economic problems it caused. With morale dropping, Chiang's troops began to defect to the Communists. Sometimes whole divisions, officers as well as ordinary soldiers, changed sides. By 1948, the PLA was advancing south out of Manchuria and had encircled Beijing. Communist troops took the old imperial capital, crossed the Yangtze the following spring, and occupied the commercial hub of Shanghai. During the next few months, Chiang's government and two million of his followers fled to Taiwan, which the Japanese had returned to Chinese control after World War II.

The Truman administration reacted to the spread of Communist power in China with acute discomfort.

➤ CHIANG KAI-SHEK AND MAO ZEDONG EXCHANGE A TOAST. After World War II, the United States sent General George C. Marshall to China in an effort to prevent civil war between Chiang Kai-shek's government and the Communists. Marshall's initial success was symbolized by this toast between Chiang (on the right) and Mao. But suspicion ran too deep, and soon conflict ensued, leading to a Communist victory in 1949. Chiang Kai-shek's government retreated to the island of Taiwan.

© Jack Wilkes / TimeLife Pictures / Getty Images

# WHO LOST CHINA?

*In 1949, with China about to fall under the control of the Communists, President Harry S Truman instructed the State Department to prepare a white paper explaining why the U.S. policy of seeking to avoid a Communist victory in China had failed. The authors of the white paper concluded that responsibility lay at the door of Nationalist Chinese leader Chiang Kai-shek and that there was nothing the United States could have reasonably done to alter the result. Most China observers today would accept that assessment, but it did little at the time to deflect criticism of the administration for selling out the interests of the U.S. ally in China.*

## U.S. STATE DEPARTMENT WHITE PAPER ON CHINA, 1949

When peace came the United States was confronted with three possible alternatives in China: (1) it could have pulled out lock, stock, and barrel; (2) it could have intervened militarily on a major scale to assist the Nationalists to destroy the Communists; (3) it could, while assisting the Nationalists to assert their authority over as much of China as possible, endeavor to avoid a civil war by working for a compromise between the two sides.

The first alternative would, and I believe American public opinion at the time so felt, have represented an abandonment of our international responsibilities and of our traditional policy of friendship for China before we had made a determined effort to be of assistance. The second alternative policy, while it may look attractive theoretically, in retrospect, was wholly impracticable. The Nationalists had been unable to destroy the Communists during the ten years before the war. Now after the war the Nationalists were, as indicated above, weakened, demoralized, and unpopular. They had quickly dissipated their popular support and prestige in the areas liberated

from the Japanese by the conduct of their civil and military officials. The Communists on the other hand were much stronger than they had ever been and were in control of most of North China. Because of the ineffectiveness of the Nationalist forces, which was later to be tragically demonstrated, the Communists probably could have been dislodged only by American arms. It is obvious that the American people would not have sanctioned such a colossal commitment of our armies in 1945 or later. We therefore came to the third alternative policy whereunder we faced the facts of the situation and attempted to assist in working out a *modus vivendi* which would avert civil war but nevertheless preserve and even increase the influence of the National Government. . . .

The distrust of the leaders of both the Nationalist and Communist Parties for each other proved too deep-seated to permit final agreement, notwithstanding temporary truces and apparently promising negotiations. The Nationalists, furthermore, embarked in 1946 on an overambitious military campaign in the face of warnings by General Marshall that it not only would fail but would plunge China into economic chaos and eventually destroy the National Government. . . .

The unfortunate but inescapable fact is that the ominous result of the civil war in China was beyond the control of the government of the United States. Nothing that this country did or could have done within the reasonable limits of its capabilities could have changed that result; nothing that was left undone by this country has contributed to it. It was the product of internal Chinese forces, forces which this country tried to influence but could not. A decision was arrived at within China, if only a decision by default.

Source: *United States Relations with China* (Washington, D.C.: U.S. Department of State, 1949), pp. xv–xvi.

---

Washington had no desire to see a Communist government on the mainland, but it had little confidence in Chiang Kai-shek's ability to realize Roosevelt's dream of a strong, united, and prosperous China. In December 1946, President Truman's emissary, General George C. Marshall, sought and received permission from the White House to abandon his mission, arguing that neither side was cooperating in the effort. During the next two years, the United States gave limited military support to the Nanjing regime but refused to commit U.S. power to guarantee its survival. The administration's hands-off policy deeply angered many in Congress, who charged that the White House was "soft on communism" and declared

further that Roosevelt had betrayed Chiang at Yalta by granting privileges in Manchuria to the Soviets. In their view, Soviet troops had hindered the dispatch of Chiang's forces to the area and provided the PLA with weapons to use against their rivals.

In later years, evidence accumulated that the Soviet Union had given little assistance to the CCP in its struggle against the Nanjing regime. In fact, Stalin periodically advised Mao against undertaking the effort. Although Communist forces undoubtedly received some assistance from Soviet occupation troops in Manchuria, the underlying reasons for their victory stemmed from conditions inside China, not from the intervention of outside powers. So indeed argued the Truman administration, when in 1949 it issued a white paper that placed most of the blame for the debacle at the feet of the Chiang Kai-shek regime (see the box on p. 34).

Many Americans, however, did not agree. The Communist victory on the mainland of China injected Asia directly into American politics as an integral element of the Cold War. During the spring of 1950, under pressure from Congress and public opinion to define U.S. interests in Asia, the Truman administration adopted a new national security policy that implied that the United States would take whatever steps were necessary to stem the further expansion of communism in the region.

## The Korean War

Communist leaders in China, from their new capital at Beijing, hoped that their accession to power in 1949 would bring about an era of peace in the region and permit their new government to concentrate on domestic goals. But the desire for peace was tempered by their determination to erase a century of humiliation at the hands of imperialist powers and to restore the traditional outer frontiers of the empire. In addition to recovering territories that had been part of the Manchu Empire, such as Manchuria, Taiwan, and Tibet, the Chinese leaders also hoped to restore Chinese influence in former tributary areas such as Korea and Vietnam.

It soon became clear that these two goals were not always compatible. Negotiations with Moscow led to Soviet recognition of Chinese sovereignty over Manchuria and Xinjiang (the desolate lands north of Tibet that were known as Chinese Turkestan because many of the peoples in the area were of Turkish origin), although the Soviets retained a measure of economic influence in both areas. Chinese troops occupied Tibet in 1950 and brought it under Chinese administration for the first time in more than a century. But in Korea and Taiwan, China's efforts to re-create the imperial buffer zone threatened to provoke new conflicts with foreign powers.

The problem of Taiwan was a consequence of the Cold War. As the civil war in China came to an end, the Truman administration appeared determined to avoid entanglement in China's internal affairs and indicated that it would not seek to prevent a Communist takeover of the island, now occupied by Chiang Kai-shek's Republic of

China. But as tensions between the United States and the new Chinese government escalated during the winter of 1949–1950, influential figures in the United States began to argue that Taiwan was crucial to U.S. defense strategy in the Pacific.

The outbreak of war in Korea also helped bring the Cold War to East Asia. Korea, long a Chinese tributary, was annexed into the Japanese Empire in 1908 and remained there until 1945. The removal of Korea from Japanese control had been one of the stated objectives of the Allies in World War II, and on the eve of Japanese surrender in August 1945, the Soviet Union and the United States agreed to divide the country into two separate occupation zones at the 38th parallel. They originally planned to hold national elections after the restoration of peace to reunify Korea under an independent government. But as U.S.-Soviet relations deteriorated, two separate governments emerged in Korea, Communist in the north and anti-Communist in the south.

Tensions between the two governments ran high along the dividing line, and on June 25, 1950, with the apparent approval of Joseph Stalin, North Korean troops invaded the south. The Truman administration immediately ordered U.S. naval and air forces to support South Korea, and the United Nations Security Council (with the Soviet delegate absent to protest the failure of the UN to assign China's seat to the new government in Beijing) passed a resolution calling on member nations to jointly resist the invasion. By September, UN forces under the command of U.S. General Douglas MacArthur marched northward across the 38th parallel with the aim of unifying Korea under a single non-Communist government.

President Truman worried that by approaching the Chinese border at the Yalu River, the UN troops could trigger Chinese intervention but was assured by MacArthur that China would not respond. In November, however, Chinese "volunteer" forces intervened on the side of North Korea and drove the UN troops southward in disarray. A static defense line was eventually established near the original dividing line at the 38th parallel, although the war continued.

To many Americans, the Chinese intervention in Korea was clear evidence that China intended to promote communism throughout Asia, and recent evidence does suggest that Mao Zedong, convinced that a revolutionary wave was on the rise in Asia, argued to his colleagues that they should not fear a confrontation with the United States on the Korean peninsula. In fact, however, China's decision to enter the war was probably motivated in large part by the fear that hostile U.S. forces might be stationed on the Chinese frontier and perhaps even launch an attack across the border. MacArthur intensified such fears by calling publicly for air attacks on Manchurian cities in preparation for an attack on Communist China. In any case, the outbreak of the Korean War was particularly unfortunate for China. Immediately after the invasion, President Truman dispatched the U.S. Seventh Fleet to the Taiwan Strait to prevent a possible Chinese invasion of Taiwan. Even more unfortunate, the invasion hardened Western attitudes against the new Chinese government and led to China's isolation from the major capitalist powers for two decades. As a result, China was cut off from all forms of economic and technological assistance and was forced to rely almost entirely on the Soviet Union, with which it had signed a pact of friendship and cooperation in early 1950.

## Conflict in Indochina

During the mid-1950s, China sought to build contacts with the nonsocialist world. A cease-fire agreement brought the Korean War to an end in July 1953, and China signaled its desire to live in peaceful coexistence with other independent countries in the region. But a relatively minor conflict now began to intensify on Beijing's southern flank, in French Indochina. The struggle had begun after World War II, when Ho Chi Minh's Indochinese Communist Party, at the head of a multiparty nationalist alliance called the Vietminh Front, seized power in northern and central Vietnam after the surrender of imperial Japan. After abortive negotiations between Ho's government and the French over a proposed "free state" of Vietnam under French tutelage, war broke out in December 1946. French forces occupied the cities and the densely populated lowlands, while the Vietminh took refuge in the mountains.

For three years, the Vietminh, waging a "people's war" of national liberation under the leadership of the popular

Indochina in 1954

Ho Chi Minh, gradually increased in size and effectiveness. What had begun as an anticolonial struggle by the Vietminh Front against the French became entangled in the Cold War in the early 1950s when both the United States and the new Communist government in China began to intervene in the conflict to promote their own national security objectives. China began to provide military assistance to the Vietminh to protect its own borders from hostile forces. The Americans supported the French but pressured them to prepare for an eventual transition to non-Communist governments in Vietnam, Laos, and Cambodia.

With casualties mounting and the French public tired of fighting the "dirty war" in Indochina, the French, at the Geneva Conference, held in 1954, agreed to a peace settlement with the Vietminh. Vietnam was temporarily divided into a northern Communist half (known as the Democratic Republic of Vietnam) and a non-Communist southern half based in Saigon (eventually to be known as the Republic of Vietnam). Elections were to be held in two years to create a unified government. Cambodia and Laos were both declared independent under neutral governments. French forces, which had suffered a major defeat at the hands of Vietminh troops at the battle of Dien Bien Phu, were withdrawn from all three countries.

China had played an active role in bringing about the settlement and clearly hoped that a settlement would lead to a reduction of tensions in the area, but subsequent efforts to bring about improved relations between China and the United States foundered on the issue of Taiwan. In the fall of 1954, the United States signed a mutual security treaty with the Republic of China guaranteeing U.S. military support in case of an invasion of Taiwan. When Beijing demanded U.S. withdrawal from Taiwan as the price for improved relations, diplomatic talks between the two countries collapsed.

## FROM CONFRONTATION TO COEXISTENCE

The 1950s opened with the world teetering on the edge of a nuclear holocaust. The Soviet Union had detonated its first nuclear device in 1949, and the two blocs—capitalist and socialist—viewed each other across an ideological divide that grew increasingly bitter with each passing year. Yet as the decade drew to a close, a measure of sanity crept into the Cold War, and the leaders of the major world powers began to seek ways to coexist in an increasingly unstable world (see Map 1.2).

## Khrushchev and the Era of Peaceful Coexistence

The first clear sign occurred after Stalin's death in early 1953. His successor, Georgy Malenkov (1902–1988), hoped to improve relations with the Western powers to reduce defense expenditures and shift government spending to growing consumer needs. During his campaign to replace Malenkov two years later, Nikita Khrushchev

(1894–1971) appealed to powerful pressure groups in the party Politburo (the governing body of the Communist Party of the Soviet Union) by calling for higher defense expenditures, but once in power, he resumed his predecessor's efforts to reduce tensions with the West and improve the living standards of the Soviet people.

In an adroit public relations touch, Khrushchev publicized Moscow's appeal for a new policy of "peaceful coexistence" with the West. In 1955, he surprisingly agreed to negotiate an end to the postwar occupation of Austria by the victorious allies and allow the creation of a neutral country with strong cultural and economic ties with the West. He also called for a reduction in defense expenditures and reduced the size of the Soviet armed forces.

At first, Washington was suspicious of Khrushchev's motives, especially after the Soviet crackdown in Hungary in the fall of 1956 (see Chapter 2). A new crisis over Berlin added to the tension. The Soviets had launched their first intercontinental ballistic missile (ICBM) in August 1957, arousing U.S. fears—fueled by a partisan political debate—of a "missile gap" between the United States and the Soviet Union. Khrushchev attempted to take advantage of the U.S. frenzy over missiles to solve the problem of West Berlin, which had remained a "Western island" of prosperity inside the relatively poverty-stricken state of East Germany. Many East Germans sought to escape to West Germany by fleeing through West Berlin—a serious blot on the credibility of the GDR and a potential source of instability in East-West relations. In November 1958, Khrushchev announced that unless the West removed its forces from West Berlin within six months, he would turn over control of the access routes to the East Germans. Unwilling to accept an ultimatum that would have abandoned West Berlin to the Communists, President Eisenhower and the West stood firm, and Khrushchev eventually backed down.

Despite such periodic crises in East-West relations, there were tantalizing signs that an era of true peaceful coexistence between the two power blocs could be achieved. In the late 1950s, the United States and the Soviet Union initiated a cultural exchange program, helping the peoples of one bloc to become acquainted with the nature of life in the other. While the Leningrad Ballet appeared at theaters in the United States, Benny Goodman and the film of Leonard Bernstein's *West Side Story* played in Moscow. In 1958, Nikita Khrushchev visited the United States and had a brief but friendly encounter with President Eisenhower at Camp David, his presidential retreat in northern Maryland. Predictions of improved future relations led reporters to laud "the spirit of Camp David."

Yet Khrushchev could rarely avoid the temptation to gain an advantage over the United States in the competition for influence throughout the world, and this resulted in an unstable relationship that prevented a lasting accommodation between the two superpowers. West Berlin was an area of persistent tension (a boil on the foot of the United States, Khrushchev derisively termed it), and in January 1961, just as newly elected president John F. Kennedy (1917–1963) came into office, Moscow threatened once again to turn over responsibility for access to the East German government.

Moscow also took every opportunity to promote its interests in the Third World, as the countries of Asia, Africa, and Latin America were now popularly called. Unlike Stalin, Khrushchev viewed the dismantling of colonial regimes in the area as a potential advantage for the Soviet Union and sought especially to exploit anti-American sentiment in Latin America. To improve Soviet influence in such areas, Khrushchev established alliances with key Third World countries such as Indonesia, Egypt, India, and Cuba. In January 1961, just as Kennedy assumed the presidency, Khrushchev unnerved the new president at an informal summit meeting in Vienna by declaring that Moscow would provide active support to national liberation movements throughout the world. There were rising fears in Washington of Soviet meddling in such sensitive trouble spots as Southeast Asia, Central Africa, and the Caribbean.

## The Cuban Missile Crisis and the Move Toward Détente

The Cold War confrontation between the United States and the Soviet Union reached frightening levels during the Cuban Missile Crisis. In 1959, a left-wing revolutionary named Fidel Castro (b. 1927) overthrew the Cuban dictator Fulgencio Batista and established a Soviet-supported totalitarian regime. After the utter failure of a U.S.-supported attempt (the "Bay of Pigs" incident) to overthrow Castro in 1961, the Soviet Union decided to place nuclear missiles in Cuba. The Kennedy administration was not prepared to allow nuclear weapons within such close striking distance of the American mainland, despite the fact that it had placed nuclear weapons in Turkey within easy range of the Soviet Union, a fact that Khrushchev was quick to point out. When U.S. intelligence discovered that a Soviet fleet carrying missiles was heading to Cuba, Kennedy decided to blockade Cuba to prevent the fleet from reaching its destination. This approach to the problem had the benefit of delaying confrontation and giving the two sides time to find a peaceful solution. In a conciliatory letter to Kennedy, Khrushchev agreed to turn back the fleet if Kennedy pledged not to invade Cuba:

> We and you ought not to pull on the ends of the rope in which you have tied the knot of war, because the more the two of us pull, the tighter that knot will be tied. And a moment may come when that knot will be tied too tight that even he who tied it will not have the strength to untie it. . . . Let us not only relax the forces pulling on the ends of the rope, let us take measures to untie that knot. We are ready for this.[4]

The intense feeling that the world might have been annihilated in a few days had a profound influence on both sides. A communication hotline between Moscow and Washington was installed in 1963 to expedite rapid communication between the two superpowers in time of crisis. In the same year, the two powers agreed to ban nu-

# A PLEA FOR PEACEFUL COEXISTENCE

*The Soviet leader Vladimir Lenin had contended that war between the socialist and imperialist camps was inevitable because the imperialists would never give up without a fight. That assumption had probably guided the thoughts of Joseph Stalin, who told colleagues shortly after World War II that a new war would break out in fifteen to twenty years. But Stalin's successor, Nikita Khrushchev, feared that a new world conflict could result in a nuclear holocaust and contended that the two sides must learn to coexist, although peaceful competition would continue. In this speech given in Beijing in 1959, Khrushchev attempted to persuade the Chinese to accept his views. But Chinese leaders argued that the "imperialist nature" of the United States would never change and warned that they would not accept any peace agreement in which they had no part.*

## KHRUSHCHEV'S SPEECH TO THE CHINESE, 1959

Comrades! Socialism brings to the people peace—that greatest blessing. The greater the strength of the camp of socialism grows, the greater will be its possibilities for successfully defending the cause of peace on this earth. The forces of socialism are already so great that real possibilities are being created for excluding war as a means of solving international disputes. . . .

When I spoke with President Eisenhower—and I have just returned from the United States of America—I got the impression that the President of the U.S.A.—and not a few people support him—understands the need to relax international tension. . . .

There is only one way of preserving peace—that is the road of peaceful coexistence of states with different social systems. The question stands thus: either peaceful coexistence or war with its catastrophic consequences. Now, with the present relation of forces between socialism and capitalism being in favor of socialism, he who would continue the "cold war" is moving towards his own destruction. . . .

Already in the first years of the Soviet power the great Lenin defined the general line of our foreign policy as being directed towards the peaceful coexistence of states with different social systems. For a long time, the ruling circles of the Western Powers rejected these truly humane principles. Nevertheless the principles of peaceful coexistence made their way into the hearts of the vast majority of mankind. . . .

It is not at all because capitalism is still strong that the socialist countries speak out against war, and for peaceful coexistence. No, we have no need of war at all. If the people do not want it, even such a noble and progressive system as socialism cannot be imposed by force of arms. The socialist countries therefore, while carrying through a consistently peace-loving policy, concentrate their efforts on peaceful construction; they fire the hearts of men by the force of their example in building socialism, and thus lead them to follow in their footsteps. The question of when this or that country will take the path to socialism is decided by its own people. This, for us, is the holy of holies.

Source: From G. F. Hudson et al., eds. *The Sino–Soviet Dispute* (New York: Frederick Praeger, 1961), pp. 61–63, cited in Peking Review, No. 40, 1959.

---

clear tests in the atmosphere, a step that served to lessen the tensions between the two nations.

## The Sino-Soviet Dispute

Nikita Khrushchev had launched his slogan of peaceful coexistence as a means of improving relations with the capitalist powers; ironically, one result of the campaign was to undermine Moscow's ties with its close ally China. During the lifetime of Joseph Stalin, Beijing had accepted the Soviet Union as the official leader of the socialist camp. After Stalin's death, however, relations began to deteriorate. Part of the reason may have been Mao Zedong's contention that he, as the most experienced Marxist leader, should now be acknowledged as the most authoritative voice within the socialist community. But another determining factor was that just as Soviet poli-

cies were moving toward moderation, China's were becoming more radical.

Several other issues were involved, including territorial disputes and China's unhappiness with limited Soviet economic assistance. But the key sources of disagreement involved ideology and the Cold War. Chinese leaders were convinced that the successes of the Soviet space program confirmed that the socialists were now technologically superior to the capitalists (the East wind, trumpeted the Chinese official press, had now triumphed over the West wind), and they urged Soviet leader Nikita Khrushchev to go on the offensive to promote world revolution. Specifically, China wanted Soviet assistance in retaking Taiwan from Chiang Kai-shek. But Khrushchev was trying to improve relations with the West and rejected Chinese demands for support against Taiwan (see the box above).

By the end of the 1950s, the Soviet Union had begun to remove its advisers from China, and in 1961, the dispute broke into the open. Increasingly isolated, China voiced its hostility to what Mao described as the "urban industrialized countries" (which included the Soviet Union) and portrayed itself as the leader of the "rural underdeveloped countries" of Asia, Africa, and Latin America in a global struggle against imperialist oppression. In effect, China had applied Mao's famous concept of people's war in an international framework.

## The Second Indochina War

The Eisenhower administration had opposed the peace settlement at Geneva in 1954, which divided Vietnam temporarily into two separate regroupment zones, specifically because the provision for future national elections opened up the possibility of placing the entire country under Communist rule. But President Eisenhower had been unwilling to introduce U.S. military forces to continue the conflict without the full support of the British and the French, who preferred to seek a negotiated settlement. In the end, Washington promised not to break the provisions of the agreement but refused to commit itself to the results.

During the next several months, the United States began to provide aid to a new government in South Vietnam. Under the leadership of the anti-Communist politician Ngo Dinh Diem, the Saigon regime began to root out dissidents while refusing to hold the national elections called for by the Geneva Accords. It was widely anticipated, even in Washington, that the Communists would win such elections. In 1959, Ho Chi Minh, despairing of the peaceful unification of the country under Communist rule, returned to a policy of revolutionary war in the south.

By 1963, South Vietnam was on the verge of collapse. Diem's autocratic methods and inattention to severe economic inequality had alienated much of the population, and revolutionary forces, popularly known as the Viet Cong (Vietnamese Communists), expanded their influence throughout much of the country. In the fall of 1963, with the approval of the Kennedy administration, senior military officers overthrew the Diem regime. But factionalism kept the new military leadership from reinvigorating the struggle against the insurgent forces, and by early 1965, the Viet Cong, their ranks now swelled by military units infiltrating from North Vietnam, were on the verge of seizing control of the entire country. In desperation, President Lyndon Johnson (1908–1973) decided to send U.S. combat troops to South Vietnam to prevent a total defeat for the anti-Communist government in Saigon.

Chinese leaders observed the gradual escalation of the conflict in South Vietnam with mixed feelings. They were undoubtedly pleased to have a firm Communist ally —and indeed one that had in so many ways followed the path of Mao Zedong—just beyond their southern frontier. Yet they could not relish the possibility that renewed bloodshed in South Vietnam might enmesh China in a new conflict with the United States. Nor could they have welcomed the specter of a powerful and ambitious united Vietnam that might wish to extend its influence throughout mainland Southeast Asia, which Beijing considered its own backyard.

Chinese leaders therefore tiptoed delicately through the minefield of the Indochina conflict, seeking to maintain good relations with their ally in Hanoi while avoiding a confrontation with the United States. As the war escalated in 1964 and 1965, Beijing publicly announced that the Chinese people would give their full support to their fraternal comrades seeking national liberation in South Vietnam but privately assured Washington that China would not directly enter the conflict unless U.S. forces threatened its southern border. Beijing also refused to cooperate fully with Moscow in shipping Soviet goods to North Vietnam through Chinese territory.

Despite its dismay at the lack of full support from China, the Communist government in North Vietnam responded to U.S. escalation by infiltrating more of its own regular force troops into the south, and by 1968, the war was a virtual stalemate. The Communists were not strong enough to overthrow the Saigon regime, whose weakness was shielded by the presence of half a million U.S. troops, but President Johnson was reluctant to engage in all-out war on North Vietnam for fear of provoking a global nuclear conflict. In the fall, after the Communist-led Tet offensive aroused heightened antiwar protests in the United States, peace negotiations began in Paris.

Richard Nixon (1913–1994) came into the White House in 1969 on a pledge to bring an honorable end to the Vietnam War. With U.S. public opinion sharply divided on the issue, he began to withdraw U.S. troops while continuing to hold peace talks in Paris. But the centerpiece of his strategy was to improve relations with China and thus undercut Chinese support for the North Vietnamese war effort. During the 1960s, relations between Moscow and Beijing had reached a point of extreme tension, and thousands of troops were stationed on both sides of their long common frontier. To intimidate their Communist rivals, Soviet sources dropped the hint that they might decide to launch a preemptive strike to destroy Chinese nuclear facilities in Xinjiang. Sensing an opportunity to split the one-time allies, Nixon sent his emissary Henry Kissinger on a secret trip to China. Responding to the latter's assurances that the United States was determined to withdraw from Indochina and hoped to improve relations with the mainland regime, Chinese leaders invited President Nixon to visit China in early 1972.

Incensed at the apparent betrayal by their close allies, in January 1973 North Vietnamese leaders signed a peace treaty in Paris calling for the removal of all U.S. forces from South Vietnam. In return, the Communists agreed to seek a political settlement of their differences with the Saigon regime. But negotiations between north and south over the political settlement soon broke down, and in early 1975, convinced that Washington would not intervene, the Communists resumed the offensive. At the end of April, under a massive assault by North Vietnamese military forces, the South Vietnamese government surrendered. A year later, the country was unified under Communist rule.

The Communist victory in Vietnam was a humiliation for the United States, but its strategic impact was limited because of the new relationship with China. During the next decade, Sino-American relations continued to improve. In 1979, diplomatic ties were established between the two countries under an arrangement whereby the United States renounced its mutual security treaty with the Republic of China in return for a pledge from China to seek reunification with Taiwan by peaceful means. By the end of the 1970s, China and the United States had forged a "strategic relationship" in which each would cooperate with the other against the common threat of Soviet "hegemonism" (as China described Soviet policy) in Asia.

# AN ERA OF EQUIVALENCE

The Johnson administration sent U.S. combat troops to South Vietnam in 1965 in an effort to prevent the expansion of communism in Southeast Asia. Washington's primary concern, however, was not Moscow but Beijing. By the mid-1960s, U.S. officials viewed the Soviet Union as an essentially conservative power, more concerned with protecting its vast empire than with expanding its borders. In fact, U.S. policy makers periodically sought Soviet assistance in achieving a peaceful settlement of the Vietnam War. As long as Khrushchev was in power, they found a receptive ear in Moscow. Khrushchev had sternly advised the North Vietnamese against a resumption of revolutionary war in South Vietnam.

After October 1964, when Khrushchev was replaced by a new leadership headed by party chief Leonid Brezhnev (1906–1982) and Prime Minister Alexei Kosygin (1904–1980), Soviet attitudes about Vietnam became

AP/Wide World Photos

➤ A BRIDGE ACROSS THE COLD WAR DIVIDE. In January 1972, U.S. President Richard Nixon startled the world by visiting mainland China and beginning the long process of restoring normal relations between the two countries. Despite Nixon's reputation as a devout anti-Communist, the visit was a success, and the two sides agreed to put aside their bitterest differences in an effort to reduce tensions in Asia. Here Nixon and Chinese leader Mao Zedong exchange a historic handshake in Beijing.

more ambivalent. On the one hand, the new Soviet leadership had no desire to see the Vietnam conflict poison relations between the great powers. On the other hand, Moscow was anxious to demonstrate its support for the North Vietnamese to deflect Chinese charges that the Soviet Union had betrayed the interests of the oppressed peoples of the world. As a result, Soviet officials voiced sympathy for the U.S. predicament in Vietnam but put no pressure on their allies to bring an end to the war. Indeed, the Soviets became Hanoi's main supplier of advanced military equipment in the final years of the war.

Still, Brezhnev and Kosygin continued to pursue the Khrushchev line of peaceful coexistence with the West and adopted a generally cautious posture in foreign affairs. By the early 1970s, a new age in Soviet-American relations had emerged, often referred to by the French term *détente*, meaning a reduction of tensions between the two sides. One symbol of the new relationship was the Antiballistic Missile (ABM) Treaty, often called SALT I (for Strategic Arms Limitation Talks), signed in 1972, in which the two nations agreed to limit their missile systems.

Washington's objective in pursuing such a treaty was to make it unprofitable for either superpower to believe that it could win a nuclear exchange by launching a preemptive strike against the other. U.S. officials believed that a policy of "equivalence," in which there was a roughly equal power balance on each side, was the best way to avoid a nuclear confrontation. Détente was pursued in other ways as well. When President Nixon took office in 1969, he sought to increase trade and cultural contacts with the Soviet Union. His purpose was to set up a series of "linkages" in U.S.-Soviet relations that would persuade Moscow of the economic and social benefits of maintaining good relations with the West.

A symbol of that new relationship was the Helsinki Agreement of 1975. Signed by the United States, Canada, and all European nations on both sides of the Iron Curtain, these accords recognized all borders in Central and Eastern Europe established since the end of World War II, thereby formally acknowledging for the first time the Soviet sphere of influence. The Helsinki Agreement also committed the signatory powers to recognize and protect the human rights of their citizens, a clear effort by the Western states to improve the performance of the Soviet Union and its allies in that area.

## An End to Détente?

Protection of human rights became one of the major foreign policy goals of the next U.S. president, Jimmy Carter (b. 1924). Ironically, just at the point when U.S. involvement in Vietnam came to an end and relations with China began to improve, the mood in U.S.-Soviet relations began to sour, for several reasons.

Some Americans had become increasingly concerned about aggressive new tendencies in Soviet foreign policy. The first indication came in Africa. Soviet influence was on the rise in Somalia, across the Red Sea in South Yemen, and later in Ethiopia. Soviet involvement was also on the increase in southern Africa, where an insurgent movement supported by Cuban troops came to power in Angola, once a colony of Portugal. Then, in 1979, Soviet troops were sent to neighboring Afghanistan to protect a newly installed Marxist regime facing rising internal resistance from fundamentalist Muslims. Some observers suspected that the Soviet advance into hitherto neutral Afghanistan was to extend Soviet power into the oil fields of the Persian Gulf. To deter such a possibility, the White House promulgated the Carter Doctrine, which stated that the United States would use its military power, if necessary, to safeguard Western access to the oil reserves in the Middle East. In fact, sources in Moscow later disclosed that the Soviet advance into Afghanistan had little to do with a strategic drive toward the Persian Gulf but represented an effort to take advantage of the recent disarray in U.S. foreign policy in the aftermath of defeat in Vietnam to increase Soviet influence in a sensitive region increasingly beset with Islamic fervor. Soviet officials feared that the wave of Islamic activism could spread to the Muslim populations in the Soviet republics in central Asia and were confident that the United States was too distracted by the "Vietnam syndrome" (the public fear of U.S. involvement in another Vietnam-type conflict) to respond.

Other factors contributed to the growing suspicion of the Soviet Union in the United States. During the era of détente, Washington officials had assumed that Moscow accepted the U.S. doctrine of equivalence—the idea that both sides possessed sufficient strength to destroy the other in the event of a surprise attack. By the end of the decade, however, some U.S. defense analysts began to charge that the Soviets were seeking strategic superiority in nuclear weapons and argued for a substantial increase in U.S. defense spending. Such charges, combined with evidence of Soviet efforts in Africa and the Middle East and reports of the persecution of Jews and dissidents in the Soviet Union, helped undermine public support for détente in the United States. These changing attitudes were reflected in the failure of the Carter administration to obtain congressional approval of a new arms limitation agreement (SALT II) signed with the Soviet Union in 1979.

## Countering the Evil Empire

The early years of the administration of President Ronald Reagan (b. 1911) witnessed a return to the harsh rhetoric, if not all of the harsh practices, of the Cold War. President Reagan's anti-Communist credentials were well known. In a speech given shortly after his election in 1980, he referred to the Soviet Union as an "evil empire" and frequently voiced his suspicion of its motives in foreign affairs. In an effort to eliminate perceived Soviet advantages in strategic weaponry, the White House began a military buildup that stimulated a renewed arms race. In 1982, the Reagan administration introduced the nuclear-tipped cruise missile, whose ability to fly at low altitudes made it difficult to detect by enemy radar. Reagan also became an ardent exponent of the Strategic Defense Initiative (SDI), nicknamed "Star Wars." Its purposes were to create a space shield that could destroy incoming missiles and to force Moscow into an arms race that it could not hope to win.

The Reagan administration also adopted a more activist, if not confrontational, stance in the Third World. That attitude was most directly demonstrated in Central America, where the revolutionary Sandinista regime had come to power with the overthrow of the Somoza dictatorship in 1979. Charging that the Sandinista regime was supporting a guerrilla insurgency movement in nearby El Salvador, the Reagan administration began to provide material aid to the government in El Salvador while simultaneously applying pressure on the Sandinistas by giving support to an anti-Communist guerrilla movement (called the Contras) in Nicaragua. The administration's Central American policy caused considerable controversy in Congress, and critics charged that growing U.S. involvement there could lead to a repeat of the nation's bitter experience in Vietnam.

By providing military support to the anti-Soviet insurgents in Afghanistan, the White House helped maintain a Vietnam-like war in Afghanistan that would embed the Soviet Union in its own quagmire. Like the Vietnam War, the conflict in Afghanistan resulted in heavy casualties and demonstrated that the influence of a super-

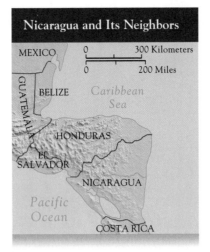

Nicaragua and Its Neighbors

power was limited in the face of strong nationalist, guerrilla-type opposition.

## CONCLUSION

At the end of World War II, a new conflict appeared in Europe as the two superpowers, the United States and the Soviet Union, began to compete for political domination. This ideological division soon spread to the rest of the world as the United States fought in Korea and Vietnam to prevent the spread of communism, promoted by the new Maoist government in China, while the Soviet Union used its influence to prop up pro-Soviet regimes in Asia, Africa, and Latin America.

What had begun, then, as a confrontation across the great divide of the Iron Curtain in Europe eventually took on global significance, much as the major European powers had jostled for position and advantage in Africa and eastern Asia prior to World War I. As a result, both Moscow and Washington became entangled in areas that in themselves had little importance in terms of real national security interests. To make matters worse, U.S. policy makers all too often applied the lessons of World War II (the "Munich syndrome," according to which efforts to appease an aggressor only encourage his appetite for conquest) to crisis points in the Third World, where conditions were not remotely comparable.

By the 1980s, however, there were tantalizing signs of a thaw in the Cold War. China and the United States, each hoping to gain leverage with Moscow, had agreed to establish diplomatic relations. Freed from its own concerns over Beijing's open support of revolutions in the Third World, the United States decided to withdraw from South Vietnam, and the war there came to an end without involving the great powers in a dangerous confrontation. While Washington and Moscow continued to compete for advantage all over the world, both sides gradually came to realize that the struggle for domination could best be carried out in the political and economic arena rather than on the battlefield.

| | 1945 | 1955 | 1965 | 1975 | 1985 |
|---|---|---|---|---|---|
| **EUROPE** | Yalta Conference | Warsaw Pact created | | SALT pact signed | |
| | NATO formed | | | | |
| | Tito expelled from Soviet bloc | Marshall Plan | | | |
| **THE AMERICAS** | | | Cuban Missile Crisis | | |
| **ASIA** | | Geneva Conference ends conflict in Indochina | U.S. sends combat troops to Vietnam | | Soviet invasion of Afghanistan |
| | Civil war in China | Korean War | Sino-Soviet dispute breaks into open | Nixon visits China | Communists seize power in South Vietnam |

## INFOTRAC COLLEGE EDITION

Visit source collections at **http://infotrac.thomsonlearning.com,** and use the Search function with the following key terms:

Cold War
Gorbachev
Korean War
Soviet Union relations with the United States
Vietnamese Conflict

## WORLD HISTORY RESOURCES

Visit the *The World Since World War II* Companion Web site for resources specific to this textbook:

**http://history.wadsworth.com/duiker_wwii/**

The Wadsworth World History Resource Center at **http://history.wadsworth.com/world/** offers a variety of tools to help you succeed in this course, including access to quizzes; images; documents; interactive simulations, maps, and timelines; movie explorations; and a wealth of other sources.

## CHAPTER NOTES

1. *Department of State Bulletin*, February 11, 1945, p. 213.
2. Quoted in Joseph M. Jones, *The Fifteen Weeks (February 21–June 5, 1947)*, 2d ed. (New York, 1964), pp. 140–141.
3. Quoted in Walter Laqueur, *Europe in Our Time* (New York, 1992), p. 111.
4. Quoted in Robert F. Kennedy, *Thirteen Days: A Memoir of the Cuban Missile Crisis* (New York, 1969), pp. 89–90.

# BRAVE NEW WORLD: THE RISE AND FALL OF COMMUNISM IN THE SOVIET UNION AND EASTERN EUROPE

According to Karl Marx, capitalism is a system that involves the exploitation of man by man; under socialism, it is the other way around. That wry joke, an ironic twist on the familiar Marxist remark a century previously, was typical of popular humor in post–World War II Moscow, where the dreams of a future Communist utopia had faded in the grim reality of life in the Soviet Union.

Nevertheless, the Communist monopoly on power seemed secure, as did Moscow's hold over its client states in Eastern Europe. In fact, for three decades after the end of World War II, the Soviet Empire appeared to be a permanent feature of the international landscape. But by the early 1980s, it became clear that there were cracks in the facade of the Kremlin wall. The Soviet economy was stagnant, the minority nationalities were restive, and Eastern European leaders were increasingly emboldened to test the waters of the global capitalist marketplace. In the United States, newly elected President Ronald Reagan boldly predicted the imminent collapse of the "evil empire."

## THE POSTWAR SOVIET UNION

World War II had left the Soviet Union as one of the world's two superpowers and its leader, Joseph Stalin, at the height of his power. As a result of the war, Stalin and his Soviet colleagues were now in control of a vast empire that included Eastern Europe, much of the Balkans, and territory gained from Japan in East Asia.

## From Stalin to Khrushchev

World War II devastated the Soviet Union. Twenty million citizens lost their lives, and cities such as Kiev, Kharkov, and Leningrad suffered enormous physical destruction. As the lands that had been occupied by the German forces were liberated, the Soviet government turned its attention to restoring their economic structures. Nevertheless, in 1945, agricultural production was only 60 percent and steel output only 50 percent of prewar levels.

The Soviet people faced incredibly difficult conditions: they worked longer hours; they ate less; they were ill-housed and poorly clothed.

In the immediate postwar years, the Soviet Union removed goods and materials from occupied Germany and extorted valuable raw materials from its satellite states in Eastern Europe. More important, however, to create a new industrial base, Stalin returned to the method he had used in the 1930s — the extraction of development capital from Soviet labor. Working hard for little pay and for precious few consumer goods, Soviet laborers were expected to produce goods for export with little in return for themselves. The incoming capital from abroad could then be used to purchase machinery and Western technology. The loss of millions of men in the war meant that much of this tremendous workload fell to Soviet women, who performed almost 40 percent of the heavy manual labor.

The pace of economic recovery in the Soviet Union was impressive. By 1947, Russian industrial production had attained 1939 levels; three years later, it had surpassed those levels by 40 percent. New power plants, canals, and giant factories were built, while new industrial enterprises and oil fields were established in Siberia and Soviet Central Asia. Stalin's new five-year plan, announced in 1946, reached its goals in less than five years.

Although Stalin's economic recovery policy was successful in promoting growth in heavy industry, primarily for the benefit of the military, consumer goods remained scarce. The development of thermonuclear weapons, MIG fighters, and the first space satellite (*Sputnik*) in the 1950s may have elevated the Soviet state's reputation as a world power abroad, but domestically, the Soviet people were shortchanged. Heavy industry grew at a rate three times that of personal consumption. Moreover, the housing shortage was acute, with living conditions especially difficult in the overcrowded cities.

When World War II ended, Stalin had been in power for more than fifteen years. During that time, he had removed all opposition to his rule and remained the undisputed master of the Soviet Union. Increasingly distrustful of competitors, Stalin exercised sole authority and pitted his subordinates against one another. One of these subordinates, Lavrenti Beria, head of the secret police, controlled a force of several hundred thousand agents, leaving Stalin's colleagues completely cowed. As Stalin remarked mockingly on one occasion, "When I die, the imperialists will strangle all of you like a litter of kittens."[1]

Stalin's morbid suspicions added to the constantly increasing repression of the regime. In 1946, government decrees subordinated all forms of literary and scientific expression to the political needs of the state. Along with the anti-intellectual campaign came political terror. By the late 1940s, there were an estimated nine million people in Siberian concentration camps. Distrust of potential threats to his power even spread to some of his closest colleagues. In 1948, Andrei Zhdanov, his presumed successor and head of the Leningrad party organization, died under mysterious circumstances, presumably at Stalin's order. Within weeks, the Leningrad party organization was purged of several top leaders, many of whom were charged with traitorous connections with Western intelligence agencies. In succeeding years, Stalin directed his suspicion at other members of the inner circle, including Foreign Minister Vyacheslav Molotov. Known as "Old Stone Butt" in the West for his stubborn defense of Soviet security interests, Molotov had been Stalin's loyal lieutenant since the early years of Stalin's rise to power. Now Stalin distrusted Molotov and had his Jewish wife placed in a Siberian concentration camp.

Stalin died in 1953 and, after some bitter infighting within the party leadership, was succeeded by Georgy Malenkov, a veteran administrator and ambitious member of the Politburo. Malenkov came to power with a clear agenda. In foreign affairs, he hoped to promote an easing of Cold War tensions and improve relations with the Western powers. For Moscow's Eastern European allies, he advocated a "new course" in their mutual relations and a decline in Stalinist methods of rule. Inside the Soviet Union, he hoped to reduce defense expenditures and assign a higher priority to improving the standard of living. Such goals were laudable and probably had the support of the majority of the Russian people, but they were not necessarily appealing to key pressure groups within the Soviet Union — the army, the Communist Party, the managerial elite, and the security services (now known as the Committee on Government Security, or KGB). In 1953, Malenkov was removed from his position as prime minister, and power shifted to his rival, the new party general secretary, Nikita Khrushchev.

During his struggle for power with Malenkov, Khrushchev had outmaneuvered him by calling for heightened defense expenditures and a continuing emphasis on heavy industry. Once in power, however, Khrushchev showed the political dexterity displayed by many an American politician and reversed his priorities. He now resumed the efforts of his predecessor to reduce tensions with the West and improve the standard of living of the Russian people. He moved vigorously to improve the performance of the Soviet economy and revitalize Soviet society. By nature, Khrushchev was a man of enormous energy as well as an innovator. In an attempt to release the stranglehold of the central bureaucracy over the national economy, he abolished dozens of government ministries and split up the party and government apparatus. Khru-

# KHRUSHCHEV DENOUNCES STALIN

*Three years after Stalin's death, the new Soviet premier, Nikita Khrushchev, addressed the Twentieth Congress of the Communist Party and denounced the former Soviet dictator for his crimes. This denunciation was the beginning of a policy of destalinization.*

## KHRUSHCHEV ADDRESSES THE TWENTIETH PARTY CONGRESS, FEBRUARY 1956

Comrades, . . . quite a lot has been said about the cult of the individual and about its harmful consequences. . . . The cult of the person of Stalin . . . became at a certain specific stage the source of a whole series of exceedingly serious and grave perversions of Party principles, of Party democracy, of revolutionary legality.

Stalin absolutely did not tolerate collegiality in leadership and in work and . . . practiced brutal violence, not only toward everything which opposed him, but also toward that which seemed to his capricious and despotic character, contrary to his concepts.

Stalin abandoned the method of ideological struggle for that of administrative violence, mass repressions and terror. . . . Arbitrary behavior by one person encouraged and permitted arbitrariness in others. Mass arrests and deportations of many thousands of people, execution without trial and without normal investigation created conditions of insecurity, fear, and even desperation.

Stalin showed in a whole series of cases his intolerance, his brutality, and his abuse of power. . . . He often chose the path of repression and annihilation, not only against actual enemies, but also against individuals who had not committed any crimes against the Party and the Soviet government. . . .

Many Party, Soviet, and economic activists who were branded in 1937–38 as "enemies" were actually never enemies, spies, wreckers, and so on, but were always honest communists; they were only so stigmatized, and often, no longer able to bear barbaric tortures, they charged themselves (at the order of the investigative judges-falsifiers) with all kinds of grave and unlikely crimes.

This was the result of the abuse of power by Stalin, who began to use mass terror against the Party cadres. . . . Stalin put the Party and the NKVD up to the use of mass terror when the exploiting classes had been liquidated in our country and when there were no serious reasons for the use of extraordinary mass terror. The terror was directed . . . against the honest workers of the Party and the Soviet state. . . .

Stalin was a very distrustful man, sickly, suspicious. . . . Everywhere and in everything he saw "enemies," "two-facers," and "spies." Possessing unlimited power, he indulged in great willfulness and choked a person morally and physically. A situation was created where one could not express one's own will. When Stalin said that one or another would be arrested, it was necessary to accept on faith that he was an "enemy of the people." What proofs were offered? The confession of the arrested. . . . How is it possible that a person confesses to crimes that he had not committed? Only in one way—because of application of physical methods of pressuring him, tortures, bringing him to a state of unconsciousness, deprivation of his judgment, taking away of his human dignity.

Source: *Congressional Record*, 84th Congress, 2d Session, vol. 102, pt. 7, pp. 9389–9402 (June 4, 1956).

---

shchev also attempted to rejuvenate the stagnant agricultural sector, long the Achilles heel of the Soviet economy. He attempted to spur production by increasing profit incentives and opened "virgin lands" in Soviet Kazakhstan to bring thousands of acres of new land under cultivation.

Like any innovator, Khrushchev had to overcome the inherently conservative instincts of the Soviet bureaucracy, as well as of the mass of the Soviet population. His plan to remove the "dead hand" of the state, however laudable in intent, alienated much of the Soviet official class, and his effort to split the party angered those who saw it as the central force in the Soviet system. Khrushchev's agricultural schemes inspired similar opposition.

Although the Kazakhstan wheat lands would eventually demonstrate their importance in the overall agricultural picture, progress was slow, and his effort to persuade the Russian people to eat more corn (an idea he had apparently picked up during a visit to the United States) led to the mocking nickname of "Cornman." Disappointing agricultural production, combined with high military spending, hurt the Soviet economy. The industrial growth rate, which had soared in the early 1950s, now declined dramatically from 13 percent in 1953 to 7.5 percent in 1964.

Khrushchev was probably best known for his policy of destalinization. Khrushchev had risen in the party hierarchy as a Stalin protégé, but he had been deeply disturbed by his mentor's excesses and, once in a position of authority, moved to excise the Stalinist legacy from Soviet society. The campaign began at the Twentieth National Congress of the Communist Party in February 1956, when Khrushchev gave a long speech criticizing some of Stalin's major shortcomings. The speech had apparently not been intended for public distribution, but it was quickly leaked to the Western press and created a sensation throughout the world (see the box on p. 47). During the next few years, Khrushchev encouraged more freedom of expression for writers, artists, and composers, arguing that "readers should be given the chance to make their own judgments" regarding the acceptability of controversial literature and that "police measures shouldn't be used."[2] At Khrushchev's order, thousands of prisoners were released from concentration camps.

Khrushchev's personality, however, did not endear him to higher Soviet officials, who frowned at his tendency to crack jokes and play the clown. Nor were the higher members of the party bureaucracy pleased when Khrushchev tried to curb their privileges. Foreign policy failures further damaged Khrushchev's reputation among his colleagues. His plan to place missiles in Cuba was the final straw (see Chapter 1). While he was away on vacation in 1964, a special meeting of the Soviet Politburo voted him out of office (because of "deteriorating health") and forced him into retirement. Although a group of leaders succeeded him, real power came into the hands of Leonid Brezhnev (1906–1982), the "trusted" supporter of Khrushchev who had engineered his downfall.

## The Brezhnev Years, 1964–1982

The ouster of Nikita Khrushchev in October 1964 vividly demonstrated the challenges that would be encountered by any Soviet leader sufficiently bold to try to reform the Soviet system. In democratic countries, pressure on the government comes from various sources within society at large — the business community and labor unions, interest groups, and the general public. In the Soviet Union, pressure on government and party leaders originated from sources essentially operating inside the system — from the government bureaucracy, the party apparatus, the KGB, and the armed forces.

Leonid Brezhnev, the new party chief, was undoubtedly aware of these realities of Soviet politics, and his long tenure in power was marked, above all, by the desire to avoid changes that might provoke instability, either at home or abroad. Brezhnev was himself a product of the Soviet system. He had entered the ranks of the party leadership under Joseph Stalin, and although he was not a particularly avid believer in party ideology — indeed, his

years in power gave rise to innumerable stories about his addiction to "bourgeois pleasures," including expensive country houses in the elite Moscow suburb of Zhukovka and fast cars (many of them gifts from foreign leaders) — he was no partisan of reform.

Still, Brezhnev sought stability in the domestic arena. He and his prime minister, Alexei Kosygin, undertook what might be described as a program of "de-Khrushchevization," returning the responsibility for long-term planning to the central ministries and reuniting the Communist Party apparatus. Despite some cautious attempts to stimulate the stagnant farm sector, increasing capital investment in agriculture and raising food prices to increase rural income and provide additional incentives to collective farmers, there was no effort to revise the basic structure of the collective system. In the industrial sector, the regime launched a series of reforms designed to give factory managers (themselves employees of the state) more responsibility for setting prices, wages, and production quotas. These "Kosygin reforms" had little effect, however, because they were stubbornly resisted by the bureaucracy and were eventually adopted by relatively few enterprises within the vast state-owned industrial sector.

### A CONTROLLED SOCIETY

Brezhnev also initiated a significant retreat from the policy of destalinization adopted by Nikita Khrushchev. Criticism of the "Great Leader" had angered conservatives both within the party hierarchy and among the public at large, many of whom still revered Stalin as a hero of the Soviet system and a defender of the Russian people against Nazi Germany. Many influential figures in the Kremlin feared that destalinization could lead to internal instability and a decline in public trust in the legitimacy of party leadership — the hallowed "dictatorship of the proletariat." Early in Brezhnev's reign, Stalin's reputation began to revive. Although his alleged "shortcomings" were not totally ignored, he was now described in the official press as "an outstanding party leader" who had been primarily responsible for the successes achieved by the Soviet Union.

The regime also adopted a more restrictive policy toward free expression and dissidence in Soviet society. Critics of the Soviet system, such as the physicist Andrei Sakharov, were harassed and arrested or, like the famous writer Alexander Solzhenitsyn, forced to leave the country. There was also a qualified return to the anti-Semitic policies and attitudes that had marked the Stalin era. Such indications of renewed repression aroused concern in the West and were instrumental in the inclusion of a statement on human rights in the 1975 Helsinki

Agreement, which guaranteed the sanctity of international frontiers throughout the continent of Europe (see Chapter 1).

The political stamp of the Brezhnev era was formally enshrined in a new state constitution, promulgated in 1977. Although the preamble declared that the Soviet Union was no longer a proletarian dictatorship but rather a "state of all the people," comprising workers, farmers, and "socialist intellectuals," it confirmed the role of the Communist Party as "the predominant force" in Soviet society. Article 49 stated that "persecution for criticism shall be prohibited," but Article 62 qualified the rights of the individual by declaring that citizens "shall be obligated to safeguard the interests of the Soviet state and to contribute to the strength of its might and prestige."

There were, of course, no rival voices to compete with the party and the government in defining national interests. The media were controlled by the state and presented only what the state wanted people to hear. The two major newspapers, *Pravda* (Truth) and *Izvestiya* (News), were the agents of the party and the government, respectively. Cynics joked that there was no news in *Pravda* and no truth in *Izvestiya*. Reports of airplane accidents in the Soviet Union were rarely publicized on the grounds that doing so would raise questions about the quality of the Soviet airline industry. The government made strenuous efforts to prevent the Soviet people from

exposure to harmful foreign ideas, especially modern art, literature, and contemporary Western rock music. When the Summer Olympic Games were held in Moscow in 1980, Soviet newspapers advised citizens to keep their children indoors to protect them from being polluted with "bourgeois" ideas passed on by foreign visitors.

For citizens of Western democracies, such a political atmosphere would seem highly oppressive, but for the people in the Soviet republics, an emphasis on law and order was an accepted aspect of everyday life inherited from the tsarist period. Conformism was the rule in virtually every corner of Soviet society, from the educational system (characterized at all levels by rote memorization and political indoctrination) to child rearing (it was forbidden, for example, to be left-handed) and even to yearly vacations (most workers took their vacations at resorts run by their employer, where the daily schedule of activities was highly regimented). Young Americans studying in the Soviet Union reported that friends there were often shocked to hear U.S. citizens criticizing their own president and to learn that they did not routinely carry identity cards.

## A STAGNANT ECONOMY

Soviet leaders also failed to achieve their objective of revitalizing the national economy. Whereas growth rates

**THE PORTALS OF DOOM.** Perhaps the most feared location in the Soviet Union was Lyubyanka Prison, an ornate prerevolutionary building in the heart of Moscow. Taken over by the Bolsheviks after the 1917 revolution, it became the headquarters of the Soviet secret police, the Cheka, later to be known as the KGB. It was here that many Soviet citizens accused of "counterrevolutionary acts" were imprisoned and executed. The figure on the pedestal is that of Felix Dzerzhinsky, first director of the Cheka. After the dissolution of the Soviet Union, the statue was removed.

Courtesy of William J. Duiker

during the early Khrushchev era had been impressive (prompting Khrushchev during one visit to the United States in the late 1950s to chortle, "We will bury you"), under Brezhnev, industrial growth declined to an annual rate of less than 4 percent in the early 1970s and less than 3 percent in the period 1975–1980. Successes in the agricultural sector were equally meager. Grain production rose from less than 90 million tons in the early 1950s to nearly 200 million tons in the 1970s but then stagnated at that level.

One of the primary problems with the Soviet economy was the absence of incentives. Salary structures offered little reward for hard labor and extraordinary achievement. Pay differentials operated within a much narrower range than in most Western societies, and there was little danger of being dismissed. According to the Soviet constitution, every Soviet citizen was guaranteed an opportunity to work.

There were, of course, some exceptions to this general rule. Athletic achievement was highly prized, and a gymnast of Olympic stature would receive great rewards in the form of prestige and lifestyle. Senior officials did not receive high salaries but were provided with countless "perquisites," such as access to foreign goods, official automobiles with a chauffeur, and entry into prestigious institutions of higher learning for their children. For the elite, it was *blat* (influence) that most often differentiated them from the rest of the population. The average citizen, however, had little material incentive to produce beyond the minimum acceptable level of effort. It is hardly surprising that overall per capita productivity was only about half that realized in most capitalist countries. At the same time, the rudeness of clerks and waiters toward their customers in Soviet society became legendary.

The problem of incentives existed at the managerial level as well, where the practice of centralized planning discouraged initiative and innovation. Factory managers, for example, were assigned monthly and annual quotas by the Gosplan (the "state plan," drawn up by the central planning commission). Because state-owned factories faced little or no competition, factory managers did not care whether their products were competitive in terms of price and quality, so long as the quota was attained. One of the key complaints of Soviet citizens was the low quality of most locally made consumer goods. Knowledgeable consumers quickly discovered that products manufactured at the end of the month were often of lower quality (because factory workers had to rush to meet their quotas at the end of their production cycle) and attempted to avoid purchasing them.

Often consumer goods were simply unavailable. Soviet citizens automatically got in line when they saw a queue forming in front of a store because they never knew when something might be available again. When they reached the head of the line, most would purchase several of the same item to swap with their friends and neighbors. Giv-

⇛ HOW TO SHOP IN MOSCOW. Because of the policy of state control over the Soviet economy, the availability of goods was a consequence not of market factors but of decisions made by government bureaucrats. As a result, needed goods were often in short supply. When Soviet citizens heard that a shipment of a particular product had arrived at a state store, they queued up to buy it. Here shoppers line up in front of a store selling dinnerware in Moscow.

ing in to this "queue psychology," of course, was a time-consuming process and inevitably served to reduce the per capita rate of productivity.

Soviet citizens often tried to overcome the shortcomings of the system by operating "on the left" (the black market). Private economic activities, of course, were illegal in the socialized Soviet system, but many workers took to "moonlighting" to augment their meager salaries. An employee in a state-run appliance store, for example, would promise to repair a customer's television set on his own time in return for a payment "under the table." Otherwise, servicing of the set might require several weeks. Knowledgeable observers estimated that as much as one-third of the entire Soviet economy operated outside the legal system.

Another major obstacle to economic growth was inadequate technology. Except in the area of national defense, the overall level of Soviet technology was not comparable to that of the West or the advanced industrial societies of East Asia. Part of the problem, of course, stemmed from the issues already described. With no competition, factory managers had little incentive to improve the quality of their products. But another reason was the high priority assigned to defense. The military sector of the economy regularly received the most resources from the government and attracted the cream of the country's scientific talent.

## PROBLEMS OF GERONTOCRACY

Such problems would be intimidating for any government; they were particularly so for the elderly generation of party leaders surrounding Leonid Brezhnev, many of whom were cautious to a fault. While some undoubtedly recognized the need for reform and innovation, they were paralyzed by the fear of instability and change. The problem worsened during the late 1970s, when Brezhnev's health began to deteriorate.

Brezhnev died in November 1982 and was succeeded by Yuri Andropov (1914–1984), a party veteran and head of the Soviet secret services. During his brief tenure as party chief, Andropov was a vocal advocate of reform, but most of his initiatives were limited to the familiar nostrums of punishment for wrongdoers and moral exhortations to Soviet citizens to work harder. At the same time, material incentives were still officially discouraged and generally ineffective. Andropov had been ailing when he was selected to succeed Brezhnev as party chief, and when he died after only a few months in office, little had been done to change the system. He was succeeded, in turn, by a mediocre party stalwart, the elderly Konstantin Chernenko (1911–1985). With the Soviet

system in crisis, Moscow seemed stuck in a time warp. As one concerned observer told an American journalist, "I had a sense of foreboding, like before a storm. That there was something brewing in people and there would be a time when they would say, 'That's it. We can't go on living like this. We can't. We need to redo everything.'"[3]

# FERMENT IN EASTERN EUROPE

The key to Moscow's security along the western frontier of the Soviet Union was the string of satellite states that had been created in Eastern Europe after World War II (see Map 2.1). Once Communist power had been assured in Warsaw, Prague, Sofia, Budapest, Bucharest, and East Berlin, a series of "little Stalins" put into power by Moscow instituted Soviet-type five-year plans that placed primary emphasis on heavy industry rather than consumer goods, on the collectivization of agriculture, and on the nationalization of industry. They also appropriated the political tactics that Stalin had perfected in the Soviet Union, eliminating all non-Communist parties and establishing the classical institutions of repression—the secret police and military forces. Dissidents were tracked down and thrown into prison, while "national Communists" who resisted total subservience to the nation were charged with treason in mass show trials and executed.

Despite such repressive efforts, however, Soviet-style policies aroused growing discontent in several Eastern European societies. Hungary, Poland, and Romania harbored bitter memories of past Russian domination and suspected that Stalin, under the guise of proletarian internationalism, was seeking to revive the empire of the Romanovs. For the vast majority of peoples in Eastern Europe, the imposition of the "people's democracies" (a euphemism invented by Moscow to refer to a society in the early stage of socialist transition) resulted in economic hardship and severe threats to the most basic political liberties.

The first indications of unrest appeared in 1953, when popular riots broke out against Communist rule in East Berlin. The riots eventually subsided, but the virus had begun to spread to neighboring countries. In Poland, public demonstrations against an increase in food prices in 1956 escalated into widespread protests against the regime's economic policies, restrictions on the freedom of Catholics to practice their religion, and the continued presence of Soviet troops (as called for by the Warsaw Pact) on Polish soil. In a desperate effort to defuse the unrest, in October the Polish party leader stepped down and

MAP **2.1** Eastern Europe and the Soviet Union. After World War II, the boundaries of Eastern Europe were redrawn as a result of Allied agreements reached at the Tehran and Yalta conferences. This map shows the new boundaries that were established throughout the region, placing Soviet power at the center of Europe. ➢ *How had the boundaries changed from the prewar era?*

was replaced by Wladyslaw Gomulka (1905–1982), a popular figure who had previously been demoted for his "nationalist" tendencies. When Gomulka took steps to ease the crisis, the new Soviet party chief, Nikita Khrushchev, flew to Warsaw to warn his Polish colleague against adopting policies that could undermine the "dictatorship of the proletariat" (the Marxist phrase for the political dominance of the party) and even weaken security links with the Soviet Union. After a brief confrontation, during which both sides threatened to use military force to punctuate their demands, Gomulka and Khrushchev reached a compromise according to which Poland would adopt a policy labeled "internal reform, external

loyalty." Poland agreed to remain in the Warsaw Pact and to maintain the sanctity of party rule. In return, Warsaw was authorized to adopt domestic reforms, such as easing restrictions on religious practice and ending the policy of forced collectivization in rural areas.

The developments in Poland sent shock waves throughout the region. The impact was the strongest in neighboring Hungary, where the methods of the local "little Stalin," Matyas Rakosi, were so brutal that he had been summoned to Moscow for a lecture. In late October, student-led popular riots broke out in the capital of Budapest and soon spread to other towns and villages throughout the country. Rakosi was forced to resign and was replaced by Imre Nagy (1896–1958), a "national Communist" who attempted to satisfy popular demands without arousing the anger of Moscow. Unlike Gomulka, however, Nagy was unable to contain the zeal of leading members of the protest movement, who sought major political reforms and the withdrawal of Hungary from the Warsaw Pact. On November 1, Nagy promised free elections, which, given the mood of the country, would probably have brought an end to Communist rule. Moscow decided on firm action. Soviet troops, recently withdrawn at Nagy's request, returned to Budapest and installed a new government under the more pliant party leader János Kádár (1912–1989). While Kádár rescinded many of Nagy's measures, Nagy sought refuge in the Yugoslav Embassy. A few weeks later, he left the embassy under the promise of safety but was quickly arrested, convicted of treason, and executed.

The dramatic events in Poland and Hungary graphically demonstrated the vulnerability of the Soviet satellite system in Eastern Europe, and many observers throughout the world anticipated an attempt by the United States to intervene on behalf of the freedom fighters in Hungary. After all, the Eisenhower administration had promised that it would "roll back" communism, and radio broadcasts by the U.S.-sponsored Radio Liberty and Radio Free Europe had encouraged the peoples of Eastern Europe to rise up against Soviet domination. In reality, Washington was well aware that U.S. intervention could lead to nuclear war and limited itself to protests against Soviet brutality in crushing the uprising.

The year of discontent was not without its consequences, however. Soviet leaders now recognized that Moscow could maintain control over its satellites in Eastern Europe only by granting them the leeway to adopt domestic policies appropriate to local conditions. Krushchev had already embarked on this path when, during a visit to Belgrade in 1955, he assured Josip Tito that there were "different roads to socialism." Eastern European Communist leaders now took Khrushchev at his word and adopted reform programs to make socialism more palatable to their subject populations. Even János Kádár, derisively labeled the "butcher of Budapest," managed to preserve many of Imre Nagy's reforms to allow a measure of capitalist incentive and freedom of expression in Hungary.

Czechoslovakia did not share in the thaw of the mid-1950s and remained under the rule of Antonin Novotny (1904–1975), who had been placed in power by Stalin himself. By the late 1960s, however, Novotny's policies had led to widespread popular alienation, and in 1968, with the support of intellectuals and reformist party members, Alexander Dubček (1921–1992) was elected

first secretary of the Communist Party. He immediately attempted to create what was popularly called "socialism with a human face," relaxing restrictions on freedom of speech and the press and the right to travel abroad. Reforms were announced in the economic sector, and party control over all aspects of society was reduced. A period of euphoria erupted that came to be known as the "Prague Spring."

It proved to be short-lived. Encouraged by Dubček's actions, some Czechs called for more far-reaching reforms, including neutrality and withdrawal from the Soviet bloc. To forestall the spread of this "spring fever," the Soviet Red Army, supported by troops from other Warsaw Pact states, invaded Czechoslovakia in August 1968 and crushed the reform movement. Gustav Husak (1913–1991), a committed Stalinist, replaced Dubček and restored the old order (see the box on p. 54).

Elsewhere in Eastern Europe, Stalinist policies continued to hold sway. The ruling Communist government in East Germany, led by Walter Ulbricht (1893–1973), consolidated its position in the early 1950s and became a faithful Soviet satellite. Industry was nationalized and agriculture collectivized. After the 1953 workers' revolt was crushed by Soviet tanks, a steady flight of East Germans to West Germany ensued, primarily through the city of Berlin. This exodus of mostly skilled laborers (soon only party chief Ulbricht would be left, remarked one Soviet observer sardonically) created economic problems and in 1961 led the East German government to erect the infamous Berlin Wall separating West from East Berlin, as well as even more fearsome barriers along the entire border with West Germany.

After walling off the West, East Germany succeeded in developing the strongest economy among the Soviet Union's Eastern European satellites. In 1971, Walter Ulbricht was succeeded by Erich Honecker (1912–1994), a party hard-liner who was deeply committed to the ideological battle against détente. Propaganda increased, and the use of the Stasi, the secret police, became a hallmark of Honecker's virtual dictatorship. Honecker ruled unchallenged for the next eighteen years.

# CULTURE AND SOCIETY IN THE SOVIET BLOC

In his occasional musings about the future Communist utopia, Karl Marx had predicted the emergence of a classless society to replace the exploitative and hierarchical systems of feudalism and capitalism. Workers would take part in productive activities but would share equally in the fruits of their labor. In their free time, they would help

# THE BREZHNEV DOCTRINE

*In the summer of 1968, when the new Communist Party leaders in Czechoslovakia were seriously considering proposals for reforming the totalitarian system there, the Warsaw Pact nations met under the leadership of Soviet party chief Leonid Brezhnev to assess the threat to the socialist camp. Shortly after, military forces of several Soviet bloc nations entered Czechoslovakia and imposed a new government subservient to Moscow. The move was justified by the spirit of "proletarian internationalism" and was widely viewed as a warning to China and other socialist states not to stray too far from Marxist-Leninist orthodoxy, as interpreted by the Soviet Union. The principle came to be known as the Brezhnev Doctrine.*

## A LETTER TO CZECHOSLOVAKIA

To the Central Committee of the Communist Party of Czechoslovakia                    Warsaw, July 15, 1968

Dear comrades!

On behalf of the Central Committees of the Communist and Workers' Parties of Bulgaria, Hungary, the German Democratic Republic, Poland, and the Soviet Union, we address ourselves to you with this letter, prompted by a feeling of sincere friendship based on the principles of Marxism-Leninism and proletarian internationalism and by the concern of our common affairs for strengthening the positions of socialism and the security of the socialist community of nations.

The development of events in your country evokes in us deep anxiety. It is our firm conviction that the offensive of the reactionary forces, backed by imperialists, against your Party and the foundations of the social system in the Czechoslovak Socialist Republic, threatens to push your country off the road of socialism and that consequently it jeopardizes the interests of the entire socialist system. . . .

We neither had nor have any intention of interfering in such affairs as are strictly the internal business of your Party and your state, nor of violating the principles of respect, independence, and equality in the relations among the Communist Parties and socialist countries. . . .

At the same time we cannot agree to have hostile forces push your country from the road of socialism and create a threat of severing Czechoslovakia from the socialist community. . . . This is the common cause of our countries, which have joined in the Warsaw Treaty to ensure independence, peace, and security in Europe, and to set up an insurmountable barrier against aggression and revenge. . . . We shall never agree to have imperialism, using peaceful or non-peaceful methods, making a gap from the inside or from the outside in the socialist system, and changing in imperialism's favor the correlation of forces in Europe. . . .

That is why we believe that a decisive rebuff of the anti-communist forces, and decisive efforts for the preservation of the socialist system in Czechoslovakia are not only your task but ours as well. . . .

We express the conviction that the Communist Party of Czechoslovakia, conscious of its responsibility, will take the necessary steps to block the path of reaction. In this struggle you can count on the solidarity and all-round assistance of the fraternal socialist countries.

Source: *Moscow News*, Supplement to No. 30 (917), 1968, pp. 3–6.

---

produce a new, advanced culture, proletarian in character and egalitarian in content.

## Cultural Expression

The reality in the post–World War II Soviet Union and in Eastern Europe was somewhat different. Under Stalin, the Soviet cultural scene was a wasteland. Beginning in 1946, a series of government decrees made all forms of literary and scientific expression dependent on the state. All Soviet culture was expected to follow the party line. Historians, philosophers, and social scientists all grew accustomed to quoting Marx, Lenin, and above all, Stalin as their chief authorities. Novels and plays, too, were supposed to portray Communist heroes and their efforts to create a better society. No criticism of existing social conditions was permitted. Even distinguished composers such as Dmitri Shostakovich were compelled to heed Stalin's criticisms, including his view that contemporary Western music was nothing but a "mishmash." Some areas of intellectual activity were virtually abolished; the science of genetics disappeared, and few movies were made during Stalin's final years.

Stalin's death brought a modest respite from cultural repression. Writers and artists banned during Stalin's years were again allowed to publish. Still, Soviet authorities, including Khrushchev, were reluctant to allow cultural freedom to move far beyond official Soviet ideology.

These restrictions, however, did not prevent the emergence of some significant Soviet literature, although authors paid a heavy price if they alienated the Soviet authorities. Boris Pasternak (1890–1960), who began his literary career as a poet, won the Nobel Prize in 1958 for his celebrated novel *Doctor Zhivago*, published in Italy in 1957. But the Soviet government condemned Pasternak's anti-Soviet tendencies, banned the novel from the Soviet Union, and would not allow him to accept the prize. The author had alienated the authorities by describing a society scarred by the excesses of Bolshevik revolutionary zeal.

Alexander Solzhenitsyn (b. 1918) caused an even greater furor than Pasternak. Solzhenitsyn had spent eight years in forced-labor camps for criticizing Stalin, and his *One Day in the Life of Ivan Denisovich*, which won him the Nobel Prize in 1970, was an account of life in those camps (see the box on p. 56). Later, Solzhenitsyn wrote *The Gulag Archipelago*, a detailed indictment of the whole system of Soviet oppression. Soviet authorities denounced Solzhenitsyn's efforts to inform the world of Soviet crimes against humanity and arrested and expelled him from the Soviet Union after he published *The Gulag Archipelago* abroad in 1973.

Exile abroad rather than imprisonment in forced-labor camps was perhaps a sign of modest progress. But even the limited freedom that had arisen during the Khrushchev years was rejected after his removal from power. Cultural controls were reimposed, destalinization was halted, and authors were again sent to labor camps for expressing outlawed ideas. These restrictive policies continued until the late 1980s.

In the Eastern European satellites, cultural freedom varied considerably from country to country. In Poland, intellectuals had access to Western publications as well as greater freedom to travel to the West. Hungarian and Yugoslav Communists, too, tolerated a certain level of intellectual activity that was not liked but not prohibited. Elsewhere, intellectuals were forced to conform to the regime's demands. After the Soviet invasion of Czechoslovakia in 1968, Czech Communists pursued a policy of strict cultural control.

The socialist camp also experienced the many facets of modern popular culture. By the early 1970s, there were 28 million television sets in the Soviet Union, although state authorities controlled the content of the programs that the Soviet people watched. Tourism, too, made inroads into the Communist world as state-run industries provided vacation time and governments facilitated the establishment of resorts for workers on the coasts of the Black Sea and the Adriatic. In Poland, the number of vacationers who used holiday retreats increased from 700,000 in 1960 to 2.8 million in 1972.

Spectator sports became a large industry and were also highly politicized as the result of Cold War divisions. Victory in international athletic events was viewed as proof of the superiority of the socialist system over its capitalist rival. Accordingly, the state provided money for the construction of gymnasiums and training camps and portrayed athletes as superheroes.

**STALINIST HEROIC: AN EXAMPLE OF SOCIALIST REALISM.** Under Stalin and his successors, art was assigned the task of indoctrinating the Soviet population on the public virtues, such as hard work, loyalty to the state, and patriotism. Grandiose statuary erected to commemorate the heroic efforts of the Red Army during World War II appeared in every Soviet city. Here is an example in Minsk, today the capital of Belarus.

# ONE DAY IN THE LIFE OF IVAN DENISOVICH

*O*n November 20, 1962, a Soviet magazine published a work by Alexander Solzhenitsyn that created a literary and political furor. The short novel related one day in the life of its chief character, Ivan Denisovich, at a Siberian concentration camp, to which he had been sentenced at the end of World War II for supposedly spying for the Germans while a Soviet soldier. This excerpt narrates the daily journey from the prison camp to a work project through the 17 degrees-below-zero cold of Siberia. Many Soviets identified with Ivan as a symbol of the suffering they had endured under Stalin.

## ALEXANDER SOLZHENITSYN, *ONE DAY IN THE LIFE OF IVAN DENISOVICH*

There were escort guards all over the place. They flung a semicircle around the column on its way to the power station, their machine guns sticking out and pointing right at your face. And there were guards with gray dogs. One dog bared its fangs as if laughing at the prisoners. The escorts all wore short sheepskins, except for half a dozen whose coats trailed the ground. The long sheepskins were interchangeable: they were worn by anyone whose turn had come to man the watchtowers.

And once again as they brought the squads together the escort recounted the entire power-station column by fives. . . .

Out beyond the camp boundary the intense cold, accompanied by a headwind, stung even Shukhov's face, which was used to every kind of unpleasantness. Realizing that he would have the wind in his face all the way to the power station, he decided to make use of his bit of rag. To meet the contingency of a headwind he, like many other prisoners, had got himself a cloth with a long tape on each end. The prisoners admitted that these helped a bit. Shukhov covered his face up to the eyes, brought the tapes around below his ears, and fastened the ends together at the back of his neck. Then he covered his nape with the flap of his hat and raised his coat collar. The next thing was to pull the front flap of the hat down into his brow. Thus in front only his eyes remained unprotected. He fixed his coat tightly at the waist with the rope. Now everything was in order except for his hands, which were already stiff with cold (his mittens were worthless). He rubbed them, he clapped them together, for he knew that in a moment he'd have to put them behind his back and keep them there for the entire march.

The chief of the escort guard recited the "morning prayer," which every prisoner was heartily sick of:

"Attention, prisoners. Marching orders must be strictly obeyed. Keep to your ranks. No hurrying, keep a steady pace. No talking. Keep your eyes fixed ahead and your hands behind your backs. A step to right or left is considered an attempt to escape and the escort has orders to shoot without warning. Leading guards, on the double."

The two guards in the lead of the escort must have set out along the road. The column heaved forward, shoulders swaying, and the escorts, some twenty paces to the right and left of the column, each man at a distance of ten paces from the next, machine guns held at the ready, set off too.

From *One Day in the Life of Ivan Denisovich* by Alexander Solzhenitsyn, translated by Ralph Parker. Translation copyright © 1963 by E. P. Dutton and Victor Gollancz, Ltd. Copyright renewed © 1991 by Penguin USA and Victor Gollancz, Ltd. Used by permission of Dutton Signet, a division of Penguin Books USA Inc.

## Social Changes in the Soviet Union and Eastern Europe

The imposition of Marxist systems in Eastern Europe had far-reaching social consequences. Most Eastern European countries made the change from peasant societies to modern industrialized economies. In Bulgaria, for example, 80 percent of the labor force was in agriculture in 1950, but only 20 percent was still there in 1980. Although the Soviet Union and its Eastern European satellites never achieved the high standards of living of the West, they did experience some improvement. In 1960, the average real income of Polish peasants was four times higher than before World War II. Consumer goods also became more widespread. In East Germany, only 17 percent of families had television sets in 1960, but 75 percent had acquired them by 1972.

According to Marxist doctrine, government control of industry and the elimination of private property were supposed to lead to a classless society. Although the classless society was never achieved, that ideal did have important social consequences. For one thing, traditional ruling classes were stripped of their special status after 1945. The Potocki family in Poland, for example, which had owned 9 million acres of land before the war, lost all of its possessions, and family members were reduced to the ranks of common laborers.

The desire to create a classless society led to noticeable changes in education. In some countries, the desire to provide equal educational opportunities led to laws that mandated quota systems based on class. In East Germany, for example, 50 percent of the students in secondary schools had to be children of workers and peasants. The sons of manual workers constituted 53 percent of university students in Yugoslavia in 1964 and 40 percent in East Germany, compared to only 15 percent in Italy and 5.3 percent in West Germany. Social mobility also increased. In Poland in 1961, half of the white-collar workers came from blue-collar families. A significant number of judges, professors, and industrial managers stemmed from working-class backgrounds.

Education became crucial in preparing for new jobs in the communist system and led to higher enrollments in both secondary schools and universities. In Czechoslovakia, for example, the number of students in secondary schools tripled between 1945 and 1970, and the number of university students quadrupled between the 1930s and the 1960s. The type of education that students received also changed. In Hungary before World War II, 40 percent of students studied law, 9 percent engineering and technology, and 5 percent agriculture. In 1970, the figures were 35 percent in engineering and technology, 9 percent in agriculture, and only 4 percent in law.

By the 1970s, the new managers of society, regardless of class background, realized the importance of higher education and used their power to gain special privileges for their children. By 1971, fully 60 percent of the children of white-collar workers attended a university, and even though blue-collar families constituted 60 percent of the population, only 36 percent of their children attended institutions of higher learning. Even East Germany dropped its requirement that 50 percent of secondary students had to be the offspring of workers and peasants.

This shift in educational preferences demonstrates yet another aspect of the social structure in the Communist world: the emergence of a new privileged class, made up of members of the Communist Party, state officials, high-ranking officers in the military and secret police, and a few special professional groups. The new elite not only possessed political power but also received special privileges, including the right to purchase high-quality goods in special stores (in Czechoslovakia, the elite could obtain organically grown produce not available to anyone else), paid vacations at special resorts, access to good housing and superior medical services, and advantages in education and jobs for their children.

Ideals of equality did not include women. Men dominated the leadership positions of the Communist parties in the Soviet Union and Eastern Europe. Women did have greater opportunities in the workforce and even in the professions, however. In the Soviet Union, women comprised 51 percent of the labor force in 1980; by the mid-1980s, they constituted 50 percent of the engineers, 80 percent of the doctors, and 75 percent of the teachers and teachers' aides. But many of these were low-paying jobs; most female doctors, for example, worked in primary care and were paid less than skilled machinists. The chief administrators in hospitals and schools were still men.

Moreover, although women were part of the workforce, they were never freed of their traditional roles in the home. Most women confronted what came to be known as the "double shift." After working eight hours in their

Courtesy of William J. Duiker

**GHOSTS OF SOVIET OLYMPIC GLORY.** A poignant legacy of the collapse of the Soviet Union is reflected in this abandoned skating rink and ski jump in Almaty, Kazakhstan. It was in this rink and on the adjacent ski jump in the mountains of Central Asia that the Soviet Union trained its best athletes to win international competitions for gold medals and glory during the Cold War. Here we sense the ghosts of former skaters, subsidized darlings of the Soviet Empire, as they attempt the difficult triple jump.

jobs, they came home to face the housework and care of the children. They might spend two hours a day in long lines at a number of stores waiting to buy food and clothes. Because of the housing situation, they were forced to use kitchens that were shared by a number of families.

Nearly three-quarters of a century after the Bolshevik Revolution, then, the Marxist dream of an advanced, egalitarian society was as far away as ever. Although in some respects conditions in the socialist camp were an improvement over those before World War II, many problems and inequities were as intransigent as ever.

# THE DISINTEGRATION OF THE SOVIET EMPIRE

On the death of Konstantin Chernenko in 1985, party leaders selected the talented and vigorous Soviet official Mikhail Gorbachev to succeed him. The new Soviet leader had shown early signs of promise. Born into a peasant family in 1931, Gorbachev combined farmwork with school and received the Order of the Red Banner for his agricultural efforts. This award and his good school record enabled him to study law at the University of Moscow. After receiving his law degree in 1955, he returned to his native southern Russia, where he eventually became first secretary of the Communist Party in the city of Stavropol and then first secretary of the regional party committee. In 1978, Gorbachev was made a member of the party's Central Committee in Moscow. Two years later, he became a full member of the ruling Politburo and secretary of the Central Committee.

During the early 1980s, Gorbachev began to realize the extent of Soviet problems and the crucial importance of massive reform to transform the system. During a visit to Canada in 1983, he discovered to his astonishment that Canadian farmers worked hard on their own initiative. "We'll never have this for fifty years," he reportedly remarked.[4] On his return to Moscow, he established a series of committees to evaluate the situation and recommend measures to improve the system.

## The Gorbachev Era

With his election as party general secretary in 1985, Gorbachev seemed intent on taking earlier reforms to their logical conclusions. The cornerstone of his reform program was *perestroika*, or "restructuring." At first, it meant only a reordering of economic policy, as Gorbachev called for the beginning of a market economy with limited free enterprise and some private property. Initial economic reforms were difficult to implement, however.

Radicals demanded decisive measures; conservatives feared that rapid changes would be too painful. In his attempt to achieve compromise, Gorbachev often pursued partial liberalization, which satisfied neither faction and also failed to work, producing only more discontent.

Gorbachev soon perceived that in the Soviet system, the economic sphere was intimately tied to the social and political spheres. Any efforts to reform the economy without political or social reform would be doomed to failure. One of the most important instruments of *perestroika* was *glasnost,* or "openness." Soviet citizens and officials were encouraged to openly discuss the strengths and weaknesses of the Soviet Union. This policy could be seen in *Pravda,* the official newspaper of the Communist Party, where disasters such as the nuclear accident at Chernobyl in 1986 and collisions of ships in the Black Sea received increasing coverage. Soon this type of reporting was extended to include reports of official corruption, sloppy factory work, and protests against government policy. The arts also benefited from the new policy as previously banned works were now allowed to circulate and motion pictures began to depict negative aspects of Soviet life. Music based on Western styles, such as jazz and rock, began to be performed openly.

Political reforms were equally revolutionary. In June 1987, the principle of two-candidate elections was introduced; previously, voters had been presented with only one candidate. Most dissidents, including Andrei Sakharov, who had spent years in internal exile, were released. At the Communist Party conference in 1988, Gorbachev called for the creation of a new Soviet parliament, the Congress of People's Deputies, whose members were to be chosen in competitive elections. It convened in 1989, the first such meeting since 1918. Now as an elected member of the Congress, Sakharov called for an end to the Communist monopoly of power and on December 11, 1989, the day he died, urged the creation of a new, non-Communist party. Early in 1990, Gorbachev legalized the formation of other political parties and struck out Article 6 of the Soviet constitution, which guaranteed the "leading role" of the Communist Party. Hitherto, the position of first secretary of the party was the most important post in the Soviet Union, but as the Communist Party became less closely associated with the state, the powers of this office diminished. Gorbachev attempted to consolidate his power by creating a new state presidency, and in March 1990, he became the Soviet Union's first president.

One of Gorbachev's most serious problems stemmed from the nature of the Soviet Union. The Union of Soviet Socialist Republics was a truly multiethnic country, containing 92 nationalities and 112 recognized languages. Previously, the iron hand of the Communist Party, centered in Moscow, had kept a lid on the centuries-old ethnic tensions that had periodically erupted throughout the history of this region. As Gorbachev released this iron grip, tensions resurfaced, a by-product of *glasnost* that Gorbachev had not anticipated. Ethnic groups took advantage of the new openness to protest what they perceived to be ethnically motivated slights. As violence erupted, the Soviet army, in disarray since the Soviet intervention in Afghanistan in 1979, had difficulty controlling the situation. In some cases, independence movements and ethnic causes became linked, as in Azerbaijan, where the National Front became the spokesgroup for the Muslim Azerbaijanis in the conflict with Christian Armenians.

The period from 1988 to 1990 witnessed the emergence of nationalist movements in all fifteen republics of the Soviet Union. Often motivated by ethnic concerns, many of them called for sovereignty of the republics and independence from Russian-based rule centered in Moscow. Such movements sprang up first in Georgia in late 1988 and then in Moldavia, Uzbekistan, Azerbaijan, and the three Baltic republics.

In December 1989, the Communist Party of Lithuania declared itself independent of the Communist Party of the Soviet Union. Gorbachev made it clear that he supported self-determination but not secession, which he believed would be detrimental to the Soviet Union. Nevertheless, on March 11, 1990, the Lithuanian Supreme Council unilaterally declared Lithuania independent. Its formal name was now the Lithuanian Republic; the adjectives *Soviet* and *Socialist* had been dropped. On March 15, the Soviet Congress of People's Deputies, though recognizing a general right to secede from the Union of Soviet Socialist Republics, declared the Lithuanian declaration null and void; the Congress stated that proper procedures must be established and followed before secession would be acceptable.

During 1990 and 1991, Gorbachev struggled to deal with the problems unleashed by his reforms. On the one hand, he tried to appease the conservative forces who complained about the growing disorder within the Soviet Union. On the other hand, he tried to accommodate the liberal forces who increasingly favored a new kind of decentralized Soviet federation. Gorbachev especially labored to cooperate more closely with Boris Yeltsin (b. 1931), elected president of the Russian Republic in June 1991. Conservative elements from the army, the party, and the KGB, however, had grown increasingly worried about the potential dissolution of the Soviet Union. On August 19, 1991, a group of these discontented rightists arrested Gorbachev and attempted to seize power. Gorbachev's unwillingness to work with the conspirators and the brave resistance in Moscow of Yeltsin and thousands of Russians who had grown accustomed to their new liberties caused the coup to disintegrate rapidly. The actions of these right-wing plotters served to accelerate the very process they had hoped to stop—the disintegration of the Soviet Union.

Despite desperate pleas from Gorbachev, all fifteen republics soon opted for complete independence (see Map 2.2). Ukraine voted for independence on December 1, 1991. A week later, the leaders of Russia, Ukraine, and Belarus announced that the Soviet Union had "ceased to exist" and would be replaced by a much looser federation, the Commonwealth of Independent States. Gorbachev resigned on December 25, 1991, and turned over his responsibilities as commander in chief to Boris Yeltsin, the president of Russia. By the end of 1991, one of the largest empires in world history had come to an end, and a new era had begun in its lands.

## The New Russia: From Empire to Nation

In Russia, by far the largest of the former Soviet republics, a new power struggle soon ensued. Yeltsin, a onetime engineer who had been dismissed from the Politburo in 1987 for his radicalism, was committed to introducing a free market economy as quickly as possible. In December 1991, the Congress of People's Deputies granted Yeltsin temporary power to rule by decree. But former Communist Party members and their allies in the Congress were opposed to many of Yeltsin's economic reforms and tried to place new limits on his powers. Yeltsin fought back. After winning a vote of confidence on April 25, 1993, Yeltsin pushed ahead with plans for a new Russian constitution that would abolish the Congress of People's Deputies, create a two-chamber parliament, and establish a strong presidency. A hard-line parliamentary minority resisted and in early October took the offensive, urging supporters to take over government offices and the central television station. Yeltsin responded by ordering military forces to storm the parliament building and arrest hard-line opponents. Yeltsin used his victory to consolidate his power in parliamentary elections held in December.

During the mid-1990s, Yeltsin was able to maintain a precarious grip on power while seeking to implement reforms that would place Russia on a firm course toward a pluralistic political system and a market economy. But the new post-Communist Russia remained as fragile as ever. Burgeoning economic inequality and rampant corruption aroused widespread criticism and shook the confidence of the Russian people in the superiority of the

**MAP 2.2** Eastern Europe and the Former Soviet Union. After the disintegration of the Soviet Union in 1991, Soviet republics declared their independence. This map shows the new configuration of the states that emerged in the 1990s, including the boundaries after the dissolution of Czechoslovakia and Yugoslavia. ➤ *What new nations have appeared since the end of the Cold War?*

capitalist system over the one that existed under Communist rule. A nagging war in the Caucasus—where the Muslim people of Chechnya sought national independence from Russia—drained the government budget and exposed the decrepit state of the once vaunted Red Army. In presidential elections held in 1996, Yeltsin was re-elected, but the rising popularity of a revived Communist Party and the growing strength of nationalist elements, combined with Yeltsin's precarious health, raised serious questions about the future of the country.

At the end of 1999, Yeltsin suddenly resigned his office and was replaced by Vladimir Putin (b. 1952), a former member of the KGB. Putin vowed to bring an end to the rampant corruption and inexperience that permeated

Russian political culture and to strengthen the role of the central government in managing the affairs of state. During succeeding months, his proposal to centralize power in the hands of the federal government in Moscow was given approval by the parliament; in early 2001, he presented a new plan to regulate political parties, which had risen in number to more than fifty. Parties at both extremes of the political spectrum, the Yabloko (apple) faction representing Western-style liberal policies and Gennadi Zyuganov's revived Communist Party, opposed the legislation, without success. Putin has not used his enhanced powers, however, to introduce market reforms and rein in the powerful forces that have impeded Russia's transition to an advanced capitalist society.

Putin also vowed to bring the breakaway state of Chechnya back under Russian authority and to adopt a more assertive role in international affairs. The new president took advantage of growing public anger at Western plans to expand the NATO alliance into Eastern Europe, as well as aggressive actions by NATO countries against Serbia in the Balkans (see Chapter 4) to restore Russia's position as an influential force in the world. To undercut U.S. dominance on the political scene, Moscow has improved relations with neighboring China and simultaneously sought to cooperate with European nations on issues of common concern. To assuage national pride, Putin has entered negotiations with such former republics of the old Soviet Union as Belarus and Ukraine to tighten forms of mutual political economic cooperation.

What had happened to derail Yeltsin's plan to transform Soviet society? To some critics, Yeltsin and his advisers tried to achieve too much too fast. Between 1991 and 1995, state firms that had previously provided about 80 percent of all industrial production and employment had been privatized, and the price of goods (previously subject to government regulation) was opened up to market forces. Only agriculture—where the decision to privatize collective farms had little impact in rural areas—was left substantially untouched. The immediate results were disastrous: industrial output dropped by more than one-third, and unemployment levels and prices rose dramatically. Many Russian workers and soldiers were not paid their salaries for months on end, and many social services came to an abrupt halt.

With the harsh official and ideological constraints of the Soviet system suddenly removed, corruption—labeled by one observer "criminal gang capitalism"—became rampant, and the government often appeared inept in coping with complexities of a market economy. Few Russians appeared to grasp the realities of modern capitalism and understandably reacted to the inevitable transition pains from the old system by heaping all the blame on the new one. The fact is that Yeltsin had attempted to change the structure of the Soviet system without due regard to the necessity of changing the mentality of the people as well. The result was a high level of disenchantment. A new joke circulated among the Russian people: "We know now that everything they told us about communism was false. And everything they told us about capitalism was true."

## Eastern Europe: From Soviet Satellites to Sovereign Nations

The disintegration of the Soviet Union had an immediate impact on its neighbors to the west. First to respond, as in 1956, was Poland, where popular protests of high food prices had erupted in the early 1980s, leading to the rise of an independent labor movement called Solidarity. Led by Lech Walesa (b. 1943), Solidarity rapidly became an influential force for change and a threat to the government's monopoly of power. The union was outlawed in 1981, but martial law did not solve Poland's serious economic problems, and in 1988, the Communist government bowed to the inevitable and permitted free national elections to take place, resulting in the election of Walesa as president of Poland in December 1990. Unlike the situation in 1956, when Khrushchev had intervened to prevent the collapse of the Soviet satellite system in Eastern Europe, in the late 1980s, Moscow—inspired by Gorbachev's policy of encouraging "new thinking" to improve relations with the Western powers—took no action to reverse the verdict in Warsaw.

In Hungary, as in Poland, the process of transition had begun many years previously. After crushing the Hungarian revolution of 1956, the Communist government of János Kádár had tried to assuage popular opinion by enacting a series of far-reaching economic reforms (labeled "communism with a capitalist face-lift"), but as the 1980s progressed, the economy sagged, and in 1989, the regime permitted the formation of opposition political parties, leading eventually to the formation of a non-Communist coalition government in elections held in March 1990.

The transition in Czechoslovakia was more abrupt. After Soviet troops crushed the Prague Spring in 1968, hard-line Communists under Gustav Husak followed a policy of massive repression to maintain their power. In 1977, dissident intellectuals formed an organization called Charter 77 as a vehicle for protest against violations of human rights. Regardless of the repressive atmosphere, dissident activities continued to grow during the 1980s, and when massive demonstrations broke out in several major cities in 1989, President Husak's government, lacking any real popular support, collapsed. At the end of December, he was replaced by Václav Havel, a dissident playwright who had been a leading figure in Charter 77.

But the most dramatic events took place in East Germany, where a persistent economic slump and the ongoing oppressiveness of the regime of Erich Honecker led to a flight of refugees and mass demonstrations against the regime in the summer and fall of 1989. Capitulating to popular pressure, the Communist government opened its entire border with the West. The Berlin Wall, the most tangible symbol of the Cold War, became the site of a massive celebration, and most of it was dismantled by joyful Germans from both sides of the border. In March 1990, free elections led to the formation of a non-

Communist government that rapidly carried out a program of political and economic reunification with West Germany.

The dissolution of the Soviet Union and its satellite system in Eastern Europe brought a dramatic end to the Cold War. At the dawn of the 1990s, a generation of global rivalry between two ideological systems had come to a close, and world leaders turned their attention to the construction of what U.S. President George Herbert Walker Bush called the New World Order. But what sort of new order would it be?

# CONCLUSION

The Soviet Union had emerged from World War II as one of the world's two superpowers. Its armies had played an instrumental role in the final defeat of the powerful German war machine and had installed pliant Communist regimes throughout Eastern Europe. No force of comparable strength had occupied the plains of western Russia since the Mongols in the thirteenth and fourteenth centuries.

During the next four decades, the Soviet Union appeared to be secure in its power. Its military and economic performance during the first postwar decade was sufficiently impressive to produce an atmosphere of incipient panic in Washington. By the mid-1980s, however, fears that the Soviet Union would surpass the United States as an economic power had long since dissipated, and the Soviet system appeared to be mired in a state of near paralysis. Economic growth had slowed to a snail's pace, corruption had reached epidemic levels, and

leadership had passed to a generation of elderly party bureaucrats who appeared incapable of addressing the burgeoning problems that affected Soviet society.

What had happened to tarnish the dream that had inspired Lenin and his fellow Bolsheviks to believe they could create a Marxist paradise? Some analysts argue that the ambitious defense policies adopted by the Reagan administration forced Moscow into an arms race it could not afford and thus ultimately led to a collapse of the Soviet economy. Others suggest that Soviet problems were more deeply rooted and would have led to the disintegration of the Soviet Union even without outside stimulation. Both arguments have some validity, but the latter is surely closer to the mark. For years, if not decades, leaders in the Kremlin had disguised or ignored the massive inefficiencies of the Soviet system. It seems clear in retrospect that the Soviet command economy proved better at managing the early stages of the Industrial Revolution than at moving on to the next stage of an advanced technological society and that the Leninist concept of democratic centralism failed to provide the quality of leadership and political courage needed to cope with the challenges of nation building. By the 1980s, behind the powerful shield of the Red Army, the system had become an empty shell.

In the years immediately preceding his ascent to power in the Politburo, the perceptive Mikhail Gorbachev had recognized the crucial importance of instituting radical reforms. At the time, he hoped that by doing so, he could save the socialist system. By then, however, it was too late. In the classic formulation of dictatorial regimes the world over, the most dangerous period is when leaders adopt reform measures to prevent collapse.

| | 1945 | 1955 | 1965 | 1975 | 1985 | 1995 | 2000 |

**SOVIET UNION AND RUSSIA**

Death of Stalin and emergence of Khrushchev

Breshnev era

Dissolution of the Soviet Union

Gorbachev years

Yeltsin era

**EASTERN EUROPE**

"Prague Spring"

Communist governments in Eastern Europe

Revolutions in Eastern Europe

## INFOTRAC COLLEGE EDITION

Visit source collections at **http://infotrac.thomsonlearning.com,** and use the Search function with the following key terms:

Gorbachev
Khrushchev
Perestroika
Stalin

## WORLD HISTORY RESOURCES

Visit the *The World Since World War II* Companion Web site for resources specific to this textbook:

**http://history.wadsworth.com/duiker_wwii/**

The Wadsworth World History Resource Center at **http://history.wadsworth.com/world/** offers a variety of tools to help you succeed in this course, including access to quizzes; images; documents; interactive simulations, maps, and timelines; movie explorations; and a wealth of other sources.

# CHAPTER NOTES

1. Vladislav Zubok and Constantin Pleshakov, *Inside the Kremlin's Cold War: From Stalin to Khrushchev* (Cambridge, England, 1996), p. 166.
2. Nikita Khrushchev, *Khrushchev Remembers*, trans. Strobe Talbott (Boston, 1970), p. 77.
3. Quoted in Hedrick Smith, *The New Russians* (New York, 1990), p. 30.
4. Hedrick Smith, *The New Russians*, p. 74.

*Chapter*

**3**

# POSTWAR EUROPE:
# ON THE PATH
# TO UNITY?

At the end of World War II, European civilization was in ruins. Almost forty million people had been killed in six years. Massive air raids and artillery bombardments had reduced many of the great cities of Europe to rubble. An American general described Berlin: "Wherever we looked, we saw desolation. It was like a city of the dead. Suffering and shock were visible in every face. Dead bodies still remained in canals and lakes and were being dug out from under bomb debris." Millions of Europeans faced starvation as grain harvests were only half of what they had been in 1939. Millions were also homeless. Millions more had been uprooted by the war; now they became "displaced persons," trying to find food and then their way home.

Between 1945 and 1970, Europe not only recovered from the devastating effects of World War II but also experienced an economic resurgence that seemed nothing less than miraculous. Economic growth and virtually full employment continued so long that the first postwar recession, in 1973, came as a shock to Western Europe. It was short-lived, however, and economic growth returned. After the collapse of Communist governments in the revolutions of 1989, a number of Eastern European states sought to create market economies and join the military and economic unions first formed by Western European states.

# WESTERN EUROPE: RECOVERY AND RENEWAL

In the immediate postwar era, the challenge was clear and intimidating. The peoples of Europe needed to rebuild their national economies and reestablish and strengthen their democratic institutions. They needed to find the means to cooperate in the face of a potential new threat from the east in the form of the Soviet Union. Above all, they needed to restore their confidence in the continuing vitality and future promise of European civilization—a civilization whose image had been badly tarnished by two bitter internal conflicts in the space of a quarter century.

In confronting the challenge, the Europeans possessed one significant trump card: the support and assistance of the United States. The United States had entered World War II as a major industrial power, but its global influence had been limited by the effects of the Great Depression and a self-imposed policy of isolation that had removed it from active involvement in world affairs. But after the United States helped bring the conflict to a close, the nation bestrode the world like a colossus. Its military power was enormous, its political influence was unparalleled, and its economic potential, fueled by the demands of building a war machine to defeat the Axis, seemed unlimited. When on June 5, 1947, Secretary of State George C. Marshall told the graduating class at Harvard University that the United States was prepared to assist the nations of Europe in the task of recovery from "hun-

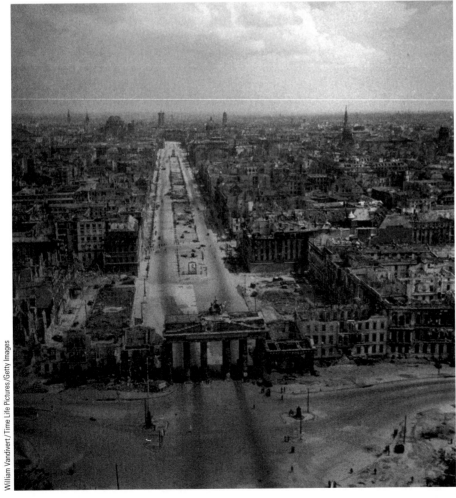

➤ ARMAGEDDON, 1945. In the last months of World War II, the German capital of Berlin was exposed to a relentless bombing campaign by the Allied forces. As the war came to an end in May 1945, the once-stylish city was in ruins. Shown here is a view of Berlin's most fashionable street, Unter den Linden. In the foreground is Brandenburg Gate, soon to become the point of division between East and West Berlin.

ger, poverty, desperation, and chaos," he offered a beacon of hope to a region badly in need of reasons for optimism.

## The Triumph of Democracy in Postwar Europe

With the economic aid of the Marshall Plan, the countries of Western Europe (see Map 3.1) recovered relatively rapidly from the devastation of World War II. Between 1947 and 1950, European countries received $9.4 billion to be used for new equipment and raw materials. By the late 1970s, industrial production had surpassed all previous records, and Western Europe experienced virtually full employment. Social welfare programs included affordable health care; housing; family allowances to provide a minimum level of material care for children; increases in sickness, accident, unemployment, and old-age benefits; and educational opportunities. Despite economic recessions in the mid-1970s and early 1980s, caused in part by a dramatic increase in the price of oil in 1973, the economies of Western Europe had never been so prosperous, leading some observers to label the period a "golden age" of political and economic achievement. Western Europeans were full participants in the technological advances of the age and seemed quite capable of standing up to competition from the other global economic powerhouses, Japan and the United States.

At the end of World War II, confidence in the ability of democratic institutions to meet the challenge of the industrial era was at an ebb. The Western democracies had been unable to confront the threat of fascism until the armies of the Wehrmacht began their march across Europe at the end of the 1930s, and most succumbed rapidly to the Nazi juggernaut. As the war finally came to a close, many Europeans, their confidence shaken by bleak prospects for the future, turned their eyes to the Soviet model. In France and Italy, local Communist parties received wide support in national elections, raising fears in the United States that they might eventually be voted into power in Paris and Rome.

By the late 1940s, however, confidence in democratic institutions began to revive as economic conditions started to improve. Even Spain and Portugal, which retained their prewar dictatorial regimes until the mid-1970s, established democratic systems in the late 1970s. Moderate political parties, especially the Christian Democrats in Italy and Germany, played a particularly important role in Europe's economic restoration. Overall, the influence of Communist parties declined, although reformist mass parties only slightly left of center, such as the Labour Party in Britain and the Social Democrats in West Germany, continued to share power. During the mid-1970s, a new variety of communism, called Eurocommunism, emerged briefly when Communist parties tried to work within the democratic system as mass movements committed to better government. But by the 1980s, internal political developments in Western Europe and events within the Communist world had combined to undermine the Eurocommunist experiment.

### FRANCE: EXPECTATIONS OF GRANDEUR

The history of France for nearly a quarter century after the war was dominated by one man, Charles de Gaulle (1890–1970), who possessed an unshakable faith in his own historic mission to reestablish the greatness of the French nation. During the war, de Gaulle had assumed leadership of resistance groups known as the "Free French," and he played an important role in ensuring the establishment of a French provisional government after the war. But the creation immediately following the war of the Fourth Republic, with a return to a multiparty parliamentary system that de Gaulle considered inefficient, led him to withdraw temporarily from politics. Eventually, he formed the French Popular Movement, a political organization based on conservative principles that blamed the party system for France's political mess and called for a stronger presidency, a goal—and role—that de Gaulle finally achieved in 1958.

At the time of his election as president, the fragile political stability of the Fourth Republic was shaken by a crisis in Algeria, France's large North African colony. The French army, having suffered a humiliating defeat in Indochina in 1954, was determined to resist demands for independence by Algeria's Muslim majority. Independence was also opposed by the large French community living in Algeria. But a strong antiwar movement among French intellectuals and church leaders led to bitter divisions in France that opened the door to the possibility of civil war. The panic-stricken leaders of the Fourth Republic offered to let de Gaulle take over the government and revise the constitution.

In 1958, de Gaulle drafted a new constitution for a Fifth Republic that greatly enhanced the power of the French president, who now had the right to choose the prime minister, dissolve parliament, and supervise both defense and foreign policy. As the new president, de Gaulle sought to return France to a position of power and influence. In the belief that an independent role in the Cold War might enhance France's stature, he pulled France out of the NATO high command. He sought to

MAP **3.1** Europe After World War II. At the Yalta Conference in February 1945, Allied leaders altered the prewar map of Europe, primarily in the east, where the boundaries of the Soviet Union were moved westward from the Baltic to the Black Sea.

increase French prestige in the Third World by consenting to Algerian independence despite strenuous opposition from the army and offered French colonies in Africa membership in a new French community of nations under French tutelage. France invested heavily in the nuclear arms race and exploded its first nuclear bomb in 1960. Despite his successes, however, de Gaulle did not really achieve his ambitious goals of world power.

Although the cost of the nuclear program increased the defense budget, de Gaulle did not neglect the French economy. Economic decision making was centralized, a reflection of the overall centralization undertaken by

the Gaullist government. Between 1958 and 1968, the French gross national product (GNP) experienced an annual increase of 5.5 percent, faster than that of the United States. By the end of the Gaullist era, France was a major industrial producer and exporter, particularly in such areas as automobiles and armaments. Nevertheless, problems remained. The expansion of traditional industries, such as coal, steel, and railroads, which had all been nationalized, led to large government deficits. The cost of living increased faster than in the rest of Europe.

Public dissatisfaction with the government's inability to deal with these problems soon led to more violent action. In May 1968, a series of student protests, provoked by conditions in the country's anachronistic educational system as well as the ongoing war in Vietnam, was followed by a general strike by the labor unions. Although de Gaulle managed to restore order, the events of May 1968 seriously undermined popular respect for the aloof and imperious president. Tired and discouraged, de Gaulle resigned from office in April 1969 and died within a year.

During the 1970s, the French economic situation worsened, bringing about a political shift to the left. By 1981, the Socialists had become the dominant party in the National Assembly, and the veteran Socialist leader, François Mitterrand (1916–1996), was elected president. Mitterrand's first concern was to resolve France's economic difficulties. In 1982, he froze prices and wages in the hope of reducing the huge budget deficit and high inflation. Mitterrand also passed a number of measures to aid workers: an increased minimum wage, expanded social benefits, a mandatory fifth week of paid vacation for salaried workers, a thirty-nine-hour workweek, and higher taxes for the rich. Mitterrand's administrative reforms included both centralization (nationalization of banks and industry) and decentralization (granting local governments greater powers). Their victory also convinced the Socialists that they could enact some of their more radical reforms. Consequently, the government nationalized the steel industry, major banks, the space and electronics industries, and important insurance firms.

## WEST GERMANY: THE ECONOMIC MIRACLE

The unification of the three Western zones into the Federal Republic of Germany (West Germany) became a reality in 1949. Konrad Adenauer (1876–1967), the leader of the Christian Democratic Union (CDU), served as chancellor from 1949 to 1963 and became the "founding hero" of the FRG. Adenauer, who had opposed Hitler and

**STUDENT REVOLT IN PARIS, 1968.** The discontent of university students exploded in the late 1960s in a series of student revolts. Perhaps best known was the movement in Paris in 1968. This photograph shows the barricades erected on a Paris street on the morning of May 11 at the height of the revolt.

his tyrannical regime, sought respect for Germany by co-operating with the United States and the other Western European nations. He was especially desirous of reconciliation with France—Germany's longtime rival. The beginning of the Korean War in June 1950 had unexpected repercussions for West Germany. The fear that South Korea might fall to the Communists led many in the West to worry about the security of West Germany and inspired calls for German rearmament. Although some people, concerned about a revival of German militarism, condemned this proposal, Cold War tensions were decisive. West Germany rearmed in 1955 and became a member of NATO.

The Adenauer era witnessed the resurrection of the West German economy, often referred to as the "economic miracle." Although West Germany had only 75 percent of the population and 52 percent of the territory of prewar Germany, by 1955 the West German GNP exceeded that of prewar Germany. Real wages doubled between 1950 and 1965, even though work hours were cut by 20 percent. Unemployment fell from 8 percent in 1950 to 0.4 percent in 1965. To maintain its economic expansion, West Germany imported hundreds of thousands of "guest" workers, primarily from Italy, Spain, Greece, Turkey, and Yugoslavia.

The capital of the Federal Republic had been placed at Bonn, a sleepy market town on the Rhine River, to erase memories of the Nazi era, when the capital was at Berlin. Still, the country was troubled by its past. The surviving major Nazi leaders had been tried and condemned as war criminals at the Nuremberg war crimes trials in 1945 and 1946. As part of the denazification of Germany, the victorious Allies continued to try lesser officials for war crimes, but these trials diminished in number as the Cold War produced a shift in attitudes. By 1950, German courts had begun to take over the war crimes trials, and the German legal machine persisted in prosecuting cases. Beginning in 1953, the West German government also began to make payments to Israel and to Holocaust survivors and their relatives to make some restitution for, in the words of German president Richard von Weizsäcker, "the unspeakable sorrow that occurred in the name of Germany."

After the Adenauer era ended in the mid-1960s, the Social Democrats became the leading party. By forming a ruling coalition with the small Free Democratic Party, the Social Democrats remained in power until 1982. The first Social Democratic chancellor was Willy Brandt (1913–1992). Brandt was especially successful with his "opening toward the east" (known as *Ostpolitik*), for which he received the Nobel Peace Prize in 1972. On March 19, 1971, Brandt met with Walter Ulbricht, the leader of East Germany, and worked out the details of a treaty that was signed in 1972. This agreement did not establish full diplomatic relations with East Germany but did call for "good neighborly" relations. As a result, it led to greater cultural, personal, and economic contacts between West and East Germany. Despite this success, the discovery of an East German spy among Brandt's advisers caused his resignation in 1974.

His successor, Helmut Schmidt (b. 1918), was more of a technocrat than a reform-minded socialist and concentrated on the economic problems brought about largely by high oil prices between 1973 and 1975. Schmidt was successful in eliminating a deficit of 10 billion marks in three years. In 1982, when the coalition of Schmidt's Social Democrats with the Free Democrats fell apart over the reduction of social welfare expenditures, the Free Democrats joined with the Christian Democratic Union of Helmut Kohl (b. 1930) to form a new government.

## GREAT BRITAIN: SUNSET FOR THE EMPIRE

The end of World War II left Britain with massive economic problems. In elections held immediately after the war, the Labour Party overwhelmingly defeated Churchill's Conservative Party. It had promised far-reaching reforms, particularly in the area of social welfare—an appealing platform in a country with a tremendous shortage of consumer goods and housing. Clement Atlee (1883–1967), the new prime minister, was a pragmatic reformer rather than the leftist revolutionary that Churchill had warned against during the election campaign. His Labour government proceeded to enact reforms that created a modern welfare state.

The establishment of the British welfare state began with the nationalization of the Bank of England, the coal and steel industries, public transportation, and public utilities such as electricity and gas. In the area of social welfare, the new government enacted the National Insurance Act and the National Health Service Act, both in 1946. The insurance act established a comprehensive social security program and nationalized medical insurance, thereby enabling the state to subsidize the unemployed, the sick, and the aged. The health act created a system of socialized medicine that forced doctors and dentists to work with state hospitals, although private practices could be maintained. This measure was especially costly for the state, but within a few years, 90 percent of the medical profession was participating. The British welfare state became the model for most European countries after the war.

The cost of building a welfare state at home forced the British to reduce expenses abroad. This meant dismantling the British Empire and reducing military aid to such countries as Greece and Turkey, a decision that inspired the enunciation in Washington of the Truman Doctrine (see Chapter 1). It was not only a belief in the morality of self-determination but also economic necessity that brought an end to the British Empire.

Continuing economic problems brought the Conservatives back into power from 1951 to 1964. Although they favored private enterprise, the Conservatives accepted the welfare state and even extended it, undertaking an ambitious construction program to improve British housing. Although the British economy had recovered from the war, it had done so at a slower rate than other European countries. This slow recovery masked a long-term economic decline caused by a variety of factors, including trade union demands for wages that rose faster than productivity and the unwillingness of factory owners to invest in modern industrial machinery and to adopt new methods. Underlying the immediate problems, however, was a deeper issue. As a result of World War II, Britain had lost much of its prewar revenue from abroad but was left with a burden of debt from its many international commitments. At the same time, with the rise of the United States and the Soviet Union, Britain's ability to play the role of a world power declined substantially.

Between 1964 and 1979, Conservatives and Labour alternated in power. Both parties faced seemingly intractable problems. Although separatist movements in Scotland and Wales were overcome, a dispute between Catholics and Protestants in Northern Ireland was marked by violence as the rebel Irish Republican Army (IRA) staged a series of dramatic terrorist acts in response to the suspension of Northern Ireland's parliament in 1972 and the establishment of direct rule by London. The problem of Northern Ireland remained unresolved. Nor was either party able to deal with Britain's ailing economy. Failure to modernize made British industry less and less competitive. Britain was also hampered by frequent labor strikes, many of them caused by conflicts between rival labor unions.

In 1979, after five years of Labour government and worsening economic problems, the Conservatives returned to power under Margaret Thatcher (b. 1925), the first woman prime minister in British history. Thatcher pledged to lower taxes, reduce government bureaucracy, limit social welfare, restrict union power, and end inflation. The "Iron Lady," as she was called, did break the power of the labor unions. Although she did not eliminate the basic components of the social welfare system, she did use austerity measures to control inflation. "Thatcherism," as her economic policy was termed, improved the British economic situation, but at a price. The south of England, for example, prospered, but the old industrial areas of the Midlands and north declined and were beset by high unemployment, poverty, and sporadic violence. Cutbacks in funding for education seriously undermined the quality of British schools, long regarded as among the world's finest.

In foreign policy, Thatcher took a hard-line approach against communism. She oversaw a large military buildup aimed at replacing older technology and reestablishing Britain as a world policeman. In 1982, when Argentina attempted to take control of the Falkland Islands (one of Britain's few remaining colonial outposts, known to Argentines as the Malvinas) 300 miles off its coast, the British successfully rebuffed the Argentines, although at considerable economic cost and the loss of 255 lives. The Falklands War, however, did generate popular support for Thatcher, as many in Britain reveled in memories of the nation's glorious imperial past.

## Western Europe: The Search for Unity

As we have seen, the divisions created by the Cold War led the nations of Western Europe to form the North Atlantic Treaty Organization in 1949. But military cooperation was not the only kind of unity fostered in Europe after 1945. The destructiveness of two world wars caused many thoughtful Europeans to consider the need for additional forms of integration. National feeling was still too powerful, however, for European nations to give up their political sovereignty. Consequently, the quest for unity focused primarily on the economic arena rather than the political one.

In 1951, France, West Germany, the Benelux countries (Belgium, the Netherlands, and Luxembourg), and Italy formed the European Coal and Steel Community (ECSC). Its purpose was to create a common market for coal and steel products among the six nations by eliminating tariffs and other trade barriers. The success of the ECSC encouraged its members to proceed further, and in 1957, they created the European Atomic Energy Community (EURATOM) to further European research on the peaceful uses of nuclear energy.

In the same year, the same six nations signed the Rome Treaty, which created the European Economic Community (EEC), also known as the Common Market. The EEC eliminated customs barriers among the six member nations and created a large free-trade area protected from the rest of the world by a common external tariff. By promoting free trade, the EEC also encouraged cooperation and standardization in many aspects of the six nations' economies. All the member nations benefited economically.

Europeans moved toward further integration of their economies after 1970. The European Economic Community expanded in 1973 when Great Britain, Ireland, and Denmark gained membership in what its members now began to call the European Community (EC). By 1986, three more members—Spain, Portugal, and Greece—had been added. The economic integration of the members of the EC led to cooperative efforts in international and political affairs as well. The foreign ministers of the twelve members consulted frequently and provided a common front in negotiations on important issues.

# EUROPE REUNITED: THE CURTAIN RISES

The fall of Communist governments in Eastern Europe during the revolutions of 1989 brought a wave of euphoria to Europe. The new structures meant an end to a postwar European order that had been imposed on unwilling peoples by the victorious forces of the Soviet Union. In 1989 and 1990, new governments throughout Eastern Europe worked diligently to scrap the remnants of the old system and introduce the democratic procedures and market systems they believed would revitalize their scarred lands. But this process proved to be neither simple nor easy.

Most Eastern European countries had little or no experience with democratic systems. Then, too, ethnic divisions, which had troubled these areas before World War II and had been forcibly submerged under Communist rule, reemerged with a vengeance. Finally, the rapid conversion to market economies also proved painful. The adoption of "shock therapy" austerity measures produced much suffering. Unemployment, for example, climbed to over 13 percent in Poland in 1992.

Nevertheless, by the beginning of the twenty-first century, many of these states, especially Poland and the Czech Republic, were making a successful transition to both free markets and democracy. In Poland, Aleksander Kwasniewski, although a former Communist, was elected president in November 1995 and pushed Poland toward an increasingly prosperous free market economy. His success brought his reelection in October 2000. In Czechoslovakia, the shift to non-Communist rule was complicated by old problems, especially ethnic issues. Czechs and Slovaks disagreed over the makeup of the new state but were able to agree to a peaceful division of the country. On January 1, 1993, Czechoslovakia split into the Czech Republic and Slovakia (see Map 3.2). Václav Havel was elected the first president of the new Czech Republic.

## The Disintegration of Yugoslavia

The most difficult transition to the post–Cold War era in Eastern Europe was undoubtedly in Yugoslavia. From its beginning in 1919, Yugoslavia had been an artificial creation. After World War II, the dictatorial Marshal Tito had managed to hold its six republics and two autonomous provinces together. After his death in 1980, no strong leader emerged, and his responsibilities passed to a collective state presidency and the League of Communists of Yugoslavia. At the end of the 1980s, Yugoslavia was caught up in the reform movements sweeping through Eastern Europe. The League of Communists collapsed, and new parties quickly emerged.

The Yugoslav political scene was complicated by the development of separatist movements. In 1990, the republics of Slovenia, Croatia, Bosnia-Herzegovina, and Macedonia began to lobby for a new federal structure of Yugoslavia that would fulfill their separatist desires. Slobodan Milošević, who had become the leader of the Serbian Communist Party in 1987 and had managed to stay in power by emphasizing his Serbian nationalism, rejected these efforts. He asserted that these republics could be independent only if new border arrangements were made to accommodate the Serb minorities in those republics who did not want to live outside the boundaries of Serbia. Serbs constituted about 12 percent of Croatia's population and 32 percent of Bosnia's.

After negotiations among the six republics failed, Slovenia and Croatia declared their independence in June 1991. Milošević's government sent the Yugoslavian army, which it controlled, into Slovenia, without much success. In September 1991, it began a full assault against Croatia. Increasingly, the Yugoslavian army was becoming the Serbian army, while Serbian irregular forces played a growing role in military operations. Before a cease-fire was arranged, the Serbian forces had captured one-third of Croatia's territory in brutal and destructive fighting.

The recognition of Slovenia, Croatia, and Bosnia-Herzegovina by many European states and the United States early in 1992 did not stop the Serbs from turning their guns on Bosnia. By mid-1993, Serbian forces had acquired 70 percent of Bosnian territory. The Serbian policy of "ethnic cleansing"—killing or forcibly removing Bosnian Muslims from their lands—revived memories of Nazi atrocities in World War II. Nevertheless, despite

MAP 3.2 Europe, 2000. After the collapse of the Communist order in Eastern Europe and the Soviet Union, a new order and a number of new states appeared in Central and Eastern Europe. At the same time, the European Union expanded and included fifteen states by 2000. ➤ *What new countries emerged from the breakup of the Soviet Union?*

worldwide outrage, European governments failed to take a decisive and forceful stand against these Serbian activities, and by the spring of 1993, the Muslim population of Bosnia was in desperate straits. As the fighting spread, European nations and the United States began to intervene to stop the bloodshed, and in the fall of 1995, a fragile cease-fire agreement was reached at a conference held in Dayton, Ohio. An international peacekeeping force was stationed in the area to maintain tranquillity and monitor the accords.

Peace in Bosnia, however, did not bring peace to Yugoslavia. A new war erupted in 1999 over Kosovo, which had been made an autonomous province within Yugoslavia by Tito in 1974. Kosovo's inhabitants were mainly ethnic Albanians. But the province was also home to a Serbian minority that considered it sacred territory where Serbian forces in the fourteenth century had been defeated by the Ottoman Turks.

In 1989, Yugoslav President Milošević stripped Kosovo of its autonomous status and outlawed any official use of the Albanian language. In 1993, some groups of ethnic Albanians founded the Kosovo Liberation Army (KLA) and began a campaign against Serbian rule in Kosovo. When Serb forces began to massacre ethnic Albanians in an effort to crush the KLA, the United States and its NATO allies sought to arrange a settlement. When Milošević refused to sign the agreement, the United States and its NATO allies began a bombing campaign that forced the Yugoslavian government into compliance. In the fall elections of 2000, Milošević himself was ousted from power and later put on trial by an international tribunal for war crimes against humanity for his ethnic cleansing policies throughout the disintegration of Yugoslavia, which has recently changed its name to Serbia and Montenegro.

## Germany: The Party's Over

For the peoples of Western Europe as well, the end of the Cold War brought changes in their lives. Perhaps the most challenging situation was faced in Germany, where the decision to unify the two zones created serious strains on the economy. Chancellor Helmut Kohl had benefited greatly from an economic boom in the mid-1980s. Gradually, however, discontent with the Christian Democrats increased, and by 1988, their political prospects seemed diminished. But unexpectedly, the 1989 revolution in East Germany led to the reunification of the two Germanies, leaving the new Germany, with its 79 million people, the leading power in Europe. Reunification, accomplished during Kohl's administration, brought rich political dividends to the Christian Democrats. In the first all-German federal election, Kohl's Christian Democrats won 44 percent of the vote, and their coalition partners, the Free Democrats, received 11 percent.

But the euphoria over reunification soon dissipated as the realization set in that the revitalization of eastern Germany would take far more money than was originally thought, and Kohl's government was soon forced to face the politically undesirable task of raising taxes substantially. Moreover, the virtual collapse of the economy in eastern Germany led to extremely high levels of unemployment and severe discontent. One reason for the problem was the government's decision to establish a 1:1 ratio between the East and West German marks. This policy raised salaries for East German workers, but it increased labor costs and provoked many companies into hiring workers abroad.

Increasing unemployment in turn led to growing resentment against foreigners. For years, foreigners seeking asylum or employment found haven in Germany because of its extremely liberal immigration laws. In 1992, more than 440,000 immigrants came to Germany seeking asylum, 123,000 of them from former Yugoslavia alone. Attacks against foreigners by right-wing extremists—many of them espousing neo-Nazi beliefs—killed seventeen people in 1992 and became an all too frequent occurrence in German life.

East Germans were also haunted by another memory from their recent past. The opening of the files of the secret police (the Stasi) showed that millions of East Germans had spied on their neighbors and colleagues, and even their spouses and parents, during the Communist era. A few senior Stasi officials were placed on trial for their past actions, but many Germans preferred simply to close the door on an unhappy period in their lives.

As the century neared its close, then, Germans struggled to cope with the challenge of building a new, united nation. To reduce the debt incurred because of economic reconstruction in the east, the government threatened to cut back on many of the social benefits West Germans had long been accustomed to receiving. This in turn sharpened resentments that were already beginning to emerge between the two zones. Although the Berlin Wall had been removed, the gap between East and West remained (see box on p. 74). In 1998, voters took out their frustations at the ballot box. Helmut Kohl's conservative coalition was defeated in national elections, and a new prime minister, Social Democrat Gerhard Schroder, came into office. Schroder had no better luck than his predecessor, however, in reviving the economy. In 2003, with nearly five million workers unemployed, the government announced plans to scale back welfare benefits that had long become a familiar part of life for the German people.

## France: A Season of Discontent

Although France did not face the challenge of integrating two different systems into a single society, it encountered many of the same economic and social problems as its neighbor Germany. The policies adopted during the early 1980s by the Socialist majority under President Mitterrand failed to work, and within three years the Mitterrand government returned some of the economy to private enterprise. Mitterrand was able to win a second seven-year term in the 1988 presidential election, but France's economic decline continued. In 1993, French unemployment stood at 10.6 percent, and in the elections in March of that year, the Socialists won only 28 percent of the vote while a coalition of conservative parties won 80 percent of the seats in the National As-

# THE GREAT WALL OF GERMANY

*he unification of the two Germanys after the fall of the Berlin Wall was widely hailed as a signal of the end of the Cold War in Europe. It even inspired fear among many Europeans living in neighboring countries as the harbinger of the rise of a new and more powerful Germany. In fact, unification has given birth to a number of major political, economic, and social problems. Although the new Germany is administratively united, it remains divided in culture and outlook, as the following article suggests.*

## REMEMBRANCE OF THINGS PAST

There's a widespread feeling among East Germans that something new should have emerged out of unification, combining the best of both worlds.

"We suddenly saw that there is a different mentality, even a different language in some areas," says Western psychologist Uwe Wetter, "a different tradition, and cultural differences all around. But we tried to address these differences by giving our knowledge—what we thought was the best—to the Easterners. We thought that would be the way to handle the situation."

Many Easterners have not been able to reestablish the sense of identity. They pine for what they regard to be the sunny side of the former East German state: a sense of belonging, and a cozy feeling that they were being taken care of by the system. Some former East Germans continue to gather at frequently held nostalgia parties.

Stefan Winkler, from the eastern part of Berlin, is one of them: "I have mixed emotions about these nostalgia parties. I still have a GDR flag. I don't think it's for nostalgia reasons; it's more of a political statement. I think people tend to forget about the bad things after a while and only remember the good. There were a couple of really good things in East Germany. A lot of [East Germans] feel quite unsafe at the moment. Not only because they lost their jobs. It's also because many lost their identity—and that's where their nostalgia comes in."

(Hardy Graupner, *Deutsche Welle* [independent world radio], Cologne, November 1999.)

Source: *World Press Review*, January 2000, p. 9.

---

sembly. The move to the right was strengthened when the conservative mayor of Paris, Jacques Chirac, was elected president in May 1995. The center-right government remained in power as the new century opened.

As in Germany, resentment against foreign-born residents was a growing political reality. Spurred by rising rates of unemployment and large numbers of immigrants from North Africa (often identified in the public mind with terrorist actions committed by militant groups based in the Middle East), many French voters gave their support to Jean-Marie Le Pen's National Front, which openly advocated a restriction on all new immigration and limited assimilation of immigrants already living in France.

## Great Britain: Move to the Left

In Great Britain, Conservative Prime Minister Margaret Thatcher dominated politics in the 1980s. The Labour Party, beset by divisions between moderate and radical wings, offered little effective opposition. Only in 1990 did Labour's fortunes seem to revive when Thatcher's government attempted to replace local property taxes with a flat-rate tax payable by every adult to his or her local authority. Although Thatcher argued that this would make local government more responsive to popu-

lar needs, many argued that this was nothing more than a poll tax that would enable the rich to pay the same rate as the poor. After antitax riots broke out, Thatcher's once legendary popularity plummeted to an all-time low. At the end of November, a revolt within her own party caused Thatcher to resign as prime minister. Her replacement was John Major, whose Conservative Party won a narrow victory in the general elections held in April 1992. But Major's lackluster leadership failed to capture the imagination of many Britons, and in new elections in May 1997, the Labour Party won a landslide victory. The new prime minister, Tony Blair, was a moderate whose youth and energy immediately instilled a new vigor on the political scene. Adopting centrist policies reminiscent of those followed by President Bill Clinton in the United States (see Chapter 4), his party dominated the political arena into the new century.

## The Move Toward European Unity: Staying the Course?

With the formation of NATO in 1949 and other regional organizations such as EURATOM and the European Community, Western European governments took the initial moves toward creating a more unified continent.

By 1992, the EC included nearly 350 million people and constituted the world's largest single trading bloc, transacting almost one-quarter of the world's commerce. In the early 1990s, EC members drafted the Treaty on European Union (known as the Maastricht Treaty, after the city in the Netherlands where the agreement was reached), seeking to create a true economic and monetary union of all members of the organization. The treaty would not take effect, however, until all members agreed. On January 1, 1994, the European Community became the European Union (EU).

One of its first goals was to introduce a common currency, called the euro. But problems soon arose. Voters in many countries opposed the austerity measures that their governments would be compelled to take to reduce growing budget deficits. Germans in particular feared that replacing the rock-solid mark with a common European currency could lead to economic disaster. Yet the logic of the new union appeared inescapable if European nations were to improve their capacity to compete with the United States and the powerful industrializing nations of the Pacific Rim. On January 1, 2002, eleven of the EC nations abandoned their national currencies in favor of the euro.

In the meantime, plans got under way to extend the EU into Eastern Europe, where several nations were just emerging from decades of domination by the Soviet Union. In December 2002, the EU voted to add ten new members, including Poland, the Baltic states, Hungary, Slovakia, and the Czech Republic, in 2004. Yet not all are convinced that European integration is a good thing. Eastern Europeans fear that their countries will be dominated by investment from their prosperous neighbors, while their counterparts in Western Europe express concerns at a possible influx of low-wage workers from the new member countries. All in all, a true sense of a unified Europe is still lacking among the population throughout the region, and the rising wave of antiforeign sentiment (see the box on p. 76) and anger at government belt tightening are issues that will not go away in the near future.

The NATO alliance continues to serve as a powerful force for European unity. Yet it too faces new challenges as Moscow's former satellites in Eastern Europe clamor for membership in the hope that it will spur economic growth and reduce the threat from a revival of Russian expansionism. In 1999, the Czech Republic, Hungary, and Poland joined the alliance, and the Baltic states have expressed an interest in doing so in the future. Some observers express concern, however, that an expanded NATO will not only reduce the cohesiveness of the organization but also provoke Russia into a new posture of hostility to the outside world.

# ASPECTS OF SOCIETY IN POSTWAR EUROPE

Socially, intellectually, and culturally, Western Europe changed significantly during the second half of the twentieth century. Although many trends represented a continuation of prewar developments, in other cases the changes were quite dramatic, leading some observers in the 1980s to begin speaking of the gradual emergence of a postmodern age.

## An Age of Affluence

In the decades following the end of World War II, Western Europe witnessed remarkably rapid change. Such products of new technologies as computers, television, jet planes, contraceptive devices, and new surgical techniques all dramatically and quickly altered the pace and nature of human life. Called variously a technocratic society, an affluent society, or the consumer society, postwar Europe was characterized by changing social values and new attitudes toward the meaning of the human experience.

The structure of European society was also altered in major respects after 1945. Especially noticeable were changes in the nature of the middle class. Traditional occupations such as merchants and the professions (law, medicine, and the universities) were greatly augmented by a new group of managers and technicians, as large companies and government agencies employed increasing numbers of white-collar supervisory and administrative personnel. In most cases, success depended on specialized knowledge acquired from some form of higher education. Since their jobs usually depended on their skills, these individuals took steps to ensure that their children would be similarly educated.

Changes occurred in other areas as well. Especially noticeable was the dramatic shift from the countryside to the cities. The number of people in agriculture declined by 50 percent. Yet the industrial working class did not expand. In West Germany, industrial workers made up 48 percent of the labor force throughout the 1950s and 1960s. Thereafter, the number of industrial workers began to dwindle as the number of white-collar service employees increased. At the same time, a substantial increase in their real wages enabled the working classes to aspire to the consumption patterns of the middle class. Buying on the installment plan, introduced in the 1930s, became widespread in the 1950s and gave workers a chance to imitate the middle class by buying such products as televisions, washing machines, refrigerators, vac-

# THE EUROPE THAT CAN SAY NO

*R*ecent attacks by neo-Nazi groups against immigrants living in Germany have aroused concern that xenophobia may be on the rise in that country. But such attacks are not an isolated phenomenon and are a reflection of the rise of antiforeign sentiment throughout the European continent as a slowing economy and the inexorable impact of European unification have aroused fears among many Europeans that their traditional culture is being rapidly eroded by the forces of globalization. According to a recent estimate, more than half a million illegal immigrants enter the EU countries each year. The following two excerpts are from articles written after the election of Jorg Haider, an outspoken opponent of European union, in Austria.

## THE HAIDER PHENOMENON

For half a century, European politics has been dominated by the center-left. The past decade has seen a burgeoning of nationalist, anti-immigration, anti-foreigner sentiment as the realities of European union hit home and the fear of economic, cultural, and racial hegemony grows. Its expression has taken various forms, from acts of sabotage by anti-American farming unions in France to the rise of nationalist soccer hooliganism and xenophobic attacks on migrants.

This is the civilized face of xenophobia, without the skinhead haircuts and the swastika tattoos. The leader of Austria's Freedom Party, Jorg Haider, is besuited, clean-cut, and well educated. His policies include curbing immigration and giving money to ethnically pure Austrian women to encourage them to breed. He is opposed to European union.

The recent upsurge in xenophobic nationalism is no less worrying for the apparent lack of a trigger. . . . Austria and Switzerland [where federal elections held in October 1999 led to the emergence of a nationalist party as the leading party in the country] may be isolated and unrelated instances of a shift to the nationalistic right. If not, all Europe should be worried. European unity itself could be at risk.

(*The Canberra Times*, October 27, 1999)

Right-wing extremists are now celebrating all over Europe. They feel victorious after Jorg Haider's record results in Austria. . . . Haider and his Freedom Party are best known for being strongly anti-immigrant and for their right-wing populism. They campaigned with such promises as putting a stop to immigration and denying welfare benefits to immigrant families. Those slogans garnered Haider 27 percent of the vote. . . . Right-wing extremist parties have become a factor in power all over Europe. In France, and in Italy, Austria and Belgium, they received the support of more than 10 percent of the voters in the last elections. They are also strongly represented in the European parliament.

"[Haider's] victory is a victory for democracy," said Tor Paulsson, party organizer for Sweden Democracy, which cooperates closely with Jean-Marie Le Pen and his National Front in France. . . . When Le Pen created the National Front, he told the racists to quit fighting and to work together instead. In the last French parliamentary elections, this recipe produced 14.9 percent of the vote. In Vitrolles the mayor has implemented the Front's slogan, "Frenchmen first." Parents who give birth to a "real French baby" get 5,000 francs plus a nanny, while Arab parents get nothing.

(Markus Gustafsson, *Aftonbladet*, Stockholm, October 5, 1999)

Source: *World Press Review*, January 2000, p. 10.

---

uum cleaners, and stereos. But the most visible symbol of mass consumerism was the automobile. Before World War II, cars were reserved mostly for the upper classes. In 1948, there were 5 million cars in all of Europe, but by 1957, the number had tripled. By the mid-1960s, there were almost 45 million cars.

Rising incomes, combined with shorter working hours, created an even greater market for mass leisure activities. Between 1900 and 1980, the workweek was reduced from sixty hours to about forty hours, and the number of paid holidays increased. All aspects of popular culture—music, sports, media—became commercialized and offered opportunities for leisure activities, including concerts, sporting events, and television viewing.

Another very visible symbol of mass leisure was the growth of tourism. Before World War II, most persons who traveled for pleasure were from the upper and middle classes. After the war, the combination of more vacation time, increased prosperity, and the flexibility provided by package tours with their lower rates and low-budget rooms enabled millions to expand their travel possibilities. By the mid-1960s, some 100 million tourists were crossing European borders each year.

Social change was also evident in new educational patterns. Before World War II, higher education was largely the preserve of Europe's wealthier classes. Even in 1950, only 3 or 4 percent of Western European young people were enrolled in a university. European higher education remained largely centered on the liberal arts, pure science, and preparation for the professions of law and medicine.

Much of this changed in the 1950s and 1960s. European states began to foster greater equality of opportunity in higher education by eliminating fees, and universities experienced an influx of students from the middle and lower classes. Enrollments grew dramatically. In France, 4.5 percent of young people went to a university in 1950; by 1965, the figure had increased to 14.5 percent. Enrollments in European universities more than tripled between 1940 and 1960.

With growth came problems. Overcrowded classrooms, unapproachable professors, and authoritarian administrators aroused student resentment. In addition, despite changes in the curriculum, students often felt that the universities were not providing an education relevant to the modern age. This discontent led to an outburst of student revolts in the late 1960s. In part, these protests were an extension of the disruptions in American universities in the mid-1960s, which were often sparked by student opposition to the Vietnam War. Protesters also criticized other aspects of Western society, such as its materialism, and expressed concern about becoming cogs in the large and impersonal bureaucratic jungles of the modern world.

The most famous student revolt occurred in France in 1968. It erupted at the University of Nanterre outside Paris but soon spread to the Sorbonne, the main campus of the University of Paris. French students demanded a greater voice in the administration of the university, took over buildings, and then expanded the scale of their protests by inviting workers to support them. Half of France's workforce went on strike in May 1968. After the Gaullist government instituted a hefty wage hike, the workers returned to work, and the police repressed the remaining student protesters.

One source of anger among the student revolutionaries of the late 1960s was the lingering influence of traditional institutions and values. World War I had seen the first significant crack in the rigid code of manners and morals of the nineteenth century. The 1920s had witnessed experimentation with drugs, the appearance of hard-core pornography, and a new sexual freedom. But these changes appeared mostly in major cities and touched only small numbers of people. After World War II, they were more extensive and far more noticeable.

Sweden took the lead in the so-called sexual revolution of the 1960s, but the rest of Europe soon followed. Sex education in the schools and the decriminalization of homosexuality were but two aspects of Sweden's liberal legislation. Introduction of the birth control pill, which became widely available by the mid-1960s, gave people more freedom in sexual behavior. Meanwhile, sexually explicit movies, plays, and books broke new ground in the treatment of once-hidden subjects.

The new standards were evident in the breakdown of the traditional family. Divorce rates increased dramatically, especially in the 1960s, while premarital and extramarital sexual experiences also rose substantially. The 1960s also saw the emergence of a drug culture. Marijuana use was widespread among college and university students, and Timothy Leary, a professor who had done research at Harvard on the effects of LSD (lysergic acid diethylamide), promulgated the purported "mind-expanding" effects of hallucinogenics.

## Expanding Roles for Women

One area of significant change in postwar European society was the role of women. Although women were found in professional careers and a number of other vocations in the 1920s and 1930s, the place for most women was still in the home. Half a century later, there were almost as many women as men in the workplace, many of them employed in professions hitherto reserved for men.

One consequence of the trend toward greater employment outside the home for women was a drop in the birthrate. The percentage of married women in the female labor force in Sweden, for example, increased from 47 to 66 percent between 1963 and 1975. In many European countries, zero population growth was reached in the 1960s, and increases since then have been due solely to immigration. In Italy and Spain, the flood of women into the workplace resulted in a dramatic reduction in the number of children born annually, leading to fears of an absolute decline in total population. In newly united Germany, it has been estimated that nearly half a million immigrants will be required annually to maintain the current level of economic growth in the country.

But the increased number of women in the workforce has not changed some old patterns. Working-class women in particular still earn salaries lower than those paid to men for equal work. Women still tend to enter traditionally female jobs. A 1980 study of twenty-five European nations revealed that women still made up more than 80 percent of typists, nurses, tailors, and dressmakers in those countries. Many European women also still faced the double burden of earning income on the one hand and raising a family and maintaining the household on the other. Such inequalities led increasing numbers of women to rebel against their conditions.

The participation of women in World Wars I and II helped them achieve one of the major aims of the nineteenth-century feminist movement—the right to vote. After World War I, many governments acknowledged the contributions of women to the war effort by granting them the vote—Sweden, Great Britain, Germany, Poland, Hungary, Austria, and Czechoslovakia. Women in France and Italy finally gained the right to vote in 1945.

After World War II, European women tended to fall back into the traditional roles expected of them, and little was heard of feminist concerns. But with the student upheavals of the late 1960s came a renewed interest in feminism, or the women's liberation movement, as it was now called. Increasingly, women protested that the acquisition of political and legal equality had not brought true equality with men.

A leading role in the movement was played by French writer Simone de Beauvoir (1908–1986). Born into a middle-class Catholic family and educated at the Sorbonne in Paris, she joined the existentialist movement, which was the leading intellectual movement of its time in Western Europe, and became active in political causes. In 1949, she published *The Second Sex*, in which she argued that living in male-dominated societies, women had been defined by their differences from men and consequently received second-class status. "What particularly signalizes the situation of woman is that she—a free autonomous being like all human creatures—nevertheless finds herself in a world where men compel her to assume the status of the Other." De Beauvoir played an active role in the women's movement during the 1970s, and her book was a major influence on women in both Western Europe and the United States.

Feminists in Europe came to believe that women must transform the fundamental conditions of their lives. They did so in a variety of ways, forming numerous "consciousness-raising" groups to further awareness of women's issues and working to legalize both contraception and abortion. A French law passed in 1968 legalized the sale of contraceptive devices. In 1979, abortion became legal in France. Even in countries where the Catholic church remained strongly opposed to contraception and legalized abortion, legislation allowing them passed in the 1970s and 1980s.

## The Environment and the Green Movements

Beginning in the 1970s, environmentalism became a serious item on the political agenda throughout the Western world. By that time, serious ecological problems had become all too apparent in the crowded countries of Western Europe. Air pollution, produced by nitrogen oxide and sulfur dioxide emissions from road vehicles, power plants, and industrial factories, was causing respiratory illnesses and having corrosive effects on buildings as well as on historical monuments such as the Parthenon in Athens. Many rivers, lakes, and seas had become so polluted that they posed serious health risks. Dying forests (such as the famous Black Forest in southern Germany) and disappearing wildlife alarmed more and more people.

Although the environment movement first began to gain broad public attention in the United States (see Chapter 4), the problem was more serious in Europe, with its higher population density and high levels of industrial production in such countries as Great Britain and West Germany. The problem was compounded by the lack of antipollution controls in the industrial sectors of the Soviet satellite states to the east.

Growing ecological awareness gave rise to Green movements and Green parties throughout Europe in the 1970s. They came about in various ways. Some grew out of the antinuclear movement; others arose out of such causes as women's liberation and concern for foreign workers. Most started at the local level and then gradually extended their activities to the national level, where they became formally organized as political parties. Most visible was the Green Party in Germany, which was officially organized in 1979 and eventually elected forty-one delegates to the West German parliament, but Green parties also competed successfully in Sweden, Austria, and Switzerland.

As in the United States, however, the movement has been hindered by concerns that strict environmental regulations could sap economic growth and exacerbate unemployment. National rivalries and disagreements over how to deal with rising levels of pollution along international waterways such as the Rhine River also impeded cooperation. Nevertheless, public alarm over potential effects of global warming has focused attention on the global character of environmental issues.

# ASPECTS OF CULTURE IN POSTWAR EUROPE

During the German occupation of France, the French intellectual Jean-Paul Sartre (1905–1980) developed a philosophy of resistance and individual freedom called existentialism, whose fundamental premise was the absence of a god in the universe, thereby denying any preordained destiny to mankind. Humans were thus deprived of any absolute purpose or meaning, set adrift in an absurd world. Often reduced to despair and depression, the protagonists of Sartre's literary works were left with only one hope—themselves, voluntarily reaching out and becoming involved in their community. In the early 1950s, Sartre became a devout Marxist, hitching his philosophy of freedom to one of political engagement to the Communist ideal.

One of Sartre's contemporaries, Albert Camus (1913–1960), greatly influenced generations of young people in the postwar era with writings that focused on the notion of the absurd. In his seminal novel, *The Stranger* (1942), the protagonist, having stumbled through a lethargic existence, realizes just before dying that regardless of the absurdity of life, humans still have the opportunity to embrace the joyful dimensions of experience—in his case, the warmth and splendor of the Algerian skies. Neither a political activist nor an ideologue, Camus broke with Sartre and other French leftists upon the disclosure of the Stalinist atrocities in the Soviet gulags.

The existentialist worldview found expression in the Paris of the 1950s in the "theater of the absurd." One of its foremost proponents was the Irish dramatist Samuel Beckett (1906–1990), who lived in France. In his trailblazing play *Waiting for Godot* (1952), two nondescript men eagerly await the appearance of someone who never arrives. While they wait, they pass the time exchanging hopes and fears, with humor, courage, and touching friendship. This waiting represents the existential meaning of life, which is found in the daily activities and fellowship of the here and now, despite the absence of any absolute salvation to the human condition.

With the Soviet suppression of the Hungarian Revolution in 1956, many Europeans became disenchanted with political systems of any kind and began to question the validity of reason, history, progress, and universal truths. Leading the way toward the adoption of a new perspective was the French structuralist Claude Lévi-Strauss (b. 1908). An anthropologist, he examined world cultures as autonomous units, each different and worthy of respect, thus helping to reinforce the dismantling of the French colonial empire and empower the newly emerging postcolonial nations in Africa and Asia.

In the late 1960s, the negation of prewar ideologies and the proliferation of structural methodology, now applied to all branches of learning, fused into a new doctrine of skepticism called deconstruction. Deconstruction cast doubt on all Western political and philosophical traditions, leaving a world in which human beings have lost their status as free agents dealing with universal verities and are reduced to empty vessels programmed by language and culture.

For deconstructionists, language was like quicksand, constantly moving, its intermittent layers hiding unlimited and opposing meanings. A word does not signify an objective meaning but rather is open to different associations by each speaker or listener. Consequently, a given text can never have one single meaning, since the intention of the author and the understanding of the reader will never be precisely the same. By denying any ultimate meaning to language, deconstruction thus negated the existence of any objective truth.

The philosophical skepticism reflected in this new approach quickly manifested itself in European literature as authors grappled with new ways to present reality in an uncertain and nonsensical world. Whereas the modernists at the beginning of the century had celebrated the power of art to benefit humankind, placing their faith in the written word, much of the new "postmodern" literature reflected the lack of belief in anything, especially the written word (see Chapter 10).

Following in the footsteps of the modernists, French authors in the 1960s experimented so radically with literary forms and language that they pushed fiction well beyond its traditional limits of rational understanding. In the "new novel," for example, authors like Alain Robbe-Grillet (b. 1922) and Nathalie Sarraute (1900–1999) delved deeply into stream-of-consciousness writing, literally abandoning the reader in the disorienting obsessions of the protagonist's unconscious mind (see Chapter 4).

Some authors, however, preferred to retrieve literary forms and values that modernists had rejected, choosing to tell a "good" chronological story, to entertain as well as to deliver a moral message. Graham Greene (1904–1991) was one of Britain's more prolific, popular, and critically acclaimed authors of the century. He succeeded in combining psychological and moral depth with enthralling stories, often dealing with political conflicts set in exotic locales. A longtime critic of the United States, Greene forecast the American defeat in Vietnam in his 1955 novel *The Quiet American*. This and many of his other novels have been made into films.

Two other European authors who combined a gripping tale with seriousness of intent, written in fresh exciting narrative, were the German writer Günter Grass (b. 1927) and the Portuguese novelist José Saramago (b. 1922). Grass's 1959 novel, *The Tin Drum*, blasted German consciousness out of the complacency that had been induced by his country's postwar economic miracle, reexamining Germany's infatuation with Hitler and warning German readers of the ever-present danger of repeating the evils of the past. In *Crabwalk* (2002), Grass chronicled a 1945 Soviet submarine attack on a German ship carrying thousands of civilian refugees, thus breaking the taboo of silence by Germans, who had suppressed the memory of their own suffering during World War II.

In *The Cave* (2001), Saramago focused on global issues, such as the erosion of individual cultures stemming from the tyranny of globalization, which, in his view, had not only led to the exploitation of poor countries but also had robbed the world's cultures of their uniqueness, thus reducing humankind to living in caves where communication is impossible and the only place of worship is the ubiquitous shopping mall. Like Grass, Saramago believed strongly in the Western humanist tradition and viewed authors as society's moral guardians and political mobilizers.

Since the end of World War II, serious music has witnessed a wide diversity of experimental movements, each searching for new tonal and rhythmic structures. Striving to go beyond Schoenberg's atonality, European composers in the 1950s set out to free their music from the traditional constraints of meter, form, and dynamics. Of special consideration are Frenchman Pierre Boulez (b. 1925) and German Karlheinz Stockhausen (b. 1928). They devised a new procedure called serialism, which is a mathematical ordering of musical components that, once set in motion, essentially writes itself automatically.

The second half of the century witnessed a profusion of diverse movements in European painting and architecture, many of which were initiated in the United States. For that reason, the issue will be discussed in Chapter 10.

# CONCLUSION

During the immediate postwar era, Western Europe emerged from the ashes of World War II and achieved a level of political stability and economic prosperity unprecedented in its long history. By the 1970s, European leaders were beginning to turn their attention to bringing about further political and economic unity among the nations in the region. With the signing of the Maastricht Treaty in 1994, a schedule had been established to put the dream into effect. But there have been some bumps along the way, as the pains of transition become more apparent and long-standing structural and cultural differences hinder the process of unification. A truly united Europe still remains a long way off.

**GLASS PYRAMID AT THE LOUVRE.** The Louvre, residence of French kings since the sixteenth century and an art museum since the French Revolution, has traditionally represented classical symmetry and grandeur. In 1988, under the auspices of French President François Mitterrand, architect I. M. Pei added this imaginative and daring symmetrical pyramid of glass. It functions as an expedient entrance to the mammoth museum, while also allowing natural light to flood the lower floors. Its form incorporates the grandeur of Egypt with modernist simplicity.

Courtesy of William J. Duiker

| 1945 | 1955 | 1965 | 1975 | 1985 | 1995 | 2000 |

**EUROPE**

De Gaulle's rule in France

Expansion of
European Economic Community

Reunification
of Germany

Student protest
in France

Era of Margaret
Thatcher in
Great Britain

Tony Blair elected
prime minister of
Great Britain

Treaty of Rome
creates common
market

Emergence of
Green movement

Introduction
of the euro

# INFOTRAC
## COLLEGE EDITION

Visit source collections at **http://infotrac.thomsonlearning.com**, and use the Search function with the following key terms:

Europe Communism
Feminism
Germany reunification
Green parties
Single European market

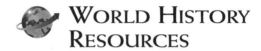

# WORLD HISTORY
## RESOURCES

Visit the *The World Since World War II* Companion Web site for resources specific to this textbook:

**http://history.wadsworth.com/duiker_wwii/**

The Wadsworth World History Resource Center at **http://history.wadsworth.com/world/** offers a variety of tools to help you succeed in this course, including access to quizzes; images; documents; interactive simulations, maps, and timelines; movie explorations; and a wealth of other sources.

# THE UNITED STATES, CANADA, AND LATIN AMERICA

*T*he United States emerged from World War II as one of the world's two superpowers. Reluctantly, it remained deeply involved in international affairs and, as its Cold War confrontation with the Soviet Union intensified, directed much of its energy toward combating the spread of communism throughout the world. Internally, Americans turned their attention to continuing the prewar recovery from the Great Depression.

American prosperity reached new proportions in the two decades after World War II, but a series of nagging economic and social problems—including racial divisions and pockets of chronic poverty—showed that the American dream still did not apply to everyone.

The end of the Cold War and the collapse of the Soviet Empire briefly raised hopes of the emergence of a new world order, but as the world entered the twenty-first century, the rise of militant terrorism raised the specter of a new era of international instability.

To the south of the United States lay the vast world of Latin America with its own unique heritage. Although there were some welcome signs during the last years of the twentieth century that military regimes were being replaced by governments elected by democratic procedures, most of the nations in the region continued to struggle with economic and political instability, and suspicion of the United States for seeking to dominate the hemisphere continued.

# The Emergence of the United States

Between 1945 and 1970, the legacy of Franklin Roosevelt's New Deal largely determined the parameters of American domestic politics. The New Deal gave rise to a distinct pattern that signified a basic transformation in American society. This pattern included a dramatic increase in the role and power of the federal government, the rise of organized labor as a significant force in the economy and politics, a commitment to the welfare state, albeit a restricted one (Americans did not have access to universal health care as most other industrialized societies did), a grudging acceptance of the need to resolve minority problems, and a willingness to experiment with deficit spending as a means of spurring the economy. The influence of New Deal politics was bolstered by the election of Democratic presidents—Harry Truman in 1948, John F. Kennedy in 1960, and Lyndon B. Johnson in 1964. Even the election of a Republican president, Dwight D. Eisenhower, in 1952 and 1956, did not significantly alter the fundamental direction of the New Deal. As Eisenhower conceded in 1954, "Should any political party attempt to abolish Social Security and eliminate labor laws and farm programs, you would not hear of that party again in our political history."

No doubt, the economic boom that took place after World War II fueled public confidence in the new American way of life. A shortage of consumer goods during the war left Americans with both surplus income and the desire to purchase these goods after the war. Then, too, the growing power of organized labor enabled more and more workers to obtain the wage increases that fueled the growth of the domestic market. Increased government expenditures (justified by the theory of English economist John Maynard Keynes that government spending could stimulate a lagging economy to reach higher levels of productivity) also indirectly subsidized the American private enterprise system. Especially after the Korean War began in 1950, outlays on defense provided money for scientific research in the universities and markets for weapons industries. After 1955, tax dollars built a massive system of interstate highways, and tax deductions for mortgages subsidized homeowners. Between 1945 and 1973, real wages grew at an average rate of 3 percent a year, the most prolonged advance in American history.

The prosperity of the 1950s and 1960s also translated into significant social changes. More workers left the factories and fields and moved into white-collar occupations, finding jobs as professional and technical employees, managers, proprietors, and clerical and sales workers. In 1940, blue-collar workers made up 52 percent of the labor force; farmers and farmworkers, 17 percent; and white-collar workers, 31 percent. By 1970, blue-collar workers constituted 50 percent; farmers and farmworkers, 3 percent; and white-collar workers, 47 percent. One consequence of this process was a movement from rural areas and central cities into the suburbs. In 1940, just 19 percent of the American population lived in suburbs, 49 percent in rural areas, and 32 percent in central cities. By 1970, those figures had changed to 38, 31, and 31 percent, respectively. The move to the suburbs also produced an imposing number of shopping malls and reinforced the American passion for the automobile, which provided the means of transport from suburban home to suburban mall and workplace. Finally, the search for prosperity led to new migration patterns. As the West and South experienced rapid economic growth through the development of new industries, especially in the defense field, massive numbers of people made the exodus from the cities of the Northeast and Midwest to the Sunbelt of the South and West. Between 1940 and 1980, cities like Chicago, Philadelphia, Detroit, and Cleveland lost between 13 and 36 percent of their populations, while Los Angeles, Dallas, and San Diego grew between 100 and 300 percent.

Although the country was becoming more affluent, it was also feeling more vulnerable as Cold War confrontations abroad had repercussions at home. The Communist victory in China aroused fears that Communists had infiltrated the United States. A demagogic senator from Wisconsin, Joseph McCarthy, helped intensify a massive "Red scare" with his (unsubstantiated) allegations that there were hundreds of Communists in high government positions. But McCarthy went too far when he attacked alleged "Communist conspirators" in the U.S. Army, and he was censured by Congress in 1954. Shortly after, his anti-Communist crusade came to an end. The pervasive fear of communism and the possibility of a nuclear war, however, remained at a peak.

While the 1950s have been characterized (erroneously) as a tranquil age, the period between 1960 and 1973 was clearly a time of upheaval that brought to the fore some of the problems that had been glossed over in the 1950s. The era began on an optimistic note. At age forty-three, John F. Kennedy (1917–1963) became the youngest president in the history of the United States and the first born in the twentieth century. His own administration, cut short by an assassin's bullet on November 22, 1963, focused primarily on foreign affairs, although it inaugurated an extended period of increased economic growth. Kennedy's successor, Lyndon B. Johnson (1908–

1973), who won a new term as president in a landslide in 1964, used his stunning mandate to pursue the growth of the welfare state, first begun in the New Deal. Johnson's programs included health care for the elderly, a "war on poverty" to be fought with food stamps and a "job corps," the new Department of Housing and Urban Development to deal with the problems of the cities, and federal assistance for education.

Johnson's other domestic passion was the achievement of equal rights for African Americans. The civil rights movement began in earnest in 1954 when the U.S. Supreme Court took the dramatic step of striking down the practice of maintaining racially segregated public schools. According to Chief Justice Earl Warren, "Separate educational facilities are inherently unequal." A year later, during a boycott of segregated buses in Montgomery, Alabama, the eloquent Martin Luther King Jr. (1929–1968) surfaced as the leader of a growing movement for racial equality.

By the early 1960s, a number of groups, including King's Southern Christian Leadership Conference (SCLC), were organizing demonstrations and sit-ins across the South to end racial segregation. In August 1963, King led the March on Washington for Jobs and Freedom. This march and King's impassioned plea for racial equality had an electrifying effect on the American people. By the end of 1963, a majority of Americans (52 percent) called civil rights the most significant national issue; only 4 percent had done so eight months earlier.

President Johnson took up the cause of civil rights. As a result of his initiative, Congress in 1964 enacted the Civil Rights Act, which ended segregation and discrimination in the workplace and all public accommodations. The Voting Rights Act, passed the following year, eliminated racial obstacles to voting in southern states. But laws alone could not guarantee a "great society," and Johnson soon faced bitter social unrest, both from African Americans and from the burgeoning antiwar movement.

In the North and West, African Americans had had voting rights for many years, but local patterns of segregation resulted in considerably higher unemployment rates for blacks (and Hispanics) than for whites and left blacks segregated in huge urban ghettos. In these ghettos, calls for militant action by radical black nationalist leaders, such as Malcolm X of the Black Muslims, attracted more attention than the nonviolent appeals of Martin Luther King. In the summer of 1965, race riots erupted in the Watts district of Los Angeles that led to thirty-four deaths and the destruction of more than one thousand buildings. Cleveland, San Francisco, Chicago, Newark,

and Detroit likewise exploded in the summers of 1966 and 1967. After the assassination of Martin Luther King in 1968, more than one hundred cities experienced rioting, including Washington, D.C., the nation's capital. The combination of riots and extremist comments by radical black leaders led to a "white backlash" and a severe division of American society. In 1964, only 34 percent of white Americans agreed with the statement that blacks were asking for "too much"; by late 1966, that number had risen to 85 percent.

Antiwar protests also divided the American people after President Johnson committed American troops to a costly war in Vietnam (see the box on p. 85). The antiwar movement arose out of the free speech movement that began in 1964 at the University of California at Berkeley as a protest against the impersonality and authoritarianism of the large university. As the war progressed and U.S. casualties mounted, protests escalated. Teach-ins, sit-ins, and the occupation of university buildings alternated with more radical demonstrations that increasingly led to violence. The killing of four students at Kent State University in 1970 by the Ohio National Guard caused a reaction, and the antiwar movement began to subside. By that time, however, antiwar demonstrations had helped weaken the willingness of many Americans to continue the war. But the combination of antiwar demonstrations and ghetto riots in the cities also prepared many people to embrace "law and order," an appeal used by Richard M. Nixon (1913–1995), the Republican presidential candidate in 1968. With Nixon's election in 1968, a shift to the right in American politics had begun.

## The United States Moves Right

Nixon eventually ended U.S. involvement in Vietnam by gradually withdrawing American troops and appealing to the "silent majority" of Americans for patience in bringing the conflict to an end. A slowdown in racial desegregation appealed to southern whites, who ordinarily tended to vote Democratic. The Republican strategy also gained support among white Democrats in northern cities, where court-mandated busing to achieve racial integration had produced a white backlash. Nixon was less conservative on other issues, notably when, breaking with his strong anti-Communist past, he visited China in 1972 and opened the door toward the eventual diplomatic recognition of that Communist state.

However, Nixon was paranoid about conspiracies and began to use illegal methods of gaining political intelli-

# THE AGE OF AQUARIUS

*he election of John F. Kennedy to the presidency in the fall of 1960 sparked a vast wave of enthusiasm among young people across the United States. In his inaugural address, the new president dramatically declared that the "torch of liberty" had passed to "a new generation of Americans," who were now admonished to ask not what their country could do for them, but what they could do for their country.*

Within a few short years, however, the optimism engendered by the Kennedy presidency had dissipated, to be replaced by an era of discontent marked by antiwar protests on college campuses, urban riots, and a widespread distaste for the shallowness of life in the postwar United States. By the 1970s, many Americans had lost faith in their government and in its ability to adequately service their needs and realize their aspirations.

What had happened to tarnish the dream of the Kennedy years? In part, of course, the disillusionment was a direct consequence of the Vietnam War, a war for which President Kennedy himself bore part of the responsibility and which eventually aroused massive unrest on college campuses across the country. But it is clear that the public discontent over U.S. foreign policy in the 1960s was only one symptom of a deeper current of protest over domestic issues in the United States — over civil rights for racial minorities, over inequalities between men and women, and even over the materialistic lifestyle that characterized the country's capitalist civilization. According to one political scientist, Samuel P. Huntington, the "age of protest" actually began in February 1960, months before the Kennedy election, when four young African Americans demanded service at a lunch counter in Greensboro, North Carolina.

What puzzled many Americans was that the discontent of the 1960s and early 1970s took place during a period marked by the greatest material prosperity that the country had ever known. To seasoned observers, however, the ferment was a product of deep-seated cyclical changes that were an integral part of the rhythm of American society. Huntington notes that there has historically been a large gap between the nation's ideals of freedom and equality and the degree to which such aspirations have actually been achieved in American society. In that sense, Kennedy may have helped unleash the era of protest with his campaign pledge to "get this country moving again." That legacy continued to fester after his assassination in November 1963.

To participants, the fires of such intense social energy may seem unquenchable. Folk musician Bob Dylan—whose song "The Times They Are A-Changin'," published in 1964, became the anthem of the protest movement—wrote that the old order was rapidly fading, and anyone who was not ready to follow the new road had better get out of the way. In fact, however, such creedal passion cannot be sustained. As the historian Arthur F. Schlesinger Jr. has noted, life in America has always been a process of ebb and flow between innovation and conservatism, with each phase bearing the seeds of its own contradiction. Sustained public action is emotionally exhausting, breeding a desire to return to a calmer private life. But when social problems begin to fester and people grow weary of selfish motives and the concentration on material pleasures, the process begins again.

So it has happened periodically in American history. And so it was in the 1960s, when a generation of young Americans grew bored with the complacency of the Eisenhower years and welcomed the "Age of Aquarius," marked by "harmony and understanding, sympathy and trust abounding." All too soon, the dream died, and an exhausted country returned to its private concerns in the self-indulgent years of the 1980s.

Sources: Arthur F. Schlesinger Jr., *The Cycles of American History* (Boston: Houghton Mifflin, 1986); Samuel P. Huntington, *American Politics: The Promise of Disharmony* (Cambridge, Mass.: Belknap Press of Harvard University, 1981); Bob Dylan, *Lyrics, 1962–1985* (New York: Knopf, 1992); "Aquarius," from the American rock musical *Hair*, words by James Rado and Gerome Ragni (New York: United Artists, 1968).

gence about his political opponents. One of the president's advisers explained that their intention was to "use the available federal machinery to screw our political enemies." Nixon's zeal led to the infamous Watergate scandal—the attempted bugging of Democratic National Headquarters. Although Nixon repeatedly lied to the American public about his involvement in the affair, secret tapes of his own conversations in the White House revealed the truth. On August 9, 1974, Nixon resigned from office, an act that saved him from almost certain impeachment and conviction.

After Watergate, American domestic politics focused on economic issues. Gerald B. Ford (b. 1913) became president when Nixon resigned, only to lose in the 1976 election to the Democratic former governor of Georgia, Jimmy Carter (b. 1924), who campaigned as an outsider against the Washington establishment. Both Ford and Carter faced severe economic problems. The period from 1973 to the mid-1980s was one of economic stagnation, which came to be known as stagflation—a combination of high inflation and high unemployment. In 1984, median family income was 6 percent below that of 1973.

The economic downturn stemmed at least in part from a dramatic rise in oil prices. Oil had been a cheap and abundant source of energy in the 1950s, but by the late 1970s, half of the oil used in the United States came from the Middle East. An oil embargo imposed by the Organization of Petroleum Exporting Countries (OPEC) cartel as a reaction to the Arab-Israeli War in 1973 and OPEC's subsequent raising of prices led to a quadrupling of the cost of oil. By the end of the 1970s, oil prices had increased twentyfold, encouraging inflationary tendencies throughout the entire economy. Although the Carter administration produced a plan for reducing oil consumption at home while spurring domestic production, neither Congress nor the American people could be persuaded to follow what they regarded as drastic measures.

By 1980, the Carter administration was facing two devastating problems. High inflation and a noticeable decline in average weekly earnings were causing a perceptible drop in American living standards. At the same time, a crisis abroad had erupted when fifty-three Americans were taken and held hostage by the Iranian government of Ayatollah Khomeini. Although Carter had little control over the situation, his inability to gain the release of the American hostages led to the perception at home that he was a weak president. His overwhelming loss to Ronald Reagan (b. 1911) in the election of 1980 brought forward the chief exponent of conservative Republican policies and a new political order.

## Return to Hegemony

The conservative trend continued in the 1980s. The election of Ronald Reagan changed the direction of American policy on several fronts. Reversing decades of the expanding welfare state, Reagan cut spending on food stamps, school lunch programs, and job programs. At the same time, his administration fostered the largest peacetime military buildup in American history. Total federal spending rose from $631 billion in 1981 to more than $1 trillion by 1986. But instead of raising taxes to pay for the new expenditures, which far outweighed the budget cuts in social areas, Reagan convinced Congress to support supply-side economics. Massive tax cuts were designed to stimulate rapid economic growth and produce new revenues. Much of the tax cut went to the wealthy.

Between 1980 and 1986, the income of the lowest 40 percent of the workforce fell 9 percent, while the income of the highest 20 percent rose by 5 percent.

Reagan's policies seemed to work in the short run, and the United States experienced an economic upturn that lasted until the end of the 1980s. But the spending policies of the Reagan administration also produced record government deficits, which loomed as an obstacle to long-term growth. In the 1970s, the total deficit was $420 billion; between 1981 and 1987, Reagan budget deficits were three times that amount. The inability of George H. W. Bush (b. 1924), Reagan's successor, to deal with the deficit problem or with the continuing economic downslide led to the election of a Democrat, Bill Clinton (b. 1946), in November 1992.

The new president was a southerner who claimed to be a new Democrat—one who favored fiscal responsibility and a more conservative social agenda—a clear indication that the rightward drift in American politics had not been ended by his victory. During his first term in office, Clinton reduced the budget deficit and signed a bill turning the welfare program back to the states while pushing measures to strengthen the educational system and provide job opportunities for those Americans removed from the welfare rolls. By seizing the center of the American political agenda, Clinton was able to win reelection in 1996, although the Republican Party now held a majority in both houses of Congress.

President Clinton's political fortunes were helped considerably by a lengthy economic revival. Thanks to downsizing, major U.S. corporations began to recover the competitive edge they had lost to Japanese and European firms in previous years. At the same time, a steady reduction in the annual government budget deficit strengthened confidence in the performance of the national economy. Although wage increases were modest, inflation was securely in check, and public confidence in the future was on the rise.

Many of the country's social problems, however, remained unresolved. Although crime rates were down, drug use, smoking, and alcoholism among young people were on the rise, and the specter of rising medical costs loomed as a generation of baby boomers neared retirement age. Americans remained bitterly divided over such issues as abortion and affirmative action programs to rectify past discrimination on the basis of gender, race, or sexual orientation.

President Clinton contributed to the national sense of unease by becoming the focus of a series of financial and sexual scandals that aroused concerns among many Americans that the moral fiber of the country had been severely undermined. Accused of lying under oath in a judicial hearing, he was impeached by the Republican-led majority in Congress. Although the effort to remove Clinton from office failed, his administration was tarnished, and in 2000, Republican candidate George W. Bush (b. 1946), the son of Clinton's predecessor, narrowly defeated Clinton's vice president, Albert Gore, in the race for the presidency. Bush too sought to occupy the center of the political spectrum while heeding the concerns of his conservative base.

## TERRORIST ATTACK ON THE UNITED STATES

On September 11, 2001, terrorists hijacked four commercial jet planes shortly after taking off from Boston, Newark, and Washington, D.C. Two of the planes were flown directly into the twin towers of the World Trade Center in New York City, causing both buildings to collapse; a third slammed into the Pentagon, near Washington, D.C.; and the fourth crashed in a field in central Pennsylvania. About three thousand people were killed, including everyone aboard the four airliners.

The hijackings were carried out by a terrorist organization known as al-Qaeda, which had been suspected of bombing two U.S. embassies in Africa in 1998 and attacking a U.S. naval ship, the U.S.S. *Cole*, two years later. Its leader, Osama bin Laden, was a native of Saudi Arabia who was allegedly angry at the growing U.S. presence in the Middle East. U.S. President George W. Bush vowed to wage an offensive war on terrorism, and in October, with broad international support, U.S. forces attacked al-Qaeda bases in Afghanistan (see Chapter 8). The Bush administration had less success in gaining United Nations approval for an attack on the brutal regime of Saddam Hussein in Iraq, which Washington accused of amassing weapons of mass destruction and providing support to terrorist groups in the region.

## CANADA: IN THE SHADOW OF GOLIATH

Canada experienced many of the same developments as the United States in the postwar years. For twenty-five years after World War II, Canada realized extraordinary economic prosperity as it set out on a new path of industrial development. Canada had always had a strong export economy based on its abundant natural resources. Now it also developed electronic, aircraft, nuclear, and chemical engineering industries on a large scale. Much of

*AP/Wide World Photos*

➤➤ **TERRORIST ATTACK ON THE WORLD TRADE CENTER IN NEW YORK CITY.** On September 11, 2001, hijackers flew two commercial jetliners into the twin towers of the World Trade Center. Shown is the second of the jetliners about to hit one of the towers while smoke billows from the site of the first attack. Both towers soon collapsed, killing thousands.

the Canadian growth, however, was financed by capital from the United States, which resulted in U.S. ownership of Canadian businesses. While many Canadians welcomed the economic growth, others feared U.S. economic domination of Canada and its resources.

Canada's close relationship with the United States has been a notable feature of its postwar history. In addition to fears of economic domination, Canadians have also worried about playing a subordinate role politically and militarily to their neighboring superpower. Canada agreed to join the North Atlantic Treaty Organization in 1949 and even sent military contingents to fight in Korea the following year. But to avoid subordination to the United States or any other great power, Canada has consistently and actively supported the United Nations. Nevertheless, concerns about the United States have not kept Canada from maintaining a special relationship with its southern neighbor. The North American Air Defense Command (NORAD), formed in 1957, was based on close cooperation between the air forces of the two countries for the defense of North America against missile attack. As another example of their close cooperation, in 1972, Canada and the United States signed the Great Lakes Water Quality Agreement to regulate water quality of the lakes that border both countries.

After 1945, the Liberal Party continued to dominate Canadian politics until 1957, when John Diefenbaker (1895–1979) achieved a Conservative victory. But a major recession returned the Liberals to power, and under Lester Pearson (1897–1972), they created Canada's welfare state by enacting a national social security system (the Canada Pension Plan) and a national health insurance program.

The most prominent Liberal government, however, was that of Pierre Trudeau (1919–2000), who came to power in 1968. Although French Canadian in background, Trudeau was dedicated to Canada's federal union. In 1968, his government passed the Official Languages Act, creating a bilingual federal civil service and encouraging the growth of French culture and language in Canada. Although Trudeau's government vigorously pushed an industrialization program, high inflation and Trudeau's efforts to impose the will of the federal government on the powerful provincial governments alienated voters and weakened his government.

For Canada, the vigor of the U.S. economy in the 1980s and 1990s was a mixed blessing, for the American behemoth was all too often inclined to make use of its power to have its way with its neighbors. Economic recession had brought Brian Mulroney (b. 1939), leader of the Progressive Conservative Party, to power in Canada in 1984. Mulroney's government sought to privatize many of Canada's state-run corporations and negotiated a free trade agreement with the United States. Bitterly resented by many Canadians as a sellout, the agreement cost Mulroney's government much of its popularity. In 1993, the ruling Conservatives were drastically defeated in national elections, winning only two seats in the House of Commons. The Liberal leader, Jean Chrétien, took over as prime minister with the charge of stimulating the nation's sluggish economy.

The new Liberal government also faced an ongoing crisis over the French-speaking province of Quebec. In the late 1960s, the Parti Québécois, headed by René Lévesque, campaigned on a platform of Quebec's secession from the Canadian confederation. In 1970, the party won 24 percent of the popular vote in Quebec's provin-

cial elections. To pursue their dream of separation, some underground separatist groups even used terrorist bombings and kidnapped two prominent government officials. In 1976, the Parti Québécois won Quebec's provincial elections and in 1980 called for a referendum that would enable the provincial government to negotiate Quebec's independence from the rest of Canada. But voters in Quebec rejected the plan in 1995, and debate over Quebec's status continued to divide Canada as the decade came to a close. Provincial elections held in April 2003 delivered a stunning defeat to the Parti Québécois and a decisive victory to federalist elements.

# DEMOCRACY, DICTATORSHIP, AND DEVELOPMENT IN LATIN AMERICA SINCE 1945

The Great Depression of the 1930s caused political instability in many Latin American countries that led to military coups and militaristic regimes. But it also helped transform Latin America from a traditional to a modern economy. Since the nineteenth century, Latin Americans had exported raw materials, especially minerals and foodstuffs, while buying the manufactured goods of the industrialized countries, particularly Europe and the United States. Despite a limited degree of industrialization, Latin America was still dependent on an export-import economy. As a result of the Great Depression, however, exports were cut in half, and the revenues available to buy manufactured goods declined. In response, many Latin American countries encouraged the development of new industries to produce goods that were formerly imported. Due to a shortage of capital in the private sector, governments often invested in the new industries, thereby leading, for example, to government-run steel industries in Chile and Brazil and petroleum industries in Argentina and Mexico.

In the 1960s, however, Latin American countries were still dependent on the United States, Europe, and now Japan for the advanced technology needed for modern industries. To make matters worse, poverty conditions in

MAP **4.1**  Political Trends in Latin America in the 1960s and 1970s.
Latin America experienced considerable political upheaval after World War II,
especially as a result of severe economic problems. The result was a move
toward military regimes as well as strong leftist movements, especially
Marxism. ➢ *Which Latin American countries experienced military regimes,
and which were troubled by leftist movements?*

Atlantic
Ocean

Caracas
VENEZUELA
Bogotá
COLOMBIA
Quito
ECUADOR

GUYANA (1966)
SURINAME (1975)
FRENCH GUIANA

BRAZIL

PERU
Lima

BOLIVIA
La Paz
Sucre

Brasília

PARAGUAY

Pacific
Ocean

CHILE
Asunción

Atlantic
Ocean

Santiago
Buenos Aires
ARGENTINA
URUGUAY
Montevideo

0     500    1,000   1,500 Kilometers
0         500        1,000 Miles

Falkland
Islands (Br.)

( )   Date of independence

Urban terrorism,
1960–1979

Rightist military coups,
1960–1979

Leftist guerrilla warfare

European colonial
possession

some Latin American countries limited the size of domestic markets, and many countries were unable to find markets abroad for their products.

These failures resulted in takeovers by military regimes that sought to curb the demands of the new industrial middle class and a working class that had increased in size and power as a result of industrialization (see Map 4.1). In the 1960s, repressive military regimes in Chile, Brazil, and Argentina abolished political parties and turned to export-import economies financed by foreigners while encouraging multinational corporations to come into their countries. Because these companies were primarily interested in taking advantage of Latin America's raw materials and abundant supply of cheap labor, their presence often offered little benefit to the local economy and contributed to the region's dependence on the industrially developed nations.

In the 1970s, Latin American regimes grew even more reliant on borrowing from abroad, especially from banks in Europe and the United States. Between 1970 and 1982, debt to foreigners increased from $27 billion to $315.3 billion. By 1982, a number of governments announced that they could no longer pay interest on their debts to foreign banks, and their economies began to crumble. Wages fell, and unemployment skyrocketed. Governments were forced to undertake fundamental reforms to qualify for additional loans, reducing the size of the state sector and improving agricultural production in order to stem the flow of people from the countryside to the cities and strengthen the domestic market for Latin American products.

In the 1990s, the opening of markets to free trade practices and other consequences of the globalization process began to exert a growing impact on Latin American economies. As some countries faced the danger of bankruptcy, belt-tightening measures undertaken to reassure foreign investors provoked social protests and threatened to undermine the precarious political stability in the region.

Other factors have also played important roles in the history of Latin America since 1945. The Catholic church had been a powerful force in Latin America for centuries, but its hold over people diminished as cities and industrial societies developed. Eventually, the church adopted a middle stance in Latin American society, advocating a moderate capitalist system that would respect workers' rights, institute land reform, and provide for the poor. Some Catholics, however, took a more radical path to change by advocating a theology of liberation. Influenced by Marxist ideas, advocates of liberation theology believed that Christians must fight to free the oppressed, using violence if necessary. Some Catholic clergy recommended armed rebellions and even teamed up with Marxist guerrillas in rural areas. Other radical priests worked in factories alongside workers or carried on social work among the poor in the slums. Liberation theology was by no means the ideology of the majority of Latin American Catholics and was rejected by the church hierarchy. Nevertheless, the Catholic church continued to play an important role in Latin America by becoming the advocate of human rights against authoritarian regimes.

The United States continued to cast a large shadow over Latin America. In 1948, the nations of the region formed the Organization of American States (OAS), which was intended to eliminate unilateral action by one state in the internal or external affairs of another state, while encouraging regional cooperation to maintain peace. It did not end U.S. interference in Latin American affairs, however. The United States returned to a policy of unilateral action when it believed that Soviet agents were attempting to use local Communists or radical reformers to establish governments hostile to U.S. interests. In the 1960s, President Kennedy's Alliance for Progress encouraged social reform and economic development by providing private and public funds to elected governments whose reform programs were acceptable to the United States. But the Alliance failed to work, and when Marxist-led insurrections began to spread throughout the region, the United States responded by providing massive military aid to anti-Communist regimes, regardless of their nature.

## The Threat of Marxist Revolutions

Until the 1960s, Marxism played little role in the politics of Latin America. The success of Fidel Castro in Cuba, however, opened the door for other revolutionary movements that aimed to gain the support of peasants and industrial workers and bring radical change to Latin America.

### THE CUBAN REVOLUTION

An authoritarian regime, headed by Fulgencio Batista (1901–1973) and closely tied economically to U.S. investors, had ruled Cuba since 1934. A strong opposition movement to Batista's government developed, led by Fidel Castro (b. 1926) and assisted by Ernesto "Ché" Guevara (1928–1967), an Argentinian who believed that revolutionary upheaval was necessary for change to occur. Castro maintained that only armed force could overthrow Batista, but when their initial assaults on Batista's regime brought little success, Castro's forces, based in the Sierra Maestra mountains, turned to guerrilla warfare. As the rebels gained more support, Batista responded with such brutality that he alienated his own supporters. The dictator fled in December 1958, and Castro's revolutionaries seized Havana on January 1, 1959.

Relations between Cuba and the United States quickly deteriorated. An agrarian reform law in May 1959 nationalized all landholdings over 1,000 acres. A new level of antagonism arose early in 1960 when the Soviet Union agreed to buy Cuban sugar and provide $100 million in credits. On March 17, 1960, President Eisenhower directed the Central Intelligence Agency (CIA) to "organize the training of Cuban exiles, mainly in Guatemala, against a possible future day when they might return to their homeland."[1] Arms from Eastern Europe began to arrive in Cuba, the United States cut its purchases of Cuban sugar, and the Cuban government nationalized U.S. companies and banks. In October 1960, the United States declared a trade embargo of Cuba, driving Castro closer to the Soviet Union.

On January 3, 1961, the United States broke diplomatic relations with Cuba. The new U.S. president, John F. Kennedy, approved a plan originally drafted by the previous administration to launch an invasion to overthrow Castro's government, but the landing of fourteen hundred CIA-assisted Cubans in Cuba on April 17, 1961, known as the Bay of Pigs, turned into a total military disaster. This fiasco encouraged the Soviets to make an even greater commitment to Cuban independence by attempting to place nuclear missiles in the country, an act that led to a showdown with the United States (see Chapter 1). As its part of the bargain to defuse the missile crisis, the United States agreed not to invade Cuba.

But the missile crisis affected Cuba in another way as well. Castro, who had urged Khrushchev to stand firm even at the risk of nuclear war with the United States, now realized that the Soviet Union was unreliable. If revolutionary Cuba was to be secure and no longer encircled by hostile states tied to U.S. interests, the Cubans would have to instigate social revolution in the rest of Latin America. He believed that once guerrilla wars were launched, peasants would flock to the movement and overthrow the old regimes. Guevara attempted to instigate a guerrilla war in Bolivia but was caught and killed by the Bolivian army in the fall of 1967. The Cuban strategy had failed.

In Cuba, however, Castro's socialist revolution proceeded, with mixed results. The Cuban Revolution did secure some social gains for its people, especially in health care and education. The regime provided free medical services for all citizens, and a new law code expanded the rights of women. Illiteracy was wiped out by creating new schools and establishing teacher-training institutes that tripled the number of teachers within ten years. Eschewing the path of rapid industrialization, Castro encouraged agricultural diversification. But the Cuban economy continued to rely on the production and sale of sugar. Economic problems forced the Castro regime to depend on Soviet subsidies and the purchase of Cuban sugar by Soviet bloc countries.

The disintegration of the Soviet Union was a major blow to Cuba, as the new government in Moscow no longer had a reason to continue to subsidize the onetime Soviet ally. During the 1990s, Castro began to introduce limited market reforms and to allow the circulation of U.S. dollars. But although most Cubans remained locked in poverty, the regime refused to liberalize the political system, and although limited Cuban contacts with the United States were permitted by the Clinton administration, the U.S. embargo remained in place as the new century dawned.

CHILE

Another challenge to U.S. influence in Latin America appeared in 1970 when a Marxist, Salvador Allende (1908–1973), was elected president of Chile and attempted to create a socialist society by constitutional means. Chile suffered from a number of economic problems. Wealth was concentrated in the hands of large landowners and a few large corporations. Inflation, foreign debts, and a decline in the mining industry (copper exports accounted for 80 percent of Chile's export income) caused untold difficulties. Right-wing control of the government failed to achieve any solutions, especially since foreign investments were allowed to expand. There was growing resentment of U.S. corporations, especially Anaconda and Kennecott, which controlled the copper industry.

In the 1970 elections, a split in the moderate forces enabled Allende to become president of Chile as head of a coalition of Socialists, Communists, and Catholic radicals. A number of labor leaders, who represented the interests of the working classes, were given the ministries of labor, finance, public works, and interior in the new government. Allende increased the wages of industrial workers and began to move toward socialism by nationalizing the largest domestic and foreign-owned corporations. Nationalization of the copper industry—essentially without compensation for the owners—caused the Nixon administration to cut off all aid to Chile, creating serious problems for the Chilean economy. At the same time, the government offered only halfhearted resistance to radical workers who were beginning to take control of the landed estates.

These actions brought growing opposition from the upper and middle classes, who began, with covert support from the CIA, to organize strikes against the government. Allende attempted to stop the disorder by bringing three military officers into his cabinet. They succeeded in ending the strikes, but when Allende's coalition increased its vote in the congressional elections of March 1973, the Chilean army, under the direction of General Augusto Pinochet, decided on a coup d'état. In September 1973, Allende and thousands of his supporters were killed. Contrary to the expectations of many right-wing politicians, the military remained in power and set up a dictatorship. The regime moved quickly to outlaw all political parties, disband the congress, and restore many nationalized industries and landed estates to their original owners. The copper industry, however, remained in government hands. Although Pinochet's regime liberalized the economy, its flagrant abuse of human rights led to growing unrest against the government in the mid-1980s. In 1989, free elections produced a Christian Democratic president who advocated free market economics.

The shadow of the Pinochet era continued to hover over Chilean politics, however, as many citizens demanded that the general, now living in exile, be brought to justice for his crimes against humanity. In 2000, he was returned to the country from Europe and placed on trial for crimes that had allegedly taken place under his rule.

## NICARAGUA

The United States intervened in Nicaraguan domestic affairs in the early twentieth century, and U.S. marines actually remained there for long periods of time. The leader of the U.S.-supported National Guard, Anastasio Somoza (1896–1956), seized control of the government in 1937, and his family remained in power for the next forty-three years. U.S. support for the Somoza military regime enabled the family to overcome any opponents while enriching themselves at the expense of the state.

Opposition to the regime finally arose from Marxist guerrilla forces known as the Sandinista National Liberation Front. By mid-1979, military victories by the Sandinistas left them in virtual control of the country. Inheriting a poverty-stricken nation, the Sandinistas organized a provisional government and aligned themselves with the Soviet Union. The Reagan and Bush administrations, believing that Central America faced the danger of another Communist state, financed the counterrevolutionary Contra rebels in a guerrilla war against the Sandinista government. The Contra war and a U.S. economic embargo undermined support for the Sandinistas, and in

1990, they agreed to hold free elections. Although they lost to a coalition headed by Violetta Barrios de Chamorro (b. 1929), the Sandinistas remained a significant political force in Nicaragua.

## Nationalism and the Military: The Examples of Argentina and Brazil

The military became the power brokers of twentieth-century Latin America. Especially in the 1960s and 1970s, Latin American armies portrayed themselves as the guardians of national honor and orderly progress. In the mid-1970s, only Colombia, Venezuela, and Costa Rica maintained democratic governments.

A decade later, pluralistic systems had been installed virtually everywhere except in Cuba, Paraguay, and some of the Central American states. The establishment of democratic institutions, however, has not managed to solve all the chronic problems that have plagued the states of Latin America. Official corruption continued in many countries, and the gap between rich and poor is growing, most notably in Brazil and Venezuela, where a leftist regime led by President Hugo Chavez aroused massive protests by adopting policies designed to redistribute the wealth in this oil-rich country.

### ARGENTINA

Fearful of the forces unleashed by the development of industry, the military intervened in Argentinian politics in 1930 and propped up the cattle and wheat oligarchy that had controlled the government since the beginning of the twentieth century. In 1943, restless military officers staged a coup and seized power. But the new regime was not sure how to deal with the working classes. One of its members, Juan Perón (1895–1974), thought that he could manage the workers and used his position as labor secretary in the military government to curry favor with them. He encouraged workers to join labor unions and increased job benefits as well as the number of paid holidays and vacations. But as Perón grew more popular, other army officers began to fear his power and arrested him. An uprising by workers forced the officers to back down, and in 1946, Perón was elected president.

Perón pursued a policy of increased industrialization to please his chief supporters—labor and the urban middle class. At the same time, he sought to free Argentina from foreign investors. The government bought the railways; took over the banking, insurance, shipping, and communications industries; and assumed regulation of imports and exports. But Perón's regime was also authoritarian.

His wife, Eva Perón, organized women's groups to support the government while Perón created fascist gangs, modeled after Hitler's Storm Troops, that used violence to overawe his opponents. But growing corruption in the Perón government and the alienation of more and more people by the regime's excesses encouraged the military to overthrow him in September 1955. Perón went into exile in Spain.

It had been easy for the military to seize power, but it was harder to rule, especially now that Argentina had a party of *Peronistas* clamoring for the return of the exiled leader. In the 1960s and 1970s, military and civilian governments (the latter closely watched by the military) alternated in power. When both failed to provide economic stability, military leaders decided to allow Juan Perón to return. Reelected president in September 1973, Perón died one year later. In 1976, the military installed a new regime, using the occasion to kill more than six thousand leftists. With the economic problems still unsolved, the regime tried to divert people's attention by invading the Falkland Islands in April 1982. Great Britain, which had controlled the islands since the nineteenth century, decisively defeated the Argentine forces. The loss discredited the military and opened the door once again to civilian rule. In 1983, Raúl Alfonsín (b. 1927) was elected president and sought to reestablish democratic processes.

In 1989, however, Alfonsín was defeated in the presidential elections by the Peronist candidate, Carlos Saúl Menem (b. 1930). During his first term, the charismatic Menem won broad popularity for his ability to control the army, long an active force in politics, and he was reelected in 1995. But when he sought to control rampant inflation by curbing government spending, rising unemployment and an economic recession cut into his public acclaim. In 1999, Fernando de la Rúa was elected president on a promise to reduce unemployment—now running at nearly 20 percent—and to bring an end to official corruption. But with Argentina suffering from low growth, rising emigration (a growing number of descendants of European settlers were returning to live in Europe), and shrinking markets abroad, the new government soon collapsed, initiating an era of political chaos. In May 2003, Nestor Kirchner (b. 1950) assumed the presidency and sought to revive public confidence in an economy in paralysis.

## BRAZIL

After Getúlio Vargas was forced to resign from the presidency in 1945, a second Brazilian republic came into being. In 1949, Vargas was elected to the presidency. But he was unable to solve Brazil's economic problems, especially its soaring inflation, and in 1954, after the armed

➤ **THE PERÓNS.** Elected president of Argentina in 1946, Juan Perón soon established an authoritarian regime that nationalized some of Argentina's basic industries and organized fascist gangs to overwhelm its opponents. He is shown here with his wife, Eva, during the inauguration ceremonies initiating his second term as president in 1952.

© CORBIS

forces called on him to resign, Vargas committed suicide. Subsequent democratically elected presidents had no better success in controlling inflation while trying to push rapid industrialization. In the spring of 1964, the military decided to intervene and took over the government.

The armed forces remained in direct control of the country for twenty years, setting a new economic course, cutting back somewhat on state control of the economy and emphasizing market forces. The new policies seemed to work, and during the late 1960s, Brazil experienced an "economic miracle" as it moved into self-sustaining economic growth, generally the hallmark of a modern economy.

Rapid economic growth carried with it some potential drawbacks. The economic exploitation of the Amazon River basin opened the region to farming but in the view of some critics threatened the ecological balance not only of Brazil but of the earth itself. Ordinary Brazilians hardly benefited as the gulf between rich and poor, always wide, grew even wider. In 1960, the wealthiest 10 percent of Brazil's population received 40 percent of the nation's income; in 1980, they received 51 percent. At the same time, rapid development led to an inflation rate of 100 percent a year, and an enormous foreign debt added to the problems. By the early 1980s, the economic miracle was turning into an economic nightmare. Overwhelmed, the generals retreated and opened the door for a return to democracy in 1985.

In 1990, national elections brought a new president into office—Fernando Collor de Mello (b. 1949). The new administration promised to reduce inflation with a drastic reform program based on squeezing money out of the economy by stringent controls on wages and prices, drastic reductions in public spending, and cuts in the number of government employees. But Collor de Mello's efforts—reminiscent of Menem's in Argentina—were undermined by reports of official corruption, and he resigned at the end of 1992 after having been impeached. In new elections two years later, Fernando Cardoso (b. 1931) was elected president by an overwhelming majority of the popular vote.

Cardoso, a member of the Brazilian Social Democratic Party, introduced measures to privatize state-run industries and to reform social security and the pension system. He rode a wave of economic prosperity to reelection in 1998. But economic problems, combined with allegations of official corruption and rising factionalism within the ruling party, undermined his popularity, leading to the victory of the Workers' Party in elections held in 2003. The new president, ex-lathe operator Luiz Inacio "Lula"

da Silva, however, immediately cautioned his supporters that the party's ambitious plans could not be realized until urgent financial reforms had been enacted.

## The Mexican Way

During the presidency of Lázaro Cárdenas in the 1930s, the Mexican government returned to some of the original revolutionary goals by distributing 44 million acres of land to landless Mexican peasants, thereby appealing to the rural poor.

In the 1950s and 1960s, Mexico's ruling party, the Institutional Revolutionary Party (PRI), focused on a balanced industrial program. Fifteen years of steady economic growth combined with low inflation and real gains in wages for more and more people made those years appear to be a golden age in Mexico's economic development. But at the end of the 1960s, one implication of Mexico's domination by one party became apparent with the rise of the student protest movement. On October 2, 1968, a demonstration by university students in Tlatelolco Square in Mexico City was met by police, who opened fire and killed hundreds of students. Leaders of the PRI became concerned about the need to change the system.

The next two presidents, Luis Echeverría (b. 1922) and José López Portillo (b. 1920), introduced political reforms. The government eased rules for the registration of political parties and allowed greater freedom of debate in the press and universities. But economic problems continued to trouble Mexico.

In the late 1970s, vast new reserves of oil were discovered in Mexico. As the sale of oil abroad rose dramatically, the government became increasingly dependent on oil revenues. When world oil prices dropped in the mid-1980s, Mexico was no longer able to make payments on its foreign debt, which had reached $80 billion in 1982. The government was forced to adopt new economic policies, including the sale of publicly owned companies to private parties.

The debt crisis and rising unemployment increased dissatisfaction with the government. In the 1988 elections, the PRI's choice for president, Carlos Salina, who had been expected to win in a landslide, won by only a 50.3 percent majority. The new president continued the economic liberalization of his predecessors and went even further by negotiating the North American Free Trade Agreement (NAFTA) with the United States and Canada. Although NAFTA was highly controversial in the United States because of the fear that U.S. firms would move factories to Mexico, where labor costs are cheaper and environmental standards less stringent, some observers asserted that the impact of NAFTA has been more beneficial to the U.S. economy than to its southern neighbor. Reflecting Mexico's continuing economic problems was rising popular unrest in southern parts of the country, where unhappy farmers, many of whom are native Amerindians, have grown increasingly vocal in protesting endemic poverty and widespread neglect of the needs of the indigenous peoples, who comprise about 10 percent of the total population of 100 million people.

In the summer of 2000, a national election suddenly swept the ruling PRI from power. The new president, Vicente Fox (b. 1942), promised to address the many problems affecting the country, including political corruption, widespread poverty, environmental concerns, and a growing population. But he faces vocal challenges from the PRI, which still controls many state legislatures and a plurality in Congress, as well as from the protest movement in rural areas in the south. Calling themselves Zapatistas in honor of the revolutionary leader Emiliano Zapata, the rebels demand passage of legislation to protect the rights of the indigenous Indian population and increasing autonomy for regions such as the southern state of Chiapas, where Amerindians make up a substantial percentage of the population. President Fox has expressed his support for legislative action to bring about reforms, but the movement has aroused such a groundswell of support from around the country that he will be under considerable pressure to deal with generations of neglect in solving the problems of Mexico.

# SOCIAL CHANGES IN THE UNITED STATES

As in Europe (see Chapter 3), major changes took place in American society in the decades following World War II. New technologies such as television, jet planes, medical advances, and the computer revolution all dramatically altered the pace and nature of American life. Increased prosperity led to the growth of the middle class, the expansion of higher education, and a rapid increase in consumer demand for the products of a mass society. The building of a nationwide system of superhighways, combined with low fuel prices and steady improvements in the quality and operability of automobiles, produced a more highly mobile society in which the average American family moved at least once every five years, sometimes from one end of the continent to the other.

## The Melting Pot in Action

One of the primary visual factors that helped shape American society in the postwar era was the increasing pace of new arrivals from abroad. As restrictions on immigration were loosened after World War II, millions of immigrants began to arrive from all over the world. Although the majority came from Latin America, substantial numbers came from China, Vietnam, and the countries of southern Asia. By 2003, people of Hispanic origin surpassed African Americans as the largest minority in the country. Although illegal immigration—especially from Mexico and the Caribbean islands—became a controversial issue in American politics, there was little doubt that the face of America was changing rapidly. Whether the country's traditional role as a "melting pot"—integrating new arrivals into the mainstream of American society—can continue to function remains to be seen.

## Women and Society

Many of the changes taking place in American life reflected the fact that the role of women was in a state of rapid transition. In the years immediately following the war, many women gave up their jobs in factories and returned to their traditional role as homemakers, sparking the "baby boom" of the late 1940s and 1950s. Eventually, however, many women became restive with their restrictive role as wives and mothers and began to enter the workforce at an increasing rate. Unlike the situation before World War II, many of them were married. In 1900, for example, married women made up about 15 percent of the female labor force. By 1970, their number had increased to 62 percent.

As in Europe, however, American women were still not receiving equal treatment in the workplace, and by the late 1960s, some began to assert their rights and speak as feminists. Leading advocates of women's rights in the United States were Betty Friedan and Gloria Steinem. A journalist and the mother of three children, Friedan (b. 1921) grew increasingly uneasy with her attempt to fulfill the traditional role of housewife and mother. In 1963, she published *The Feminine Mystique*, in which she analyzed the problems of middle-class women in the 1950s and argued that women were systematically being denied equality with men. *The Feminine Mystique* became a best-seller and transformed Friedan into a prominent spokeswoman for women's rights in the United States.

As women became more actively involved in public issues, their role in education increased as well. Beginning in the 1980s, women's studies programs began to proliferate on college campuses throughout the United States. Women also became active in promoting women's rights in countries around the world, and they helped organize international conferences on the subject in Mexico City, Copenhagen, Nairobi, and Beijing.

## The Environment

Concern over environmental problems first began to engage public opinion in the United States during the 1950s, when high pollution levels in major cities such as Los Angeles, Chicago, and Pittsburgh, combined with the popularity of Rachel Carson's book, *Silent Spring*, aroused concerns over the impact that unfettered industrialization was having on the quality of life and the health of the American people. During the next several decades, federal, state, and local governments began to issue regulations directed at reducing smog in urban areas and improving the quality of rivers and streams throughout the country. In general, most Americans reacted favorably to such regulations, but by the 1980s, the environmental movement had engendered a backlash as some people complained that excessively radical measures could threaten the pace of economic growth and a loss of jobs in the workforce. By the end of the century, concern over the environment was deeply entangled with concerns over the state of the national economy. Still, it was clear that the quality of life in environmental terms was much improved for the vast majority of Americans compared to what had existed prior to World War II.

# TRENDS IN THE ARTS

After World War II, the capital of the Western art world shifted from Paris to New York. Continuing the avant-garde quest to express reality in new ways, a group of New York artists known as Abstract Expressionists began to paint large nonrepresentational canvases in an effort to express a spiritual essence beyond the material world. Among the first was Jackson Pollock (1912–1956), who developed the technique of dripping and flinging paint onto a canvas spread out on the floor. Pollock's large paintings of swirling colors expressed the energy of primal forces as well as the vast landscapes of his native Wyoming.

During the 1960s, many American artists began to reject the emotional style of the previous decade and chose to deal with familiar objects from everyday experience. Some feared that art was being drowned out by popular culture, which bombarded Americans with the images of mass culture in newspapers, in the movies, or on television. In the hope of making art more relevant and accessible to the public, artists sought to pattern their work on aspects of everyday life to reach and manipulate the masses. Works such as those by Andy Warhol (1930–1987), which repeated images such as soup cans, dollar bills, and the faces of the *Mona Lisa* and Marilyn Monroe, often left the viewer with a detached numbness and a sense of being trapped in an impersonal, mechanized world. Repetitious and boring, most such paintings did little to close the gap between popular culture and serious art.

Perhaps the most influential American artist of the postwar era was Robert Rauschenberg (b. 1925), whose works broke through the distinctions between painting and other art forms such as sculpture, photography, dance, and theater. In his "collages" or "combines," he juxtaposed disparate images and everyday objects—photographs, clothing, letters, even dirt and cigarette butts—to reflect the energy and disorder of the world around us. He sought to reproduce the stream of images projected by flicking the channels on a TV set. His works represented an encapsulated documentary of American life in the 1960s, filled with news events, celebrities, war, sports, and advertisements.

Following in Duchamp's footsteps, Rauschenberg helped free future artists to find art in anything under the sun. Beginning in the late 1960s, a new school of conceptual art began to reject the commercial marketability of an art object and seek the meaning of art in ideas. Art as idea could be philosophy, linguistics, mathematics, or social criticism, existing solely in the mind of the artist and the audience. In a related attempt to free art from the shackles of tradition, a school of performance art used the body as a means of living sculpture. Often discomfiting or shocking in its intimate revelations, performance art offended many viewers. Such works expanded the horizons of modern creativity but also widened the gap between modern art and the public, many of whom now considered art as socially dysfunctional and totally lacking in relevance to their daily lives.

By the early 1970s, Postmodernism became the new art of revolt. It replaced Modernism, which was no longer considered sufficiently outrageous. Although some artists persevered in the Modernist tradition of formal experimentation, many believed that art should serve society, and therefore their work expressed political concerns, seeking to redress social inequities by addressing issues of gender, race, sexual orientation, ecology, and globalization. This new style was called conceptual art, because it was primarily preoccupied with ideas. Using innovative techniques such as photography, video, and even representational painting, such artists (many of them women, persons of color, gays, or lesbians) produced shocking works with the intent of motivating the viewer to political action.

One powerful example of such Postmodern art is found in the haunting work of the Colombian artist Doris Salcedo (b. 1959). Her art evokes disturbing images of her country's endless civil war and violent drug trade. Salcedo often presents everyday wooden furniture, over which she has applied a thin layer of cement and fragments of personal mementos from the owner's past life: a remnant of lace curtain, a lock of hair, or a handkerchief. Frozen in time, these everyday souvenirs evoke the pain of those who were dragged from their homes in the middle of the night and senselessly murdered. Salcedo's work can be experienced as an impassioned plea to stop the killing of innocent civilians or as the fossilized artifact from some future archaeologist's dig, showing traces of our brief and absurd sojourn on earth.

One of the most popular genres in the 1990s was the installation. The artist "installs" machine- or human-made objects, sometimes filling a large room, with the aim of transporting the viewer to another environment so as to experience new ideas and self-awareness. A powerful example is found in the untitled installation of 1997 by Robert Gober (b. 1955), in the center of which a stereotypical statue of the Virgin Mary stands over an open drain while a wide steel pipe pierces her body. Such a violent violation of the Madonna can be viewed by

Christians as the victory and resilience of faith despite the century's philosophical discourse denying the existence of God.

Musical composers also experimented with radically new concepts. One such innovator was American John Cage (1912–1992), who by the 1950s had developed the extreme procedure of "indeterminacy," or the use of chance in both musical composition and performance. Since Cage defined music as the "organization of sound," he included all types of noise in his music. Any unconventional sound was welcomed: electronic buzzers and whines, tape recordings played at altered speeds, or percussion from any household item. In wanting to make music "purposeless," Cage removed the composer's control over the sounds. Rather, he sought to let the sounds, unconnected to one another, exist on their own. His most discussed work, called "4′ 33″," was four minutes and thirty-three seconds of silence—the "music" being the sounds the audience heard in the hall during the "performance," such as coughing, the rustling of programs, the hum of air conditioning, and the shuffling of feet.

In the 1960s, minimalism took hold in the United States. Largely influenced by Indian music, minimalist composers such as Philip Glass (b. 1937) focus on the subtle nuances in the continuous repetitions of a melodic or rhythmic pattern. Yet another musical development was microtonality, which expands the traditional twelve-tone chromatic scale to include quarter tones and even smaller intervals. Since the 1960s, there has also been

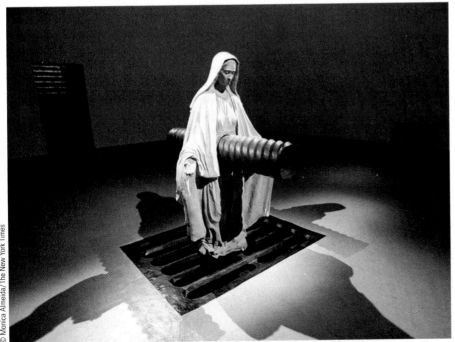

⇒ ROBERT GOBER'S MADONNA INSTALLATION. Here the Virgin Mary is welcoming the faithful with outstretched arms, inviting them to unburden their suffering and tears down the drain at her feet. By combining such dramatically opposed visual objects, Gober succeeds in making the Madonna's pain palpably real, bringing her down to our level, overwhelming us with sadness and awe. For the unbeliever, Gober's installation is equally moving, representing as it does humankind's indomitable spirit. For despite the absurdity of one's existence, like this statue with its insides pierced, we are somehow still standing, still persevering in our quest for joy and meaning in life.

much experimental electronic and computer music. However, despite the excitement of such musical exploration, much of it is considered too cerebral and alien, even by the educated public.

One of the most accomplished and accessible contemporary American composers, John Adams (b. 1947), has labeled much of twentieth-century experimental composition as the "fussy, difficult music of transition." His music blends modernist elements with classical traditions using much minimalist repetition interspersed with dynamic rhythms. Critics applaud his opera *Nixon in China* (1987), as well as his oratorio *El Niño* (2000), for their dramatic effects and haunting music.

Architecture best reflects the extraordinary global economic expansion of the second half of the twentieth century, from the rapid postwar reconstruction of Japan and Europe to the phenomenal prosperity of the West and the newfound affluence of emerging Third World nations. No matter where one travels today, from Kuala Lumpur to Johannesburg, from Buenos Aires to Shanghai, the world's cities boast the identical monolithic rectangular skyscraper, which is the international symbol of modernization, money, and power.

A major failure of Modernist architecture, inspired by the utopian schemes of the 1920s and built in the 1960s, was the creation of a new capital in Brazil. Brasília, a glistening but sterile city of glass and steel erected as a futuristic ideal, totally ignored the human factor and as a consequence has suffered from its impractical limitations. A more realistic example of city planning is to be found in Singapore, which since the 1980s has housed 80 percent of its three million inhabitants in government-built high-rise buildings grouped together in independent communities called estates. These estates have been adapted to local conditions on a human scale and include schools, places of worship, stores, a subway system, day care, and entertainment.

The arts are affected by the technological discoveries of their age, and today's marvel is undoubtedly the computer. In recent years, all the arts have been grappling with computerizing their medium. In architecture, for example, the computer is used as an engineering tool to solve construction problems for buildings imagined on the drawing board. What is more, architects today bypass the drawing board completely and let the computer conceive the building all by itself. In the visual arts, many artists compose abstract designs or representational paintings directly on the computer, forsaking canvas and brush entirely.

Of all the arts, music has been dealing with electronic devices the longest, so the computer represents just the latest technology in composing mathematically formed atonal works. Computer technology has also invented "hyperinstruments," which translate colors or movement into sounds. The "electric glove," for example, reacts to the motion of the fingers, producing changing tones—instant music.

Not to be undone, "hypertext" fiction offers a thoroughly postmodern, open-ended text, created by the reader, who must direct the nonlinear chronology of the story on the computer. Actually, such a procedure was first developed during the 1960s by the Argentine author Julio Cortazar (1914–1984). In his seminal novel *Hopscotch* (1966), the reader selects the chronology of the story by turning the pages forward or backward. For other trends in contemporary literature, see the box on p. 99.

## Popular Culture

Popular culture in the twentieth century, especially since World War II, has played an important role in helping Western people define themselves. It also reflects the economic system that supports it, for it is this system that manufactures, distributes, and sells the images that people consume as popular culture. As popular culture and its economic support system have become increasingly intertwined, leisure industries have emerged. Modern popular culture is thus inextricably tied to the mass consumer society in which it has emerged. This consumer-oriented aspect of popular culture delineates it clearly from the folk culture of preceding centuries; folk culture is something people make, whereas popular culture is something people buy.

The United States has been the most influential force in shaping popular culture in the West and, to a lesser degree, throughout the world. Through movies, music, advertising, and television, the United States has spread its particular form of consumerism and the American dream to millions around the world.

Motion pictures were the primary vehicle for the diffusion of American popular culture in the years immediately following the war and continued to dominate both European and American markets in the next decades. Although developed in the 1930s, television did not become readily available until the late 1940s. By 1954, there were 32 million sets in the United States as television became the centerpiece of middle-class life. In the 1960s, as television spread around the world, American networks unloaded their products on Europe and developing countries at extraordinarily low prices. Only the establishment of quota systems prevented American television from completely inundating these countries.

The United States has also dominated popular music since the end of World War II. Jazz, blues, rhythm and

# THE SEARCH FOR A NEW LITERATURE

*Ever since James Joyce at the beginning of the twentieth century, Western authors have been searching for new literary means of expressing the complexities of modern life. Their often radical experiments culminated in the years after World War II. In this process, American literature has followed its own independent path, led by two authors, William Faulkner (1897–1962) and Ernest Hemingway (1899–1961). Although both wrote masterpieces before the war, they continued to write important works in the 1950s and influenced subsequent generations of authors with their unique styles. Under the impact of these two masters, postwar writing in the United States omitted authorial explanation and commentary and made its point by suggestion rather than assertion, by prying coherence and meaning from the text.*

Faulkner's world was the Old South. Admired for their stylistic innovations regarding chronology and inner monologue, Faulkner's novels chronicled the history of an imaginary county in Mississippi from its early settlers to his own day. In novels such as *The Sound and the Fury* (1929), *Absalom, Absalom!* (1936), and *Intruder in the Dust* (1948), he expressed his outrage at the moral decay of the modern-day South and its failure to solve its social problems.

Hemingway's world was that of the American expatriate, roaming the world to find purpose and identity in a larger global culture. Using his patented laconic style (he once explained his stripped-down prose by referring to the principle of an iceberg, that "there is seven-eighths of it underwater for every part that shows"), his works—including *The Sun Also Rises* (1926), *For Whom the Bell Tolls* (1940), and *The Old Man and the Sea* (1952)—explored the psychological meaning of masculinity under the pressures of different aspects of modern life. Injured in a plane crash on safari in Africa, he committed suicide in 1961.

Fictional writing in the 1960s reflected growing concerns about the materialism and superficiality of American culture and often took the form of exuberant and comic verbal fantasies. As the decade intensified with the pain of the Vietnam War and the ensuing social and political turmoil, authors turned to satire, using "black humor" and cruelty, hoping to shock the American public into a recognition of its social ills. Many of these novels—such as Thomas Pynchon's *V* (1953), Joseph Heller's *Catch-22* (1961), and John Barth's *Sotweed Factor* (1961)—were wildly imaginative, highly entertaining, and very different from the writing of the first half of the century, which had detailed the "real" daily lives of small-town or big-city America.

In the 1970s and 1980s, American fiction relinquished the extravagant verbal displays of the 1960s, returning to a more sober exposition of social problems, this time related to race, gender, and sexual orientation. Much of the best fiction explored the moral dimensions of contemporary life from Jewish, African American, feminist, or gay perspectives. Some outstanding women's fiction was written by foreign-born writers from Asia and Latin America, who examined the problems of immigrants, such as cultural identity and assimilation into the American mainstream.

Postwar writing in Latin America has been equally vibrant. Nobel Prize–winning writers such as Mario Vargas Llosa, Gabriel García Márquez, José Luis Borges, and Carlos Fuentes are among the most respected literary names of the postwar half century. These authors often use dazzling language and daring narrative experimentation to make their point. Master of this new style is Gabriel García Márquez (b. 1938), from Colombia. In *One Hundred Years of Solitude* (1967), he explores the transformation of a small town under the impact of political violence, industrialization, and the arrival of a U.S. banana company. Especially noteworthy is his use of magical realism, relating the outrageous events that assail the town in a matter-of-fact voice, thus transforming the fantastic into the commonplace.

Unlike novelists in the United States and Western Europe, who tend to focus their attention on the interior landscape within the modern personality in an industrial society, fiction writers in Latin America, like their counterparts in Africa and much of Asia, have sought to project an underlying political message. Many have been inspired by a sense of social and political injustice, a consequence of the economic inequality and authoritarian politics that marked the local scene throughout much of the twentieth century. Some, like the Peruvian José Maria Arguedas, have championed the cause of the Amerindian and lauded the diversity that marks the ethnic mix throughout the continent. Others have run for high political office as a means of remedying social problems. Some have been women, reflecting the rising demand for sexual equality in a society traditionally marked by male domination. The memorable phrase of the Chilean poet Gabriela Mistral—"I have chewed stones with woman's gums"—encapsulates the plight of Latin American women.

Sources: *The Norton Anthology of American Literature*, 4th ed. (New York: Norton, 1995); Naomi Lindstrom, *Twentieth Century Spanish American Fiction* (Austin: University of Texas Press, 1994).

blues, rock, rap, and hip-hop have been the most popular music forms in the Western world—and much of the non-Western world—during this time. All of them originated in the United States, and all are rooted in African American musical innovations. These forms later spread to the rest of the world, inspiring local artists, who then transformed the music in their own way.

In the postwar years, sports became a major product of both popular culture and the leisure industry. The development of satellite television and various electronic breakthroughs helped make spectator sports a global phenomenon. The Olympic Games could now be broadcast around the world from anywhere on earth. Sports became a cheap form of entertainment for consumers, as fans did not have to leave their homes to enjoy athletic competitions. In fact, some sports organizations initially resisted television, fearing that it would hurt ticket sales. However, the tremendous revenues possible from television contracts overcame this hesitation. As sports television revenue escalated, many sports came to receive the bulk of their yearly revenue from broadcasting contracts.

Sports became big politics as well as big business. Politicization was one of the most significant trends in sports during the second half of the twentieth century. Football (soccer) remains the dominant world sport and more than ever has become a vehicle for nationalist sentiment and expression. The World Cup is the most watched event on television. Although the sport can be a positive outlet for national and local pride, all too often it has been marred by violence as nationalistic fervor has overcome rational behavior.

## Science and Technology

Since the Scientific Revolution of the seventeenth century and the Industrial Revolution of the nineteenth, science and technology have played increasingly important roles in world civilization. Many of the scientific and technological achievements since World War II have revolutionized people's lives. When American astronauts walked on the moon, millions watched the event on their television sets in the privacy of their living rooms.

Before World War II, theoretical science and technology were largely separated. Pure science was the domain of university professors, far removed from the practical technological matters of technicians and engineers. But during World War II, university scientists were recruited to work for their governments to develop new weapons and practical instruments of war. British physicists played a crucial role in developing an improved radar system in 1940 that helped defeat the German air force in the Battle of Britain. The computer, too, was a wartime crea-

tion. British mathematician Alan Turing designed a primitive computer to assist British intelligence in breaking the secret codes of German ciphering machines. The most famous product of wartime scientific research was the atomic bomb, created by a team of American and European scientists under the guidance of the physicist J. Robert Oppenheimer. Obviously, most wartime devices were created for destructive purposes, but computers and breakthrough technologies such as nuclear energy were soon adapted for peacetime uses.

The sponsorship of research by governments and the military during World War II led to a new scientific model. Science had become very complex, and only large organizations with teams of scientists, huge laboratories, and complicated equipment could undertake such large-scale projects. Such facilities were so expensive, however, that only governments and large corporations could support them. Because of its postwar prosperity, the United States was able to lead in the development of the new science. Almost 75 percent of all scientific research funds in the United States came from the government in 1965. Unwilling to lag behind, especially in military development, the Soviet Union was also forced to provide large outlays for scientific and technological research and development. In fact, the defense establishments of the United States and the Soviet Union generated much of the scientific research of the postwar era. One of every four scientists and engineers trained after 1945 was engaged in the creation of new weapons systems. Universities found their research agendas increasingly determined by government funding for military-related projects.

There was no more stunning example of how the new scientific establishment operated than the space race of the 1960s. In 1957, the Soviets announced that they had sent the first space satellite, *Sputnik I*, into orbit around the earth. In response, the United States launched a gigantic project to land a manned spacecraft on the moon within a decade. Massive government funding financed the scientific research and technological advances that attained this goal in 1969.

The postwar alliance of science and technology led to an accelerated rate of change that became a fact of life throughout Western society. The emergence of the computer has revolutionized American business practices and transformed the way individuals go about their lives and communicate with each other. Although early computers, which required thousands of vacuum tubes to function, were quite large, the development of the transistor and the silicon chip enabled manufacturers to reduce the size of their products dramatically. By the 1990s, the personal computer had become a fixture in businesses, schools, and homes around the country. The Internet—

the world's largest computer network—provides millions of people around the world with quick access to immense quantities of information, as well as rapid communication and commercial transactions. By 2000, an estimated 500 million people were using the Internet. The United States has been at the forefront of this process, and the Clinton administration established the goal of providing instruction in computers to every school in the country.

# CONCLUSION

During the second half of the twentieth century, the United States emerged as the preeminent power in the world, dominant in its economic and technological achievements as well as in terms of military hardware. Although the Soviet Union was a serious competitor in the arms race engendered by the Cold War, its economic achievements paled in comparison with those of the U.S. behemoth. Beginning in the 1970s, Japan began to rival the United States in the realm of industrial production, but the challenge faded in the 1990s, when structural weaknesses began to tarnish the Japanese miracle.

The worldwide dominance of the United States was a product of a combination of political, economic, and cultural factors and showed no signs of abating as the new century began. But there were some warning signs that bore watching: a growing gap in the distribution of wealth that could ultimately threaten the steady growth in consumer spending; an educational system that all too often fails to produce graduates with the skills needed to master the challenges of a technology-driven economy; and a racial divide that threatens to undermine America's historical role as a melting pot of peoples.

As the new century dawned, America's global hegemony was also threatened from abroad in the form of a militant terrorist movement originating in the Middle East. So far, the U.S. response, led by the administration of President George W. Bush, has been primarily military, but whether the politics and social forces driving the movement can be defeated by such means alone has been a matter of vigorous debate. As Americans become increasingly concerned about the threat to national security, the future remains in serious doubt.

For most of the nations elsewhere in the Americas, U.S. dominance has mixed consequences. As a vast consumer market and a source of capital, the dynamism of the U.S. economy helped stimulate growth throughout the region. But recent studies suggest that for many countries in Latin America, the benefits of globalization have been slower to appear than originally predicted and have often flowed primarily to large transnational corporations at the expense of smaller domestic firms. At the same time, the U.S. penchant for interfering in the affairs of its neighbors has aroused anger and frequently undermined efforts by local governments to deal with problems within their own borders. At the end of the twentieth century, the United States was still finding it difficult to be a good neighbor.

## INFOTRAC COLLEGE EDITION

Visit source collections at **http://infotrac.thomsonlearning.com**, and use the Search function with the following key terms:

Cold War
Jimmy Carter
Fidel Castro
Richard Nixon
Ronald Reagan
Soviet Union relations with the United States

## WORLD HISTORY RESOURCES

Visit the *The World Since World War II* Companion Web site for resources specific to this textbook:

**http://history.wadsworth.com/duiker_wwii/**

The Wadsworth World History Resource Center at **http://history.wadsworth.com/world/** offers a variety of tools to help you succeed in this course, including access to quizzes; images; documents; interactive simulations, maps, and timelines; movie explorations; and a wealth of other sources.

## CHAPTER NOTES

1. Dwight D. Eisenhower, *The White House Years: Waging Peace, 1956–1961* (Garden City, 1965), p. 533.

# Chapter 5

# THE EAST IS RED: CHINA UNDER COMMUNISM

"A revolution is not a dinner party, or writing an essay, or painting a picture, or doing embroidery; it cannot be so refined, so leisurely and gentle, so temperate and kind, courteous, restrained, and magnanimous. A revolution is an insurrection, an act of violence by which one class overthrows another."[1] With these words—written in 1926, at a time when the Communists, in cooperation with Chiang Kai-shek's Nationalist Party, were embarked on their Northern Expedition to defeat the warlords and reunify China—the young revolutionary Mao Zedong warned his colleagues that the road to victory in the struggle to build a Communist society would be arduous and would inevitably involve acts of violence against the class enemy.

During the next twenty years, the mettle of the Communist Party was severely tested. It was harassed to near extinction by the Nationalist government and then attacked by the armed forces of imperial Japan. In the summer of 1949, it finally triumphed over Chiang in a bruising civil war that led to the latter's abandonment of the mainland and retreat to the island of Taiwan. By then, Mao had become the most powerful man in China, and people began to speculate about his future intentions. Did Mao's words two decades previously portend a new reign of terror that would—not for the first time—drown the Chinese Revolution in a sea of blood? Or were Mao and his colleagues—as some American observers had speculated in Mao's wartime capital of Yan'an—really "agrarian reformers," more patriots than revolutionaries, who would bind the wounds of war and initiate a period of peace and prosperity? As Mao and his colleagues mounted the rostrum of Beijing's Gate of Heavenly Peace in early October 1949 to declare their intentions, the fate of a nation lay in the balance.

# CHINA UNDER MAO ZEDONG

The first signs were reassuring. In the fall of 1949, China was at peace for the first time in twelve years. The newly victorious Communist Party, under the leadership of its chairman, Mao Zedong, turned its attention to consolidating its power base and healing the wounds of war. Its long-term goal was to construct a socialist society, but its leaders realized that popular support for the revolution was based on the party's platform of honest government, land reform, social justice, and peace rather than on the utopian goal of a classless society. Accordingly, the new regime followed Soviet precedent in adopting a moderate program of political and economic recovery known as New Democracy.

## New Democracy

Under New Democracy—patterned roughly after Lenin's New Economic Policy in Soviet Russia in the 1920s— the capitalist system of ownership was retained in the industrial and commercial sectors. A program of land redistribution was adopted, but the collectivization of agriculture was postponed. Only after the party had consolidated its rule and brought a degree of prosperity to the national economy would the difficult transformation to a socialist society begin.

In following Soviet precedent, Chinese leaders tacitly recognized that time and extensive indoctrination would be needed to convince the Chinese people of the superiority of socialism. In the meantime, the party would rely on capitalist profit incentives to spur productivity. Manufacturing and commercial firms were permitted to remain in private hands, but they were placed under stringent government regulations and were encouraged to form "joint enterprises" with the government. To win the support of the poorer peasants, who made up the majority of the population, the land reform program that had long been in operation in "liberated areas" was now expanded throughout the country. This strategy was designed not only to win the gratitude of the rural masses but also to undermine the political and economic influence of counterrevolutionary elements still loyal to Chiang Kai-shek.

In some ways, New Democracy was a success. About two-thirds of the peasant households in the country received property under the land reform program and thus had reason to be grateful to the new regime. Spurred by official tolerance for capitalist activities and the end of the civil war, the national economy began to rebound, although agricultural production still lagged behind both official targets and the growing population, which was increasing at an annual rate of more than 2 percent. But there were a number of blemishes in the picture. In the course of carrying out land redistribution, thousands if not millions of landlords and rich farmers lost their lands, their personal property, their freedom, and sometimes their lives. Many of those who died had been tried and convicted of "crimes against the people" in tribunals set up in towns and villages around the country. As Mao himself later conceded, many were innocent of any crime, but in the eyes of the party, their deaths were necessary to destroy the power of the landed gentry in the countryside (see the box on p. 105).

## The Transition to Socialism

Originally, party leaders intended to follow the Leninist formula of delaying the building of a fully socialist society until China had a sufficient industrial base to permit the mechanization of agriculture. In 1953, they launched the nation's first five-year plan (patterned after earlier Soviet plans), which called for substantial increases in industrial output. Lenin had believed that the lure of mechanization would provide Russian peasants with an incentive to join collective farms, which, because of their greater size, could better afford to purchase expensive farm machinery. But the enormous challenge of providing tractors and reapers for millions of rural villages eventually convinced Mao Zedong and some of his colleagues that it would take years, if not decades, for China's infant industrial base to meet the burgeoning needs of a modernizing agricultural sector. He therefore decided to change the equation and urged that collectivization be undertaken immediately, in the hope that collective farms would increase food production and release land, labor, and capital for the industrial sector.

Accordingly, in 1955 the Chinese government launched a new program to build a socialist society. Beginning in that year, virtually all private farmland was collectivized, although peasant families were allowed to retain small plots for their private use (a Chinese version of the private plots adopted in the Soviet Union). In addition, most industry and commerce were nationalized.

Collectivization was achieved without provoking the massive peasant unrest that had taken place in the Soviet Union during the 1930s, perhaps because the Chinese government followed a policy of persuasion rather than compulsion (Mao remarked that Stalin had "drained the pond to catch the fish") and because the land reform program had already earned the support of millions of rural Chinese. But the hoped-for production increases did not materialize, and in 1958, at Mao's insistent urging, party

# LAND REFORM IN ACTION

*One of the great achievements of the new Communist regime was the land reform program, which resulted in the distribution of farmland to almost two-thirds of the rural population in China. The program consequently won the gratitude of millions of Chinese. But it also had a dark side as local land reform tribunals routinely convicted "wicked landlords" of crimes against the people and then put them to death. The following passage, written by a foreign observer, describes the process in one village.*

## REVOLUTION IN A CHINESE VILLAGE

T'ien-ming [a Party cadre] called all the active young cadres and the militiamen of Long Bow [village] together and announced to them the policy of the county government, which was to confront all enemy collaborators and their backers at public meetings, expose their crimes, and turn them over to the county authorities for punishment. He proposed that they start with Kuo Te-yu, the puppet village head. Having moved the group to anger with a description of Te-yu's crimes, T'ien-ming reviewed the painful life led by the poor peasants during the occupation and recalled how hard they had all worked and how as soon as they harvested all the grain the puppet officials, backed by army bayonets, took what they wanted, turned over huge quantities to the Japanese devils, forced the peasants to haul it away, and flogged those who refused.

As the silent crowd contracted toward the spot where the accused man stood, T'ien-ming stepped forward. . . . "This is our chance. Remember how we were oppressed. The traitors seized our property. They beat us and kicked us. . . .

"Let us speak out the bitter memories. Let us see that the blood debt is repaid. . . ."

He paused for a moment. The peasants were listening to every word but gave no sign as to how they felt. . . .

"Come now, who has evidence against this man?"

Again there was silence.

Kuei-ts'ai, the new vice-chairman of the village, found it intolerable. He jumped up, struck Kuo Te-yu on the jaw with the back of his hand. "Tell the meeting how much you stole," he demanded.

The blow jarred the ragged crowd. It was as if an electric spark had tensed every muscle. Not in living memory had any peasant ever struck an official. . . .

The people in the square waited fascinated as if watching a play. They did not realize that in order for the plot to unfold they themselves had to mount the stage and speak out what was on their minds.

That evening T'ien-ming and Kuei-ts'ai called together the small groups of poor peasants from various parts of the village and sought to learn what it was that was really holding them back. They soon found the root of the trouble was fear of the old established political forces and their military backers. The old reluctance to move against the power of the gentry, the fear of ultimate defeat and terrible reprisal that had been seared into the consciousness of so many generations, lay like a cloud over the peasants' minds and hearts.

Emboldened by T'ien-ming's words, other peasants began to speak out. They recalled what Te-yu had done to them personally. Several vowed to speak up and accuse him the next morning. After the meeting broke up, the passage of time worked its own leaven. In many a hovel and tumble-down house talk continued well past midnight. Some people were so excited they did not sleep at all. . . .

On the following day the meeting was livelier by far. It began with a sharp argument as to who would make the first accusation, and T'ien-ming found it difficult to keep order. Before Te-yu had a chance to reply to any questions, a crowd of young men, among whom were several militiamen, surged forward ready to beat him.

Source: Richard Solomon, *Mao's Revolution and the Chinese Political Culture*, pages 198–199. Copyright © 1971 Center for Chinese Studies, University of Michigan. Used with permission of the University of California Press.

leaders approved a more radical program known as the Great Leap Forward. Existing rural collectives, normally the size of a traditional village, were combined into vast "people's communes," each containing more than thirty thousand people. These communes were to be responsible for all administrative and economic tasks at the local level. The party's official slogan promised "Hard work for a few years, happiness for a thousand."[2]

Mao hoped this program would mobilize the population for a massive effort to accelerate economic growth and ascend to the final stage of communism before the end of the twentieth century. It is better, he said, to "strike while the iron is hot" and advance the revolution without interruption. Some party members were concerned that this ambitious program would threaten the government's rural base of support, but Mao argued that

Chinese peasants were naturally revolutionary in spirit. The Chinese rural masses, he said, are

first of all, poor, and secondly, blank. That may seem like a bad thing, but it is really a good thing. Poor people want change, want to do things, want revolution. A clean sheet of paper has no blotches, and so the newest and most beautiful words can be written on it, the newest and most beautiful pictures can be painted on it.[3]

Those words, of course, were *socialism* and *communism*.

The Great Leap Forward was a disaster. Administrative bottlenecks, bad weather, and peasant resistance to the new system (which, among other things, attempted to eliminate work incentives and destroy the traditional family as the basic unit of Chinese society) combined to drive food production downward, and over the next few years, as many as fifteen million people may have died of starvation. Many peasants were reportedly reduced to eating the bark off trees and in some cases allowing infants to starve. In 1960, the commune experiment was essentially abandoned. Although the commune structure was retained, ownership and management were returned to the collective level. Mao was severely criticized by some of his more pragmatic colleagues (one remarked bitingly that "one cannot reach Heaven in a single step"), provoking him to complain that he had been relegated to the sidelines "like a Buddha on a shelf."

## The Great Proletarian Cultural Revolution

But Mao was not yet ready to abandon either his power or his dream of an egalitarian society. In 1966, he returned to the attack, mobilizing discontented youth and disgruntled party members into revolutionary units known as Red Guards who were urged to take to the streets to cleanse Chinese society—from local schools and factories to government ministries in Beijing—of impure elements who in Mao's mind were guilty of "taking the capitalist road." Supported by his wife, Jiang Qing, and other radical party figures, Mao launched China on a new forced march toward communism.

The so-called Great Proletarian Cultural Revolution lasted for ten years, from 1966 to 1976. Some Western observers interpreted it as a simple power struggle between Mao and some of his key rivals such as head of state Liu Shaoqi (1898–1969) and Deng Xiaoping (1904–1997), the party's general secretary. Both were removed from their positions, and Liu later died, allegedly of torture, in a Chinese prison. But real policy disagreements were involved. One reason Mao had advocated the Great Leap Forward was to bypass the party and government bureau-

cracy, which in his view had lost their revolutionary zeal and were primarily concerned with protecting their power. Now he and his supporters feared that capitalist values and the remnants of "feudalist" Confucian ideas and practices would undermine ideological fervor and betray the revolutionary cause. Mao himself was convinced that only an atmosphere of constant revolutionary fervor (what he termed "uninterrupted revolution") could enable the Chinese to overcome the lethargy of the past and achieve the final stage of utopian communism. "I care not," he once wrote, "that the winds blow and the waves beat. It is better than standing idly in a courtyard."

His opponents, on the other hand, worried that Mao's "heaven-storming" approach could delay economic growth and antagonize the people. They argued for a more pragmatic strategy that gave priority to nation building over the ultimate Communist goal of spiritual transformation. But with Mao's supporters now in power, the party carried out vast economic and educational reforms that virtually eliminated any remaining profit incentives, established a new school system that emphasized "Mao Zedong Thought," and stressed practical education at the elementary level at the expense of specialized training in science and the humanities in the universities. School learning was discouraged as a legacy of capitalism, and Mao's famous *Little Red Book* (a slim volume of Maoist aphorisms to encourage good behavior and revolutionary zeal) was hailed as the most important source of knowledge in all areas.

Such efforts to destroy all vestiges of traditional society were reminiscent of the Reign of Terror in revolutionary France, when the Jacobins sought to destroy organized religion and even replaced the traditional Christian chronological system with a new revolutionary calendar. Red Guards rampaged through the country attempting to eradicate the "four olds" (old thought, old culture, old customs, and old habits). They destroyed temples and religious sculptures; they tore down street signs and replaced them with new ones carrying revolutionary names. At one point, the city of Shanghai even ordered that the significance of colors in stoplights be changed, so that red (the revolutionary color) would indicate that traffic could move.

But a mood of revolutionary enthusiasm is difficult to sustain. Key groups, including party bureaucrats, urban professionals, and many military officers, did not share Mao's belief in the benefits of "uninterrupted revolution" and constant turmoil. Many were alienated by the arbitrary actions of the Red Guards, who indiscriminately accused and brutalized their victims in a society where legal safeguards had almost entirely vanished. Whether the Cultural Revolution led to declining productivity is a matter of debate. Inevitably, however, the sense of anarchy and uncertainty caused popular support for the movement to erode, and when the end came with Mao's death in 1976, the vast majority of the population may well have welcomed its demise.

Personal accounts by young Chinese who took part in the Cultural Revolution clearly show that their initial enthusiasm often turned to disillusionment. According to Liang Heng, author of a book titled *Son of the Revolution*, at first he helped friends organize Red Guard groups: "I thought it was a great idea. We would be following Chairman Mao just like the grownups, and Father would be proud of me. I suppose I too resented the teachers who had controlled and criticized me for so long, and I looked forward to a little revenge."[4] Later, he had reason to repent. His sister ran off to join the local Red Guard group. Prior to her departure, she denounced her mother and the rest of her family as "rightists" and enemies of the revolution. Their home was regularly raided by Red Guards, and

their father was severely beaten and tortured for having three neckties and "Western shirts." Books, paintings, and writings were piled in the center of the floor and burned before his eyes. On leaving, a few of the Red Guards helped themselves to his monthly salary and his transistor radio.

## From Mao to Deng

In September 1976, Mao Zedong died at the age of eighty-three. After a short but bitter succession struggle, the pragmatists led by Deng Xiaoping seized power from the radicals and brought the Cultural Revolution to an end. Mao's widow, Jiang Qing, and three other radicals (derisively called the "Gang of Four" by their opponents) were placed on trial and sentenced to death or to long terms in prison. The egalitarian policies of the previous decade were reversed, and a new program emphasizing economic modernization was introduced.

**PUNISHING CHINESE ENEMIES DURING THE CULTURAL REVOLUTION.** The Cultural Revolution, which began in 1966, was a massive effort by Mao Zedong and his radical supporters to eliminate rival elements within the Chinese Communist Party and the government. Accused of being "capitalist roaders," such individuals were subjected to public criticism and removed from their positions. Some were imprisoned or executed. Here Red Guards parade a victim wearing a dunce cap through the streets of Beijing.

Under the leadership of Deng, who placed his supporters in key positions throughout the party and the government, attention focused on what were called the "Four Modernizations": industry, agriculture, technology, and national defense. Deng had been a leader of the faction that opposed Mao's program of rapid socialist transformation, and during the Cultural Revolution, he had been forced to perform menial labor to "sincerely correct his errors." But Deng continued to espouse the pragmatic approach and reportedly once remarked, "Black cat, white cat, what does it matter so long as it catches the mice?" Under the program of Four Modernizations, many of the restrictions against private activities and profit incentives were eliminated, and people were encouraged to work hard to benefit themselves and Chinese society. The familiar slogan "Serve the people" was replaced by a new one repugnant to the tenets of Mao Zedong Thought: "Create wealth for the people."

Crucial to the program's success was the government's ability to attract foreign technology and capital. For more than two decades, China had been isolated from technological advances taking place elsewhere in the world. Although China's leaders understandably prided themselves on their nation's capacity for "self-reliance," their isolationist policy had been exceedingly costly for the national economy. China's post-Mao leaders blamed the country's backwardness on the "ten lost years" of the Cultural Revolution, but the "lost years," at least in technological terms, extended back to 1949 and in some respects even before. Now, to make up for lost time, the government encouraged foreign investment and sent thousands of students and specialists abroad to study capitalist techniques.

By adopting this pragmatic approach in the years after 1976, China made great strides in ending its chronic problems of poverty and underdevelopment. Per capita income roughly doubled during the 1980s; housing, education, and sanitation improved; and both agricultural and industrial output skyrocketed. Clearly, China had begun to enter the Industrial Age.

But critics, both Chinese and foreign, complained that Deng Xiaoping's program had failed to achieve a "fifth modernization": democracy. Official sources denied such charges and spoke proudly of restoring "socialist legality" by doing away with the arbitrary punishments applied during the Cultural Revolution. Deng himself encouraged the Chinese people to speak out against earlier excesses. In the late 1970s, ordinary citizens began to paste posters criticizing the abuses of the past on the so-called Democracy Wall near Tiananmen Square in downtown Beijing.

Yet it soon became clear that the new leaders would not tolerate any direct criticism of the Communist Party or of Marxist-Leninist ideology. Dissidents were suppressed, and some were sentenced to long prison terms. Among them was the well-known astrophysicist Fang Lizhi, who spoke out publicly against official corruption and the continuing influence of Marxist-Leninist concepts in post-Mao China, telling an audience in Hong Kong that "China will not be able to modernize if it does not break the shackles of Maoist and Stalinist-style socialism." Fang immediately felt the weight of official displeasure. He was refused permission to travel abroad, and articles that he submitted to official periodicals were rejected. Deng Xiaoping himself reportedly remarked, "We will not suppress people who hold differing political views from our own. But as for Fang Lizhi, he has been indulging in mudslinging and spreading slander without any basis, and we should take legal action against him." Replied Fang, "I have never criticized any Chinese leader by name, nor accused any of them of illegal acts or immoral activities. But some perhaps feel guilty. If the cap fits, wear it."[5]

The problem began to intensify in the late 1980s, as more Chinese began to study abroad and more information about Western society reached educated individuals inside the country. Rising expectations aroused by the economic improvements of the early 1980s led to increasing pressure from students and other urban residents for better living conditions, relaxed restrictions on study abroad, and increased freedom to select employment after graduation.

## Incident at Tiananmen Square

As long as economic conditions for the majority of Chinese were improving, other classes did not share the students' discontent, and the government was able to isolate them from other elements in society. But in the late 1980s, an overheated economy led to rising inflation and growing discontent among salaried workers, especially in the cities. At the same time, corruption, nepotism, and favored treatment for senior officials and party members were provoking increasing criticism. In May 1989, student protesters carried placards demanding Science and Democracy (reminiscent of the slogan of the May Fourth Movement, whose seventieth anniversary was celebrated in the spring of 1989), an end to official corruption, and the resignation of China's aging party leadership. These demands received widespread support from the urban population (although notably less in rural areas) and led to massive demonstrations in Tiananmen Square (see the box on p. 109).

The demonstrations divided the Chinese leaders. Reformist elements around party general secretary Zhao

# STUDENTS APPEAL FOR DEMOCRACY

*In the spring of 1989, thousands of students gathered in Tiananmen Square in downtown Beijing to provide moral support to their many compatriots who had gone on a hunger strike in an effort to compel the Chinese government to reduce the level of official corruption and enact democratic reforms, opening the political process to the Chinese people. The statement that follows was printed on flyers and distributed to participants and passersby on May 17, 1989, to explain the goals of the movement.*

## "WHY DO WE HAVE TO UNDERGO A HUNGER STRIKE?"

By 2:00 P.M. today, the hunger strike carried out by the petition group in Tiananmen Square has been under way for 96 hours. By this morning, more than 600 participants have fainted. When these democracy fighters were lifted into the ambulances, no one who was present was not moved to tears.

Our petition group now undergoing the hunger strike demands that at a minimum the government agree to the following two points:

1. to engage on a sincere and equal basis in a dialogue with the "higher education dialogue group." In addition, to broadcast the actual dialogue in its entirety. We absolutely refuse to agree to a partial broadcast, to empty gestures, or to fabrications that dupe the people.

2. to evaluate in a fair and realistic way the patriotic democratic movement. Discard the label of "trouble-making" and redress the reputation of the patriotic democratic movement.

It is our view that the request for a dialogue between the people's government and the people is not an unreasonable one. Our party always follows the principle of seeking truths from actual facts. It is therefore only natural that the evaluation of this patriotic democratic movement should be done in accordance with the principle of seeking truths from actual facts.

Our classmates who are going through the hunger strike are the good sons and daughters of the people! One by one, they have fallen. In the meantime, our "public servants" are completely unmoved. Please, let us ask where your conscience is.

Ziyang were sympathetic to the protesters, but veteran leaders such as Deng saw the student demands for more democracy as a disguised call for an end to Communist Party rule. After some hesitation, the government sent tanks and troops into Tiananmen Square to crush the demonstrators. Dissidents were arrested, and the regime once again began to stress ideological purity and socialist values. Although the crackdown provoked widespread criticism abroad, Chinese leaders insisted that economic reforms could only take place in conditions of party leadership and political stability.

Deng and other aging party leaders turned to the army to protect their base of power and suppress what they described as "counterrevolutionary elements." Deng was undoubtedly counting on the fact that many Chinese, particularly in rural areas, feared a recurrence of the disorder of the Cultural Revolution and craved economic prosperity more than political reform. In the months following the confrontation, the government issued new regulations requiring courses on Marxist-Leninist ideology in the schools, winnowed out dissidents in the intellectual community, and made it clear that while economic reforms would continue, the CCP's monopoly of power would not be allowed to decay. Harsh punishments were imposed on those accused of undermining the Communist system and supporting its enemies abroad.

## From Marx to Confucius

In the 1990s, the government began to nurture urban support by reducing the rate of inflation and guaranteeing the availability of consumer goods in great demand among the rising middle class. Under Deng's successor, Jiang Zemin (b. 1926) who served as both party chief and president of China, the government promoted rapid economic growth while cracking down harshly on political dissent. That policy paid dividends in bringing about a perceptible decline in alienation among the population in the cities. Industrial production continued to surge, leading to predictions that China would become one of the economic superpowers of the twenty-first century. But problems in rural areas began to increase, as lagging farm income, high taxes, and official corruption sparked resentment among the rural populace.

Partly out of fear that such developments could undermine the socialist system and the rule of the CCP,

**GIVE ME LIBERTY—OR GIVE ME DEATH!** The demonstrations that erupted in Tiananmen Square in the spring of 1989 spread rapidly to other parts of China, where students and other local citizens gave their vocal support to the popular movement in Beijing. Here students from a high school march to the city of Guilin to display their own determination to take part in the reform of Chinese society. Their call to "give me liberty or give me death" (in Patrick Henry's famous phrase) echoed the determination expressed by many of their counterparts in Beijing.

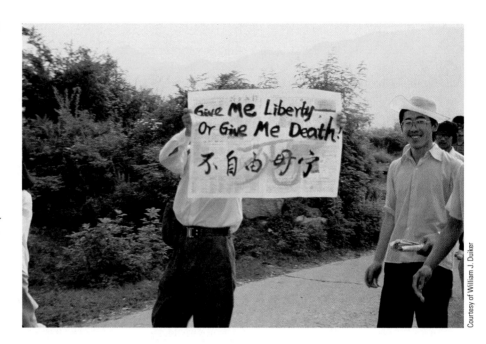

Courtesy of William J. Duiker

conservative leaders have attempted to curb Western influence and restore faith in Marxism-Leninism. Recently, in what may be a tacit recognition that Marxist exhortations are no longer an effective means of enforcing social discipline, the party has turned to Confucianism as an antidote. Ceremonies celebrating the birth of Confucius now receive official sanction, and the virtues he promoted, such as righteousness, propriety, and filial piety, are now widely cited as the means to counter antisocial behavior.

Beijing's decision to emphasize traditional Confucian themes as a means of promoting broad popular support for its domestic policies is paralleled on the world stage, where it relies on the spirit of nationalism to achieve its goals. Today, China conducts an independent foreign policy and is playing an increasingly active role in the region. To some of its neighbors, including Japan, India, and Russia, China's new posture is cause for disquiet and gives rise to suspicions that it is once again preparing to assert its muscle as in the imperial era. A striking example of this new attitude took place as early as 1979, when Chinese forces briefly invaded Vietnam as punishment for the Vietnamese occupation of neighboring Cambodia. In the 1990s, China aroused concern in the region by claiming sole ownership over the Spratly Islands in the South China Sea and over Diaoyu Island (also claimed by Japan) near Taiwan (see Map 5.1).

To Chinese leaders, however, such actions simply represent legitimate efforts to resume China's rightful role in the affairs of the region. After a century of humiliation at the hands of the Western powers and neighboring Japan,

the nation, in Mao's famous words of 1949, "has stood up" and no one will be permitted to humiliate it again. For the moment, at least, a fervent patriotism seems to be on the rise in China, actively promoted by the party as a means of holding the country together. Pride in the achievement of national sports teams is intense, and two young authors recently achieved wide acclaim with the publication of their book *The China That Can Say No,* a response to criticism of the country in the United States and Europe. The decision by the International Olympic Committee to award the 2008 Summer Games to Beijing led to widespread celebration throughout the country.

Whether the current leadership will be able to prevent further erosion of the party's power and prestige is unclear. In the short term, efforts to slow the process of change may succeed because many Chinese are understandably fearful of punishment and concerned for their careers. And high economic growth rates can sometimes obscure a multitude of problems as many individuals will opt to chase the fruits of materialism rather than the less tangible benefits of personal freedom. But in the long run, the party leadership must resolve the contradiction between political authoritarianism and economic prosperity. One is reminded of Chiang Kai-shek's failed attempt during the 1930s to revive Confucian ethics as a standard of behavior for modern China: dead ideologies cannot be revived by decree.

Unrest is also growing among China's national minorities: in Xinjiang, where restless Muslim peoples observe with curiosity the emergence of independent Islamic states in Central Asia, and in Tibet, where the

MAP 5.1 The People's Republic of China. This map shows China's current boundaries. Major regions are indicated in capital letters. Areas in dispute are shown by darker shading. ➤ *In which regions are there movements against Chinese rule?*

official policy of quelling separatism has led to the violent suppression of Tibetan culture and an influx of thousands of ethnic Chinese immigrants. In the meantime, the Falun Gong religious movement, which the government has attempted to suppress as a potentially serious threat to its authority, is an additional indication that with the disintegration of the old Maoist utopia, the Chinese people will need more than a pallid version of Marxism-Leninism or a revived Confucianism to fill the gap.

New leaders installed in 2002 and 2003 appear to recognize the challenge. Hu Jintao (b. 1943), who replaced Jiang Zemin as CCP general secretary and head of state, appears to recognize the need for further reforms to open up Chinese society and bridge the yawning gap between rich and poor. In recent years, the government has shown a growing tolerance for the public exchange of ideas, which has surfaced with the proliferation of bookstores, avant-garde theater, experimental art exhibits, and the Internet.

## SERVE THE PEOPLE: CHINESE SOCIETY UNDER COMMUNISM

Enormous changes took place in Chinese society after the Communist rise to power in 1949. Yet beneath the surface of rapid change were tantalizing hints of the survival of elements of the old China. Despite all the efforts of Mao Zedong and his colleagues, the ideas of Confucius and Sons had still not been irrevocably discarded. China under communism remained a society that in many respects was enthralled by its past.

### The Politics of the Mass Line

Nowhere was this uneasy balance between the old and the new more clearly demonstrated than in politics and government.

In its broad outlines, the new political system followed the Soviet pattern. Yet from the start, CCP leaders made it clear that the Chinese model would differ from the Soviet in important respects. Whereas the Bolsheviks had severely distrusted nonrevolutionary elements in Russia and established a minority government based on the radical left, Mao and his colleagues were more confident that they possessed the basic support of the majority of the Chinese people. Under New Democracy, the party attempted to reach out to all progressive classes in the population to maintain the alliance that had brought it to power in the first place.

The primary link between the regime and the population was the system of "mass organizations," representing peasants, workers, women, religious groups, writers, and artists. The party had established these associations during the 1920s to mobilize support for the revolution. Now they served as a conduit between party and people, enabling the leaders to assess the attitude of the masses while at the same time seeking their support for the party's programs. Behind this facade of representative institutions stood the awesome power of the CCP.

Initially, this "mass line" system worked fairly well. True, opposition to the regime was ruthlessly suppressed, but on the positive side, China finally had a government that appeared to be "for the people." Although there was no pretense at Western-style democracy, and official corruption and bureaucratic mismanagement and arrogance had by no means been entirely eliminated, the new ruling class came preponderantly from workers and peasants and was more willing than its predecessors to listen to the complaints and aspirations of its constituents.

A good example of the party's mass line policy was the land reform program, which redistributed farmland to the poor. The program was carried out at the village level by land reform cadres who urged local farmers to establish tribunals to confiscate the lands of the landlord class and assign them to poor or landless peasants, thus giving the impression that the policy was locally inspired rather than imposed, Soviet-style, from the top down.

But the adoption of the Great Leap Forward betrayed a fundamental weakness in the policy of the mass line. While declaring his willingness to listen to the concerns of the population, Mao was also determined to build a utopian society based on Marxist-Leninist principles. Popular acceptance of nationalization and collectivization during the mid-1950s indicates that the Chinese people were not entirely hostile to socialism, but when those programs were carried to an extreme during the Great Leap Forward, many Chinese, even within the party, resisted and forced the government to abandon the program.

The failure of the Great Leap Forward split the CCP and led to the revolutionary disturbances of the following decade. Some of Mao's associates had opposed his radical approach and now sought to adopt a more cautious road to nation building. To Mao, such views were a betrayal of the party's revolutionary principles. The Cultural Revolution, which he launched in 1966, can be seen above all as his attempt to cleanse the system of its impurities and put Chinese society back on the straight road to egalitarian communism.

Many of his compatriots evidently shared his beliefs. Young people in particular, alienated by the lack of job opportunities, flocked to his cause and served with enthusiasm in the Red Guard organizations that became the shock troops of the revolution. But the enthusiasms aroused by the Cultural Revolution did not last. As in the French Revolution, the efforts to achieve revolutionary purity eventually alienated all except the most radical elements in the country, and a period of reaction inevitably set in. In China, revolutionary fervor gave way to a new era in which belief in socialist ideals was replaced by a more practical desire for material benefits.

## Economics in Command

Deng Xiaoping recognized the need to restore a sense of "socialist legality" and credibility to a system that was on the verge of breakdown and hoped that rapid economic growth would satisfy the Chinese people and prevent them from demanding political reforms. The post-Mao leaders demonstrated a willingness to place economic performance over ideological purity. To stimulate the stagnant industrial sector, which had been under state control since the end of the era of New Democracy, they reduced bureaucratic controls over state industries and allowed local managers to have more say over prices, salaries, and quality control. Productivity was encouraged by permitting bonuses to be paid for extra effort, a policy that had been discouraged during the Cultural Revolution. State firms were no longer guaranteed access to precious resources and were told to compete with each other for public favor and even to export goods on their own initiative. The regime also tolerated the emergence of a small private sector. Unemployed youth were encouraged to set up restaurants, bicycle or radio repair shops, and handicraft shops on their own initiative.

Finally, the regime opened up the country to foreign investment and technology. The Maoist policy of self-reliance was abandoned, and China openly sought the advice of foreign experts and the money of foreign capitalists. Special economic zones were established in urban centers near the coast (ironically, many were located in the old nineteenth-century treaty ports), where lucrative concessions were offered to encourage foreign firms to build factories. The tourist industry was encouraged, and students were sent abroad to study.

The new leaders especially stressed educational reform. The system adopted during the Cultural Revolution, emphasizing practical education and ideology at the expense of higher education and modern science, was rapidly abandoned (Mao's *Little Red Book* itself was withdrawn from circulation and could no longer be found on bookshelves), and a new system based generally on the Western model was instituted. Admission to higher education was based on success in merit examinations, and courses on science and mathematics received high priority.

No economic reform program could succeed unless it included the countryside. Three decades of socialism had done little to increase food production or to lay the basis for a modern agricultural sector. China, with a population now numbering one billion, could still barely feed itself. Peasants had little incentive to work and few opportunities to increase production through mechanization, the use of fertilizer, or better irrigation.

Under Deng Xiaoping, agricultural policy made a rapid about-face. Under the new "rural responsibility system," adopted shortly after Deng had consolidated his authority, collectives leased land on contract to peasant families, who paid a quota as rent to the collective. Anything produced on the land above that payment could be sold on the private market or consumed. To soak up excess labor in the villages, the government encouraged the formation of so-called sideline industries, a modern equivalent of the traditional cottage industries in premodern China. Peasants raised fish or shrimp, made consumer goods, and even assembled living room furniture and appliances for sale to their newly affluent compatriots.

The reform program had a striking effect on rural production. Grain production increased rapidly, and farm income doubled during the 1980s. Yet it also created problems. In the first place, income at the village level became more unequal as some enterprising farmers (known locally as "ten thousand dollar" households) earned profits several times those realized by their less fortunate or less industrious neighbors. When some farmers discovered they could earn more by growing cash crops or other specialized commodities, they devoted less land to rice and other grain crops, thus threatening to reduce the supply of China's most crucial staple. Finally, the agricultural policy threatened to undermine the government's population control program, which party leaders viewed as crucial to the success of the Four Modernizations.

Since a misguided period in the mid-1950s when Mao had argued that more labor would result in higher productivity, China had been attempting to limit its population growth. By 1970, the government had launched a stringent family planning program—including education, incentives, and penalties for noncompliance—to persuade the Chinese people to limit themselves to one child per family. The program did have some success, and the rate of population growth was reduced drastically in the early 1980s. The rural responsibility system, however, undermined the program because it encouraged farm families to pay the penalties for having additional children in the belief that the labor of these offspring would increase family income and provide the parents with greater security in their old age.

Still, the overall effects of the modernization program were impressive. The standard of living improved for the majority of the population. Whereas a decade earlier the average Chinese had struggled to earn enough to buy a bicycle, radio, watch, or washing machine, by the late 1980s many were beginning to purchase videocassette recorders, refrigerators, and color television sets. The government popularized the idea that all Chinese would prosper, although not necessarily at the same speed. Earlier slogans such as "Serve the people" and "Uphold the banner of Marxist-Leninist-Maoist thought" were replaced by others that announced that "Time is money" and instructed citizens to "Create wealth for the people." The party announced that China was still at the "primary stage of socialism" and might not reach the state of utopian communism for generations.

Yet the rapid growth of the economy created its own problems: inflationary pressures, greed, envy, increased corruption, and—most dangerous of all for the regime—rising expectations. When the economy failed to live up to those expectations, as in the late 1980s, disillusionment ran high, especially in the cities, where high living by officials and rising prices for goods aroused widespread alienation and cynicism. Such attitudes undoubtedly contributed to the anger and frustration that burst out during the spring of 1989, when many workers, peasants, and functionaries joined the demonstrations in Tiananmen Square against official corruption and one-party rule.

During the 1990s, growth rates in the industrial sector remained high as domestic capital became increasingly available to compete with the growing presence of foreign enterprises. The government began to adopt a serious attitude to the need to close down inefficient state enterprises, and by the end of the decade, the private sector, with official encouragement, accounted for over 10 percent of the gross domestic product. A stock market opened, and China's prowess in the international marketplace improved dramatically.

As a result of these developments, China now possesses a large and increasingly affluent middle class. The domestic market for consumer goods has burgeoned, as indicated by the fact that over 80 percent of all urban Chinese now possess a color television set, a refrigerator, and a washing machine. One-third own their homes, and nearly as many have an air conditioner. Like their counterparts elsewhere in Asia, urban Chinese are increasingly brand-name conscious, a characteristic that provides a considerable challenge to local manufacturers.

But as Chinese leaders discovered, rapid economic change never comes without cost. The closing of state-run factories has led to the dismissal of millions of workers each year, and the private sector, although growing at more than 20 percent annually, is unable to absorb them all. Discontent has been increasing in the countryside as well, where farmers earn only about half the salary of their urban counterparts (in recent years, the government tried to increase the official purchase price for grain but rescinded the order when it became too expensive). China's recent entry into the World Trade Organization (WTO) may help the nation as a whole, but is less likely to benefit farmers, who must now face the challenge of cheap foreign imports. Taxes and local corruption add to their complaints. In desperation, millions of rural people have left for the big cities, where many of them are unable to find steady employment and are forced to live in squalid conditions in crowded tenements or in the sprawling suburbs. Millions of others remain on the farm but attempt to maximize their income by producing for the market or increasing the size of their families. Although China's population control program continues to limit rural couples to two children, such regulations are widely flouted despite stringent penalties. Chinese leaders must now face the reality that the pains of industrialization are not limited to capitalist countries.

# THE LEGACY OF THE PAST: CONTINUITY AND CHANGE IN CHINESE SOCIETY

Originally, the Chinese Communist Party intended to bring an end to the Confucian legacy in modern China. At the root of Marxist-Leninist ideology is the idea of building a new citizen free from the prejudices, ignorance, and superstition of the "feudal" era and the capitalist desire for self-gratification. This new citizen would be characterized not only by a sense of racial and sexual equality but also by the selfless desire to contribute his or her utmost for the good of all. In the words of Mao Zedong's famous work "The Foolish Old Man Who Removed the Mountains," the people should "be resolute, fear no sacrifice, and surmount every difficulty to win victory."[6]

The new government wasted no time in keeping its promise. During the early 1950s, it took a number of steps to bring a definitive end to the old system in China. Women were permitted to vote and encouraged to become active in the political process. At the local level, an increasing number of women became active in the CCP and in collective organizations. In 1950, a new marriage law guaranteed women equal rights with men. Most important, perhaps, it permitted women for the first time to initiate divorce proceedings against their husbands. Within a year, nearly one million divorces had been granted. The regime also undertook to destroy the influence of the traditional family system. To the Communists, loyalty to the family, a crucial element in the Confucian social order, undercut loyalty to the state and to the dictatorship of the proletariat.

At first, the new government moved carefully to avoid alienating its supporters in the countryside unnecessarily. When collective farms were established in the mid-1950s, each member of a collective accumulated "work points" based on the number of hours worked during a specified time period. Payment for work points was made not to the individual but to the family head. The payments, usually in the form of ration coupons, could then be spent at the collective community store. Because the payments went to the head of the family, the traditionally dominant position of the patriarch was maintained. When people's communes were established in the late 1950s, payments went to the individual.

During the political radicalism of the Great Leap Forward, children were encouraged to report to the authorities any comments by their parents that criticized the system. Such practices continued during the Cultural Revolution, when children were expected to report on their parents, students on their teachers, and employees on their superiors. Some have suggested that Mao deliberately encouraged such practices to bring an end to the traditional "politics of dependency." According to this theory, historically the famous "five relationships" forced individuals to swallow their anger and frustration (known in Chinese as "to eat bitterness") and accept the hierarchical norms established by Confucian ethics. By encouraging the oppressed elements in society—the young, the female, and the poor—to voice their bitterness, Mao was breaking down the tradition of dependency. Such denunciations had been issued against landlords and other "local tyrants" in the land reform tribunals of the late 1940s and early 1950s. Later, during the Cultural Revolution, they were applied to other authority figures in Chinese society.

The post-Mao era brought a decisive shift away from revolutionary utopianism and a return to the pragmatic approach to nation building. For most people, it meant improved living conditions and a qualified return to family traditions. For the first time in more than a decade, enterprising Chinese began to concentrate on improving their standard of living. For the first time, millions of Chinese saw the prospect of a house or an urban flat with a washing machine, television set, and indoor plumbing. Young people whose parents had given them patriotic names such as Build the Country, Protect Mao Zedong, and Assist Korea began to choose more elegant and cosmopolitan names for their own children. Some names, such as Surplus Grain or Bring a Younger Brother, expressed hope for the future.

The new attitudes were also reflected in physical appearance. For a generation after the civil war, clothing had been restricted to the traditional baggy "Mao suit" in olive drab or dark blue, but by the 1980s, young people craved such fashionable Western items as designer jeans, trendy sneakers, and sweat suits (or reasonable facsimiles). Cosmetic surgery to create a more buxom figure or a more Western facial look became increasingly common among affluent young women in the cities. Many had the epicanthic fold over their eyelids removed or even added to their noses—a curious decision in view of the tradition of referring derogatorily to foreigners as "big noses."

Religious practices and beliefs also changed. As the government became more tolerant, some Chinese began returning to the traditional Buddhist faith or to folk religions, and Buddhist and Taoist temples were once again crowded with worshipers. Despite official efforts to suppress its more evangelical forms, Christianity became increasingly popular; like the "rice Christians" (persons who supposedly converted for economic reasons) of the past, many viewed it as a symbol of success and cosmopolitanism.

As with all social changes, China's reintegration into the outside world has had a price. Arranged marriages, nepotism, and mistreatment of females (for example, many parents in rural areas reportedly killed female infants in the hope of having the next one be a son) have returned, although such behavior had likely continued under the cloak of revolutionary purity for a generation.

**REACH FOR THE SKY.** This eighty-story television tower, shown here on the left, is an example of Shanghai's monumental effort to become one of the most modern cities in the world. Pudong was once an uninhabited mudflat on the eastern shores of the Huang Pu River. It is now a dynamic sector of the city teeming with hotels, office buildings, and entertainment centers.

© Bob Krist/CORBIS

Materialistic attitudes are highly prevalent among young people, along with a corresponding cynicism about politics and the CCP. Expensive weddings are now increasingly common, and bribery and favoritism are all too frequent. Crime of all types, including an apparently growing incidence of prostitution and sex crimes against women, appears to be on the rise. To discourage sexual abuse, the government now seeks to provide free legal services for women living in rural areas.

There is also a price to pay for the trend toward privatization. Under the Maoist system, the elderly and the sick were provided with retirement benefits and health care by the state or by the collective organizations. Under current conditions, with the latter no longer playing such a social role and more workers operating in the private sector, the safety net has been removed. The government recently attempted to fill the gap by enacting a social security law, but because of a lack of funds, eligibility is limited primarily to individuals in the urban sector of the economy. Those living in the countryside—who still represent 60 percent of the population—are essentially left to their own devices.

# China's Changing Culture

Like their contemporaries all over Asia, Chinese artists were strongly influenced by the revolutionary changes that were taking place in the art world of the West in the early twentieth century. In the decades following the 1911 revolution, Chinese creative artists began to experiment with Western styles, although the more extreme schools, such as Surrealism and Abstract painting, had little impact.

The rise to power of the Communists in 1949 added a new dimension to the debate over the future of culture in China. Spurred by comments made by Mao Zedong at a cultural forum in Yan'an in 1942, leaders rejected the Western slogan of "Art for art's sake" and, like their Soviet counterparts, viewed culture as an important instrument of indoctrination. The standard would no longer be aesthetic quality or the personal preference of the artist but "Art for life's sake," whereby culture would serve the interests of socialism.

At first, the new emphasis on socialist realism did not entirely extinguish the influence of traditional culture. Mao and his colleagues saw the importance of traditional values and culture in building a strong new China and tolerated—and even encouraged—efforts by artists to synthesize traditional ideas with socialist concepts and Western techniques. During the Cultural Revolution, however, all forms of traditional culture came to be viewed as reactionary. Socialist realism became the only standard of acceptability in literature, art, and music. All forms of traditional expression were forbidden.

Characteristic of the changing cultural climate in China was the experience of author Ding Ling. Born in 1904 and educated in a school for women set up by leftist intellectuals during the hectic years after the May Fourth Movement, she began writing in her early twenties. At first, she was strongly influenced by prevailing Western styles, but after her husband, a struggling young poet and a member of the CCP, was executed by Chiang Kai-shek's government in 1931, she became active in party activities and sublimated her talent to the revolutionary cause.

In the late 1930s, Ding Ling settled in Yan'an, where she became a leader in the party's women's and literary associations. She remained dedicated to revolution, but years of service to the party had not stifled her individuality, and in 1942, she wrote critically of the incompetence, arrogance, and hypocrisy of many party officials, as well as the treatment of women in areas under Communist authority. Such conduct raised eyebrows, but she was able to survive criticism and in 1948 wrote her most famous novel, *The Sun Shines over the Sangan River*, which described the CCP's land reform program in favorable terms. It was awarded the Stalin Prize three years later.

During the early 1950s, Ding Ling was one of the most prominent literary lights of the new China, but in the more ideological climate at the end of the decade, she was attacked for her individualism and her previous criticism of the party. Although temporarily rehabilitated, during the Cultural Revolution she was sentenced to hard labor on a commune in the far north and was only released in the late 1970s after the death of Mao Zedong. Although crippled and in poor health, she began writing a biography of her mother that examined the role of women in twentieth-century China. She died in 1981. Ding Ling's story mirrored the fate of thousands of progressive Chinese intellectuals who, despite their efforts, were not able to satisfy the constantly changing demands of a repressive regime.

After Mao's death, Chinese culture was once again released from the shackles of socialist realism. In painting, the new policies led to a revival of interest in both traditional and Western forms. The revival of traditional art was in part a matter of practicality as talented young Chinese were trained to produce traditional paintings for export to earn precious foreign currency for the state. But the regime also showed a new tolerance for the imitation of Western styles as a necessary by-product of development, thus unleashing an impressive outpouring of artistic creativity later dubbed the "Beijing Spring." A new generation of Chinese painters began to experiment with a wide range of previously prohibited art styles, including Cubism and Abstract Expressionism.

An excellent illustration of Chinese artists' tireless battle for creative freedom is the painting *My Dream* (1988) by Xu Mangyao. On the canvas, an artist, having freed his hands from manacles, seeks to escape from the confinement of a red brick wall. The painting represents the worldwide struggle by all the twentieth-century artists silenced by totalitarian regimes in the Soviet Union, Latin America, and Africa.

In music, too, the post-Mao era brought significant changes. Music academies closed during the Cultural Revolution for sowing the seeds of the bourgeois mentality were reopened. Students were permitted to study both Chinese and Western styles, but the vast majority selected the latter. To provide examples, leading musicians and composers, such as violinist Isaac Stern, were invited to China to lecture and perform before eager Chinese students.

The limits to freedom of expression were most apparent in literature. During the early 1980s, party leaders encouraged Chinese writers to express their views on the mistakes of the past, and a new "literature of the wounded" began to describe the brutal and arbitrary nature of the Cultural Revolution. One of the most prominent writers was Bai Hua, whose script for the film *Bitter Love* described the life of a young Chinese painter who joined the revolutionary movement during the 1940s but was destroyed during the Cultural Revolution when his work was condemned as counterrevolutionary. The film depicted the condemnation through a view of a street in Beijing "full of people waving the *Quotations of Chairman Mao*, all those devout and artless faces fired by a feverish fanaticism." Driven from his home for posting a portrait of a third-century B.C.E. defender of human freedom on a Beijing wall, the artist flees the city. At the end of the film, he dies in a snowy field, where his corpse and a semicircle made by his footprints form a giant question mark.

In criticizing the excesses of the Cultural Revolution, Bai Hua was only responding to Deng Xiaoping's appeal for intellectuals to speak out, but he was soon criticized for failing to point out the essentially beneficial role of the CCP in recent Chinese history, and his film was withdrawn from circulation in 1981. Bai Hua was compelled to recant his errors and to state that the great ideas of Mao Zedong on art and literature were "still of universal guiding significance today."[7]

As the attack on Bai Hua illustrates, many party leaders remained suspicious of the impact that "decadent" bourgeois culture could have on the socialist foundations of Chinese society, and the official press periodically warned that China should adopt only the "positive" aspects of Western culture (notably, its technology and its work ethic) and not the "negative" elements such as drug use, pornography, and hedonism. One of the chief targets in China's recent "spiritual civilization" campaign is author Wang Shuo (b. 1958), whose writings have been banned for exhibiting a sense of "moral decay." In his novels *Playing for Thrills* (1989) and *Please Don't Call Me Human* (2000), Wang highlighted the seamier side of contemporary urban society, peopled with hustlers, ex-convicts, and other assorted hooligans. Spiritually depleted, hedonistic, and amoral in their approach to life, his characters represent the polar opposite of the socialist ideal.

Conservatives were especially incensed by the tendency of many writers to dwell on the shortcomings of the socialist system and to come uncomfortably close to direct criticism of the role of the CCP. The outstanding works of author Mo Yan (b. 1956) are a case in point. Viewed as China's greatest writer, in his novels *The Garlic Ballads* (1988) and *The Republic of Wine* (2000), Mo exposes the rampant corruption of contemporary Chinese society, the roots of which he attributes to one-party rule (see the box on p. 118).

# CONCLUSION

To the outside observer, since the Communist takeover of power on the mainland, China has projected an image of almost constant turmoil and rapid change. That portrayal is not an inaccurate one, for Chinese society has undergone a number of major transformations since the establishment of the People's Republic of China in the fall of 1949. Even in the relatively stable 1980s, many a prudent China watcher undoubtedly wondered whether the prosperous and tolerant conditions of the era of Deng Xiaoping would long endure.

An extended period of political instability and domestic violence is hardly unusual in the years following a major revolutionary upsurge. Similar conditions existed in late-eighteenth-century France after the revolt that overthrew the ancient regime and in Russia after the Bolshevik seizure of power in 1917. In both cases, pragmatists in the pursuit of national wealth and power clashed with radicals who were determined to create a utopian society. In the end, the former were victorious, in a process sometimes known as the "routinization of the revolution." "The revolution," it has been astutely observed, "eats its own."

# TROUBLE IN THE GARLIC FIELDS

*Considered one of the masterpieces of modern Chinese literature, Mo Yan's novel* The Garlic Ballads *(1988) describes with passion and intimacy the suffering of contemporary Chinese peasants in northern China. Based on real-life riots in northern China in the summer of 1987, the novel is a plea for social reform as it exposes the greed, corruption, and inhumanity of the local government and the legacy of the feudal mentality. Oppressed and betrayed by their cadres, a group of garlic farmers are swept up into a riot against the local administrator. Mo Yan depicts the resilience and courage of Chinese peasants in the face of incredible hardship and violent oppression. In the closing pages of the novel, at the trial of the peasant rioters, a young military officer, speaking for the author and human decency, accuses the local judge of turning the court into a travesty of justice. In a more recent novel,* The Republic of Wine *(2000), Mo exposes the greed and inhumanity of party officials, whose corrupt practices mock the ideals of a just socialist society.*

## MO YAN, *THE GARLIC BALLADS*

He turned to face the spectators, speaking with a passion that touched everyone who heard him. "Your Honors, ladies and gentlemen, the situation in our farming villages has changed drastically in the wake of the Party's Third Plenary Session of the Eleventh Central Committee, including those here in Paradise County. The peasants are much better off than they were during the Cultural Revolution. This is obvious to everyone. But the benefits they enjoyed as a result of rural economic reforms are gradually disappearing."

"Please don't stray too far from the subject," the presiding judge broke in.

"Thank you for reminding me, Your Honor: I'll get right to the point. In recent years the peasants have been called upon to shoulder ever heavier burdens: fees, taxes, fines, and inflated prices for just about everything they need. No wonder you hear them talk about plucking the wild goose's tail feathers as it flies by. Over the past couple of years these trends have gotten out of control, which is why, I believe, the Paradise County garlic incident should have come as no surprise."

The presiding judge glanced down at his wrist-watch.

"Not being able to sell their crops was the spark that ignited this explosive incident, but the root cause was the un-

enlightened policies of the Paradise County government!" the officer continued. "Before Liberation only about a dozen people were employed by the district government, and things worked fine. Now even a township government in charge of the affairs of a mere thirty thousand people employs more than sixty people! And when you add those in the communes it's nearly a hundred, seventy percent of whose salaries are paid by peasants through township fees and taxes. Put in the bluntest possible terms, they are feudal parasites on the body of society! So in my view, the slogans 'Down with corrupt officials!' and 'Down with bureaucrats!' comprise a progressive call for the awakening of the peasants. . . .

"What I want to say is this," the young officer continued. "The people have the right to overthrow any party or government that disregards their well-being. If an official assumes the role of public master rather than public servant, the people have the right to throw him out! . . . In point of fact, things have improved in the wake of the party rectification, and most of Paradise County's responsible party members are doing a fine job. But one rat turd can spoil a whole pot of porridge, and the unprincipled behavior of a single party member adversely affects the party's reputation and the government's prestige. The people aren't always fair and discerning, and can be forgiven if their dissatisfaction with a particular official carries over into their attitudes toward officials in general. But shouldn't that be a reminder to officials to act in such a way as to best represent the party and the government?

". . . If we endorse the proposition that all people are equal under the law, then we must demand that the Paradise County People's Procuratorate indict Paradise County administrator Zhong Weimin on charges of official misconduct! I have nothing more to say."

The young officer remained standing for a moment before wearily taking a seat behind the defense table. Thunderous applause erupted from the spectator section behind him.

Source: *The Garlic Ballads* by Yan Mo, translated by Howard Goldblatt. Translation copyright © 1995 by Howard Goldblatt. Used by permission of Penguin, a Division of Penguin Books USA Inc., Penguin Books, New York, 1995, pp. 268–271.

A similar course of events has been taking place in China since the Communist ascent to power. Radical elements grew restive at what they perceived as a relapse into feudal habits by "capitalist roaders" within the party and launched the Great Proletarian Cultural Revolution.

What was distinctive about the Chinese case was that the movement was led by Mao Zedong himself, who risked the destruction of the very organization that had brought him to power in the first place — the Communist Party. Clearly, much about the Chinese Revolution cannot be explained without an understanding of the complex personality of its great leader.

With the death of Mao in 1976, the virulent phase of the revolution appeared to be at an end, and a more stable era of economic development is under way. Yet the Communist Party remains in power.

Why has communism survived in China, albeit in a substantially altered form, when it collapsed in Eastern Europe and the Soviet Union? One of the primary reasons is probably cultural. Although the doctrine of Marxism-Leninism originated in Europe, many of its main precepts, such as the primacy of the community over the individual and the denial of the concept of private property, run counter to the trends in Western civilization. This inherent conflict is especially evident in the societies of Central and Western Europe, which were strongly influenced by Enlightenment philosophy and the Industrial Revolution. These forces were weaker in the countries farther to the east, but both had begun to penetrate tsarist Russia by the end of the nineteenth century.

By contrast, Marxism-Leninism found a more receptive climate in China and other countries in the region influenced by Confucian tradition. In its political culture, the Communist system exhibits many of the same characteristics as traditional Confucianism—a single truth, an elite governing class, and an emphasis on obedience to the community and its governing representatives—while feudal attitudes regarding female inferiority, loyalty to the family, and bureaucratic arrogance are hard to break. On the surface, China today bears a number of uncanny similarities to the China of the past.

Yet these similarities should not blind us to the real changes that are taking place in the China of today, which is fundamentally different from that of the late Qing or even the early republic. Literacy rates and the standard of living, on balance, are far higher; the pressures of outside powers are less threatening; and China has entered the opening stages of its own industrial and technological revolution. For many Chinese, independent talk radio and the Internet are a greater source of news and views than the official media. Where Sun Yat-sen, Chiang Kai-shek, and even Mao Zedong broke their lances on the rocks of centuries of tradition, poverty, and ignorance, China's present leaders rule a country much more aware of the world and its place in it.

## INFOTRAC COLLEGE EDITION

Visit source collections at **http://infotrac.thomsonlearning.com**, and use the Search function with the following key terms:

Mao Zedong
Deng Xiaoping
Tiananmen Square

## WORLD HISTORY RESOURCES

Visit the *The World Since World War II* Companion Web site for resources specific to this textbook:

**http://history.wadsworth.com/duiker_wwii/**

The Wadsworth World History Resource Center at **http://history.wadsworth.com/world/** offers a variety of tools to help you succeed in this course, including access to quizzes; images; documents; interactive simulations, maps, and timelines; movie explorations; and a wealth of other sources.

# CHAPTER NOTES

1. "Report on an Investigation of the Peasant Movement in Hunan (March 1927)," *Quotations from Chairman Mao Tse-tung* (Beijing, 1976), p. 12.
2. Quoted in Stanley Karnow, *Mao and China: Inside China's Cultural Revolution* (New York, 1972), p. 95.
3. Quoted from an article by Mao Zedong in the June 1, 1958, issue of the journal *Red Flag*. See Stuart R. Schram, *The Political Thought of Mao Tse-tung* (New York, 1963), p. 253. The quotation "strike while the iron is hot" is from Karnow, *Mao and China*, p. 93.
4. Liang Heng with Judith Shapiro, *Son of the Revolution* (New York, 1983).
5. Quoted in *Time*, March 13, 1989, pp. 10–11.
6. "The Foolish Old Man Who Removed the Mountains," *Quotations from Chairman Mao*, p. 182.
7. Quoted in Jonathan Spence, *Chinese Roundabout: Essays in History and Culture* (New York, 1992), p. 285.

# Reflection

# PART I

As World War II came to an end, the survivors of that bloody struggle could afford to face the future with at least a measure of cautious optimism. With the death of Adolf Hitler in his bunker in Berlin, there were reasons to hope that the bitter rivalry that had marked relations among the Western powers would finally be put to an end and that the wartime alliance of the United States, Great Britain, and the Soviet Union could be maintained into the postwar era. In the meantime, the peoples of Asia and Africa saw the end of the war as a gratifying sign that the colonial system would soon end, ushering in a new era of political stability and economic development on a global scale.

With the perspective of more than half a century, we can see that these hopes have been only partly realized. In the decades following the war, the capitalist nations managed to recover from the extended economic depression that had contributed to the start of World War II and advanced to a level of economic prosperity never before seen in world history. The bloody conflicts that had erupted among European nations during the first half of the twentieth century came to an end, and Germany and Japan were fully integrated into the world community.

On the other hand, the prospects for a stable, peaceful world and an end to balance-of-power politics were hampered by the emergence of the grueling and sometimes tense ideological struggle between the socialist and capitalist camps, a competition headed by the only remaining great powers, the Soviet Union and the United States. Although the two superpowers were able to avoid a nuclear confrontation, the postwar world was divided into two heavily armed camps in a balance of terror that on one occasion—the Cuban Missile Crisis—brought the world briefly to the brink of nuclear holocaust.

Europe again became divided into hostile camps as the Cold War rivalry between the United States and the Soviet Union forced the European nations to ally with one or the other of the superpowers. The creation of two mutually antagonistic military alliances—NATO in 1949 and the Warsaw Pact in 1955—confirmed the new division of Europe, while a divided Germany, and within it, a divided Berlin, remained its most visible symbols. Repeated crises over the status of Berlin only intensified the fears in both camps.

In the midst of this rivalry, the Western European nations, with the assistance of the United States, made a remarkable economic recovery and attained unprecedented levels of prosperity. In Eastern Europe, Soviet domination, both political and economic, seemed so complete that many doubted it could ever be undone. Soviet military intervention, as in Hungary in 1956 and Czechoslovakia in 1968, reminded the Soviet satellites of their real condition; communism appeared, at least for the time being, too powerful to be dislodged. The Helsinki Agreement, signed in 1975, appeared to be a tacit admission by the West that the Iron Curtain had taken on a near-permanent status.

In the meantime, behind a shield of Soviet troops and tanks, the Soviet Union and its Eastern European satellites acted to stabilize the socialist system and realize the promise of a better society. Although Nikita Khrushchev appeared to harbor a sincere belief in the superiority of Marxist-Leninist ideas over those of the capitalist West, by the 1960s for the average citizen in the socialist bloc countries, the dream of a utopian society had begun to fade, and party leaders cynically manipulated the system for their own benefit.

Only in China was the dream still alive, actively promoted by Mao Zedong and his radical disciples during the frenetic years between the Great Leap Forward and Mao's death at the end of the Cultural Revolution. Whether or not his "uninterrupted revolution" was simply a last-ditch effort to retain power, Mao appeared to have a real awareness that even in China there lurked the danger of creeping bourgeoisification. His failure is a striking testimonial to the difficulties of continually stoking the fires of social revolution.

In the West, economic affluence appeared to give birth to its own set of problems. The voracious focus on material possessions, an intrinsic characteristic of the capitalist ethos, helped promote high levels of productivity in office and factory but at the same time produced a spiritual malaise in individual members of society, who increasingly began to question the meaning and purpose of life beyond the sheer accumulation of things. As the spread of scientific knowledge eroded religious belief, increasing social mobility undermined the traditional base-level structural units of human society—the family and the community. Modernity, as postwar society in the West was now commonly described, appeared to have no answer to the search for meaning in life beyond an unconfirmed and complacent belief in the Enlightenment doctrine of progress.

For the have-nots of capitalist society, the sources of discontent were more immediate, focusing on a lack of equal access to the cornucopia of goods produced by the capitalist machine. To their credit, political leaders in many countries sought ways to extend the benefits of an affluent society to their disadvantaged constituents, but success was limited, and experts searched without result for the ultimate cause.

Nowhere was this more the case than in Latin America, where resource-rich nations like Brazil, Chile, Mexico, and Venezuela continue to be plagued with political instability, flagrant corruption, and a widening gap in the distribution of wealth between the rich and the poor.

The driving force behind many of these changes in the postwar world was the Industrial Revolution, which continued to undermine the political, social, and economic foundations of traditional society, without disclosing the final destination. Human beings could only hope that as old ways were inexorably ground up and chucked aside in the new industrial world, the expanding power of scientific knowledge would provide them with clues on how to manipulate the situation to their ultimate benefit.

In the early 1990s, the Soviet Union and its system of satellites suddenly came tumbling down, leading to the emergence of truly independent nations in Eastern Europe and rising hopes for the emergence of a New World Order. But it soon became clear that the end of the Cold War had also unleashed long-dormant ethnic and religious forces in various parts of the world, producing a new round of civil conflicts and a level of terrorist activity reminiscent of the early part of the twentieth century. In Part II of this book, we will explore the impact of these events on the continents of Africa and Asia.

# THIRD WORLD RISING

# EMERGING
# AFRICA

At the end of World War II, Africa had already been exposed to over half a century of colonial rule. Although many Europeans complacently assumed that colonialism was a necessary evil in the process of introducing civilization to the backward peoples of Africa and Asia, to some African intellectuals, the Western drive for economic profit and political hegemony was a plague that threatened ultimately to destroy civilization. It was the obligation of Africans to use their own humanistic and spiritual qualities to help save the human race. The Ghanaian official Michael Francis Dei-Anang agreed. In *Whither Bound Africa*, written in 1946, he scathingly unmasked the pretensions of Western superiority:

*Forward! To what?*
*The Slums, where man is dumped upon man,*
*Where penury*
*And misery*
*Have made their hapless homes,*
*And all is dark and drear?*
*Forward! To what?*
*The factory*
*To grind hard hours*
*In an inhuman mill,*
*In one long ceaseless spell?*

*Forward! To what?*
*To the reeking round*
*Of medieval crimes,*
*Where the greedy hawks*
*of Aryan stock*

*Prey with bombs and guns*
*On men of lesser breed?*
*Forward to CIVILIZATION.*[1]

To Africans like Dei-Anang, the new Africa that emerged from imperialist rule had a duty to seek new ways of resolving the problems of humanity.

In the three decades following the end of World War II, the peoples of Africa were gradually liberated from the formal trappings of European colonialism. The creation of independent states in Africa began in the late 1950s and proceeded gradually until the last colonial regimes were finally dismantled. But the transition to independence has not been an unalloyed success. The legacy of colonialism in the form of political inexperience and continued European economic domination has combined with overpopulation and climatic disasters to frustrate the new states' ability to achieve political stability and economic prosperity. At the same time, arbitrary boundaries imposed by the colonial powers and ethnic and religious divisions within the African countries have led to bitter conflicts, which have posed a severe obstacle to the dream of continental solidarity and cooperation in forging a common destiny. Today, the continent of Africa, although blessed with enormous potential, is one of the most volatile and conflict-ridden areas of the world. Michael Dei-Anang's dream of a unique African road has not yet been realized. •

# UHURU: THE STRUGGLE FOR INDEPENDENCE

After World War II, Europeans reluctantly recognized that the end result of colonial rule in Africa would be African self-government, if not full independence. Accordingly, the African population would have to be trained to handle the responsibilities of representative government. In many cases, however, relatively little had been done to prepare the local population for self-rule. Early in the colonial era, during the late nineteenth century, African administrators had held influential positions in several British colonies, and one even served as governor of the Gold Coast. Several colonies had legislative councils with limited African participation, although their functions were solely advisory. But with the formal institution of colonial rule, senior positions were reserved for the British, although local authority remained in the hands of native rulers.

After World War II, most British colonies introduced reforms that increased the representation of the local population. Members of legislative and executive councils were increasingly chosen through elections, and Africans came to constitute a majority of these bodies. Elected councils at the local level were introduced in the 1950s to reduce the power of the tribal chiefs and clan heads, who had controlled local government under indirect rule. An exception was South Africa, where European domination continued. In the Union of South Africa, the franchise was restricted to whites except in the former territory of the Cape Colony, where persons of mixed ancestry had enjoyed the right to vote since the mid-nineteenth century. Black Africans did win some limited electoral rights in Northern and Southern Rhodesia (now Zambia and Zimbabwe), although whites generally dominated the political scene.

A similar process of political liberalization was taking place in the French colonies. At first, the French tried to assimilate the African peoples into French culture. By the 1920s, however, racist beliefs in Western cultural superiority and the tenacity of traditional beliefs and practices among Africans had somewhat discredited this ideal. The French therefore substituted a more limited program of assimilating African elites into Western culture and using them as administrators at the local level as a link to the remainder of the population. This policy resembled the British policy of indirect rule, although it placed more emphasis on French culture in training local administrators. It had only limited success, however, because many Western-educated Africans refused to leave the urban centers to live in the countryside. Others, who were exposed to radical ideas while studying abroad, rejected the prevailing forms of Western civilization and called for the restoration of national independence.

The Nazi occupation of northern France had an effect on black Africans somewhat like that of the Japanese occupation of Southeast Asia on Asians. In 1944, the Free French movement under General Charles de Gaulle issued the Brazzaville Declaration, which promised equal rights, though not self-government, in a projected French Union composed of France and its overseas possessions.

After the war, a legislative assembly for the new organization was created, although its political powers were limited. At the same time, African representatives were elected to the French National Assembly in Paris. But even this new community of nations had separate categories of citizenship based on education and ethnic background, and decisions on major issues were still made in France or by French officials in French Africa.

## The Colonial Legacy

As in Asia, colonial rule had a mixed impact on the societies and peoples of Africa. The Western presence brought a number of short-term and long-term benefits to Africa, such as improved transportation and communication facilities, and in a few areas laid the foundation for a modern industrial and commercial sector. Improved sanitation and medical care in all probability increased life expectancy. The introduction of selective elements of Western political systems laid the basis for the gradual creation of democratic societies.

Yet the benefits of Westernization were distributed unequally, and the vast majority of Africans found their lives little improved, if at all. Only South Africa and French-held Algeria, for example, developed modern industrial sectors, extensive railroad networks, and modern communications systems. In both countries, European settlers were numerous, most investment capital for industrial ventures was European, and whites comprised almost the entire professional and managerial class. Members of the native population were generally restricted to unskilled or semiskilled jobs at wages less than one-fifth of those enjoyed by Europeans. Those who worked in industry or on infrastructure projects often suffered from inhumane working conditions. Several thousand African conscripts reportedly died on press gangs building the new railroad system.

Many colonies concentrated on export crops—peanuts from Senegal and Gambia, cotton from Egypt and Uganda, coffee from Kenya, and palm oil and cocoa products from the Gold Coast. Here the benefits of development were somewhat more widespread. In some cases, the crops were grown on plantations, which were usually owned by Europeans. But plantation agriculture was not always suitable in Africa, and much farming was done by free or tenant farmers. In some areas, where land ownership was traditionally vested in the community, the land was owned and leased by the corporate village.

Even here, however, the vast majority of the profits from the export of tropical products accrued to Europeans or to merchants from other foreign countries, such as India and the Arab emirates. While a fortunate few bene- fited from the increase in exports, the vast majority of Africans continued to be subsistence farmers growing food for their own consumption. The gap was particularly wide in places like Kenya, where the best lands had been reserved for European settlers to make the colony self-sufficient. As in other parts of the world, the early stages of the Industrial Revolution were especially painful for the rural population, and ordinary subsistence farmers reaped few benefits from colonial rule.

## The Rise of Nationalism

The African response to the loss of independence can be traced through several stages, beginning with resistance. In some cases, the opposition came from an organized state, such as Ashanti, which fought against the British takeover of the Gold Coast in the 1860s. Where formal states did not exist, the colonial takeover was often easier and more gradual; in a few instances, however, such as the Zulu tribesmen in South Africa in the 1880s and Abdel Qadir's rebellion against the French in Algeria, resistance to white rule was quite fierce.

But formal nationalist movements and parties generally arose later in Africa than in Asia. The first nationalist groups were formed in urban areas, primarily among people who had been exposed to Western civilization. The first Afro-Europeans, as such people are sometimes called, often benefited from the European presence, and some, as we have seen, held responsible positions in the colonial bureaucracy. But as the system became more formalized in the early twentieth century, more emphasis was placed on racial distinctions, and opportunities in government and other professional positions diminished, especially in the British colonies, where indirect rule was based on collaboration with the local tribal aristocracy. The result was a dissatisfied urban educated elite, who were all the angrier when they realized they would not benefit from the improved conditions.

Political organizations for African rights did not arise until after World War I, and then only in a few areas, such as British-ruled Kenya and the Gold Coast. At first, organizations such as the National Congress of British West Africa (formed in 1919 in the Gold Coast) and Jomo Kenyatta's Kikuyu Central Association in Kenya focused on improving African living conditions in the colonies rather than on national independence. After World War II, however, following the example of independence movements elsewhere, these groups became organized political parties with independence as their objective. In the Gold Coast, Kwame Nkrumah (1909–1972) led the Convention People's Party, the first formal political party in black Africa. In the late 1940s, Jomo Kenyatta (1894–

1978) founded the Kenya African National Union (KANU), which focused on economic issues but had an implied political agenda as well.

For the most part, these political activities were basically nonviolent and were led by Western-educated African intellectuals. Their constituents were primarily urban professionals, merchants, and members of labor unions. But the demand for independence was not entirely restricted to the cities. In Kenya, for example, the widely publicized Mau Mau movement among the Kikuyu people used terrorism as an essential element of its program to achieve *uhuru* (Swahili for "freedom") from the British. Although most of the violence was directed against other Africans—only about a hundred Europeans were killed in the violence, compared with an estimated seventeen hundred Africans who lost their lives at the hands of the rebels—the specter of Mau Mau terrorism alarmed the European population and convinced the British government in 1959 to promise eventual independence.

A similar process was occurring in Egypt, which had been a protectorate of Great Britain (and under loose Turkish suzerainty until the breakup of the Ottoman Empire) since the 1880s. National consciousness had existed in Egypt since well before the colonial takeover, and members of the legislative council were calling for independence even before World War I. In 1918, a formal political party called the Wafd was formed to promote Egyptian independence. The intellectuals were opposed as much to the local palace government as to the British, however, and in 1952, an army coup overthrew King Farouk, the grandson of Khedive Ismail, and established an independent republic.

In areas such as South Africa and Algeria, where the political system was dominated by European settlers, the transition to independence was more complicated. In South Africa, political activity by local Africans began with the formation of the African National Congress (ANC) in 1912. Initially, the ANC was dominated by Western-oriented intellectuals and had little mass support. Its goal was to achieve economic and political reforms, including full equality for educated Africans, within the framework of the existing system. But the ANC's efforts met with little success, while conservative white parties managed to stiffen the segregation laws. In response, the ANC became increasingly radicalized, and by the 1950s, the prospects for a violent confrontation were growing.

In Algeria, resistance to French rule by Berbers and Arabs in rural areas had never ceased. After World War II, urban agitation intensified, leading to a widespread rebellion against colonial rule in the mid-1950s.

At first, the French government tried to maintain its authority in Algeria, which was considered an integral part of metropolitan France. But when Charles de Gaulle became president in 1958, he reversed French policy, and Algeria became independent under President Ahmad Ben Bella (b. 1918) in 1962. The armed struggle in Algeria hastened the transition to statehood in its neighbors as well. Tunisia won its independence in 1956 after some urban agitation and rural unrest but retained close ties with Paris. The French attempted to suppress the nationalist movement in Morocco by sending Sultan Muhammad V into exile, but the effort failed, and in 1956, he returned as the ruler of the independent state of Morocco.

Most black African nations achieved their independence in the late 1950s and 1960s, beginning with the Gold Coast, now renamed Ghana, in 1957 (see Map 6.1). Nigeria, the Belgian Congo (renamed Zaire and later the Democratic Republic of the Congo), Kenya, Tanganyika (renamed Tanzania after merging with Zanzibar), and several other countries soon followed. Most of the French colonies agreed to accept independence within the framework of de Gaulle's French Community. By the late 1960s, only parts of southern Africa and the Portuguese possessions of Mozambique and Angola remained under European rule.

Independence came later to Africa than to most of Asia. Several factors help explain the delay. For one thing, colonialism was established in Africa somewhat later than in most areas of Asia, and the inevitable reaction from the local population was consequently delayed. Furthermore, with the exception of a few areas in West Africa and along the Mediterranean, coherent states with a strong sense of cultural, ethnic, and linguistic unity did not exist in most of Africa. Most traditional states, such as Ashanti in West Africa, Songhai in the southern Sahara, and Bakongo in the Congo basin, were collections of heterogeneous peoples with little sense of national or cultural identity. Even after colonies were established, the European powers often practiced a policy of "divide and rule," while the British encouraged political decentralization by retaining the authority of the traditional native chieftains. It is hardly surprising that when opposition to colonial rule emerged, unity was difficult to achieve.

# THE ERA OF INDEPENDENCE

The newly independent African states faced intimidating challenges. Like the new states in South and Southeast Asia, they had been profoundly affected by colonial rule.

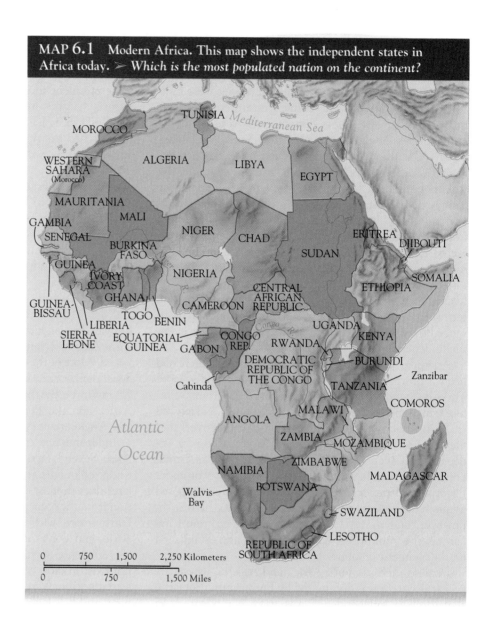

**MAP 6.1** Modern Africa. This map shows the independent states in Africa today. ➤ *Which is the most populated nation on the continent?*

Yet the experience had been highly unsatisfactory in most respects. Although Western political institutions, values, and technology had been introduced, at least into the cities, the exposure to European civilization had been superficial at best for most Africans and tragic for many. At the outset of independence, most African societies were still primarily agrarian and traditional, and their modern sectors depended mainly on imports from the West.

## Pan-Africanism and Nationalism: The Destiny of Africa

Like the leaders of the new states in South and Southeast Asia, most African leaders came from the urban middle class. They had studied in Europe or the United States and spoke and read European languages. Although most were profoundly critical of colonial policies, they appeared to accept the relevance of the Western model to Africa and gave at least lip service to Western democratic values.

Their views on economics were somewhat more diverse. Some, like Jomo Kenyatta of Kenya and General Mobutu Sese Seko (1930–1998) of Zaire, were advocates of Western-style capitalism. Others, like Julius Nyerere (b. 1922) of Tanzania, Kwame Nkrumah of Ghana, and Sékou Touré (1922–1984) of Guinea, preferred an "African form of socialism," which bore slight resemblance to the Marxist-Leninist socialism practiced in the Soviet Union and was more like the syndicalist movement in Western Europe. According to its advocates, it was descended from traditional communal practices in precolonial Africa.

Like the leaders of other developing countries, the new political leaders in Africa were strongly nationalistic and generally accepted the colonial boundaries. But as we have seen, these boundaries were artificial creations of the colonial powers. Virtually all of the new states included widely diverse ethnic, linguistic, and territorial groups. Zaire, for example, was composed of more than two hundred territorial groups speaking seventy-five different languages.

Some African leaders themselves harbored attitudes that undermined the fragile sense of common identity needed to knit these diverse groups together. A number of leaders—including Nkrumah of Ghana, Touré of Guinea, and Kenyatta of Kenya—were enticed by the dream of pan-Africanism, a concept of continental unity that transcended national boundaries and was to find its concrete manifestation in the Organization of African Unity (OAU), which was founded in Addis Ababa, Ethiopia, in 1963 (see the box on p. 130).

Pan-Africanism originated among African intellectuals during the first half of the twentieth century. A basic element was the conviction that there was a distinctive "African personality" that owed nothing to Western materialism and provided a common sense of destiny for all black African peoples. According to Aimé Césaire, a West Indian of African descent and a leading ideologist of the movement, whereas Western civilization prized rational thought and material achievement, African culture emphasized emotional expression and a common sense of humanity.

The concept of a unique African destiny (known to its originators by the French term négritude, or "blackness"), was in part a natural defensive response to the social Darwinist concepts of Western racial superiority and African inferiority that were popular in Europe and the United States during the early years of the twentieth century. At the same time, it was stimulated by growing self-doubt among many European intellectuals after World War I, who feared that Western civilization was on a path of self-destruction. Aimé Césaire compared the white world,

*appalling weary from its immense effort*
*the crack of its joints rebelling under the hardness of the stars*

with that of the Africans,

*Those who invented neither gunpowder nor compass*
*those who tamed neither steam nor electricity*
*those who explored neither sea nor sky*
*but those who know the humblest corners of the country*
*    suffering*
*those whose only journeys were uprooting*
*those who went to sleep on their knees*
*those who were domesticated and christianized*
*those who were inoculated with degeneration.*[2]

The idea had more appeal to Africans from French colonies than to those from British possessions. Yet it also found adherents in the British colonies, as well as in the United States and elsewhere in the Americas. African American intellectuals such as W. E. B. Dubois and George Padmore and the West Indian politician Marcus Garvey attempted to promote a "black renaissance" by popularizing the idea of a distinct African personality. Their views were shared by several of the new African leaders, including Leopold Senghor (b. 1906) of Senegal, Kwame Nkrumah of Ghana, and Jomo Kenyatta of Kenya. Nkrumah in particular appeared to hope that a pan-African union could be established that would unite all of the new countries of the continent in a broader community.

## Dream and Reality: Political and Economic Conditions in Contemporary Africa

The program of the OAU had forecast a future Africa based on freedom, equality, justice, and dignity and on the unity, solidarity, and territorial integrity of African states. It did not take long for reality to set in. Vast disparities in education and income made it hard to establish democracy in much of Africa. Expectations that independence would lead to stable political structures based on "one person, one vote" were soon disappointed as the initial phase of pluralistic governments gave way to a series of military regimes and one-party states. Between 1957 and 1982, more than seventy leaders of African countries were overthrown by violence, and the pace has increased since then.

# TOWARD AFRICAN UNITY

*I*n May 1963, the leaders of thirty-two African states met in Addis Ababa, the capital of Ethiopia, to discuss the creation of an organization that would represent the interests of all the newly independent countries of Africa. The result was the Organization of African Unity. An excerpt from its charter is presented here. Although the organization has by no means realized all of the aspirations of its founders, it provides a useful forum for the discussion and resolution of its members' common problems.

## CHARTER OF THE ORGANIZATION OF AFRICAN UNITY

We, the Heads of African States and Governments assembled in the City of Addis Ababa, Ethiopia;

CONVINCED that it is the inalienable right of all people to control their own destiny;

CONSCIOUS of the fact that freedom, equality, justice, and dignity are essential objectives for the achievement of the legitimate aspirations of the African peoples;

CONSCIOUS of our responsibility to harness the natural and human resources of our continent for the total advancement of our peoples in spheres of human endeavor;

INSPIRED by a common determination to promote understanding among our peoples and cooperation among our States in response to the aspirations of our peoples for brotherhood and solidarity, in a larger unity transcending ethnic and national differences;

CONVINCED that, in order to translate this determination into a dynamic force in the cause of human progress, conditions for peace and security must be established and maintained;

DETERMINED to safeguard and consolidate the hard-won independence as well as the sovereignty and territorial integrity of our States, and to fight against neocolonialism in all its forms;

DEDICATED to the general progress of Africa; . . .

DESIROUS that all African States should henceforth unite so that the welfare and well-being of their peoples can be assured;

RESOLVED to reinforce the links between our states by establishing and strengthening common institutions;

HAVE agreed to the present Charter.

Source: *Organizing African Unity* by Jon Woronoff, pp. 642–649. Copyright © 1970 by Scarecrow Press, Inc. Used with permission of the publisher.

---

Hopes that independence would inaugurate an era of economic prosperity and equality were similarly dashed. Part of the problem could be (and was) ascribed to the lingering effects of colonialism. Most newly independent countries in Africa were dependent on the export of a single crop or natural resource. When prices fluctuated or dropped, they were at the mercy of the vagaries of the international market. In several cases, the resources were still controlled by foreigners, leading to the charge that colonialism had been succeeded by "neocolonialism," in which Western domination was maintained by economic rather than by political or military means. To make matters worse, most African states had to import technology and manufactured goods from the West, and the prices of those goods rose more rapidly than those of the export products.

The new states also contributed to their own problems. Scarce national resources were squandered on military equipment or expensive consumer goods rather than on building up their infrastructure to provide the foundation for an industrial economy. Corruption, a painful reality throughout the modern world, became almost a way of life in Africa, as bribery (known variously as *dash, chai,* or *bonsella*) became necessary to obtain even the most basic services. The Nigerian author Cyprian Ekwensi expressed his disillusionment with African politics in his novel *Jagua Nana*. When the heroine's boyfriend Freddie states, "I wan' money quick-quick; an' politics is de only hope," she replies, "No Freddie. I no wan' you to win. . . . Politics not for you, Freddie. You got education. You got culture. You're a gentleman an' proud. Politics be a game for dog. And in dis Lagos, is a rough game. De roughest game in de whole worl'. Is smell an' dirty an' you too clean an' sweet."[3]

Finally, population growth, which has hindered economic growth more severely than anything else in the new nations of Asia and Africa, became a serious problem and crippled efforts to build modern economies. By the mid-1980s, annual population growth averaged nearly 3 percent throughout Africa, the highest rate of any continent. Drought conditions and the inexorable spread of the Sahara (usually known as desertification, a condition caused partly by overpopulation) have led to widespread hunger and starvation, first in West African countries such as Niger and Mali and then in Ethiopia, Somalia, and the Sudan. Despite global efforts to provide food, millions are in danger of starvation and malnutrition, and countless others have fled to neighboring countries in search of sustenance.

In recent years, the spread of AIDS in Africa has reached epidemic proportions. According to one estimate, one-third of the entire population of sub-Saharan Africa is infected with the virus, including a high percentage of the urban middle class. Over 75 percent of the AIDS cases reported around the world are on the continent of Africa. Some observers estimate that without measures to curtail the effects of the disease, it will have a significant impact on several African countries by reducing population growth, which is presently predicted to increase throughout the continent by at least 300 million in the next fifteen years.

Poverty is endemic in Africa, particularly among the three-quarters of the population still living off the land. Urban areas have grown tremendously, but as in much of Asia, most are surrounded by massive squatter settlements of rural peoples who had fled to the cities in search of a better life. The expansion of the cities has overwhelmed fragile transportation and sanitation systems and led to rising pollution and perpetual traffic jams, while millions are forced to live without water and electricity. Meanwhile, the fortunate few (all too often government officials on the take) live the high life and emulate the consumerism of the West (in a particularly expressive phrase, the rich in many East African countries are know as *wabenzi*, or "Mercedes-Benz people").

Courtesy of William J. Duiker

⇒ **MANIOC, FOOD FOR THE MILLIONS.** Manioc, a tuber like the potato, was brought to Africa from the New World soon after the voyages of Columbus. Although low in nutrient value, it can be cultivated in poor soil with little moisture and is reportedly the staple food for nearly one-third of the population of sub-Saharan Africa. Manioc is also widely grown in tropical parts of Asia and South America and is familiar to Westerners as the source of tapioca (it is also called cassava or yuca). In the illustration shown here, village women in Senegal rhythmically pound manioc to the chanting of those standing nearby.

## THE SEARCH FOR SOLUTIONS

Concern over the dangers of economic inequality inspired a number of African leaders—including Nkrumah in Ghana, Nyerere in Tanzania, and Samora Michel in Mozambique—to restrict foreign investment and nationalize the major industries and utilities while promoting social ideals and values. Nyerere was the most consistent, promoting the ideals of socialism and self-reliance through his Arusha Declaration of 1967. Taking advantage of his powerful political influence, Nyerere placed limitations on income and established village collectives to avoid the corrosive effects of economic inequality and government corruption. Sympathetic foreign countries provided considerable economic aid to assist the experiment, and many observers noted that levels of corruption, political instability, and ethnic strife were lower in Tanzania than in many other African countries. Unfortunately, corruption has increased in recent years, while political elements on the island of Zanzibar, citing the stagnation brought by decades of socialism, are agitating for autonomy or even total separation from the mainland. Tanzania also has poor soil, inadequate rainfall, and limited resources, all of which have contributed to its slow growth and continuing rural and urban poverty.

In 1985, Nyerere voluntarily retired from the presidency. In his farewell speech, he confessed that he had failed to achieve many of his ambitious goals to create a socialist society in Africa. In particular, he admitted that his plan to collectivize the traditional private farm (*shamba*) had run into strong resistance from conservative peasants. "You can socialize what is not traditional," he remarked. "The *shamba* can't be socialized." But Nyerere insisted that many of his policies had succeeded in improving social and economic conditions, and he argued that the only real solution was to consolidate the multitude of small countries in the region into a larger East African Federation.[4]

The countries that opted for capitalism faced their own dilemmas. Neighboring Kenya, blessed with better soil in the highlands, a local tradition of aggressive commerce, and a residue of European settlers, welcomed foreign investment and profit incentives. The results have been mixed. Kenya has a strong current of indigenous African capitalism and a substantial middle class, mostly based in the capital, Nairobi. But landlessness, unemployment, and income inequities are high, even by African standards (almost one-fifth of the country's 27 million people are squatters, and unemployment is currently estimated at 45 percent). The rate of population growth —more than 4 percent annually—is one of the highest in the world. Eighty percent of the population remains rural, and 40 percent live below the poverty line. The result has been widespread unrest in a country formerly admired for its successful development.

Beginning in the mid-1970s, a few African nations decided to adopt Soviet-style Marxism-Leninism. In Angola and Ethiopia, Marxist parties followed the Soviet model and attempted to create fully socialist societies with the assistance of Soviet experts and Cuban troops and advisers. Economically, the results were disappointing, and both countries faced severe internal opposition. In Ethiopia, the revolt by Muslim tribal peoples in the province of Eritrea led to the fall of the Marxist leader Mengistu and his regime in 1990. A similar revolt erupted against the government in Angola, with the rebel group UNITA controlling much of the rural population and for a time threatening the capital city, Luanda. With the death of the rebel leader Julius Savimbi in 2002, the revolt finally appeared to be at an end.

## THE SEARCH FOR COMMUNITY

Finally, Africans were disappointed that the dream of a united Africa was not realized. Most Africans felt a shared sense of continuing victimization at the hands of the West and were convinced that independence had not ended Western interference in and domination of African affairs. Many African leaders were angered when Western powers, led by the United States, conspired to overthrow the radical Congolese politician Patrice Lumumba in Zaire in the early 1960s. The episode reinforced their desire to form the Organization of African Unity as a means of reducing Western influence. But aside from agreeing to adopt a neutral stance during the Cold War, African states had difficulty achieving a united position on many issues, and their disagreements left the region vulnerable to external influence and even led to conflict. During the late 1980s and early 1990s, border disputes festered in many areas of the continent and in some cases—as with Morocco and a rebel movement in the Western Sahara and between Kenya and Uganda— flared into outright war.

Even within many African nations, the concept of nationhood was undermined by the renascent force of regionalism or tribalism. Nigeria, with the largest population on the continent, was rent by civil strife during the late 1960s when dissident Ibo groups in the southeast attempted unsuccessfully to form the independent state of Biafra. Ethnic conflicts broke out among hostile territorial groups in Zimbabwe (the former Southern Rhodesia)

and in several nations in Central Africa. In Kenya, Luo tribal leader Tom Mboya was assassinated, presumably because rival groups feared that he would be selected to succeed the charismatic Kikuyu president Jomo Kenyatta.

Another force undermining nationalism in Africa was pan-Islamism. Its prime exponent in Africa was Egyptian president Gamal Abdel Nasser. After Nasser's death in 1970, the torch of Islamic unity in Africa passed to Libyan president Muammar Qadhafi, whose ambitions to create a greater Muslim nation in the Sahara under his authority led to conflict with neighboring Chad. The Islamic resurgence also surfaced in Ethiopia, where Muslim tribesmen in Eritrea (the former Italian colony of Eritrea had been joined with Ethiopia in 1952) rebelled against the Marxist regime of Colonel Mengistu in Addis Ababa.

## RECENT TRENDS

Not all the news in Africa has been bad. Stagnant economies have led to the collapse of one-party regimes and the emergence of fragile democracies in several countries. Dictatorships were brought to an end in Ethiopia, Liberia, and Somalia, although in each case the fall of the regime was later followed by political instability or civil war. In Senegal, national elections held in the summer of 2000 brought an end to four decades of rule by the once dominant Socialist Party. The new president, Abdoulaye Wade, promised to introduce comprehensive reforms to stimulate the economy.

Perhaps the most notorious case was that of Idi Amin of Uganda. Colonel Amin led a coup against Prime Minister Milton Obote in 1971. After ruling by terror and brutal repression of dissident elements, he was finally deposed in 1979. In recent years, stability has returned to the country, which in May 1996 had its first presidential election in more than fifteen years.

Africa has also benefited from the end of the Cold War, as the superpowers have virtually ceased to compete for power and influence in Africa. When the Soviet Union withdrew its support from the Marxist government in Ethiopia, the United States allowed its right to maintain military bases in neighboring Somalia to lapse, resulting in the overthrow of the authoritarian government there. Unfortunately, clan rivalries led to such turbulence that many inhabitants were in imminent danger of starvation, and in the winter of 1992, U.S. military forces occupied the country in an effort to provide food to the starving population. Since the departure of foreign troops in 1993, the country has been divided into clan fiefdoms while Islamic groups struggle to bring a return to law and order.

Perhaps Africa's greatest success story is South Africa, where the white government—which long maintained a policy of racial segregation (apartheid) and restricted black sovereignty to a series of small "Bantustans" in relatively infertile areas of the country—finally accepted the inevitability of African involvement in the political process and the national economy. In 1990, the government of President F. W. de Klerk (b. 1936) released ANC leader Nelson Mandela (b. 1918) from prison, where he had been held since 1964. In 1993, the two leaders agreed to hold democratic national elections the following spring. In the meantime, ANC representatives agreed to take part in a transitional coalition government with de Klerk's National Party. Those elections resulted in a substantial majority for the ANC, and Mandela became president.

In May 1996, a new constitution was approved, calling for a multiracial state. The coalition government quickly collapsed, however, as the National Party immediately went into opposition, claiming that the new charter did not adequately provide for joint decision making by members of the coalition. The third group in the coalition, the Zulu-based Inkatha Freedom Party, agreed to remain within the government, but rivalry with the ANC intensified. Zulu chief Mangosuthu Buthelezi, drawing on the growing force of Zulu nationalism, began to invoke the memory of the great nineteenth-century ruler Shaka in a possible bid for future independence.

In 1999, a major step toward political stability was taken when Nelson Mandela stepped down from the presidency, to be replaced by his longtime disciple Thabo Mbeki. The new president faced a number of intimidating problems, including rising unemployment, widespread lawlessness, chronic corruption, and an ominous flight of capital and professional personnel from the country. Mbeki's conservative economic policies earned the support of some white voters and the country's new black elite but was criticized by labor leaders, who contend that the benefits of independence are not seeping down to the poor. Still, with all its problems, South Africa remains the wealthiest and most industrialized state on the continent, and many of its citizens still support the premise that a multiracial society can succeed in Africa.

If the situation in South Africa provides grounds for modest optimism, the situation in Nigeria provides reason for serious concern. Africa's largest country in terms of population, and one of its wealthiest because of substantial oil reserves, Nigeria until recent years was in the grip of military strongmen. During his rule, General Sani Abacha ruthlessly suppressed all opposition and in late 1995 ordered the execution of a writer despite widespread protests from human rights groups abroad. Ken Saro-Wiwa had criticized environmental damage caused by foreign interests in southern Nigeria, but the regime's major concern was his support for separatist activities in an area that had previously launched the Biafran insurrection in the late 1960s. In a protest against the brutality of the Abacha regime, Nobel Prize–winning author Wole Soyinka published from exile a harsh exposé of the crisis inside the country. His book, *The Open Sore of a Continent,* places the primary responsibility for failure not on Nigeria's long list of dictators but on the very concept of the modern nation-state, which was introduced into Africa arbitrarily by Europeans during the later stages of the colonial era. A nation, he contends, can only emerge from below, as the expression of the moral and political will of the local inhabitants; nationhood cannot be imposed artificially from above, as was the case throughout Africa.

In 1998, Abacha died, and national elections led to the creation of a civilian government under Olusegun Obasanjo. Civilian leadership has not been a panacea for Nigeria's problems, however. Northerners, who had traditionally dominated Nigerian politics, became irritated at the new president's efforts to address economic problems in the southern part of the country. In early 2000, religious riots broke out in several northern cities as the result of a decision by provincial officials to apply Islamic law throughout their jurisdiction. President Obasanjo has attempted to defuse the unrest by delaying in carrying out the decision, but the issue raises tensions between Christian peoples in the southern part of the country and the primarily Islamic north while threatening the fragile unity of Africa's most populous country.

The religious tensions that erupted in Nigeria have spilled over into neighboring states. In the nearby Ivory Coast, the death of President Felix Houphouet-Boigny in 1993 led to an outbreak of long-simmering resentment between Christians in the south and recently arrived Muslim immigrants in the north. National elections held in the fall of 2000, resulting in the election of a Christian president, were marked by sporadic violence and widespread charges of voting irregularities. In the meantime, pressure to apply the *Shari'a* is spreading to Nigeria's northern neighbor Niger, where the president has opposed Islamic law on the grounds that it would unsettle his country. Christian churches have been attacked, and bars and brothels have been sacked or burnt to the ground.

Currently, the most tragic situation is in the central African states of Rwanda and Burundi, where a chronic conflict between the minority Tutsis and the Hutu majority has led to a bitter civil war, with thousands of refugees fleeing to the neighboring Democratic Republic of the Congo (formerly Zaire). In a classic example of conflict between pastoral and farming peoples, the nomadic Tutsis had long dominated the sedentary Hutu population. It was the attempt of the Bantu-speaking Hutus to bring an end to Tutsi domination that initiated the recent conflict, marked by massacres on both sides. In the meantime, the presence of large numbers of foreign troops and refugees intensified centrifugal forces inside Zaire, where General Mobutu Sese Seko had long ruled with an iron hand. In 1997, military forces led by Mobutu's longtime opponent Lauren Kabila managed to topple the general's corrupt government in Kinshasa. Once in power, Kabila renamed the country the Democratic Republic of the Congo and promised a return to democratic practices. The new government systematically suppressed political dissent, however, and in January 2001, Kabila was assassinated and was succeeded shortly afterward by his son. Peace talks are now under way.

It is clear that African societies have not yet begun to surmount the challenges they have faced since independence. Most African states are still poor and their populations illiterate. According to a World Bank report published in 2000, sub-Saharan Africa is the only major region in the world where the population is living less well than it did in the 1960s. But a significant part of the problem is, as Wole Soyinka contended, that the nation-state system is not particularly well suited to the African continent. Africans must find better ways to cooperate with each other and to protect and promote their own interests. A first step in that direction was taken in 1991, when the Organization for African Unity agreed to establish the African Economic Community (AEC). In 2001, the OAU was replaced by the African Union, which is intended to provide greater political and economic integration throughout the continent in years to come. As a first step, West African states have set up a peacekeeping force to monitor fragile cease-fires in Liberia and neighboring Sierra Leone, where civil wars have caused widespread devastation.

As Africa evolves, it is useful to remember that economic and political change is often an agonizingly slow and painful process. Introduced to industrialization and concepts of Western democracy only a century ago, African societies are still groping for ways to graft Western political institutions and economic practices onto a native structure still significantly influenced by traditional values and attitudes. As one African writer recently observed, it is easy to be cynical in Africa because changes in political regimes have had little effect on people's livelihood. Still, he said, "let us welcome the wind of change. This, after all, is a continent of winds. The trick is to keep hope burning, like a candle protected from the wind."[5]

# CONTINUITY AND CHANGE IN MODERN AFRICAN SOCIETIES

Although generalizations are difficult on this most diverse of continents, it is clear that the impact of the West has been greater on urban and educated Africans and more limited on their rural and illiterate compatriots. After all, the colonial presence was first and most firmly established in the cities. Many cities, including Dakar, Lagos, Johannesburg, Cape Town, Brazzaville, and Nairobi, are direct products of the colonial experience. Most African cities today look like their counterparts elsewhere in the world. They have high-rise buildings, blocks of residential apartments, wide boulevards, neon lights, movie theaters, and traffic jams.

The cities are also where the African elites live and work. Affluent Africans, like their contemporaries in other developing countries, have been strongly attracted to the glittering material aspects of Western culture. They live in Western-style homes or apartments and eat Western foods stored in Western refrigerators, and those who can afford it drive Western cars. It has been said, not wholly in praise, that there are more Mercedes-Benzes in Nigeria than in Germany, where they are manufactured.

The furniture of their minds has become increasingly Western as well, in part because of the educational system. In the precolonial era, education as we know it did not really exist in Africa except for parochial schools in Christian Ethiopia and academies to train young males in Islamic doctrine and law in Muslim societies in North and West Africa. For the average African, education took place at the home or in the village courtyard and stressed socialization and vocational training.

Traditional education in Africa was not necessarily inferior to that in Europe. Social values and customs were transmitted to the young by storytellers, often village elders who could gain considerable prestige through their performance. Among the Luo people in Kenya, for example, children were taught in a *siwindhe*, or the house of a widowed grandmother. Here they would be instructed in the ways and thinking of their people. A favorite saying for those who behaved stupidly was "you are uneducated, like one who never slept in a *siwindhe*."[6]

Europeans introduced modern Western education into Africa in the nineteenth century, although some Africans had already become literate in one or more Western languages by taking part in commerce. The French set up the first state-run schools in Senegal in 1818. In British colonies and protectorates, the earliest schools were established by missionaries. At first, these schools concentrated on vocational training with some instruction in European languages and Western civilization. Most courses were taught in the vernacular, although many schools later switched to English or French. Eventually, pressure from Africans led to the introduction of professional training, and the first institutes of higher learning were established in the early twentieth century. Most college-educated Africans, called "been-to's," however, received their higher training abroad.

With independence, African countries established their own state-run schools. The emphasis was on the primary level, but high schools and universities were established in major cities. The basic objectives have been to introduce vocational training and improve literacy rates. Unfortunately, both funding and trained teachers are scarce in most countries, and few rural areas have schools. As a result, illiteracy remains high, estimated at about 70 percent of the population across the continent. There has been a perceptible shift toward education in the vernacular languages. In West Africa, only about one in four adults is conversant in a Western language.

One interesting vehicle for popular education that emerged during the transition to independence in Nigeria was the Onitsha Market pamphlet. Produced prima-rily by the Ibo people in the southeast, who traditionally valued egalitarianism and individual achievement, the pamphlets were "how-to" books advising readers on how to succeed in a rapidly changing Africa. They tended to be short, inexpensive, and humorous, with flashy covers to attract the potential buyer's attention. One, titled "The Nigerian Bachelor's Guide," sold 40,000 copies. Unfortunately, the Onitsha Market and the pamphlet tradition were destroyed during the Nigerian civil war of the late 1960s, but they undoubtedly played an important role during a crucial period in the country's history. Recently, Onitsha has become the largest producer of video movies in sub-Saharan Africa.

Outside the major cities, where about three-quarters of the continent's inhabitants live, Western influence has had less of an impact. Millions of people throughout Africa (as in Asia) live much as their ancestors did, in thatch huts without modern plumbing and electricity; they farm or hunt by traditional methods, practice time-honored family rituals, and believe in the traditional deities. Even here, however, change is taking place. Slavery has been eliminated, for the most part, although there have been persistent reports of raids by slave traders on defenseless villages in the southern Sudan. Economic need, though, has brought about massive migrations as

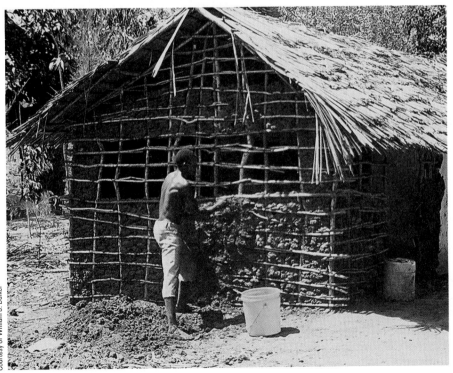

Courtesy of William J. Duiker

≫ BUILDING HIS DREAM HOUSE.
In Africa, the houses of rural people are often constructed with a wood frame, known as wattle, daubed with mud, and then covered with a thatch roof. Such houses are inexpensive to build and remain cool in the hot tropical climate. In this Kenyan village not far from the Indian Ocean, a young man is applying mud to the wall of his future home. Houses are built in a similar fashion throughout the continent, as well as in much of southern Asia.

some leave to work on plantations, others move to the cities, and still others flee to refugee camps to escape starvation. Migration itself is a wrenching experience, disrupting familiar family and village ties and enforcing new social relationships.

Nowhere, in fact, is the dichotomy between old and new, native and foreign, rural and urban so clear and painful as in Africa. Urban dwellers regard the village as the repository of all that is backward in the African past, while rural peoples view the growing urban areas as a source of corruption, prostitution, hedonism, and the destruction of communal customs and values. The tension between traditional ways and Western culture is particularly strong among African intellectuals, many of whom are torn between their admiration for things Western and their desire to retain an African identity. "Here we stand," wrote one Nigerian,

> infants overblown
> poised between two civilizations
> finding the balancing irksome,
> itching for something to happen,
> to tip us one way or the other,
> groping in the dark for a helping hand
> and finding none.[7]

## African Women

One of the consequences of colonialism and independence has been a change in the relationship between men and women. In most precolonial African societies, men and women had distinctly different roles. Women in sub-Saharan Africa, however, generally did not live under the severe legal and social disabilities that we have seen in such societies as China and India, and their relationship with men was complementary rather than subordinate.

Within the family, wives normally showed a degree of deference to their husbands, and polygamy was not uncommon. But because society was usually arranged on communal lines, property was often held in common, and production tasks were divided on a cooperative rather than hierarchical basis. The status of women tended to rise as they moved through the life cycle. Women became more important as they reared children; in old age, they often became eligible to serve in senior roles within the family, lineage, or village. In some societies, such as the Ashanti kingdom in West Africa, women such as the queen mother were eligible to hold senior political positions. Some observers argue that polygamy was beneficial for women because it promoted communal and cooperative attitudes within the community and divided up the task of motherhood among several wives.

Sexual relationships changed profoundly during the colonial era, sometimes in ways that could justly be described as beneficial. Colonial governments attempted to bring an end to forced marriage, bodily mutilation such as clitoridectomy, and polygamy. Missionaries introduced women to Western education and encouraged them to organize themselves to defend their interests.

But the new system had some unfavorable consequences as well. Like men, women now became a labor resource. As African males were taken from the villages to serve as forced labor on construction projects, the traditional division of labor was disrupted, and women were forced to play a more prominent role in the economy. At the same time, their role in the broader society was constricted. In British colonies, Victorian attitudes of sexual repression and female subordination led to restrictions on women's freedom, and the positions in government they had formerly held were closed to them.

Independence also had a significant impact on gender roles in African society. Almost without exception, the new governments established the principle of sexual equality and permitted women to vote and run for political office. Yet as elsewhere, women continue to operate at a disability in a world dominated by males. Politics remains a male preserve, and although a few professions, such as teaching, child care, and clerical work, are dominated by women, most African women are employed in menial positions such as agricultural labor, factory work, and retail trade or as domestics. Education is open to all at the elementary level, but women comprise less than 20 percent of students at the upper levels in most African societies today.

Not surprisingly, women have made the greatest strides in the cities. Most urban women, like men, now marry on the basis of personal choice, although a significant minority are still willing to accept their parents' choice. After marriage, African women appear to occupy a more equal position than their counterparts in most Asian countries. Each marriage partner tends to maintain a separate income, and women often have the right to possess property separate from their husbands. While many wives still defer to their husbands in the traditional manner, others are like the woman in Abioseh Nicol's story "A Truly Married Woman," who, after years as living as a common-law wife with her husband, is finally able to provide the price and finalize the marriage. After the wedding, she declares, "For twelve years I have got up every morning at five to make tea for you and breakfast. Now I am a truly married woman [and] you must treat me with a little more respect. You are now my husband and not a lover. Get up and make yourself a cup of tea."[8]

In general, sexual relationships between men and women in contemporary Africa are relatively relaxed, as they were in traditional society. Sexual activity among adolescents is customary in most societies, and only a minority of women are still virgins at the time of marriage. Most marriages are monogamous. Males seem to be more likely to have extramarital relationships, often with bar girls or prostitutes (sometimes known as "walk-about women"), but adultery on the part of women is not rare. In some Muslim societies, efforts to apply *Shari'a* law have led to greater restrictions on the freedom of women. In northern Nigeria, a woman was recently sentenced to death for committing the act of adultery. The sentence was later reversed on appeal.

There is a growing feminist movement in Africa, but it is firmly based on conditions in the local environment. Many African women writers, for example, refuse to be defined by Western dogma and opt instead for a brand of African feminism much like that of Ama Ata Aidoo, a Ghanaian novelist, whose ultimate objective is to free African society as a whole, not just its female inhabitants. After receiving her education at a girls' school in the Gold Coast and attending classes at Stanford University in the United States, she embarked on a writing career in which, as she notes, she has committed herself to the betterment of the African people. Every African women and every man, she insists, "should be a feminist, especially if they believe that Africans should take charge of our land, its wealth, our lives, and the burden of our development. Because it is not possible to advocate independence for our continent without also believing that African women must have the best that the environment can offer."[9]

In a few cases, women are even going into politics. One example is Margaret Dongo of Zimbabwe, where a black African government under Robert Mugabe succeeded white rule in the former Southern Rhodesia in 1980. Now an independent member of Zimbabwe's Parliament, she is labeled "the ant in the elephant's trunk" for her determined effort to root out corruption and bring about social and economic reforms to improve the lot of the general population. "We didn't fight to remove white skins," she remarks. "We fought discrimination against blacks in land distribution, education, employment. If we are being exploited again by our black leaders, then what did we fight for?"[10]

In general, then, women in urban areas in contemporary Africa have been able to hold their own. Although they are still sometimes held to different standards than men (African men often expect their wives to be both modern and traditional, fashionable and demure, wage earners and housekeepers) and do not possess the full

**SALT OF THE EARTH.** During the precolonial era, many West African societies were forced to import salt from Mediterranean countries in exchange for tropical products and gold. Today the people of Senegal satisfy their domestic needs by mining salt deposits contained in lakes like this one in the interior of the country. These lakes are the remnants of vast seas that covered the region of the Sahara in prehistoric times. Note that it is women who are doing much of the heavy labor, while men occupy the managerial positions.

range of career opportunities that men do, they are manifestly better off than women in many Asian societies.

The same cannot necessarily be said about women in rural areas, where traditional attitudes continue to exert a strong influence and individuals may still be subordinated to communalism. In some societies, clitoridectomy is still widely practiced. Polygamy is also not uncommon, and arranged marriages are still the rule rather than the exception.

To a villager in Africa as elsewhere, an African city often looks like the fount of evil, decadence, and corruption. Women in particular have suffered from the tension between the pull of the city and the village. As men are drawn to the cities in search of employment and excitement, their wives and girlfriends are left behind, both literally and figuratively, in the native village. Nowhere has this been more vividly described than in the anguished cry of Lawino, the abandoned wife in Ugandan author p'Bitek Okot's *Song of Lawino*. Lawino laments not just her husband's decision to take a modern urban wife, who dusts powder over her face to look like a white woman and has red-hot lips like glowing charcoal, but his rejection of his roots. He in turn lashes out in frustration at what he considers the poverty, backwardness, and ignorance of the rural environment.

## African Culture

Inevitably, the tension between traditional and modern, native and foreign, and individual and communal that has permeated contemporary African society has spilled over into culture. In general, in the visual arts and music, utility and ritual have given way to pleasure and decoration. In the process, Africans have been affected to a certain extent by foreign influences but have retained their distinctive characteristics. Wood carving, metalwork, painting, and sculpture, for example, have preserved their traditional forms but are now increasingly adapted to serve the tourist industry and the export market.

No area of African culture has been so strongly affected by political and social events as literature. Except for Muslim areas in North and East Africa, precolonial Africans did not have a written literature, although their tradition of oral storytelling served as a rich repository of history, custom, and folk culture. The absence of written languages, of course, means a lack of a traditional African literature. The first written literature in the vernacular or in European languages emerged during the nineteenth century in the form of novels, poetry, and drama.

Angry at the negative portrayal of Africa in Western literature (see the box on p. 139), African authors initially wrote primarily for a European audience as a means of establishing black dignity and purpose. Embracing the ideals of *négritude*, many glorified the emotional and communal aspects of the traditional African experience.

One of the first was Guinean author Camara Laye (1928–1980), who in 1953 published *The Dark Child*, a touching and intimate initiation into village life in precolonial Africa. In the novel, which admitted the reader to the secret rituals and practices of daily life behind the protective hedges of an African village compound, the author openly regretted the lost ways of the African past while conceding that they were not appropriate to the Guinea of tomorrow.

Chinua Achebe of Nigeria was the first major African novelist to write in the English language. In his writings, he attempts to interpret African history from a native perspective and to forge a new sense of African identity. In his most famous novel, *Things Fall Apart* (1958), he recounts the story of a Nigerian who refuses to submit to the new British order and eventually commits suicide. Criticizing those of his contemporaries who have accepted foreign rule, the protagonist laments that the white man "has put a knife on the things that held us together and we have fallen apart."

After 1965, the African novel took a dramatic turn, shifting its focus from the brutality of the foreign oppressor to the shortcomings of the new native leadership.

Having gained independence, African politicians were now portrayed as mimicking and even outdoing the injustices committed by their colonial predecessors. A prominent example of this genre is the work of Kenyan Ngugi Wa Thiong'o (b. 1938). His first novel, *A Grain of Wheat*, takes place on the eve of *Uhuru*, or independence. Although it mocks local British society for its racism, snobbishness, and superficiality, its chief interest lies in its unsentimental and even unflattering portrayal of ordinary Kenyans in their daily struggle for survival.

Whereas Ngugi initially wrote in English for elite African and foreign readers, he was determined to reach a broader audience and eventually decided to write in his native Kikuyu. For that reason, perhaps, in the late 1970s, he was placed under house arrest for writing subversive literature. From prison, he secretly wrote *Devil on the Cross*, which urged his compatriots to overthrow the government of Daniel arap Moi. Published in 1980, the book sold widely and was eventually read aloud by storytellers throughout Kenyan society. Fearing an attempt on his life, in recent years Ngugi has lived in exile.

Many of Ngugi's contemporaries have followed his lead and focused their frustration on the failure of the continent's new leadership to carry out the goals of independence. One of the most outstanding is Nigerian Wole Soyinka (b. 1934). His novel *The Interpreters* (1965)

Courtesy of William J. Duiker

⇛ I ACCUSE! For many Africans, the end of European colonialism did not mark the opening of a new era of democratic achievement and economic prosperity. To the contrary, most African countries have been plagued with continuing problems of endemic poverty, internecine conflict, and authoritarian rule. In this photograph, an anonymous commentator from the city of Mombasa, in Kenya, braves official displeasure by pointing an accusing finger at African leaders who rule by dictatorial means. The focus of his anger is undoubtedly directed at Kenyan president Daniel arap Moi, one of the most authoritarian of recent African rulers. Moi agreed to retire in 2002.

# AFRICA: DARK OR RADIANT CONTINENT?

*olonialism camouflaged its economic objectives under the cloak of a "civilizing mission," which in Africa was aimed at illuminating the so-called Dark Continent with Europe's brilliant civilization. In 1899, the Polish-born English author Joseph Conrad (1857–1924) fictionalized his harrowing journey up the Congo River in the novella* Heart of Darkness. *Expressing views from his Victorian perspective, he portrayed an Africa that was incomprehensible, irrational, sensual, and therefore threatening. Conrad, however, was shocked by the horrific exploitation of the peoples of the Belgian Congo, presenting them with a compassion rarely seen during the heyday of imperialism.*

*Over the years, Conrad's work has provoked much debate, and many African writers have been prompted to counter his vision by reaffirming the dignity and purpose of the African people. One of the first to do so was the Guinean author Camara Laye (1928–1980), who in 1954 composed a brilliant novel,* The Radiance of the King, *which can be viewed as the mirror image of Conrad's* Heart of Darkness. *In Laye's work, another European protagonist undertakes a journey into the impenetrable heart of Africa. This time, however, he is enlightened by the process, thereby obtaining self-knowledge and ultimately salvation.*

## JOSEPH CONRAD, *HEART OF DARKNESS*

We penetrated deeper and deeper into the heart of darkness. It was very quiet there. At night sometimes the roll of drums behind the curtain of trees would run up the river and remain sustained faintly, as if hovering in the air high over our heads, till the first break of day. Whether it meant war, peace, or prayer we could not tell. . . . But suddenly, as we struggled round a bend, there would be a glimpse of rush walls, of peaked grass-roofs, a burst of yells, a whirl of black limbs, a mass of hands clapping, of feet stamping, of bodies swaying, of eyes rolling, under the droop of heavy and motionless foliage. The steamer toiled along slowly on the edge of a black and incomprehensible frenzy. The prehistoric man was cursing us, praying to us, welcoming us—who could tell? We were cut off from the comprehension of our surroundings; we glided past like phantoms, wondering and secretly appalled, as sane men would be before an enthusiastic outbreak in a madhouse. . . .

It was unearthly, and the men were—No, they were not inhuman. Well, you know, that was the worst of it—this suspicion of their not being inhuman. It would come slowly to one. They howled and leaped, and spun, and made horrid faces; but what thrilled you was just the thought of their humanity—like yours—the thought of your remote kinship with this wild and passionate uproar. Ugly. Yes, it was ugly enough; but if you were man enough you would admit to yourself that there was in you just the faintest trace of a response to the terrible frankness of that noise, a dim suspicion of there being a meaning in it which you—you so remote from the night of first ages—could comprehend. And why not? The mind of man is capable of anything—because everything is in it, all the past as well as the future. What was there after all? Joy, fear, sorrow, devotion, valour, rage—who can tell?—but truth—stripped of its cloak of time.

## CAMARA LAYE, *THE RADIANCE OF THE KING*

"I enjoy life . . . ," thought Clarence. "If I filed my teeth like the people of Aziana, no one could see any difference between me and them." There was, of course, the difference in pigmentation in the skin. But what difference did that make? "It's the soul that matters," he kept telling himself. "And in that respect I am exactly as they are." . . .

But where was this radiance coming from? Clarence got up and went to the right-hand window, from which this radiance seemed to be streaming. . . .

He saw the king. And then he knew where the extraordinary radiance was coming from. . . .

And he had the feeling that all was lost. But had he not already lost everything? . . . He would remain for ever chained to the South, chained to his hut, chained to everything he had so thoughtlessly abandoned himself to. His solitude seemed to him so heavy, it burdened him with such a great weight of sorrow that his heart seemed about to break. . . .

But at that very moment the king turned his head, turned it imperceptibly, and his glance fell upon Clarence. . . .

"Yes, no one is as base as I, as naked as I," he thought. "And you, lord, you are willing to rest your eyes upon me!" Or was it because of his very nakedness? . . . "Because of your very nakedness!" the look seemed to say. "That terrifying void that is within you and which opens to receive me; your hunger which calls to my hunger; your very baseness which did not exist until I gave it leave; and the great shame you feel. . . ."

When he had come before the king, when he stood in the great radiance of the king, still ravaged by the tongue of fire, but alive still, and living only through the touch of that fire, Clarence fell upon his knees, for it seemed to him that he was finally at the end of his seeking, and at the end of all seekings.

Sources: From *Heart of Darkness* by Joseph Conrad. Penguin Books, 1991. From *The Radiance of the King* by Camara Laye, translated from the French by James Kirkup. New York: Vintage, 1989.

lambasted the corruption and hypocrisy of Nigerian politics. Succeeding novels and plays have continued that tradition, resulting in a Nobel Prize in literature in 1986. The winner of the Nobel Prize in 2003 was J. M. Coetzee (b. 1940), whose novels, such as *Disgrace* (1999), exposed the social and psychological devastation of apartheid on South Africans. His plea for tolerance and compassion echoed the moral commitment to human dignity on the part of many white African authors.

Some recent African authors, like the Somali writer Nuruddin Farah (b. 1945), argue that it is time for Africans to stop blaming their present political ills on either colonialism or on their own dictators. In his writings, such as the novel *Sweet and Sour Milk*, Farah urges Africans to stop lamenting the contamination of African society from the West and take charge of their own destiny. In so doing, Farah joins other African writers in serving as the social conscience of a continent still seeking its own identity.

Among Africa's most prominent writers today, a number are women. Traditionally, African women were valued for their talents as storytellers, but writing was strongly discouraged by both traditional and colonial authorities on the grounds that women should occupy themselves with their domestic obligations. In recent years, however, a number of women have emerged as prominent writers of African fiction. Two examples are Buchi Emecheta (b. 1940) of Nigeria and Ama Ata Aidoo (b. 1942) of Ghana. Beginning with *Second Class Citizen* (1975), which chronicled the breakdown of her own marriage, Emecheta has published numerous works exploring the role of women in contemporary African society and decrying the practice of polygamy. In her own writings, Aidoo has focused on the identity of today's African women and the changing relations between men and women in society. Her novel *Changes: A Love Story* (1991) chronicles the lives of three women, none presented as a victim but all caught up in the struggle for survival and happiness. Sadly, the one who strays the furthest from traditional African values finds herself free but isolated and lonely.

One of the overriding concerns confronting African intellectuals since independence has been the problem of language. Unlike Asian societies, Africans have not inherited a long written tradition from the precolonial era. As a result, many intellectuals have written in the colonial language, a practice that sometimes results in guilt and anxiety. As we have seen, some have reacted by writing in their local languages to reach a native audience. The market for such work is limited, however, because of the high illiteracy rate and also because novels written in

African languages have no market abroad. Moreover, because of the deep financial crisis throughout the continent, there is little money for the publication of serious books. Many of Africa's libraries and universities are almost literally without books. It is little wonder that many African authors, to their discomfort, continue to write and publish in foreign languages.

Contemporary African music also reflects a hybridization or fusion with Western culture. Having traveled to the New World via the slave trade centuries earlier, African drum beats evolved into North American jazz and Latin American dance rhythms, only to return to reenergize African music. In fact, today music is one of Africans' most effective weapons for social and political protest. Easily accessible to all, African music, whether Afro-beat in Nigeria, rai in Algeria, or reggae in Benin, represents the "weapon of the future," contemporary musicians say; it "helped free Nelson Mandela" and "will put Africa back on the map." Censored by all the African dictatorial regimes, these courageous musicians persist in their struggle against corruption, what one singer calls the second slavery, "the cancer that is eating away at the system." Their voices echo the chorus "Together we can build a nation, / Because Africa has brains, youth, knowledge."[11]

# CONCLUSION: GATHERED AT THE BEACH

Nowhere in the developing world is the dilemma of continuity and change more agonizing than in contemporary Africa. Mesmerized by the spectacle of Western affluence yet repulsed by the bloody trail from slavery to World War II and the atomic bombs over Hiroshima and Nagasaki, African intellectuals have been torn between the dual images of Western materialism and African exceptionalism.

What is the destiny of Africa? Some Africans still yearn for the dreams embodied in the program of the OAU. Novelist Ngugi Wa Thiong'o argues that for his country, the starting point is a democratic Kenya. More broadly, he calls for "an internationalization of all the democratic and social struggles for human equality, justice, peace, and progress."[12] Some African political leaders, however, have apparently discarded the democratic ideal and turned their attention to what is sometimes called the "East Asian model," based on the Confucian tenet of subordination of the individual to the community as the guiding principle of national development.

Whether African political culture today is well placed to imitate the strategy adopted by the fast-growing nations of East Asia—which in any event are now encountering problems of their own—is questionable. Like all peoples, Africans must ultimately find their own solutions within the context of their own traditions and not by seeking to imitate the example of others.

For the average African, of course, such intellectual dilemmas pale before the daily challenge of survival. But the fundamental gap between the traditional village and the modern metropolis is perhaps wider in Africa than anywhere else in the world and may well be harder to bridge. The solution is not yet visible. In the meantime, writes Ghanaian author George Awoonor-Williams, all Africans are exiles:

*The return is tedious*
*And the exiled souls gathered at the beach*

*Arguing and deciding their future*
*Should they return home*
*And face the fences the termites had eaten*
*And see the dunghill that has mounted their birthplace? . . .*

*The final strokes will land them on forgotten shores*
*They committed to the impiety of self-deceit*
*Slashed, cut and wounded their souls*
*And left the mangled remainder in manacles.*

*The moon, the moon is our father's spirit*
*At the stars entrance the night revellers gather*
*To sell their chatter and inhuman sweat to the gateman*
*And shuffle their feet in agonies of birth.*
*Lost souls, lost souls, lost souls, that are*
*   still at the gate.*[13]

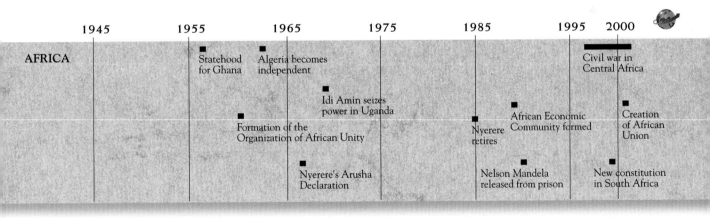

| 1945 | 1955 | 1965 | 1975 | 1985 | 1995 | 2000 |
|---|---|---|---|---|---|---|

AFRICA

Statehood for Ghana

Algeria becomes independent

Idi Amin seizes power in Uganda

Formation of the Organization of African Unity

Nyerere's Arusha Declaration

Nyerere retires

African Economic Community formed

Nelson Mandela released from prison

Civil war in Central Africa

Creation of African Union

New constitution in South Africa

# INFOTRAC COLLEGE EDITION

Visit source collections at http://infotrac.thomsonlearning.com, and use the Search function with the following key terms:

Africa
Developing countries
Nelson Mandela

# WORLD HISTORY RESOURCES

Visit the *The World Since World War II* Companion Web site for resources specific to this textbook:

http://history.wadsworth.com/duiker_wwii/

The Wadsworth World History Resource Center at http://history.wadsworth.com/world/ offers a variety of tools to help you succeed in this course, including access to quizzes; images; documents; interactive simulations, maps, and timelines; movie explorations; and a wealth of other sources.

# CHAPTER NOTES

1. Quoted in G.-C. M. Mutiso, *Socio-Political Thought in African Literature* (New York, 1974), p. 117.
2. Aimé Césaire, *Cahier d'un retour du pays natal*, trans. John Berger and Anna Bostock (Harmondsworth, England, 1969), p. 10, quoted in Emmanuel N. Obiechina, *Language and Theme: Essays on African Literature* (Washington, D.C., 1990), pp. 78–79.
3. Cyprian Ekwensi, *Jagua Nana* (Greenwich, England, 1961), pp. 146–147.
4. *New York Times*, September 1, 1996.
5. Dan Agbee, in *Newswatch* (Lagos), quoted in *World Press Review*, August 1991, p. 16.
6. Adrian Roscoe, *Uhuru's Fire: African Literature East to South* (Cambridge, England, 1977), p. 23.
7. Francis Ademola, *Reflections: Nigerian Prose and Verse* (Lagos, 1962), p. 65, quoted in Mutiso, *Socio-Political Thought in African Literature*, p. 117.
8. Abioseh Nicol, *A Truly Married Woman and Other Stories* (London, 1965), p. 12.
9. Ama Ata Aidoo, *No Sweetness Here* (New York, 1995), p. 136.
10. Quoted in *New York Times*, May 13, 1996.
11. Gilles Médioni, "Stand Up, Africa!" *World Press Review*, July 2002, p. 34. Reprinted from *L'Express*.
12. Ngugi Wa Thiong'o, *Decolonising the Mind: The Politics of Language in African Literature* (Portsmouth, N.H., 1986), p. 103.
13. George Awoonor-Williams, *Rediscovery and Other Poems* (Ibadan, Nigeria, 1964), p. 11, quoted in Mutiso, *Socio-Political Thought in African Literature*, pp. 81–82.

# FERMENT IN THE MIDDLE EAST

*W*e Muslims are of one family even though we live under different governments and in various regions."[1] So said Ayatollah Ruholla Khomeini, the Islamic religious figure and leader of the 1979 revolution that overthrew the shah in Iran. The ayatollah's remark was not just a pious wish by a religious mystic but an accurate reflection of one crucial aspect of the political dynamics in the region.

If the concept of African exceptionalism, or "blackness," represents an alternative to the system of nation-states in Africa, in the Middle East a similar role has been played by the forces of militant Islam. In both regions, a yearning for a sense of community beyond national borders tugs at the emotions and intellect of their inhabitants and counteracts the dynamic pull of nationalism that has provoked political turmoil and conflict in much of the rest of the world.

## CRESCENT OF CONFLICT

A dramatic example of the powerful force of pan-Islamic sentiment took place on September 11, 2001, when Muslim militants hijacked four U.S. airliners and turned them into missiles aimed at the center of world capitalism. Although the headquarters of the terrorist network that carried out the attack—known as al-Qaeda—was located in Afghanistan, the militants themselves came from several different Muslim states. In the months that followed, support for al-Qaeda and its mysterious leader, Osama bin Laden, intensified throughout the Muslim world (see the box on p. 144). To many observers, it appeared that the

Islamic peoples were embarking on an era of direct confrontation with the entire Western world.

What were the sources of Muslim anger? In a speech released on videotape shortly after the attack, bin Laden declared that the attacks were a response to the "humiliation and disgrace" that have afflicted the Islamic world for over eighty years, a period dating back to the end of World War I.

For the Middle East, the period between the two world wars was an era of transition. With the fall of the Ottoman and Persian Empires, new modernizing regimes emerged in Turkey and Iran, and a more traditionalist but fiercely independent government was established in Saudi Arabia. Elsewhere, European influence continued to be strong; the British and French had mandates in

# THE ROOTS OF TERRORISM

*In the weeks and months following the terrorist attack on September 11, 2001, commentators throughout the world voiced their views on the roots of the attack and how to prevent a recurrence. In many Muslim countries, horror at the violence was balanced by a conviction that the problem could not be solved simply by seeking out the perpetrators and destroying their terrorist network. Rather, terrorism was a consequence of contemporary conditions throughout much of the Arab world and could only be resolved by political and economic means. Such was the view of the author of the following editorial, published a few days following the attack in El Watan, an independent newspaper in Algiers, the capital of Algeria. Algerian society has been shattered by terrorist activities committed by Islamic militants for over a decade.*

## ALGERIA: RETHINKING THE VARIABLES

Even if the U.S. military kills bin Laden and decimates his forces, international terrorism will be only weakened, not destroyed. Experts agree on this point, and some assert that if bin Laden dies a martyr, his name will act as a stimulus for terrorist movements around the world that won't hesitate to commit further spectacular attacks.

And so as the fear and anger fade, a growing chorus of voices is calling for a comprehensive approach to terrorism, the fruit of intensive thought about its deepest nature. The first conclusion will involve the responsibility of the West-

ern world, which throughout history has allowed religious fundamentalism to thrive when it served Western interests.

Thus, the West unconditionally backed the monarchies of the Gulf, a breeding ground of fundamentalism, because of their oil resources, while at the same time lending blinkered support to Israel's expansionist policies. Against the will of their people, Arab and Muslim leaders have been coddled by the West, spurring popular anger to fever pitch during the Gulf War.

Resentment, widespread in the Arab world by the end of the 20th century, has been exploited by the fundamentalists, who have channeled it into a "holy war" (jihad) against the West. The West, and notably the United States, has learned nothing from all this. Worse, the West has aggravated frustrations the world over by canonizing laissez-faire economics, whose centerpiece—globalization—heralds the systematic impoverishment of billions of people.

But it would be hasty to blame the West alone for terrorism. Both governments and movements in the Arab-Muslim world have sought to impose their religious dogma everywhere by means of systematic terror perpetrated by fanatical groups. Their aim is to create Afghan-type states. Algeria is the clearest case in point.

Source: Excerpt from "Algeria: Rethinking the Variables" by A. Bahmane in El Watan, 9/19/01, Algiers, in *World Press Review*, November 2001. Reprinted with permission from World Press Review.

Syria, Lebanon, Jordan, and Palestine, and British influence persisted in Iraq and southern Arabia and throughout the Nile valley. Pan-Arabism was on the rise, but it lacked focus and coherence.

During World War II, the Middle East became the cockpit of European rivalries, as it had been during World War I. The region was more significant to the warring powers than previously because of the growing importance of oil and the Suez Canal's position as a vital sea route. For a brief period, the Afrika Korps, under the command of the brilliant German general Erwin Rommel, threatened to seize Egypt and the Suez Canal, but British troops defeated the German forces at El Alamein, west of Alexandria, in 1942 and gradually drove them westward until their final defeat after the arrival of U.S. troops in Morocco under the field command of General George S. Patton. From that time until the end of the war, the entire region from the Mediterranean Sea eastward was under secure Allied occupation.

## The Question of Palestine

As in other areas of Asia, the end of World Was II led to the emergence of a number of independent states. Jordan, Lebanon, and Syria, all European mandates before the war, became independent. Egypt, Iran, and Iraq, though still under a degree of Western influence, became increasingly autonomous. Sympathy for the idea of Arab unity led to the formation of the Arab League in 1945, but different points of view among its members prevented it from achieving anything of substance.

The one issue on which all Arab states in the area could agree was the question of Palestine. As tensions between Jews and Arabs in that mandate intensified during the 1930s, the British attempted to limit Jewish immigration into the area and firmly rejected proposals for independence. After World War II, the Zionists turned for support to the United States, and in March 1948, the Truman administration approved the concept of an independent Jewish state, despite the fact that only about one-third of the local population were Jews. In May, the new state of Israel was formally established.

To its Arab neighbors, the new state represented a betrayal of the interests of the Palestinian people, 90 percent of whom were Muslim, and a flagrant disregard for the conditions set out in the Balfour Declaration of 1917. Outraged at the lack of Western support for Muslim interests in the area, several Arab countries invaded the new Jewish state. The invasion did not succeed because of internal divisions among the Arabs, but both sides remained bitter, and the Arab states refused to recognize Israel.

The war had other lasting consequences as well because it led to the exodus of thousands of Palestinian refugees into neighboring Muslim states. Jordan, which had become independent under its Hashemite ruler, was now flooded by the arrival of one million urban Palestinians in a country occupied by half a million Bedouins. To the north, the state of Lebanon had been created to provide the local Christian community with a country of its own, but the arrival of the Palestinian refugees upset the delicate balance between Christians and Muslims. In any event, the creation of Lebanon had angered the Syrians, who had lost it as well as other territories to Turkey as a result of European decisions before and after the war.

## Nasser and Pan-Arabism

The dispute over Palestine placed Egypt in an uncomfortable position. Technically, Egypt was not an Arab state. King Farouk, who had acceded to power in 1936, had frequently declared support for the Arab cause, but the Egyptian people were not Bedouins and shared little of the culture of the peoples across the Red Sea. Nevertheless, Farouk committed Egyptian armies to the disastrous war against Israel.

In 1952, King Farouk, whose corrupt habits had severely eroded his early popularity, was overthrown by a military coup engineered by young military officers ostensibly under the leadership of Colonel Muhammad Nagib. The real force behind the scenes was Colonel Gamal Abdul Nasser (1918–1970), the son of a minor government functionary who, like many of his fellow officers, had been angered by the army's inadequate preparation for the war against Israel four years earlier. In 1953, the monarchy was replaced by a republic.

In 1954, Nasser seized power in his own right and immediately instituted a land reform program. He also adopted a policy of neutrality in foreign affairs and expressed sympathy for the Arab cause. The British presence had rankled many Egyptians for years, for even after granting Egypt independence, Britain had retained control over the Suez Canal to protect its route to the Indian Ocean. In 1956, Nasser suddenly nationalized the Suez Canal Company, which had been under British and French administration. Seeing a threat to their route to the Indian Ocean, the British and the French launched a joint attack on Egypt to protect their investment. They were joined by Israel, whose leaders had grown exasperated at sporadic Arab commando raids on Israeli territory and now decided to strike back. But the Eisenhower administration in the United States, concerned that the attack smacked of a revival of colonialism, supported Nasser and brought about the withdrawal of foreign forces from Egypt and of Israeli troops from the Sinai Peninsula.

Nasser now turned to pan-Arabism. In 1958, Egypt united with Syria in the United Arab Republic (UAR). The union had been proposed by the Ba'ath Party, which advocated the unity of all Arab states in a new socialist society. In 1957, the Ba'ath Party assumed power in Syria and opened talks with Egypt on a union between the two countries, which took place in March 1958 following a plebiscite. Nasser, despite his reported ambivalence about the union, was named president of the new state.

Egypt and Syria hoped that the union would eventually include all Arab states, but other Arab leaders, including young King Hussein of Jordan and the kings of Iraq and Saudi Arabia, were suspicious. The latter two in particular feared pan-Arabism on the assumption that they would be asked to share their vast oil revenues with the poorer states of the Middle East. Such fears were understandable.

Nasser opposed the existing situation, in which much of the wealth of the Middle East flowed into the treasuries of a handful of wealthy feudal states or, even worse, the pockets of foreign oil interests. In Nasser's view, through Arab unity, this wealth could be put to better use to improve the standard of living in the area. To achieve a more equitable division of the wealth of the region, natural resources and major industries would be nationalized; central planning would guarantee that resources were exploited efficiently, but private enterprise would continue at the local level.

In the end, however, Nasser's determination to extend state control over the economy brought an end to the UAR. When the government announced the nationalization of a large number of industries and utilities in 1961, a military coup overthrew the Ba'ath leaders in Damascus, and the new authorities declared that Syria would end its relationship with Egypt.

The breakup of the UAR did not end Nasser's dream of pan-Arabism. In 1962, Algeria finally received its independence from France and, under its new president, Ahmad Ben Bella, established close relations with Egypt, as did a new republic in Yemen. During the mid-1960s, Egypt took the lead in promoting Arab unity against Israel. At a meeting of Arab leaders held in Jerusalem in 1964, the Palestine Liberation Organization (PLO) was set up under Egyptian sponsorship to represent the interests of the Palestinians. According to the charter of the PLO, only the Palestinian people (and thus not Jewish immigrants from abroad) had the right to form a state in the old British mandate. A guerrilla movement called al-Fatah, led by the dissident PLO figure Yasir Arafat (b. 1929), began to launch terrorist attacks on Israeli territory, prompting Israel to raid PLO bases in Jordan in 1966.

## The Arab-Israeli Dispute

The growing Arab hostility was a constant threat to the security of Israel. In the years after independence, Israeli leaders dedicated themselves to creating a Jewish homeland. Aided by reparations paid by the postwar German government and private funds provided by Jews living abroad, notably in the United States, the government attempted to build a democratic and modern state that would be a magnet for Jews throughout the world and a symbol of Jewish achievement.

Ensuring the survival of the tiny state surrounded by antagonistic Arab neighbors was a considerable challenge, made more difficult by divisions within the Israeli population. Some were immigrants from Europe, while others came from countries of the Middle East. Some were secular and even socialist in their views, while others were politically conservative and stressed religious orthodoxy. There were also Christians as well as many Muslim Palestinians who had not fled to other countries. To balance these diverse interests, Israel established a parliament, called the Knesset, on the European model, with proportional representation based on the number of votes each party received in the general election. The parties were so numerous that none ever received a majority of votes, and all governments had to be formed from a coalition of several parties. As a result, moderate secular leaders such as longtime Prime Minister David Ben Gurion had to cater to more marginal parties composed of conservative religious groups.

During the late 1950s and 1960s, the dispute between Israel and other states in the Middle East escalated in intensity. Essentially alone except for the sympathy of the United States and several Western European countries, Israel adopted a policy of determined resistance to and immediate retaliation against alleged PLO and Arab provocations. By the spring of 1967, relations between Israel and its Arab neighbors had deteriorated as Nasser attempted to improve his standing in the Arab world by intensifying military activities and imposing a blockade against Israeli commerce through the Gulf of Aqaba. Concerned that it might be isolated, and lacking firm support from Western powers (who had originally guaranteed Israel the freedom to use the Gulf of Aqaba), in June 1967 Israel suddenly launched air strikes against Egypt and several of its Arab neighbors. Israeli armies then broke the blockade at the head of the Gulf of Aqaba and occupied the Sinai peninsula. Other Israeli forces attacked Jordanian territory on the West Bank of the Jordan River (Jordan's King Hussein had recently signed an alliance with Egypt and placed his army under Egyptian command), occupied the whole of Jerusalem, and seized Syrian military positions in the Golan Heights along the Israeli-Syrian border.

Despite limited Soviet support for Egypt and Syria, in a brief six-day war, Israel had mocked Nasser's pretensions of Arab unity and tripled the size of its territory, thus enhancing its precarious security (see Map 7.1). Yet Israel had also aroused more bitter hostility among the Arabs and included an additional million Palestinians inside its borders, most of them living on the West Bank.

During the next few years, the focus of the Arab-Israeli dispute shifted as Arab states demanded the return of the occupied territories. Meanwhile, many Israelis argued that the new lands improved the security of the beleaguered state and should be retained. Concerned that the dispute might lead to a confrontation between the superpowers, the Nixon administration tried to achieve a peace settlement. The peace effort received a mild stimulus when Nasser died of a heart attack in September 1970 and was succeeded by his vice president, ex-general Anwar al-Sadat (1918–1981). Sadat soon showed himself to be more pragmatic than his predecessor, dropping the now irrelevant name United Arab Republic in favor of the Arab Republic of Egypt and replacing Nasser's socialist policies with a new strategy based on free enterprise and encouragement of Western investment. He also agreed to sign a peace treaty with Israel on the condition that Israel retire to its pre-1967 frontiers. Concerned that other Arab countries would refuse to make peace and take advantage of its presumed weakness, Israel refused.

Rebuffed in his offer of peace, smarting from criticism of his moderate stand from other Arab leaders, and increasingly concerned over Israeli plans to build permanent Jewish settlements in the occupied territories, Sadat attempted once again to renew Arab unity through a new confrontation with Israel. In 1973, on Yom Kippur (the Jewish Day of Atonement), an Israeli national holiday,

Egyptian forces suddenly launched an air and artillery attack on Israeli positions in the Sinai just east of the Suez Canal. Syrian armies attacked Israeli positions in the Golan Heights. After early Arab successes, the Israelis managed to recoup some of their losses on both fronts. As a superpower confrontation between the United States and the Soviet Union loomed, a cease-fire was finally reached.

In the next years, a fragile peace was maintained, marked by U.S. "shuttle diplomacy" (carried out by U.S. Secretary of State Henry Kissinger) and the rise to power in Israel of the militant Likud Party under Prime Minister Menachem Begin (1913–1992). The conflict now spread to Lebanon, where many Palestinians had found refuge and the PLO had set up its headquarters. Rising tension along the border was compounded by increasingly hostile disputes between Christians and Muslims over control of the capital, Beirut.

After his election as U.S. president in 1976, Jimmy Carter began to press for a compromise peace based on Israel's return of occupied Arab territories and Arab recognition of the state of Israel (an idea originally proposed by Kissinger). By now, Sadat was anxious to reduce his military expenses and announced his willingness to visit Jerusalem to seek peace. The meeting took place in November 1977, with no concrete results, but Sadat persisted. In September 1978, he and Begin met with Carter at Camp David in the United States. Israel agreed to withdraw from the Sinai, but not from other occupied territories unless it was recognized by other Arab countries.

The promise of the Camp David agreement was not fulfilled. One reason was the assassination of Sadat by Islamic militants in October 1981. But there were deeper causes, including the continued unwillingness of many Arab governments to recognize Israel and the Israeli government's encouragement of Jewish settlements in the occupied West Bank.

During the early 1980s, the militancy of the Palestinians increased, leading to rising unrest, popularly labeled the *intifada* (uprising) among PLO supporters living inside Israel. To control the situation, a new Israeli government under Prime Minister Itzhak Shamir invaded southern Lebanon to destroy PLO commando bases near the Israeli border. The invasion provoked international condemnation and further destabilized the perilous balance between Muslims and Christians in Lebanon. As the 1990s began, U.S.-sponsored peace talks opened between Israel and a number of its neighbors. The first major breakthrough came in 1993, when Israel and the PLO reached an agreement calling for Palestinian autonomy in selected areas of Israel in return for PLO recognition of the legitimacy of the Israeli state.

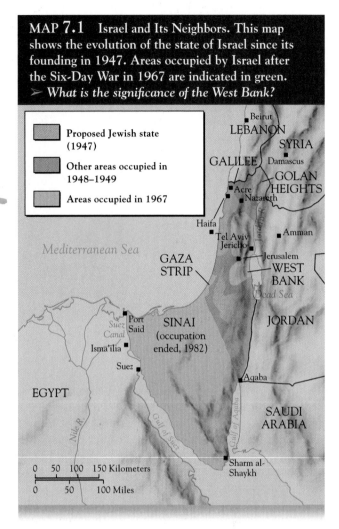

MAP **7.1**   Israel and Its Neighbors. This map shows the evolution of the state of Israel since its founding in 1947. Areas occupied by Israel after the Six-Day War in 1967 are indicated in green.
➤ *What is the significance of the West Bank?*

Progress in implementing the agreement, however, was slow. Terrorist attacks by Palestinian militants resulted in heavy casualties and shook the confidence of many Jewish citizens that their security needs could be protected under the agreement. At the same time, Jewish residents of the West Bank resisted the extension of Palestinian authority in the area. In November 1995, Prime Minister Yitzhak Rabin was assassinated by an Israeli opponent of the accords. National elections held a few months later led to the formation of a new government under Benjamin Netanyahu (b. 1949) which adopted a tougher stance in negotiations with the Palestinian Authority under Yasir Arafat.

When Netanyahu was replaced by a new Labour government under Prime Minister Ehud Barak (b. 1942) the latter promised to revitalize the peace process. Negotiations continued with the PLO and also got under way

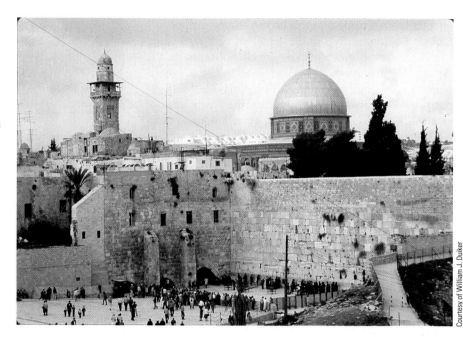

**THE TEMPLE MOUNT AT JERUSALEM.** The Temple Mount is one of the most sacred spots in the city of Jerusalem. Originally it was the site of a temple built during the reign of Solomon, king of the Jews, about 1000 B.C.E. The Western Wall of the temple is shown in the foreground. Beyond the wall is the Dome of the Rock complex, built on the place from which Muslims believe that Muhammad ascended to heaven. Sacred to both religions, the Temple Mount is now a major bone of contention between Muslims and Jews and a prime obstacle to a final settlement of the Arab-Israeli dispute.

with Syria over a peace settlement in Lebanon and the possible return of the Golan Heights. But in late 2000, peace talks broke down over the future of the city of Jerusalem, leading to massive riots by Palestinians, an Israeli crackdown, and the election of a new and more hard-line Israeli prime minister, the former Defense Minister Ariel Sharon (b. 1928). Sharon's ascent to leadership was accompanied by a rash of suicide attacks by Palestinians against Israeli targets, an intensive Israeli military crackdown on suspected terrorist sites inside Palestinian territory, and a dramatic increase in bloodshed on both sides. Although Saudi Arabia set forth a plan calling for full Arab recognition of the state of Israel in return for the latter's final withdrawal from occupied territories, prospects of reaching a peace agreement remain dim.

## Revolution in Iran

The Arab-Israeli dispute also provoked an international oil crisis. In 1960, a number of oil-producing states formed the Organization of Petroleum Exporting Countries (OPEC) to gain control over oil prices, but the organization was not recognized by the foreign oil companies. In the 1970s, a group of Arab oil states established the Organization of Arab Petroleum Exporting Countries (OAPEC) to use as a weapon to force Western governments to abandon pro-Israeli policies. During the 1973 Yom Kippur War, some OPEC nations announced significant increases in the price of oil to foreign countries. The price hikes were accompanied by an apparent oil shortage and created serious economic problems in the United States and Europe as well as in the Third World. They also proved to be a boon to oil-exporting countries, such as Libya, now under the leadership of the militantly anti-Western Colonel Muammar Qadhafi (b. 1942).

One of the key oil-exporting countries was Iran. Under the leadership of Shah Mohammad Reza Pahlavi (1919–1980), who had taken over from his father in 1941, Iran had become one of the richest countries in the Middle East. Although relations with the West had occasionally been fragile (especially after Prime Minister Mossadeq had briefly attempted to nationalize the oil industry in 1951), during the next twenty years, Iran became a prime ally of the United States in the Middle East. With encouragement from the United States, which hoped that Iran could become a force for stability in the Persian Gulf, the shah attempted to carry through a series of social and economic reforms to transform the country into the most advanced in the region.

Statistical evidence suggests that his efforts were succeeding. Per capita income increased dramatically, literacy rates improved, a modern communications infrastructure took shape, and an affluent middle class emerged in the capital of Tehran. Under the surface, however, trouble was brewing. Despite an ambitious land reform program, many peasants were still landless, unemployment among intellectuals was dangerously high, and the urban middle class was squeezed by high inflation. Housing costs had skyrocketed, provoked in part by the massive influx of foreigners attracted by oil money.

Some of the unrest took the form of religious discontent as millions of devout Muslims looked with distaste at a new Iranian civilization based on greed, sexual license, and material accumulation. Conservative *ulama* opposed rampant government corruption, the ostentation of the shah's court, and the extension of voting rights to women. Some opposition elements took to terrorism against wealthy Iranians or foreign residents in an attempt to provoke social and political disorder. In response, the shah's U.S.-trained security police, the *Savak*, imprisoned and sometimes tortured thousands of dissidents.

Leading the opposition was Ayatollah Ruholla Khomeini (1900–1989), an austere Shi'ite cleric who had been exiled to Iraq and then to France because of his outspoken opposition to the shah's regime. From Paris, Khomeini continued his attacks in print, on television, and in radio broadcasts. By the late 1970s, large numbers of Iranians began to respond to Khomeini's diatribes against the "satanic regime," and demonstrations by his supporters were repressed with ferocity by the police. But workers' strikes (some of them in the oil fields, which reduced government revenue) grew in intensity. In January 1979, the shah appointed a moderate, Shapur Bakhtiar, as prime minister and then left the country for medical treatment.

Bakhtiar attempted to conciliate the rising opposition and permitted Khomeini to return to Iran, where he demanded the government's resignation. With rising public unrest and incipient revolt within the army, the government collapsed and was replaced by a hastily formed Islamic republic. The new government, which was dominated by Shi'ite *ulama* under the guidance of Ayatollah Khomeini, immediately began to introduce traditional Islamic law. A new reign of terror ensued as supporters of the shah were rounded up and executed.

Though much of the outside world focused on the U.S. embassy in Tehran, where militants held a number of foreign hostages, the Iranian Revolution involved much more. In the eyes of the ayatollah and his followers, the United States was "the great Satan," the powerful protec-

tor of Israel, and the enemy of Muslim peoples everywhere. Furthermore, it was responsible for the corruption of Iranian society under the shah. Now Khomeini demanded that the shah be returned to Iran for trial and that the United States apologize for its acts against the Iranian people. In response, the Carter administration stopped buying Iranian oil and froze Iranian assets in the United States.

The effects of the disturbances in Iran quickly spread beyond its borders. Sunni militants briefly seized the holy places in Mecca and began to appeal to their brothers to launch similar revolutions in Islamic countries around the world, including far-off Malaysia and Indonesia. At the same time, ethnic unrest emerged among the Kurdish minorities along the border. In July 1980, the shah died of cancer in Cairo. With economic conditions in Iran rapidly deteriorating, the Islamic revolutionary government finally agreed to free the hostages in return for the release of Iranian assets in the United States. During the next few years, the intensity of the Iranian Revolution moderated slightly, as the government displayed a modest tolerance for a loosening of clerical control over freedom of expression and social activities. But rising criticism of rampant official corruption and a high rate of inflation sparked a new wave of government repression in the mid-1990s; newspapers were censored, the universities were purged of disloyal or "un-Islamic" elements, and religious militants raided private homes in search of blasphemous activities.

In 1997, the moderate Islamic cleric Mohammad Khatemi was elected president of Iran. Khatemi, whose surprising victory reflected a growing desire among many Iranians for a more pluralistic society open to the outside world, signaled the tantalizing possibility that Iran might wish to improve relations with the United States. During the next few years, press censorship was relaxed, leading to the emergence of several reformist newspapers and magazines, and restrictions on women's activities were relaxed. But the new president faced severe pressures from conservative elements to maintain the purity of Islamic laws, and in April 2000, several reformist publications were ordered to close by the judiciary for having printed materials that "disparaged Islam." Although student protests erupted into the streets in 2003, hard-liners continued to reject proposals to expand civil rights and limit the power of the clerics.

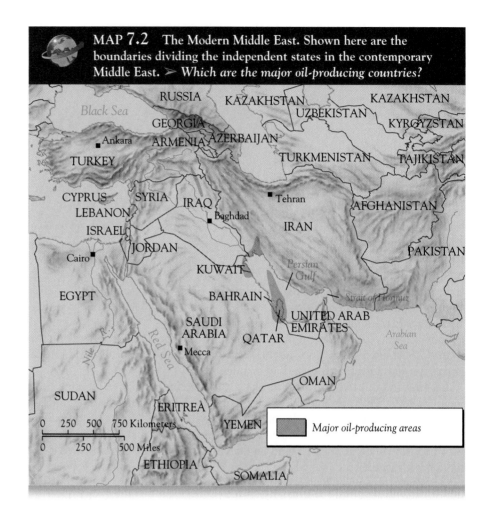

MAP 7.2 The Modern Middle East. Shown here are the boundaries dividing the independent states in the contemporary Middle East. ➤ *Which are the major oil-producing countries?*

Major oil-producing areas

## Crisis in the Gulf

Although much of the Iranians' anger was directed against the United States during the early phases of the revolution, Iran had equally hated enemies closer to home. To the north, the immense power of the Soviet Union, driven by atheistic communism, was viewed as a modern-day version of the Russian threat of previous centuries. To the west was a militant and hostile Iraq, now under the leadership of the ambitious Saddam Hussein (b. 1937). Problems from both directions appeared shortly after Khomeini's rise to power. Soviet military forces occupied Afghanistan to prop up a weak Marxist regime there. The following year, Iraqi forces suddenly attacked along the Iranian border.

Iraq and Iran had long had an uneasy relationship, fueled by religious differences (Iranian Islam is predominantly Shi'ite, while the ruling caste in Iraq is Sunni) and a perennial dispute over borderlands adjacent to the Persian Gulf, the vital waterway for the export of oil from both countries. Like several of its neighbors, Iraq had long dreamed of unifying the Arabs but had been hindered by internal factions and suspicion among its neighbors.

During the mid-1970s, Iran gave some support to a Kurdish rebellion in the mountains of Iraq. In 1975, the government of the shah agreed to stop aiding the rebels in return for territorial concessions at the head of the gulf. Five years later, however, the Kurdish revolt had been suppressed, and President Saddam Hussein, who had assumed power in Baghdad in 1979, accused Iran of violating the territorial agreement and launched an attack on his neighbor. The war was a bloody one, involving the use of poison gas against civilians and the employment of children to clear minefields, and lasted for nearly ten years. Other countries, including the two superpowers, watched nervously in case the conflict should spread throughout the region. Finally, with both sides virtually exhausted, a cease-fire was arranged in the fall of 1988.

The bitter conflict with Iran had not slaked Saddam Hussein's appetite for territorial expansion. In early August 1990, Iraqi military forces suddenly moved across the border and occupied the small neighboring country of Kuwait at the head of the gulf. The immediate pretext was the claim that Kuwait was pumping oil from fields inside Iraqi territory. Baghdad was also angry over the Kuwaiti government's demand for repayment of loans it had made to Iraq during the war with Iran. But the underlying reason was Iraq's contention that Kuwait was legally a part of Iraq. Kuwait had been part of the Ottoman Empire until the opening of the twentieth century, when the local prince had agreed to place his patrimony under British protection. When Iraq became independent in 1932, it claimed the area on the grounds that the state of Kuwait had been created by British imperialism, but opposition from major Western powers and other countries in the region, who feared the consequences of a "greater Iraq," prevented an Iraqi takeover.

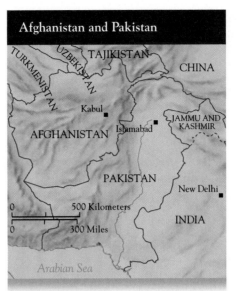

Afghanistan and Pakistan

The Iraqi invasion of Kuwait in 1990 sparked an international outcry, and the United States amassed an international force that liberated the country and destroyed a substantial part of Iraq's armed forces. President George H. W. Bush had promised the American people that U.S. troops would not fight with one hand tied behind their backs (a clear reference to the Vietnam War), but the allied forces did not occupy Baghdad at the end of the war because the allies feared that doing so would cause a total breakup of the country, an eventuality that would operate to the benefit of Iran. The allies hoped instead that the Hussein regime would be ousted by an internal revolt. In the meantime, harsh economic sanctions were imposed on the Iraqi government as the condition for peace. The anticipated overthrow of Saddam Hussein did not materialize, however, and his tireless efforts to evade the conditions of the cease-fire continued to bedevil the administrations of Presidents Bill Clinton and George W. Bush.

The terrorist attacks launched against the United States in September 2001 added a new dimension to the Middle Eastern equation. After the failure of the Soviet Union to quell the rebellion in Afghanistan during the 1980s, a fundamentalist Muslim group known as the Taliban seized power in Kabul and ruled the country with a fanaticism reminiscent of the Cultural Revolution in China. Backed by conservative religious forces in Pakistan, the Taliban provided a base of operations for Osama bin Laden's terrorist network. After the attacks of September 11, a coalition of forces led by the United States overthrew the Taliban and attempted to build a new and moderate government. But the country's long history of bitter internecine tribal warfare represents a severe challenge to such efforts.

In the meantime, the Bush administration, charging that Iraqi dictator Saddam Hussein not only had provided support to bin Laden's terrorist organization but also sought to develop weapons of mass destruction, threatened to invade Iraq and remove him from power. The plan, widely debated in the media and opposed by many of the United States' traditional allies, disquieted Arab leaders and fanned anti-American sentiment throughout the Muslim world. Nevertheless, in March 2003, American-led forces attacked Iraq and overthrew Hussein's regime. In the months that followed, occupation forces sought to restore stability to the country while setting forth plans to lay the foundations of a future democratic society. But although Saddam Hussein was later captured by U.S. troops, armed resistance by militant Muslim elements continues to hinder a return to stability.

# POLITICS IN THE CONTEMPORARY MIDDLE EAST

To many seasoned observers, U.S. plans in Iraq seem unrealistic, since democratic values are not deeply rooted in the region. Feudal rulers remain in power, notably on the Arabian peninsula. The kings of Saudi Arabia, for example, continue to rule by traditional precepts and, citing the distinctive character of Muslim political institutions, have been reluctant to establish representative political institutions. As a general rule, these rulers maintain and even enforce the strict observance of traditional customs. Religious police in Saudi Arabia are responsible for enforcing the Muslim dress code, maintaining the prohibition against alcohol, and making sure offices close during the time for prayer.

In other societies, traditional authority has been replaced by charismatic one-party rule or military dictatorships. Nasser's regime in Egypt is a good example of a

**RAID ON TIKRIT.** While the U.S.-led coalition won a rapid and relatively bloodless victory in Iraq in 2003, the transition to peace has been more complex, as resistance forces, supplemented by Islamic militants from abroad, have launched periodic attacks on occupation troops, as well as on Iraqis who cooperate with them, in an effort to destabilize the situation. Here U.S. infantry units carry out a raid on Tikrit, once a stronghold of support for the Saddam Hussein regime.

single-party state where the leader won political power by the force of his presence or personality. The Ayatollah Khomeini in Iran, Muammar Qadhafi in Libya, and Saddam Hussein in Iraq are other examples. Although their personal characteristics and images differ, all have sought to take advantage of their popular appeal.

In other instances, charismatic rule has given way to modernizing bureaucratic regimes. Examples include the governments of Syria, Yemen, Turkey, and Egypt since Nasser, where Anwar al-Sadat and his successor, Hosni Mubarak, have avoided dramatic personal appeal in favor of a regime focused on performance. Sometimes the authoritarian character of the regimes has been modified by some democratic tendencies, especially in Turkey, where free elections and the sharing of power have become more prevalent in recent years. A few Arab nations, such as Bahrain, Kuwait, and Jordan, have even engaged in limited forms of democratic experimentation.

In Syria, the death of longtime President Hafez al-Assad in 2000 led to a referendum that elevated his son Bashar al-Assad to the office. The new president indicated that he would not seek to continue the personality cult that had arisen during the reign of his father but warned that he would not encourage political reforms that might threaten the domination of the country's one-party political system. Noting that he would tolerate only "positive criticism" of government policies, he declared that "we have to have our own democracy to match our

history and culture, arising from the needs of our people and our reality."[2]

Only in Israel are democratic institutions firmly established. The Israeli system suffers from the proliferation of minor parties, some of which are able to dictate policy because their support is essential to keeping a government in power. In recent years, divisions between religious conservatives and secular elements within the Jewish community have become increasingly sharp, resulting in bitter disagreements over social policy and the negotiating process with the Palestinians. Nevertheless, the government generally reflects the popular will, and power is transferred by peaceful and constitutional means.

## The Economics of Oil

Few areas exhibit a greater disparity of individual and national wealth than the Middle East. Although millions live in abject poverty, a fortunate few rank among the wealthiest people in the world. The annual per capita income in Egypt is about $600 (in U.S. dollars), but in the tiny states of Kuwait and United Arab Emirates, it is nearly $20,000. Some of that disparity can be explained by the uneven distribution of fertile and barren land, but the primary reason, of course, is oil. Unfortunately for most of the peoples of the region, oil reserves are distributed unevenly and all too often are located in areas where the population density is low. Egypt and Turkey, with more than fifty million inhabitants apiece, have almost no oil reserves. The combined population of Kuwait, the United Arab Emirates, and Saudi Arabia is well under ten million people. This disparity in wealth inspired Nasser's quest for Arab unity (and perhaps Saddam Hussein's as well), but it has also posed a major obstacle to that unity.

The growing importance of petroleum has obviously been a boon to several of the states in the region, but it has been an unreliable one. Because of the violent fluctuations in the price of oil during the past thirty years, the income of oil-producing states has varied considerably. The spectacular increase in oil prices during the 1970s, when members of OPEC were able to raise the price of a barrel of oil from about $3 to $30, could not be sustained, forcing a number of oil-producing countries to scale back their economic development plans.

Not surprisingly, considering their different resources and political systems, the states of the Middle East have adopted diverse approaches to the problem of developing strong and stable economies. Some, like Nasser in Egypt and the leaders of the Ba'ath Party in Syria, attempted to create a form of Arab socialism, favoring a high level of government involvement in the economy to relieve the inequities of the free enterprise system. Others turned to the Western capitalist model to maximize growth, while using taxes or massive development projects to build a modern infrastructure, redistribute wealth, and maintain political stability and economic opportunity for all.

Whatever their approach, all the states have attempted to develop their economies in accordance with Islamic beliefs. Although the Koran has little to say about economics and can be variously understood as capitalist or socialist, it is clear in its opposition to charging interest and in its concern for the material welfare of the Muslim community, the *umma*. How these goals are to be achieved, however, is a matter of interpretation.

Socialist theories of economic development such as Nasser's were often suggested as a way to promote economic growth while meeting the requirements of Islamic doctrine. State intervention in the economic sector would bring about rapid development, while land redistribution and the nationalization or regulation of industry would prevent or minimize the harsh inequities of the marketplace. In general, however, the socialist approach has had little success, and most governments, including those of Egypt and Syria, have shifted to a more free enterprise approach while encouraging foreign investment to compensate for a lack of capital or technology.

Although the amount of arable land is relatively small, most countries in the Middle East rely to a certain degree on farming to supply food for their growing populations. In some cases, as in Egypt, Iran, Iraq, and Turkey, farmers

have until recently been a majority of the population. Often much of the fertile land was owned by wealthy absentee landlords, but land reform programs in several countries have attempted to alleviate this problem.

The most comprehensive and probably the most successful land reform program was instituted in Egypt, where Nasser and his successors managed to reassign nearly a quarter of all cultivable lands by limiting the amount a single individual could hold. Similar programs in Iran, Iraq, Libya, and Syria had less effect. In Iran, large landlords at the local and national level managed to limit the effects of the shah's reform program. After the 1979 revolution, many farmers seized lands forcibly from the landlords, giving rise to questions of ownership that the revolutionary government has tried with minimal success to resolve.

Agricultural productivity throughout the region has been plagued by the lack of water resources. With popu-

**≫ CAIRO: CITY OF MILLIONS.** Cairo, the capital of Egypt, is today a metropolis of over ten million people crowded into the lush but narrow delta of the Nile River. Shown here is a picture of downtown Cairo, where crowded apartment houses jostle for space with office buildings and mosques topped by the ubiquitous minaret.

Courtesy of William J. Duiker

lations growing at more than 2 percent annually on average in the Middle East (more than 3 percent in some countries), several governments have tried to increase the amount of water available for irrigation. Many attempts have been sabotaged by government ineptitude, political disagreements, and territorial conflicts, however. The best-known example is the Aswan Dam, which was built by Soviet engineers in the 1950s. The project was designed to control the flow of water throughout the Nile valley, but it has had a number of undesirable environmental consequences. Today, the dearth of water is reaching crisis proportions and is having a political impact as governments squabble over access to scarce water resources in the region. For example, disputes between Israel and its neighbors over water rights and between Iraq and its neighbors over the exploitation of the Tigris and the Euphrates have caused serious tensions in recent years.

Another way in which governments have attempted to deal with rapid population growth is to encourage emigration. Oil-producing states with small populations, such as Saudi Arabia and the United Arab Emirates, have imported labor from other countries in the region, mostly to work in the oil fields. By the mid-1980s, more than 40 percent of the population in those states was composed of foreign nationals, who often sent the bulk of their salaries back to their families in their home countries. The decline in oil revenues since the mid-1980s, however, has forced several governments to take measures to stabilize or reduce the migrant population. Since the Iraqi invasion, Kuwait, for example, has expelled all Palestinians and restricted migrant workers from other countries to three-year stays.

## The Islamic Revival

In recent years, many developments in the Middle East have been described in terms of a resurgence of traditional values and customs in response to the pressure of Western influence. Indeed, some conservative religious forces in the area have consciously attempted to replace foreign culture and values with allegedly "pure" Islamic forms of belief and behavior.

But the Islamic revival that has taken place in the contemporary Middle East is not a simple dichotomy between traditional and modern, native and foreign, or irrational and rational. In the first place, many Muslims in the Middle East believe that Islamic values and modern ways are not incompatible and may even be mutually reinforcing in some ways. Second, the resurgence of what are sometimes called "fundamentalist" Islamic groups may, in a Middle Eastern context, appear to be a rational

and practical response to self-destructive practices, such as corruption and hedonism, drunkenness, prostitution, and the use of drugs. Finally, the reassertion of Islamic values can be a means of establishing cultural identity and fighting off the overwhelming impact of Western ideas.

Initially, many Muslim intellectuals responded to Western influence by trying to reconcile the perceived differences between tradition and modernity and by creating an "updated" set of Islamic beliefs and practices that would not clash with the demands of the modern world. This process took place in most Islamic societies, but it was especially prevalent in Turkey, Egypt, and Iran. Mustapha Kemal Atatürk embraced the strategy when he attempted to secularize the Islamic religion in the new Turkish republic. The Turkish model was followed by Shah Reza Khan and his son Mohammad Reza Pahlavi in Iran and then by Nasser in postwar Egypt, all of whom attempted to make use of Islamic values while asserting the primacy of other issues such as political and economic development. Religion, in effect, had become the handmaiden of political power, national identity, and economic prosperity.

For obvious reasons, these secularizing trends were particularly noticeable among the political, intellectual, and economic elites in urban areas. They had less influence in the countryside, among the poor, and among devout elements within the *ulama*. Many of the latter believed that Western secular trends in the major cities had given birth to regrettable and even repugnant social attitudes and behavioral patterns, such as political and economic corruption, sexual promiscuity, individualism, and the prevalence of alcohol, pornography, and drugs. Although such practices had long existed in the Middle East, they were now far more visible and socially acceptable.

This reaction began early in the century and intensified after World War I, when the Western presence increased. In 1928, devout Muslims in Egypt formed the Muslim Brotherhood as a means of promoting personal piety. Later, the movement began to take a more activist approach, including the eventual use of terrorism by a radical minority. Despite Nasser's surface commitment to Islamic ideals and Arab unity, some Egyptians were fiercely opposed to his policies and regarded his vision of Arab socialism as a betrayal of Islamic principles. Nasser reacted harshly and executed a number of his leading opponents.

The movement to return to Islamic purity strengthened after World War II and reached its zenith in Iran. It is not surprising that Iran took the lead in light of its long tradition of ideological purity within the Shi'ite sect as well as the uncompromisingly secular character of the shah's reforms in the postwar era. In revolutionary Iran, traditional Islamic beliefs are all-pervasive and extend into education, clothing styles, social practices, and the legal system.

While the political aspects of the Iranian Revolution inspired distrust and suspicion among political elites elsewhere in the region, its cultural and social effects were profound. Although no other state in the Middle East adopted the violent approach to cultural reform applied in Iran, Iranian ideas have spread throughout the area and affected social and cultural behavior in many ways. In Algeria, the political influence of fundamentalist Islamic groups has grown substantially and enabled them to win a stunning victory in the national elections in 1992. When the military stepped in to cancel the second round of elections and crack down on the militants, the latter responded with a campaign of terrorism against moderates that has claimed thousands of lives.

A similar trend has emerged in Egypt, where militant groups such as the Muslim Brotherhood have engaged in terrorism, including the assassination of Sadat and more recent attacks on foreign tourists, who are considered carriers of corrupt Western influence. In 1994, the prominent novelist Naguid Mahfouz was stabbed outside his home, apparently in response to earlier writings that were deemed blasphemous of Muslim belief.

Even in Turkey, generally considered the most secular of Islamic societies, a militant political group, known as the Islamic Welfare Party, took power in a coalition government formed in 1996. Worried moderates voiced their concern that the secular legacy of Kemal Atatürk was being eroded, and eventually, the new prime minister, Necmettin Erbakan, agreed to resign under heavy pressure from the military. Uncomfortable with the militancy of Arab neighbors, Turkey maintains close ties with the United States and is currently adopting reforms to extend human rights and freedom of expression in the hope of gaining entry into the European Union. But religious and economic discontent simmers beneath the surface.

## Women and Islam

Nowhere have the fault lines between tradition and modernity in Muslim societies in the Middle East been so sharp as in the ongoing debate over the role of women. At the beginning of the twentieth century, women's place in Middle Eastern society had changed little since the days of the Prophet Muhammad. Women were secluded in their homes and had few legal, political, or social rights.

Early in the twentieth century, inspired in part by the Western presence, a "modernist" movement arose in several countries in the Middle East with the aim of bringing Islamic social values and legal doctrine into line with Western values and attitudes. Advocates of modernist views contended that Islamic doctrine was not inherently opposed to women's rights and that the teachings of Muhammad and his successors had actually broadened them in significant ways. To modernists, Islamic traditions such as female seclusion, wearing the veil, and even polygamy were pre-Islamic folk traditions that had been tolerated in the early Islamic era and continued to be practiced in later centuries.

During the first decades of the twentieth century, such views had considerable impact on a number of Middle Eastern societies, including Turkey and Iran. As we have seen, greater rights for women were a crucial element in the social revolution promoted by Mustapha Kemal Atatürk in Turkey. In Iran, Shah Reza Khan and his son granted female suffrage and encouraged the education of women. In Egypt, a vocal feminist movement arose in educated women's circles in Cairo as early as the 1920s.

Modernist views had somewhat less effect in other Islamic states, such as Iraq, Jordan, Morocco, and Algeria, where traditional views of women continued to prevail in varying degrees. Particularly in rural areas, notions of women's liberation made little headway. Most conservative by far was Saudi Arabia, where women were not only segregated and expected to wear the veil in public but were also restricted in education and forbidden to drive automobiles (see the box on p. 156).

Until recently, the general trend in urban areas of the Middle East was toward a greater role for women. This was particularly the case in Egypt and in Iran, where the liberal policies of the shah encouraged Western attitudes toward sexual equality. With the exception of conservative religious communities, women in Israel have achieved substantial equality with men and are active in politics, the professions, and even the armed forces. Golda Meir (1898–1978), prime minister of Israel from 1969 to 1974, became an international symbol of the ability of women to be world leaders.

Beginning in the 1970s, however, there was a shift toward a more traditional approach to gender roles in many Middle Eastern societies. It was accompanied by attacks on the growing Western influence within the media and on the social habits of young people. The reactions were especially strong in Iran, where attacks by religious conservatives on the growing role of women contributed to the emotions underlying the Iranian Revolution of 1979. Iranian women were instructed to wear the veil and to dress modestly in public. Films produced in postrevolutionary Iran expressed the new morality. They rarely featured women, and when they did, physical contact between men and women was prohibited. Still, Iranian women have many freedoms that they lacked before the

# KEEPING THE CAMEL OUT OF THE TENT

*Almighty God created sexual desire in ten parts; then he gave nine parts to women and one to men." So pronounced Ali, Muhammad's son-in-law, as he explained why women are held morally responsible as the instigators of sexual intercourse. Consequently, over the centuries Islamic women have been secluded, veiled, and in many cases genitally mutilated to safeguard male virtue. Women are forbidden to look directly at, speak to, or touch a man prior to marriage. Even today, they are often sequestered at home or limited to strictly segregated areas away from all male contact. Women normally pray at home or in an enclosed antechamber of the mosque so that their physical presence will not disturb men's spiritual concentration.*

*Especially limiting today are the laws governing women's behavior in Saudi Arabia. Schooling for girls has never been compulsory because fathers believe that "educating women is like allowing the nose of the camel into the tent; eventually the beast will edge in and take up all the room inside." The country did not establish its first girls' school until 1956. The following description of Saudi women is from* Nine Parts of Desire: The Hidden World of Islamic Women, *by journalist Geraldine Brooks.*

## GERALDINE BROOKS,
## NINE PARTS OF DESIRE

Women were first admitted to university in Saudi Arabia in 1962, and all women's colleges remain strictly segregated. Lecture rooms come equipped with closed-circuit TVs and telephones, so women students can listen to a male professor and question him by phone, without having to contaminate themselves by being seen by him. When the first dozen women graduated from university in 1973, they were devastated to find that their names hadn't been printed on the commencement program. The old tradition, that it dishon-

ors women to mention them, was depriving them of recognition they believed they'd earned. The women and their families protested, so a separate program was printed and a segregated graduation ceremony was held for the students' female relatives. . . .

But while opening of women's universities widened access to higher learning for women, it also made the educational experience much shallower. Before 1962, many progressive Saudi families had sent their daughters abroad for education. They had returned to the kingdom not only with a degree but with experience of the outside world. . . . Now a whole generation of Saudi women have completed their education entirely within the country. . . .

Lack of opportunity for education abroad means that Saudi women are trapped in the confines of an education system that still lags men's. Subjects such as geology and petroleum engineering—tickets to influential jobs in Saudi Arabia's oil economy—remain closed to women. . . . Few women's colleges have their own libraries, and libraries shared with men's schools are either entirely off limits to women or open to them only one day per week. . . .

But women and men [take] the same degree examinations. Professors quietly acknowledge the women's scores routinely outstrip the men's. "It's no surprise," said one woman professor. "Look at their lives. The boys have their cars, they can spend the evenings cruising the streets with their friends, sitting in cafés, buying black-market alcohol and drinking all night. What do the girls have? Four walls and their books. For them, education is everything."

Source: Geraldine Brooks, *Nine Parts of Desire: The Hidden World of Islamic Women* (New York: Doubleday, 1996).

---

twentieth century; for example, they can attend a university, receive military training, vote, practice birth control, and write fiction.

The Iranian Revolution helped promote a revival of traditional attitudes toward women in other Islamic societies. Women in secular countries such as Egypt, Turkey, and far-off Malaysia have begun to dress more modestly in public, while public attacks on open sexuality in the media have become increasingly frequent.

Women have won some small victories in their struggle for equal rights in the Middle East. In 1999, a governmental edict declared that women would be granted

the right to vote in Kuwait, and women have been given an equal right to divorce.

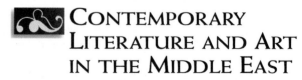 ## CONTEMPORARY LITERATURE AND ART IN THE MIDDLE EAST

As in other areas of Asia and Africa, the encounter with the West in the nineteenth and twentieth centuries stimulated a cultural renaissance in the Middle East. Muslim

**IRANIAN WOMEN PRACTICING SOCCER.** Despite the restriction of having to cover their bodies in public, young Iranian women play soccer and other sports, attend schools and universities, and partake in other activities of the modern world. Here we see young women playing a game of soccer in their black-hooded garments. Although they rarely did so before the Islamic Revolution, today about two million Iranian women take part in sports.

authors translated Western works into Arabic and Persian and began to experiment with new literary forms. The advent of modern newspapers and magazines eliminated the traditional differences between the oral and written languages. The resulting fused language included colloquial speech, borrowed Western words, and ancient words resurrected from indigenous languages.

The new literature dealt with a number of new themes. The rise in national consciousness stimulated interest in historical traditions. Writers also switched from religious to secular themes and addressed the problems of this world and the means of rectifying them. Furthermore, literature was no longer the exclusive domain of the elite but was increasingly written for the broader mass of the population.

Iran has produced one of the most prominent national literatures in the contemporary Middle East. Since World War II, Iranian literature has been hampered somewhat by political considerations, since it has been expected to serve first the Pahlavi monarchy and more recently the Islamic Republic. Nevertheless, Iranian writers are among the most prolific in the region and often write in prose, which has finally been accepted as the equal of poetry. Perhaps the most outstanding Iranian author of the twentieth century was short-story writer Sadeq Hedayat. Hedayat was obsessed with the frailty and absurdity of life and wrote with compassion about the problems of ordinary human beings. Frustrated and disillusioned at the government's suppression of individual liberties, he committed suicide in 1951. Like Japan's Mishima Yukio,

Hedayat later became a cult figure among his country's youth.

Despite the male-oriented nature of Iranian society, many of the new writers were women. Since the revolution, the chador, or veiled garment, has become the central metaphor in Iranian women's writing. Advocates praise the veil as the last bastion of defense against Western cultural imperialism. Behind the veil, the Islamic woman can breathe freely, unpolluted by foreign exploitation and moral corruption. They see the veil as the courageous woman's weapon against Western efforts to dominate the Iranian soul. Other Iranian women, however, consider the veil a "mobile prison" or an oppressive anachronism from the Dark Ages. A few use the pen as a weapon in a crusade to liberate their sisters and enable them to make their own choices. As one writer, Sousan Azadi, expressed it, "As I pulled the chador over me, I felt a heaviness descending over me. I was hidden and in hiding. There was nothing visible left of Sousan Azadi."[3]

Like Iran, Egypt in the twentieth century has experienced a flowering of literature accelerated by the establishment of the Egyptian republic in the early 1950s. The most illustrious contemporary Egyptian writer is Naguib Mahfouz (b. 1911), who won the Nobel Prize in literature in 1988. His *Cairo Trilogy*, published in 1952, chronicles three generations of a merchant family in Cairo during the tumultuous years between the two world wars. Mahfouz is particularly adept at blending panoramic historical events with the intimate lives of ordinary human beings with great compassion and energy. Unlike many other modern writers, his message is essentially optimistic and reflects his hope that religion and science can work together for the overall betterment of humankind.

No women writer has played a more active role in exposing the physical and psychological grievances of Egyptian women than Nawal el-Saadawi (b. 1931). For decades, she has battled against the injustices of religious fundamentalism and a male-dominated society—even enduring imprisonment for promoting her cause. In *Two Women in One* (1985), el-Saadawi follows the struggle of a young university student as she rebels against the life her father has programmed for her, striking out instead on an unchartered independent destiny.

The emergence of a modern Turkish literature can be traced to the establishment of the republic in 1923. The most popular contemporary writer is Orhan Pamuk (b. 1952), whose novels attempt to capture Turkey's unique blend of cultures. "I am living in a culture," he writes, "where the clash of East and West, or the harmony of East and West, is the lifestyle. That is Turkey."[4] In his novel *The Black Book* (1994), Pamuk resuscitates Istanbul's past from the multitude of Byzantine, Ottoman, and republican artifacts strewn in the muddy depths of the Bosporus.

Although Israeli literature arises from a totally different tradition from that of its neighbors, it shares with them certain contemporary characteristics and a concern for ordinary human beings. Early writers identified with the aspirations of the new nation, trying to find a sense of order in the new reality, voicing terrors from the past and hope for the future. Some contemporary Israeli authors, however, have refused to serve as promoters for Zionism and are speaking out on sensitive national issues. The internationally renowned novelist Amos Oz (b. 1939), for example, is a vocal supporter of peace with the Palestinians. Oz is a member of Peace Now and the author of a political tract titled *Israel, Palestine, and Peace*. In an interview, Oz accused both Ariel Sharon and Yasir Arafat of being "immovable, handcuffed to the past and to each other."[5] With the Arabs feeling victimized by colonialism and the Jews by Nazi Germany, each side believes that it alone is the rightful proprietor of ancient Palestine. For Oz, the only solution is compromise, which, however unsatisfactory for both sides, is preferable to mutual self-destruction.

Like literature, the art of the modern Middle East has been profoundly influenced by its exposure to Western culture. Reflecting their hopes for the new nation, Israeli painters sought to bring to life the sentiments of pioneers arriving in a promised land. Many attempted to capture the longing for community expressed in the Israeli commune, or kibbutz. Others searched for the roots of Israeli culture in the history of the Jewish people or in the horrors of the Holocaust. The experience of the Holocaust has attracted particular attention from sculptors, who work in wood and metal as well as stone.

The popular music of the contemporary Middle East has also been strongly influenced by that of the modern West, but to different degrees in different countries. In Israel, many contemporary young rock stars voice lyrics as irreverent toward the traditions of their elders as those of Europe and the United States do. One idol of many Israeli young people, rock star Aviv Ghefen, declares himself to be "a person of no values," and his music carries a shock value that attacks the country's political and social shibboleths with abandon. The rock music popular among Palestinians, on the other hand, makes greater use of Arab musical motifs and is closely tied to a political message. One recent recording, "The Song of the Engineer," lauds Yehia Ayash, a Palestinian accused of manufacturing many of the explosive devices used in terrorist attacks on Israeli citizens. The lyrics have their own shock value: "Spread the flame of revolution. Your explosive will wipe the enemy out, like a volcano, a torch, a banner." When one Palestinian rock leader from the Gaza Strip was asked why his group employed a musical style that originated in the West, he explained, "For us, this is a tool like any other. Young people in Gaza like our music, they listen to us, they buy our cassettes, and so they spread our message."

# CONCLUSION

The Middle East is one of the most unstable regions in the world today. In part, this turbulence is due to the continued interference of outsiders attracted by the massive oil reserves under the parched wastes of the Arabian peninsula and in the vicinity of the Persian Gulf. Oil is both a blessing and a curse to the peoples of the region.

Another factor contributing to the volatility of the Middle East is the tug-of-war between the sense of ethnic identity in the form of nationalism and the intense longing to be part of a broader Islamic community, a dream that dates back to the time of the Prophet Muhammad. The desire to create that community—a vision threatened by the presence of the alien state of Israel—inspired Gamal Abdul Nasser in the 1950s and Ayatollah Khomeini in the 1970s and 1980s and probably motivated many of the actions of Saddam Hussein in Iraq.

A final reason for the turmoil in the Middle East is the intense debate over the role of religion in civil society. It has been customary in recent years for Western commentators to label Muslim efforts to return to a purer form of Islam as fanatical and extremist, reflecting a misguided attempt to reverse the course of history, and there is no doubt that many of the legal and social restrictions now being enforced in various Muslim countries in the Middle East appear excessively harsh to outside observers. But it is important to remember that Muslim societies are not alone in deploring the sense of moral decline that is perceived to be occurring in societies throughout the world. Nor are they alone in advocating a restoration of traditional religious values as a means of reversing the trend. Movements dedicated to such purposes are appearing in many other societies (including Israel and the United States) and can be viewed as an understandable reaction to the rapid and often bewildering changes that are taking place in the contemporary world. Not infrequently,

members of such groups turn to violence as a means of making their point.

Whatever the reasons, it is clear that a deep-seated sense of anger is surging through much of the Islamic world today, an anger that transcends specific issues like the situation in Iraq or the Arab-Israeli dispute. Although economic privation and political oppression are undoubtedly important factors, the roots of Muslim resentment, as historian Bernard Lewis has pointed out, lie in a historical sense of humiliation that first emerged centuries ago, when Arab hegemony in the Mediterranean region was replaced by European domination, and continues today. The world is reaping the harvest of that long-cultivated bitterness, and the consequences cannot be foreseen.

## INFOTRAC COLLEGE EDITION

Visit source collections at **http://infotrac.thomsonlearning.com**, and use the Search function with the following key terms:

Israel history
Nasser
Palestine

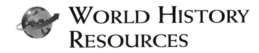

## WORLD HISTORY RESOURCES

Visit the *The World Since World War II* Companion Web site for resources specific to this textbook:

**http://history.wadsworth.com/duiker_wwii/**

The Wadsworth World History Resource Center at **http://history.wadsworth.com/world/** offers a variety of tools to help you succeed in this course, including access to quizzes; images; documents; interactive simulations, maps, and timelines; movie explorations; and a wealth of other sources.

# CHAPTER NOTES

1. Quoted in R. R. Andersen, R. F. Seibert, and J. G. Wagner, *Politics and Change in the Middle East: Sources of Conflict and Accommodation*, 4th ed. (Englewood Cliffs, N.J., 1982), p. 51.
2. *New York Times*, July 18, 2000.
3. S. Azadi, with A. Ferrante, *Out of Iran* (London, 1987), p. 223, quoted in *Stories by Iranian Women Since the Revolution*, ed. S. Sullivan (Austin, Tex., 1991), p. 13.
4. *New York Times*, August 27, 2003.
5. Amos Oz, interview, *Jim Lehrer NewsHour*, PBS, January 23, 2002.

# NATIONALISM TRIUMPHANT: THE EMERGENCE OF INDEPENDENT STATES IN SOUTH AND SOUTHEAST ASIA

First-time visitors to the Malaysian capital of Kuala Lumpur are astonished to observe a pair of twin towers thrusting up above the surrounding buildings into the clouds. The Petronas Towers rise 1,483 feet from ground level, leading to claims by Malaysian officials that they are the world's tallest buildings, at least for the time being.

More than an architectural achievement, the towers announced the emergence of Asia as a major player on the international scene. It is probably no accident that the foundations were laid on the site of the Selangor Cricket Club, symbol of colonial hegemony in Southeast Asia. "These towers," commented one local official, "will do wonders for Asia's self-esteem and confidence, which I think is very important, and which I think at this moment are at the point of takeoff."[1]

Slightly more than a year after that remark, Malaysia and several of its neighbors were mired in a financial crisis that threatened to derail their rapid advance to economic affluence and severely undermined the "self-esteem" that the Petronas Towers were meant to symbolize. Today, several years after the buildings were completed, many of their offices remain unoccupied.

The Petronas Towers, then, serve as a vivid demonstration in steel and glass of the dual face of modern Asia: a region seeking to compete with the advanced nations of the West while still struggling to overcome a legacy of economic underdevelopment and colonial rule. As Asian leaders have discovered, it is a path strewn with hidden obstacles.

# SOUTH ASIA

In 1947, nearly two centuries of British colonial rule came to an end when two new independent nations, India and Pakistan, came into being. Under British authority, the subcontinent of South Asia had been linked ever more closely to the global capitalist economy. Yet as in other areas of Asia and Africa, the experience brought only limited benefits to the local peoples; little industrial development took place, and the bulk of the profits went into the pockets of Western entrepeneurs.

For half a century, nationalist forces had been seeking reforms in colonial policy and the eventual overthrow of colonial power. But the peoples of South Asia did not regain their independence until after World War II.

## The End of the British Raj

During the 1930s, the nationalist movement in India was severely shaken by factional disagreements between Hindus and Muslims. The outbreak of World War II subdued these sectarian clashes, but they erupted again after the war ended in 1945. Battles between Hindus and Muslims broke out in several cities, and Mohammed Ali Jinnah, leader of the Muslim League, demanded the creation of a separate state for each. Meanwhile, the Labour Party, which had long been critical of the British colonial legacy on both moral and economic grounds, had come to power in Britain, and the new prime minister, Clement Attlee, announced that power would be transferred to "responsible Indian hands" by June 1948.

But the imminence of independence did not dampen communal strife. As riots escalated, the British reluctantly accepted the inevitability of partition and declared that on August 15, 1947, two independent nations— Hindu India and Muslim Pakistan—would be established. Pakistan would be divided between the main area of Muslim habitation in the Indus River valley in the west and a separate territory in east Bengal 2,000 miles to the east. Although Mahatma Gandhi warned that partition would provoke "an orgy of blood,"[2] he was increasingly regarded as a figure of the past, and his views were ignored.

The British instructed the rulers in the princely states to choose which state they would join by August 15, but problems arose in predominantly Hindu Hyderabad, where the nawab was a Muslim, and mountainous Kashmir, where a Hindu prince ruled over a Muslim population. After independence was declared, the flight of millions of Hindus and Muslims across the borders led to violence and the death of more than a million people. One of the casualties was Gandhi, who was assassinated

on January 30, 1948, as he was going to morning prayer. The assassin, a Hindu militant, was apparently motivated by Gandhi's opposition to a Hindu India.

## Independent India

With independence, the Indian National Congress, now renamed the Congress Party, moved from opposition to the responsibility of power under Jawaharlal Nehru, the new prime minister. The prospect must have been intimidating. The vast majority of India's 400 million people were poor and illiterate. The new nation encompassed a bewildering number of ethnic groups and fourteen major languages. Although Congress leaders spoke bravely of building a new nation, Indian society still bore the scars of past wars and divisions.

The government's first problem was to resolve disputes left over from the transition period. The rulers of Hyderabad and Kashmir had both followed their own preferences rather than the wishes of their subject populations. Nehru was determined to include both states within India. In 1948, Indian troops invaded Hyderabad and annexed the area. India was also able to seize most of Kashmir, but at the cost of creating an intractable problem that has poisoned relations with Pakistan to the present day.

### AN EXPERIMENT IN DEMOCRATIC SOCIALISM

Under Nehru's leadership, India adopted a political system on the British model, with a figurehead president and a parliamentary form of government. A number of political parties operated legally, but the Congress Party, with its enormous prestige and charismatic leadership, was dominant at both the central and the local levels. It was ably assisted by the Indian civil service, which had been created during the era of British colonial rule and provided solid expertise in the arcane art of bureaucracy.

Nehru had been influenced by British socialism and patterned his economic policy roughly after the program of the British Labour Party. The state took over ownership of the major industries and resources, transportation, and utilities, while private enterprise was permitted at the local and retail levels. Farmland remained in private hands, but rural cooperatives were officially encouraged. The government also sought to avoid excessive dependence on foreign investment and technological assistance. All businesses were required by law to have majority Indian ownership.

In other respects, Nehru was a devotee of Western materialism. He was convinced that to succeed, India must

# TWO VISIONS FOR INDIA

*Although Jawaharlal Nehru and Mohandas Gandhi agreed on their desire for an independent India, their visions of the future of their homeland were dramatically different. Nehru favored industrialization to build material prosperity, whereas Gandhi praised the simple virtues of manual labor. The first excerpt is from a speech by Nehru; the second is from a letter written by Gandhi to Nehru.*

## NEHRU'S SOCIALIST CREED

I am convinced that the only key to the solution of the world's problems and of India's problems lies in socialism, and when I use this word I do so not in a vague humanitarian way but in the scientific economic sense. . . . I see no way of ending the poverty, the vast unemployment, the degradation and the subjection of the Indian people except through socialism. That involves vast and revolutionary changes in our political and social structure, the ending of vested interests in land and industry, as well as the feudal and autocratic Indian states system. That means the ending of private property, except in a restricted sense, and the replacement of the present profit system by a higher ideal of cooperative service. . . . In short, it means a new civilization, radically different from the present capitalist order. Some glimpse we can have of this new civilization in the territories of the U.S.S.R. Much has happened there which has pained me greatly and with which I disagree, but I look upon that great and fascinating unfolding of a new order and a new civilization as the most promising feature of our dismal age.

## A LETTER TO JAWAHARLAL NEHRU

I believe that if India, and through India the world, is to achieve real freedom, then sooner or later we shall have to go and live in the villages—in huts, not in palaces. Millions of people can never live in cities and palaces in comfort and peace. Nor can they do so by killing one another, that is, by resorting to violence and untruth. . . . We can have the vision of . . . truth and nonviolence only in the simplicity of the villages. That simplicity resides in the spinning wheel and what is implied by the spinning wheel. . . .

You will not be able to understand me if you think that I am talking about the villages of today. My ideal village still exists only in my imagination. . . . In this village of my dreams the villager will not be dull—he will be all awareness. He will not live like an animal in filth and darkness. Men and women will live in freedom, prepared to face the whole world. There will be no plague, no cholera, and no smallpox. Nobody will be allowed to be idle or to wallow in luxury. Everyone will have to do body labor. Granting all this, I can still envisage a number of things that will have to be organized on a large scale. Perhaps there will even be railways and also post and telegraph offices. I do not know what things there will be or will not be. Nor am I bothered about it. If I can make sure of the essential thing, other things will follow in due course. But if I give up the essential thing, I give up everything.

Source: From *Sources of Indian Tradition* by William De Bary. Copyright © 1988 by Columbia University Press, New York, and excerpt from *Gandhi in India: In His Own Words*, Martin Green, ed. Copyright © 1987 by Navajian Trust, Lebanon, NH: University Press of New England.

industrialize. In advocating industrialization, Nehru departed sharply from Gandhi, who believed that materialism was morally corrupting and that only simplicity and nonviolence (as represented by the traditional Indian village and the symbolic spinning wheel) could save India, and the world itself, from self-destruction (see the box above). Gandhi, Nehru complained, "just wants to spin and weave."

The primary themes of Nehru's foreign policy were anticolonialism and antiracism. Under his guidance, India took a neutral stance in the Cold War and sought to provide leadership to all newly independent nations in Asia, Africa, and Latin America. It also sought good relations with the new People's Republic of China. India's neutrality put it at odds with the United States, which during the 1950s was trying to mobilize all nations against what it viewed as the menace of international communism.

Relations with Pakistan continued to be troubled. India refused to consider Pakistan's claim to Kashmir, even though the majority of the population there was Muslim. Tension between the two countries persisted, erupting into war in 1965. In 1971, when riots against the Pakistani government broke out in East Pakistan, India intervened on the side of East Pakistan, which declared its independence as the new nation of Bangladesh (see Map 8.1).

## THE POST-NEHRU ERA

Nehru's death in 1964 aroused concern that Indian democracy was dependent on the Nehru mystique. When his successor, a Congress Party veteran, died in 1966, Congress leaders selected Nehru's daughter, Indira Gandhi (no relation to Mahatma Gandhi), as the new

**MAP 8.1** Modern South Asia. This map shows the boundaries of all the states in contemporary South Asia. India, the largest in area and population, is highlighted by darker shading. ➤ *How many countries are there in the region?*

Map labels: KAZAKHSTAN, MONGOLIA, KYRGYZSTAN, TAJIKISTAN, TURKMENISTAN, CHINA, AFGHANISTAN, Srinagar, JAMMU, KASHMIR, Amritsar, Simla, PAKISTAN, Chandigarh, NEPAL, BHUTAN, IRAN, New Delhi, Leh, Karachi, Agra, Lucknow, Jaipur, Kanpur, Patna, Allahabad, Benares, Ahmadabad, Bhopal, Calcutta, BURMA, Bhubaneswar, BANGLADESH, *Arabian Sea*, Bombay, Hyderabad, Goa, Guntakal, *Bay of Bengal*, Bangalore, Madras, ANDAMAN AND NICOBAR IS., Calicut, Pondicherry, Port Blair, *Indian Ocean*, Cochin, Madurai, Trivandrum, SRI LANKA, INDONESIA

0   1000 Kilometers
0   600 Miles

A minority government of procapitalist parties was formed, but within two years, Gandhi was back in power. She now faced a new challenge, however, in the rise of religious strife. The most dangerous situation was in the Punjab, where militant Sikhs were demanding autonomy or even independence from India. Gandhi did not shrink from a confrontation and attacked Sikh rebels hiding in their Golden Temple in the city of Amritsar. The incident aroused widespread anger among the Sikh community, and in 1984, Sikh members of Gandhi's personal bodyguard assassinated her.

By now, Congress politicians were convinced that the party could not remain in power without a member of the Nehru family at the helm. Gandhi's son Rajiv, a commercial airline pilot with little interest in politics, was persuaded to replace his mother as prime minister. Rajiv lacked the strong ideological and political convictions of his mother and grandfather and allowed a greater role for private enterprise. But his government was criticized for cronyism, inefficiency, and corruption, as well as insensitivity to the poor.

Rajiv Gandhi also sought to play a role in regional affairs, mediating a dispute between the government in Sri Lanka and Tamil rebels (known as the "Elam Tigers") who were ethnically related to the majority population in southern India. The decision cost him his life: while campaigning for reelection in 1991, he was assassinated by a member of the Tiger organization. India faced the future without a member of the Nehru family as prime minister.

During the early 1990s, Congress remained the leading party, but the powerful hold it had once had on the Indian electorate was gone. New parties, such as the militantly Hindu Bharata Janata Party (BJP), actively vied with Congress for control of the central and state governments. Growing political instability at the center was accompanied by rising tensions between Hindus and Muslims.

When a coalition government formed under Congress leadership collapsed, the BJP, under Prime Minister A. B. Vajpayee, ascended to power and played on Hindu sensibilities to build its political base. Rajiv Gandhi's Italian-born wife Sonia has taken over the leadership of the Congress Party to improve its political fortunes.

## The Land of the Pure: Pakistan Since Independence

When in August 1947, Pakistan achieved independence, it was, unlike its neighbor India, in all respects a new nation, based on religious conviction rather than historical or ethnic tradition. The unique state united two separate territories 2,000 miles apart. West Pakistan, including the

prime minister. Gandhi was inexperienced in politics, but she quickly showed the steely determination of her father.

Like Nehru, Gandhi embraced democratic socialism and a policy of neutrality in foreign affairs, but she was more activist than her father. To combat rural poverty, she nationalized banks, provided loans to peasants on easy terms, built low-cost housing, distributed land to the landless, and introduced electoral reforms to enfranchise the poor.

Gandhi was especially worried by India's growing population and in an effort to curb the growth rate adopted a policy of enforced sterilization. This policy proved unpopular, however, and, along with growing official corruption and Gandhi's authoritarian tactics, led to her defeat in the general election of 1975, the first time the Congress Party had failed to win a majority at the national level.

Indus River basin and the West Punjab, was perennially short of water and was populated by dry crop farmers and peoples of the steppe. East Pakistan was made up of the marshy deltas of the Ganges and Brahmaputra Rivers. Densely populated with rice farmers, it was the home of the artistic and intellectual Bengalis.

Even though the new state was an essentially Muslim society, its first years were marked by intense internal conflicts over religious, linguistic, and regional issues. Mohammed Ali Jinnah's vision of a democratic state that would assure freedom of religion and equal treatment for all was opposed by those who advocated a state based on Islamic principles.

Even more dangerous was the division between east and west. Many in East Pakistan felt that the government, based in the west, ignored their needs. In 1952, riots erupted in East Pakistan over the government's decision to adopt Urdu, a language derived from Hindi and used by Muslims in northern India, as the national language of the entire country. Most East Pakistanis spoke Bengali, an unrelated language. Tensions persisted, and in March 1971, East Pakistan declared its independence as the new nation of Bangladesh. Pakistani troops attempted to restore central government authority in the capital of Dhaka, but rebel forces supported by India went on the offensive, and the government bowed to the inevitable and recognized independent Bangladesh.

The breakup of the union between East and West Pakistan undermined the fragile authority of the military regime that had ruled Pakistan since 1958 and led to its replacement by a civilian government under Zulfikar Ali Bhutto. But now religious tensions came to the fore, despite a new constitution that made a number of key concessions to conservative Muslims. In 1977, a new military government under General Zia Ul Ha'q came to power with a commitment to make Pakistan a truly Islamic state. Islamic law became the basis for social behavior as well as for the legal system. Laws governing the consumption of alcohol and the role of women were tightened in accordance with strict Muslim beliefs. But after Zia was killed in a plane crash, Pakistanis elected Benazir Bhutto, the daughter of Zulfikar Ali Bhutto and a supporter of secularism who had been educated in the United States. She too was removed from power by a military regime, in 1990, on charges of incompetence and corruption. Reelected in 1993, she attempted to crack down on opposition forces but was removed once again amid renewed charges of official corruption. Her successor soon came under fire for the same reason and in 1999 was ousted by a military coup led by General Pervaiz Musharraf, who promised to restore political stability and honest government.

In September 2001, Pakistan became the focus of international attention when a coalition of forces arrived in Afghanistan to overthrow the Taliban regime and destroy the al-Qaeda terrorist network. Despite considerable support for the Taliban among the local population, President Musharraf pledged his help in bringing terrorists to justice. He also promised to return his country to the secular principles espoused by Mohammed Ali Jinnah. His situation was complicated by renewed tensions with India over Kashmir and a series of violent clashes between Muslims and Hindus in India.

## Poverty and Pluralism in South Asia

The leaders of the new states that emerged in South Asia after World War II faced a number of problems. The peoples of South Asia were still overwhelmingly poor and illiterate, and the sectarian, ethnic, and cultural divisions that had plagued Indian society for centuries had not dissipated.

### THE POLITICS OF COMMUNALISM

Perhaps the most sincere effort to create democratic instititutions was in India, where the new constitution called for social justice, liberty, equality of status and opportunity, and fraternity. All citizens were guaranteed protection from discrimination on the grounds of religious belief, race, caste, sex, or place of birth.

In theory, then, India became a full-fledged democracy on the British parliamentary model. In actuality, a number of distinctive characteristics made the system less than fully democratic in the Western sense but may also have enabled it to survive. As we have seen, India became in essence a one-party state. By leading the independence movement, the Congress Party had gained massive public support, which enabled it to retain its preeminent position in Indian politics for three decades. The party also avoided being identified as a party exclusively for the Hindu majority by including prominent non-Hindus among its leaders and favoring measures to protect minority groups such as Sikhs, untouchables, and Muslims from discrimination.

After Nehru's death in 1964, however, problems emerged that had been disguised by his adept maneuvering. Part of the problem was the familiar one of a party too long in power. Party officials became complacent and all too easily fell prey to the temptations of corruption and pork-barrel politics.

Another problem was communalism. Beneath the surface unity of the new republic lay age-old ethnic, linguistic, and religious divisions. Because of India's vast size and complex history, no national language had ever emerged. Hindi was the most prevalent, but it was the native language of less than one-third of the population. During the colonial period, English had served as the official language of government, and many non-Hindi speakers suggested making it the official language. But English was spoken only by the educated elite, and it represented an affront to national pride. Eventually, India recognized fourteen official tongues, making the parliament sometimes sound like the Tower of Babel.

Divisiveness increased after Nehru's death, and under his successors, official corruption grew. Only the lack of appeal of its rivals and the Nehru family charisma carried on by his daughter Indira Gandhi kept the party in power. But she was unable to prevent the progressive disintegration of the party's power base at the state level, where regional or ideological parties won the allegiance of voters by exploiting ethnic or social revolutionary themes.

During the 1980s, religious tensions began to intensify, not only among Sikhs in the northwest but also between Hindus and Muslims. As we have seen, Gandhi's uncompromising approach to Sikh separatism led to her assassination in 1987. Under her son, Rajiv Gandhi, Hindu militants at Ayodhya, in northern India, demanded the destruction of a mosque built on a holy site where a Hindu temple had previously existed. In 1992, Hindu demonstrators destroyed the mosque and erected a temporary temple at the site, provoking clashes between Hindus and Muslims throughout the country. In protest, rioters in neighboring Pakistan destroyed a number of Hindu shrines in that country.

In recent years, communal divisions have intensified as militant Hindu groups agitate for a state that caters to the Hindu majority, now numbering more than 700 million people. In the spring of 2002, violence between Hindus and Muslims flared up again over plans by Hindu activists to build a permanent temple at the site of the destroyed mosque at Ayodhya.

## THE ECONOMY

Nehru's answer to the social and economic inequality that had long afflicted the subcontinent was socialism. He instituted a series of five-year plans, which led to the creation of a relatively large and reasonably efficient industrial sector, centered on steel, vehicles, and textiles. Industrial production almost tripled between 1950 and 1965, and per capita income rose by 50 percent between 1950 and 1980, although it was still less than $300 (in U.S. dollars).

By the 1970s, however, industrial growth had slowed. The lack of modern infrastructure was a problem, as was the rising price of oil, most of which had to be imported. The relative weakness of the state-owned sector, which grew at an annual rate of only about 2 percent in the 1950s and 1960s, versus 5 percent for the private sector, also became a serious obstacle.

India's major economic weakness, however, was in agriculture. At independence, mechanization was almost unknown, fertilizer was rarely used, and most farms were small and uneconomical because of the Hindu tradition of dividing the land equally among all male children. As a result, the vast majority of the Indian people lived in conditions of abject poverty. Landless laborers outnumbered landowners by almost two to one. The government attempted to relieve the problem by redistributing land to the poor, limiting the size of landholdings, and encouraging farmers to form voluntary cooperatives. But all three programs ran into widespread opposition and apathy.

Another problem was overpopulation. Even before independence, the country had had difficulty supporting its people. In the 1950s and 1960s, the population grew by more than 2 percent annually, twice the nineteenth-century rate. Beginning in the 1960s, the Indian government sought to curb population growth. Indira Gandhi instituted a program combining monetary rewards and compulsory sterilization. Males who had fathered too many children were sometimes forced to undergo a vasectomy. Popular resistance undermined the program, however, and the goals were scaled back in the 1970s. As a result, India has made little progress in holding down its burgeoning population, now estimated at more than one billion. One factor in the continued growth has been a decline in the death rate, especially the rate of infant mortality. Nevertheless, as a result of media popularization and better government programs, the trend today, even in poor rural villages, is toward smaller families. The average number of children a woman bears has been reduced from six in 1950 to three today. As has occurred elsewhere, the decline in family size began among the educated and is gradually spreading throughout Indian society.

The "Green Revolution" that began in the 1960s helped reduce the severity of the population problem. The introduction of more productive, disease-resistant strains of rice and wheat doubled grain production between 1960 and 1980. But the Green Revolution also increased rural inequality. Only the wealthier farmers were able to purchase the necessary fertilizer, while poor peasants were often driven off the land. Millions fled to the cities, where they lived in vast slums, working at menial jobs or even begging for a living.

After the death of Indira Gandhi in 1984, her son Rajiv proved more receptive to foreign investment and a greater role for the private sector in the economy. India began to export more manufactured goods, including computer software. The pace of change has accelerated under Rajiv Gandhi's successors, who have continued to transfer state-run industries to private hands. These policies have stimulated the growth of a prosperous new middle class, now estimated at more than 100 million. Consumerism has soared, and sales of television sets, automobiles, videocassette recorders, and telephones have increased dramatically. Equally important, Western imports are being replaced by new products manufactured in India with Indian brand names.

Nevertheless, Nehru's dream of a socialist society remains strong. State-owned enterprises still produce about half of all domestic goods, and high tariffs continue to stifle imports. Nationalist parties have played on the widespread fear of foreign economic influence to force the cancellation of some contracts and the relocation of some foreign firms. A combination of religious and environmental groups attempted unsuccessfully to prevent Kentucky Fried Chicken from establishing outlets in major Indian cities (see the box on p. 168).

As in the industrialized countries of the West, economic growth has been accompanied by environmental damage. Water and air pollution has led to illness and death for many people, and an environmental movement has emerged. Some critics, reflecting the traditional anti-imperialist attitude of Indian intellectuals, blame Western capitalist corporations for the problem, as in the highly publicized case of leakage from a foreign-owned chemical plant at Bhopal. Much of the problem, however, comes from state-owned factories erected with Soviet aid. And not all the environmental damage can be ascribed to industrialization. The Ganges River is so polluted by human overuse that it is risky for Hindu believers to bathe in it.

Moreover, many Indians have not benefited from the new prosperity. Nearly one-third of the population lives

**➤ INDIA'S HOPE, INDIA'S SORROW.** In India, as in many other societies in Southern Asia, overpopulation is a serious obstacle to economic development. The problem is particularly serious in large cities, where thousands of poor children are forced into begging or prostitution. Shown here are a few of the thousands of street children in the commercial hub of Bombay.

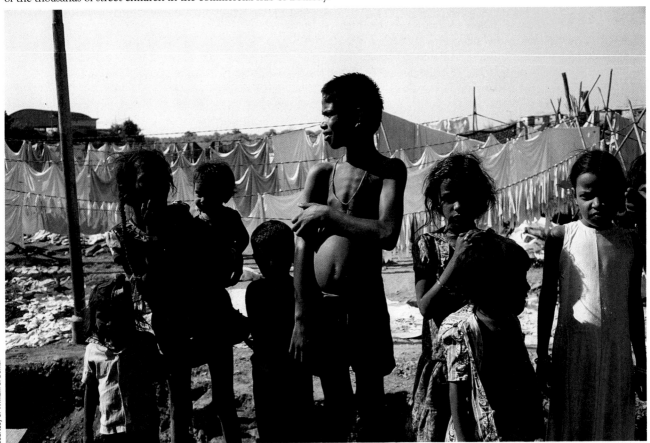

Courtesy of William J. Duiker

# SAY NO TO McDONALD'S AND KFC!

*One of the consequences of Rajiv Gandhi's decision to deregulate the Indian economy has been an increase in the presence of foreign corporations, including U.S. fast-food restaurant chains. Their arrival set off a storm of protest in India: from environmentalists concerned that raising grain for chickens is an inefficient use of land, from religious activists angry at the killing of animals for food, and from nationalists anxious to protect the domestic market from foreign competition. The author of this piece, which appeared in the Hindustan Times, was Maneka Gandhi, a daughter-in-law of Indira Gandhi and a onetime minister of the environment who has emerged as a prominent rival of Congress Party president Sonia Gandhi.*

## WHY INDIA DOESN'T NEED FAST FOOD

India's decision to allow Pepsi Foods Ltd. to open 60 restaurants in India—30 each of Pizza Hut and Kentucky Fried Chicken—marks the first entry of multinational, meat-based junk-food chains into India. If this is allowed to happen, at least a dozen other similar chains will very quickly arrive, including the infamous McDonald's.

The implications of allowing junk-food chains into India are quite stark. As the name denotes, the foods served at Kentucky Fried Chicken (KFC) are chicken-based and fried. This is the worst combination possible for the body and can create a host of health problems, including obesity, high cholesterol, heart ailments, and many kinds of cancer. Pizza Hut products are a combination of white flour, cheese, and meat—again, a combination likely to cause disease. . . .

Then there is the issue of the environmental impact of junk-food chains. Modern meat production involves misuse of crops, water, energy, and grazing areas. In addition, animal agriculture produces surprisingly large amounts of air and water pollution.

KFC and Pizza Hut insist that their chickens be fed corn and soybeans. Consider the diversion of grain for this purpose. As the outlets of KFC and Pizza Hut increase in number, the poultry industry will buy up more and more corn to feed the chickens, which means that the corn will quickly disappear from the villages, and its increased price will place it out of reach for the common man. Turning corn into junk chicken is like turning gold into mud. . . .

It is already shameful that, in a country plagued by famine and flood, we divert 37 percent of our arable land to growing animal fodder. Were all of that grain to be consumed directly by humans, it would nourish five times as many people as it does after being converted into meat, milk, and eggs. . . .

Of course, it is not just the KFC and Pizza Hut chains of Pepsi Foods Ltd. that will cause all of this damage. Once we open India up by allowing these chains, dozens more will be eagerly waiting to come in. Each city in America has an average of 5,000 junk-food restaurants. Is that what we want for India?

Source: From *World Press Review* (September 1995), p. 47.

---

below the national poverty line. Millions continue to live in urban slums, such as the famous "City of Joy" in Calcutta, and most farm families remain desperately poor. Despite the socialist rhetoric of India's leaders, the inequality of wealth in India is as pronounced as it is in capitalist nations in the West. Indeed, India has been described as two nations: an educated urban India of 100 million people surrounded by over 900 million impoverished peasants in the countryside.

## CASTE, CLASS, AND GENDER

Drawing generalizations about the life of the average Indian is difficult because of ethnic, religious, and caste differences, which are compounded by the vast gulf between town and country.

Although the constitution of 1950 guaranteed equal treatment and opportunity for all, regardless of caste, and

prohibited discrimination based on untouchability, prejudice is hard to eliminate. Untouchability persists, particularly in the villages, where *harijans*, now called *dalits*, still perform menial tasks and are often denied fundamental human rights.

In general, urban Indians appear less conscious of caste distinctions. Material wealth rather than caste identity is increasingly defining status. Still, color consciousness based on the age-old distinctions between upper-class Aryans and lower-class Dravidians remains strong. Class-conscious Hindus still express a distinct preference for light-skinned marital partners.

In recent years, low-caste Indians (who represent more than 80 percent of the voting public) have begun to demand affirmative action to relieve their disabilities and give them a more equal share in the national wealth. Officials at U.S. consulates in India have noticed a rise in visa applications from members of the *brahmin* caste, who claim that they have "no future" in the new India. But opponents of such measures are often not reluctant to fight back. Phoolan Devi, known as the "bandit queen," spent several years in jail for taking part in the murder of twenty men from a landowning caste who had allegedly gang-raped her when she was an adolescent. Her campaign for office during the 1996 elections was the occasion of violent arguments between supporters and opponents, and she was assassinated by an unknown assailant in 2001.

In few societies was the life of women more restricted than in traditional India. Hindu favoritism toward men was compounded by the Muslim custom of *purdah* to create a society in which males were dominant in virtually all aspects of life. Females received no education and had no inheritance rights. They were restricted to the home and tied to their husbands for life. Widows were expected to shave their heads and engage in a life of religious meditation or even to immolate themselves on their husband's funeral pyre.

After independence, India's leaders sought to equalize treatment of the sexes. The constitution expressly forbade discrimination based on sex and called for equal pay for equal work. Laws prohibited child marriage and the payment of a dowry by the bride's family. Women were encouraged to attend school and enter the labor market.

Such laws, along with the dynamics of economic and social change, have had a major impact on the lives of many Indian women. Middle-class women in urban areas are much more likely to seek employment outside the home, and many hold managerial and professional positions. Some Indian women, however, choose to play a dual role—a modern one in their work and in the marketplace and a more submissive, traditional one at home (see the box on p. 170).

Such attitudes are also reflected in the Indian movie industry, where aspiring actresses must often brave family disapproval to enter the entertainment world. Before World War II, female actors were routinely viewed as prostitutes or "loose women," and such views are still prevalent among conservative Indian families. Even Karisma Kapoor, one of India's current film stars and a member of the Kapoor clan, which has produced several generations of actors, had to defy her family's ban on its women's entering show business.

Nothing more strikingly indicates the changing role of women in South Asia than the fact that in recent years, three of the major countries in the area—India, Pakistan, and Sri Lanka—have had women prime ministers. It is worthy of mention, however, that all three—Indira Gandhi, Benazir Bhutto, and Srimivao Bandaranaike—came from prominent political families and owed their initial success to a husband or a father who had served as prime minister before them.

Like other aspects of life, the role of women has changed much less in rural areas. In the early 1960s, many villagers still practiced the institution of *purdah*. A

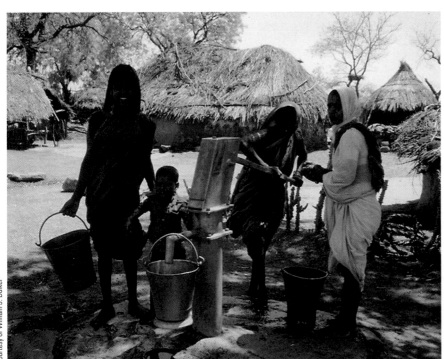

Courtesy of William J. Duiker

➤ **FETCHING WATER AT THE VILLAGE WELL.** The scarcity of water will surely become one of the planet's most crucial problems. It will affect all nations, developed and developing, rich and poor. Although many Indians live with an inadequate water supply, these women are fortunate to have a well in their village. More typical is the image of the Indian woman, dressed in a colorful sari, children encircling her as she heads to her distant home on foot, carrying a heavy pail of water on her head.

# A Critique of Western Feminism

*Organized efforts to protect the rights of women have been under way in India since the 1970s, when the Progressive Organization for Women (POW) instituted a campaign against sexual harassment and other forms of discrimination against women in Indian society. Like many of their counterparts in other parts of Asia and Africa, however, many activists for women's rights in India are critical of Western feminism, charging that it is irrelevant to their own realities. Although Indian feminists feel a bond with their sisters all over the world, they insist on resolving Indian problems with Indian solutions. As Indira Gandhi remarked, "To be liberated, a woman should be free to be herself. Rivalry between men and women is unnecessary, is destructive and itself a bondage." The author of this editorial is Madhu Kishwar, founder and editor of a women's journal in New Delhi.*

## FINDING INDIAN SOLUTIONS TO WOMEN'S PROBLEMS

Western feminism, exported to India and many other Third World countries in recent decades, has brought with it serious problems.

As products of a more homogenized culture, most Western feminists assume women's aspirations the world over must be quite similar. Yet a person's idea of a good life and her aspirations are closely related to what is valued in her particular society. This applies to feminism itself. An offshoot of individualism and liberalism, it posits that each individual is responsible primarily to herself. . . .

In societies like India, most of us find it difficult to tune in to this extreme individualism. For instance, most Indian women are unwilling to assert rights in a way that estranges them not just from their family but also from their larger community. . . .

This isn't slavery to social opinion. Rather, many of us believe life is a poor thing if our own dear ones don't honor and celebrate our rights, if our freedom cuts us off from others. In our culture, both men and women are taught to value the interests of our families more than our self-interest. . . .

Cultural issues aside, my most fundamental reservation regarding feminism is that it has strengthened the tendency among India's Western-educated elites to adopt the statist authoritarian route to social reform. The characteristic feminist response to most social issues affecting women—in the workplace, in the media, in the home—is to demand more and more stringent laws. . . .

But dearly held and deeply cherished cultural norms cannot be changed simply by applying the instruments of state repression through legal punishment. Social reform is too complex and important a matter to be left to the police and courts. The best of laws will tend to fail if social opinion is contrary to them. Therefore, the statist route of using laws as a substitute for creating a new social consensus about women's rights tends to be counterproductive.

Source: From *Far Eastern Economic Review* (May 16, 1996), p. 30.

---

woman who went about freely in society would get a bad reputation. Female children are still much less likely to receive an education. The overall literacy rate in India today is less than 40 percent, but it is undoubtedly much lower among women. Laws relating to dowry, child marriage, and inheritance are routinely ignored in the countryside. There have been a few highly publicized cases of *sati* (the immolation of widows on their deceased husband's funeral pyre) although undoubtedly more women die of mistreatment at the hands of their husband or of other members of his family.

Perhaps the most tragic aspect of continued sexual discrimination in India is the high mortality rate among girls. One-quarter of the female children born in India die before the age of fifteen as a result of neglect or even infanticide. Others are aborted before birth after gender-detection examinations. The results are striking. In most societies, the number of women equals or exceeds that of men; in India, according to one estimate, the ratio is only 933 females to 1,000 males.

## South Asian Art and Literature Since Independence

Recent decades have witnessed a prodigious outpouring of literature in India. Most works have been written in one of the Indian languages and have not been translated into a foreign tongue. Many authors, however, choose to write in English for the Indian elite or for foreign audiences. For that reason, some critics charge that such literature lacks authenticity.

Because of the vast quantity of works published (India is currently the third-largest publisher of English-language books in the world), only a few of the most prominent fiction writers can be mentioned here. Anita Desai (b. 1937) was one of the first prominent female writers in contemporary India. Her writing focuses on the struggle of Indian women to achieve a degree of independence. In her first novel, *Cry, the Peacock*, the heroine finally seeks liberation by murdering her husband, preferring freedom at any cost to remaining a captive of traditional society.

The best-known female writer in South Asia today is Taslima Nasrin (b. 1962) of Bangladesh. She first became famous when she was sentenced to death for her novel *Shame* (1993), in which she criticized official persecution of the Hindu minority. An outspoken feminist, she is critical of Islam for obstructing human progress and women's equality. She now lives in exile in Europe.

The most controversial writer in India today is Salman Rushdie (b. 1947). In *Midnight's Children*, published in 1980, the author linked his protagonist, born on the night of independence, to the history of modern India, its achievements and its frustrations. Like his contemporaries Günter Grass and Gabriel García Márquez, Rushdie used the technique of magical realism to jolt his audience into a recognition of the inhumanity of modern society and the need to develop a sense of moral concern for the fate of the Indian people and for the world as a whole.

Rushdie's later novels have tackled such problems as religious intolerance, political tyranny, social injustice, and greed and corruption. His attack on Islamic fundamentalism in *The Satanic Verses* (1988) won plaudits from literary critics but provoked widespread criticism among Muslims, including a death sentence by Ayatollah Khomeini in Iran. *The Moor's Last Sigh* (1995), which focuses on the alleged excesses of Hindu nationalism, has been banned in India.

Like Chinese and Japanese artists, Indian artists have agonized over how best to paint with a modern yet indigenous mode of expression. During the colonial period, Indian art went in several directions at once. One school of painters favored traditional themes; another experimented with a colorful primitivism founded on folk art. Many Indian artists painted representational social art extolling the suffering and silent dignity of India's impoverished millions. After 1960, however, most Indian artists adopted abstract art as their medium. Surrealism in particular, with its emphasis on spontaneity and the unconscious, appeared closer to the Hindu tradition of favoring intuition over reason. Yet Indian artists are still struggling to find the ideal way to be both modern and Indian.

## Gandhi's Vision

Indian society looks increasingly Western in form, if not in content. As in a number of other Asian and African societies, the distinction between traditional and modern, or native and westernized, sometimes seems to be a simple dichotomy between rural and urban. The major cities appear modern and westernized, but the villages have changed little since precolonial days.

Yet traditional practices appear to be more resilient in India than in many other societies, and the result is often a synthesis rather than a clash between conflicting institutions and values. Unlike China, India has not rejected its past but merely adjusted it to meet the needs of the present. Clothing styles in the streets, where the *sari* and *dhoti* continue to be popular; religious practices in the temples; and social relationships in the home all testify to the importance of tradition in India.

One disadvantage of the eclectic approach, which seeks to blend the old and the new rather than choosing one over the other, is that sometimes contrasting traditions cannot be reconciled. In *India: A Wounded Civilization*, V. S. Naipaul (b. 1932), a West Indian of Indian descent, charged that Mahatma Gandhi's glorification of poverty and the simple Indian village was an obstacle to efforts to overcome the poverty, ignorance, and degradation of India's past and build a prosperous modern society. Gandhi's vision of a spiritual India, Naipaul complained, was a balm for defeatism and an excuse for failure.

Certainly, India faces a difficult dilemma. Some problems are undoubtedly a consequence of the colonial era, but the British cannot be blamed for all of the country's economic and social ills. To build a democratic, prosperous society, the Indian people must discard many of their traditional convictions and customs. Belief in karma and inherent caste distinctions are incompatible with the democratic belief in equality before the law. These traditional beliefs also undercut the work ethic and the modern sentiment of nationalism.

So long as Indians accept their fate as predetermined, they will find it difficult to change their environment and create a new society. Yet their traditional beliefs provide a measure of identity and solace often lacking in other societies, where such traditional spiritual underpinnings have eroded. Destroying India's traditional means of coping with a disagreeable reality without changing that reality would be cruel indeed.

## SOUTHEAST ASIA

The Japanese wartime occupation had a great impact on attitudes among the peoples of Southeast Asia. It demonstrated the vulnerability of colonial rule in the region and showed that an Asian power could defeat Europeans. The Allied governments themselves also contributed—

sometimes unwittingly—to rising aspirations for independence by promising self-determination for all peoples at the end of the war. Although Winston Churchill later said that the Atlantic Charter did not apply to the colonial peoples, it would be difficult to put the genie back in the bottle.

Some did not try. In July 1946, the United States granted total independence to the Philippines. The Americans maintained a military presence on the islands, however, and U.S. citizens retained economic and commercial interests in the new country.

The British, too, under the Labour Party, were willing to bring an end to a century of imperialism in the region. In 1948, the Union of Burma received its independence. Malaya's turn came in 1957, after a Communist guerrilla movement had been suppressed.

The French and the Dutch, however, both regarded their colonies in the region as economic necessities as well as symbols of national grandeur and refused to turn them over to nationalist movements at the end of the war. The Dutch attempted to suppress a rebellion in the East Indies led by Sukarno, leader of the Indonesian Nationalist Party. But the United States, which feared a Communist victory there, pressured the Dutch to grant independence to Sukarno and his non-Communist forces, and in 1950, the Dutch finally agreed to recognize the new Republic of Indonesia.

The situation was somewhat different in Vietnam, where the leading force in the anticolonial movement was the local Indochinese Communist Party (ICP) led by the veteran Moscow-trained revolutionary Ho Chi Minh. In August 1945, virtually at the moment of Japanese surrender, the Vietminh Front, an alliance of patriotic forces under secret ICP leadership that had been founded to fight the Japanese in 1941, launched a general uprising and seized power throughout most of Vietnam.

In early September, Ho Chi Minh was declared president of a new provisional republic in Hanoi. In the meantime, French military units began arriving in Saigon, with the permission of the British occupation command there. The new government in Hanoi, formally known as the Democratic Republic of Vietnam (DRV) appealed to the victorious Allies for recognition but received no response, and by late fall, the southern part of the country was back under French rule. Ho signed a preliminary agreement with the French recognizing Vietnam as a "free state" within the French Union, but negotiations over the details broke down in the summer of 1946, and war between the two parties broke out in December. At the time, it was only an anticolonial war, but it would soon become much more (see Chapter 1).

# The Era of Independent States

Many of the leaders of the newly independent states in Southeast Asia (see Map 8.2) admired Western political institutions and hoped to adapt them to their own countries. New constitutions were patterned on Western democratic models, and multiparty political systems quickly sprang into operation.

## THE SEARCH FOR A NEW POLITICAL CULTURE

By the 1960s, most of these budding experiments in pluralist democracy had been abandoned or were under serious threat. Some had been replaced by military or one-party autocratic regimes. In Burma, a moderate government based on the British parliamentary system and dedicated to Buddhism and nonviolent Marxism had given way to a military government. In Thailand, too, the military now ruled. In the Philippines, President Ferdinand Marcos discarded democratic restraints and established his own centralized control. In South Vietnam (see Chapter 1), Ngo Dinh Diem and his successors paid lip service to the Western democratic model but ruled by authoritarian means.

One problem faced by most of these states was that independence had not brought material prosperity or ended economic inequality and the domination of the local economies by foreign interests. Most economies in the region were still characterized by tiny industrial sectors; they lacked technology, educational resources, capital investment, and leaders trained in developmental skills.

The presence of widespread ethnic, linguistic, cultural, and economic differences also made the transition to Western-style democracy difficult. In Malaya, for example, the majority Malays—most of whom were farmers—feared economic and political domination by the local Chinese minority, who were much more experienced in industry and commerce. In 1961, the Federation of Malaya, whose ruling party was dominated by Malays, integrated former British possessions on the island of Borneo into the new Union of Malaysia in a move to increase the non-Chinese proportion of the country's population. Yet periodic conflicts persisted as the Malaysian government attempted to guarantee Malay control over politics and a larger role in the economy.

The most publicized example of a failed experiment in democracy was in Indonesia. In 1950, the new leaders drew up a constitution creating a parliamentary system under a titular presidency. Sukarno was elected the first president. A spellbinding orator, Sukarno played a major role in creating a sense of national identity among the disparate peoples of the Indonesian archipelago (see the box on p. 174).

In the late 1950s, Sukarno, exasperated at the incessant maneuvering among devout Muslims, Communists, and the army, dissolved the constitution and attempted to rule on his own through what he called "guided democracy." As he described it, guided democracy was closer to Indonesian traditions and superior to the Western variety. The weakness of the latter was that it allowed the majority to dominate the minority, whereas guided democracy would reconcile different opinions and points of view in a government operated by consensus. Highly suspicious of the West, Sukarno nationalized foreign-owned enterprises and sought economic aid from China and the Soviet Union while relying for domestic support on the Indonesian Communist Party.

The army and conservative Muslims resented Sukarno's increasing reliance on the Communists, and the Muslims were further upset by his refusal to consider a state based on Islamic principles. In 1965, military officers launched a coup d'état that provoked a mass popular uprising, which resulted in the slaughter of several hundred thousand suspected Communists, many of whom were overseas Chinese, long distrusted by the Muslim majority. In 1967, a military government under General Suharto was installed.

# THE GOLDEN THROAT OF PRESIDENT SUKARNO

*President Sukarno of Indonesia was a spellbinding speaker and a charismatic leader of his nation's struggle for independence. These two excerpts are from speeches in which Sukarno promoted two of his favorite projects: Indonesian nationalism and "guided democracy." The force that would guide Indonesia, of course, was to be Sukarno himself.*

## SUKARNO ON INDONESIAN GREATNESS

What was Indonesia in 1945? What was our nation then? It was only two things, only two things. A flag and a song. That is all. (Pause, finger held up as afterthought.) But no, I have omitted the main ingredient. I have missed the most important thing of all. I have left out the burning fire of freedom and independence in the breast and heart of every Indonesian. That is the most important thing—this is the vital chord—the spirit of our people, the spirit and determination to be free. This was our nation in 1945—the spirit of our people!

And what are we today? We are a great nation. We are bigger than Poland. We are bigger than Turkey. We have more people than Australia, than Canada, we are bigger in area and have more people than Japan. In population now we are the fifth-largest country in the world. In area, we are even bigger than the United States of America. The American Ambassador, who is here with us, admits this. Of course, he points out that we have a lot of water in between our thousands of islands. But I say to him—America has a lot of mountains and deserts, too!

## SUKARNO ON GUIDED DEMOCRACY

Indonesia's democracy is not liberal democracy. Indonesian democracy is not the democracy of the world of Montaigne or Voltaire. Indonesia's democracy is not à la America, Indonesia's democracy is not the Soviet—NO! Indonesia's democracy is the democracy which is implanted in the breasts of the Indonesian people, and it is that which I have tried to dig up again, and have put forward as an offering to you. . . . If you, especially the undergraduates, are still clinging to and being borne along the democracy made in England, or democracy made in France, or democracy made in America, or democracy made in Russia, you will become a nation of copyists!

Source: From Howard Jones, *Indonesia: The Possible Dream* (New York: Harcourt Brace Jovanovich, Hoover Institute, 1971), p. 223, 237.

---

The new government made no pretensions of reverting to democratic rule, but it did restore good relations with the West and sought foreign investment to repair the country's ravaged economy. But it also found it difficult to placate Muslim demands for an Islamic state. In a few areas, including western Sumatra, militant Muslims took up arms against the state.

The one country in Southeast Asia that explicitly rejected the Western model was North Vietnam. Its leaders opted for the Stalinist pattern of national development, based on Communist Party rule and socialist forms of ownership. In 1958, stimulated by the success of collectivization in neighboring China, the government launched a three-year plan to lay the foundation for a socialist society. Collective farms were established, and all industry and commerce above the family level were nationalized.

## RECENT TRENDS TOWARD DEMOCRACY

In recent years, some Southeast Asian societies have shown signs of evolving toward more democratic forms. In the Philippines, the dictatorial Marcos regime was overthrown by a massive public uprising in 1986 and replaced by a democratically elected government under President Corazon Aquino (b. 1933), the widow of a popular politician assassinated a few years earlier. Aquino was unable to resolve many of the country's chronic economic and social difficulties, however, and political stability remains elusive; one of her successors, ex-actor Joseph Estrada, was forced to resign on the charge of corruption. At the same time, Muslims in the southern island of Mindanao have mounted a terrorist campaign in their effort to obtain autonomy or independence.

In other nations, the results have also been mixed. Although Malaysia is a practicing democracy, tensions persist between Malays and Chinese as well as between secular and orthodox Muslims who seek to create an Islamic state. In neighboring Thailand, the military has found it expedient to hold national elections for civilian governments, but the danger of a military takeover is never far beneath the surface.

In Indonesia, difficult economic conditions caused by the financial crisis of 1997 (see the next section), combined with popular anger against the Suharto government (several members of his family had reportedly used their positions to amass considerable wealth), led to violent street riots and demands for his resignation. Forced to step down in the spring of 1998, Suharto was replaced by his deputy B. J. Habibie, who called for the establishment of a national assembly to select a new government based on popular aspirations. The assembly selected a moderate Muslim leader as president, but he was charged with corruption and incompetence and was replaced in 2001 by his vice president, Sukarno's daughter Megawati Sukarnoputri (b. 1947).

The new government faced a severe challenge, not only from the economic crisis but also from dissident elements seeking autonomy or even separation from the republic. Under pressure from the international community, Indonesia agreed to grant independence to the one-time Portuguese colony of East Timor, where the majority of the people are Roman Catholics. But violence provoked by pro-Indonesian militia units forced many refugees to flee the country. Religious tensions have also erupted between Muslims and Christians elsewhere in the archipelago, and Muslim rebels in western Sumatra continue to agitate for a new state based on strict adherence to fundamentalist Islam. In the meantime, a terrorist attack directed at tourists on the island of Bali provoked fears that the Muslim nation had become a haven for terrorist elements throughout the region.

In Vietnam, the trend in recent years has been toward a greater popular role in the governing process. Elections for the unicameral parliament are more open than in the past. The government remains suspicious of Western-style democracy, however, and represses any opposition to the Communist Party's guiding role over the state.

Only in Burma (now renamed Myanmar), where the military has been in complete control since the early 1960s, have the forces of greater popular participation been virtually silenced. Even there, however, the power of the ruling regime of General Ne Win (1911–2003), known as SLORC, has been vocally challenged by Aung San Huu Kyi (b. 1952), the admired daughter of one of the heroes of the country's struggle for national liberation after World War II.

## INCREASING PROSPERITY AND FINANCIAL CRISIS

The trend toward more representative systems of government has been due in part to increasing prosperity and the growth of an affluent and educated middle class. Although Indonesia, Burma, and the three Indochinese states are still overwhelmingly agrarian, Malaysia and Thailand have been undergoing relatively rapid economic development.

In the late summer of 1997, however, these economic gains were threatened, and popular faith in the ultimate benefits of globalization was shaken as a financial crisis swept through the region. The crisis was triggered by a number of problems, including growing budget deficits caused by excessive government expenditures on ambitious development projects, irresponsible lending and investment practices by financial institutions, and an overvaluation of local currencies relative to the U.S. dollar. An underlying cause of these problems was the prevalence of backroom deals between politicians and business leaders that temporarily enriched both groups at the cost of eventual economic dislocation.

As local currencies plummeted in value, the International Monetary Fund agreed to provide assistance, but only on the condition that the governmnets concerned permit greater transparency in their economic systems and allow market forces to operate more freely, even at the price of bankruptcies and the loss of jobs. In the early 2000s, although there were signs that some political leaders recognized the serious nature of their problems and were willing to take steps to resolve them, the political cost of such changes remained uncertain.

## Regional Conflict and Cooperation: The Rise of ASEAN

In addition to their continuing internal challenges, Southeast Asian states have been hampered by serious tensions among themselves. Some of these tensions were a consequence of historical rivalries and territorial disputes that had been submerged during the long era of colonial rule. Cambodia, for example, has bickered with both of its neighbors, Thailand and Vietnam, over mutual frontiers drawn up originally by the French for their own convenience.

After the reunification of Vietnam under Communist rule in 1975, the lingering border dispute between Cambodia and Vietnam erupted again. In April 1975, a brutal revolutionary regime under the leadership of the Khmer Rouge dictator Pol Pot came to power in Cambodia and proceeded to carry out the massacre of more than one million Cambodians. Then, claiming that vast territories in the Mekong delta had been seized from Cambodia by the Vietnamese in previous centuries, the Khmer Rouge regime launched attacks across the common border. In response, Vietnamese forces invaded Cambodia in December 1978 and installed a pro-Hanoi regime in Phnom Penh. Fearful of Vietnam's increasing power in the region, China launched a brief attack on Vietnam to demonstrate its displeasure.

The outbreak of war among the erstwhile Communist allies aroused the concern of other countries in the neighborhood. In 1967, several non-Communist countries had

**HOLOCAUST IN CAMBODIA.**
When the Khmer Rouge seized power
in Cambodia in April 1975, they
immediately emptied the capital of
Phnom Penh and systematically began
to eliminate opposition elements
throughout the country. Thousands
were tortured in the infamous Tuol
Sleng prison and then marched out
to the countryside, where they were
massacred. Their bodies were thrown
into massive pits. The succeeding
government disinterred the remains,
which are now displayed at an outdoor
museum on the site.

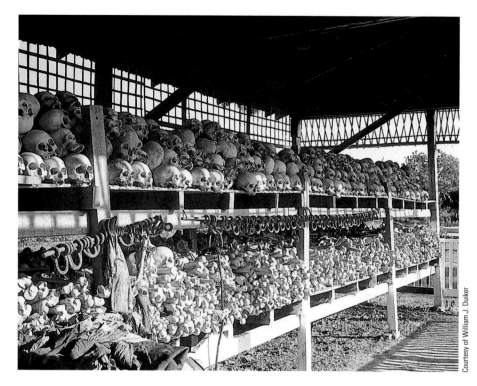

Courtesy of William J. Duiker

established the Association of Southeast Asian Nations
(ASEAN). Composed of Indonesia, Malaysia, Thailand,
Singapore, and the Philippines, ASEAN at first concentrated on cooperative social and economic endeavors,
but after the end of the Vietnam War, it cooperated with
other states in an effort to force the Vietnamese to withdraw. In 1991, the Vietnamese finally withdrew, and a
new government was formed in Phnom Penh.

The growth of ASEAN from a weak collection of diverse states into a stronger organization whose members
cooperate militarily and politically has helped provide
the nations of Southeast Asia with a more cohesive voice
to represent their interests on the world stage. They will
need it, for disagreements with Western countries over
global economic issues and the rising power of China will
present major challenges in coming years. That Vietnam
was admitted into ASEAN in 1996 should provide both
Hanoi and its neighbors with greater leverage in dealing
with their powerful neighbor to the north.

## Daily Life: Town and Country in Contemporary Southeast Asia

The urban-rural dichotomy observed in India also is
found in Southeast Asia, where the cities resemble those
in the West while the countryside often appears little

changed from precolonial days. In cities such as Bangkok,
Manila, and Jakarta, broad boulevards lined with skyscrapers alternate with muddy lanes passing through
neighborhoods packed with wooden shacks topped by
thatch or rusty tin roofs. Nevertheless, in recent decades,
millions of Southeast Asians have fled to these urban
slums. Although most available jobs are menial, the pay
is better than in the villages.

The urban migrants change not only their physical surroundings but their attitudes and values as well. Sometimes the move leads to a decline in traditional beliefs. Belief in the existence of nature and ancestral spirits, for
example, has declined among the urban populations of
Southeast Asia. In Thailand, Buddhism has come under
pressure from the rising influence of materialism, although
temple schools still educate thousands of rural youths
whose families cannot afford the cost of public education.

Nevertheless, Buddhist, Muslim, and Confucian beliefs remain strong, even in cosmopolitan cities such as
Bangkok, Jakarta, and Singapore. This preference for the
traditional also shows up in lifestyle. Native dress — or an
eclectic blend of Asian and Western attire —is still common. Traditional music, art, theater, and dance remain
popular, although Western music has become fashionable
among the young, and Indonesian filmmakers complain
that Western films are beginning to dominate the market.

The increasing inroads made by Western culture have caused anxiety in some countries. In Malaysia, for example, fundamentalist Muslims criticize the prevalence of pornography, hedonism, drugs, and alcohol in Western culture and have tried to limit their presence in their own country. The Malaysian government has attempted to limit the number of U.S. entertainment programs shown on local television stations and has replaced them with shows on traditional themes.

One of the most significant changes that has taken place in Southeast Asia in recent decades is in the role of women in society. In general, women in the region have historically faced fewer restrictions on their activities and enjoyed a higher status than women elsewhere in Asia. Nevertheless, they were not the equal of men in every respect. With independence, Southeast Asian women gained new rights. Virtually all of the constitutions adopted by the newly independent states granted women full legal and political rights, including the right to work. Today, women have increased opportunities for education and have entered careers previously reserved for men. Women have become more active in politics, and as we have seen, some have served as heads of state.

Yet women are not truly equal to men in any country in Southeast Asia. Sometimes the distinction is simply a matter of custom. In Vietnam, women are legally equal to men, yet until recently no women had served in the Communist Party's ruling Politburo. In Thailand, Malaysia, and Indonesia, women rarely hold senior positions in government service or in the boardrooms of major corporations. Similar restrictions apply in Burma, although Aung San Huu Kyi is the leading figure in the democratic opposition movement.

Sometimes, too, women's rights have been undermined by a social or religious backlash. The revival of Islamic fundamentalism has had an especially strong impact in Malaysia, where Malay women are expected to cover their bodies and wear the traditional Muslim headdress. Even in non-Muslim countries, women are still expected to behave demurely and exercise discretion in all contacts with the opposite sex.

## Cultural Trends

In most countries in Southeast Asia, writers, artists, and composers are attempting to synthesize international styles and themes with local tradition and experience. The novel has become increasingly popular as writers seek to find the best medium to encapsulate the dramatic changes that have taken place in the region in recent decades.

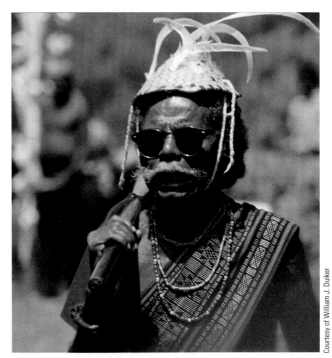

*Courtesy of William J. Duiker*

➤ ONE WORLD, ONE FASHION. One of the negative aspects of tourism is the eroding of distinctive ethnic cultures, even in previously less traveled areas. Nevertheless, fashions from other lands often seem exotic and enticing. This village chief from Flores, a remote island in the Indonesian archipelago, seems very proud of his designer sunglasses.

The best-known writer in postwar Indonesia — at least to readers abroad — is Pramoedya Toer. Born in 1925 in eastern Java, he joined the Indonesian nationalist movement in his early twenties. Arrested in 1965 on the charge of being a Communist, he spent the next fourteen years in prison. While incarcerated, he began writing his four-volume *Buru Quartet*, which recounts in fictional form the story of the struggle of the Indonesian people for freedom from colonial rule and the autocratic regimes of the independence period.

Among the most talented of contemporary Vietnamese novelists is Duong Thu Huong (b. 1947). A member of the Vietnamese Communist Party who served on the front lines during the Sino-Vietnamese war in 1979, she later became outspoken in her criticism of the party's failure to carry out democratic reforms and was briefly imprisoned in 1991. Undaunted by official pressure, she has written several novels that express the horrors experienced by guerrilla fighters during the Vietnam War and the cruel injustices perpetrated by the regime in the cause of building socialism.

Some popular musical styles have evolved out of Indonesia's growing familiarity with the West. Like young musicians in Africa, the rock group Slank, for example, uses music to attack corruption and social inequality. Shocked at the recent violent acts committed by Islamic fundamentalists, such as the 2002 bombing of a nightclub in Bali, the group promotes a nonviolent message of hope and tolerance for Indonesia's diverse ethnic and religious groups.

# A REGION IN FLUX

The image of Southeast Asia mired in the Vietnam conflict and the tensions of the Cold War has become a distant memory. In ASEAN, the states in the region have created the framework for a regional organization that can serve their common political, economic, technological, and security interests. A few members of ASEAN are already on the road to advanced development. The remainder are showing signs of undergoing a similar process within the next generation. While ethnic and religious tensions continue to exist in most ASEAN states, there are promising signs of increasing political stability and pluralism throughout the region.

To be sure, there are continuing signs of trouble. The recent financial crisis has aroused serious political unrest in Indonesia and has the potential to create similar problems elsewhere. Burma remains isolated and appears mired in a state of chronic underdevelopment and brutal military rule. The three states of Indochina remain potentially unstable and have not yet been fully integrated into the region as a whole. Finally, the increase in terrorist activity within the region, especially in Indonesia, is ominous.

All things considered, however, the situation is more promising today than would have seemed possible a generation ago. The nations of Southeast Asia appear capable of coordinating their efforts to erase the internal divisions and conflicts that have brought so much tragedy to the peoples of the region for centuries. If the original purpose of the U.S. intervention in the Indochina conflict was to buy time for the other nations of the region to develop, the gamble may have paid off. Although the war in Vietnam was lost at considerable cost and bloodshed to the participants, the dire predictions in Washington of a revolutionary reign of terror and falling dominoes were not fulfilled, and some countries in the region appear ready to join the steadily growing ranks of developing nations.

To some observers, economic success in the region has come at a high price, in the form of political authoritarianism and a lack of attention to human rights. Indeed, proponents of the view that Asian values are different from those of the West should not be too complacent in their conviction that there is no correlation between economic prosperity and democracy. Still, a look at the historical record suggests that political pluralism is often a by-product of economic advancement and that political values and institutions evolve in response to changing societal conditions. In the end, the current growing pains in Southeast Asia may prove to be beneficial in their overall impact on societies in the region.

| 1945 | 1955 | 1965 | 1975 | 1985 | 1995 | 2005 |

Southeast Asian states restore independence

Formation of ASEAN

Vietnamese invasion of Cambodia

Financial crisis in Southeast Asia

Era of guided democracy in Indonesia

Overthrow of Sukarno

Suharto steps down as president of Indonesia

Terrorist attack in Bali

Corazon Aquino elected president of the Philippines

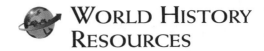

## InfoTrac College Edition

Visit source collections at **http://infotrac.thomsonlearning.com**, and use the Search function with the following key terms:

India history
Nehru
Pakistan

## World History Resources

Visit the *The World Since World War II* Companion Web site for resources specific to this textbook:

**http://history.wadsworth.com/duiker_wwii/**

The Wadsworth World History Resource Center at **http://history.wadsworth.com/world/** offers a variety of tools to help you succeed in this course, including access to quizzes; images; documents; interactive simulations, maps, and timelines; movie explorations; and a wealth of other sources.

# CHAPTER NOTES

1. *New York Times*, May 2, 1996.

2. Quoted in Larry Collins and Dominique Lapierre, *Freedom at Midnight* (New York, 1975), p. 252.

# TOWARD THE
# PACIFIC CENTURY?

*I*n August 1945, Japan was in ruins, its cities destroyed, its vast Asian empire in ashes, its land occupied by a foreign army. A decade earlier, Japanese leaders had proclaimed their national path to development as a model for other Asian nations to follow. But their Great East Asia Co-Prosperity Sphere, which had been designed to build a vast empire under Japanese tutelage, had led only to bloody war and ultimate defeat.

Half a century later, Japan had emerged as the second greatest industrial power in the world, democratic in form and content and a source of stability throughout the region. Japan's achievement spawned a number of Asian imitators. Known as the "Little Tigers," the four industrializing societies of Taiwan, Hong Kong, Singapore, and South Korea achieved considerable success by following the path originally charted by Japan. Along with Japan, they became economic powerhouses and ranked among the world's top seventeen trading nations. Other nations in Asia and elsewhere took note and began to adopt the Japanese formula. It is no wonder that observers relentlessly heralded the coming of the "Pacific Century."

The impressive success of some countries in East and Southeast Asia prompted several commentators in the region to declare that the global balance of power had shifted away from Europe and the United States toward the lands of the Pacific. When Western critics argued that eastern Asia's achievements had taken place at great cost, as authoritarian governments in the region trampled on human rights and denied their citizens the freedoms that they required to fulfill their own destiny, Asian observers retorted that freedom was not simply a matter of individuals' doing what they please but rather represented an opportunity and an obligation to serve their community and achieve the betterment of their fellow human beings. Such views not only reflected the growing self-confidence of many societies in East and Southeast Asia but also their growing inclination to defend Asian values and traditions against critics in the West. •

# JAPAN: ASIAN GIANT

For five years after the war in the Pacific, Japan was governed by an Allied administration under the command of U.S. General Douglas MacArthur. The occupation regime, which consisted of the Far Eastern Commission in Washington, D.C., and the four-power Allied Council in Tokyo, was dominated by the United States, although the country was technically administered by a new Japanese government. As commander of the occupation administration, MacArthur was responsible for demilitarizing Japanese society, destroying the Japanese war machine, trying Japanese civilian and military officials charged with war crimes, and laying the foundations of postwar Japanese society.

During the war, senior U.S. officials had discussed whether to insist on the abdication of the emperor as the symbol of Japanese imperial expansion. During the summer of 1945, the United States rejected a Japanese request to guarantee that the position of the emperor would be retained in any future peace settlement and reiterated its demand for unconditional surrender. After the war, however, the United States agreed to the retention of the emperor after he agreed publicly to renounce his divinity (see the box on p. 182). Although many historians have suggested that Emperor Hirohito opposed the war policy of his senior advisers, some recent studies have contended that he fully supported it.

Under MacArthur's firm tutelage, Japanese society was remodeled along Western lines. The centerpiece of occupation policy was the promulgation of a new constitution to replace the Meiji Constitution of 1889. The new charter, which was drafted by U.S. planners and imposed on the Japanese despite their objections to some of its provisions, was designed to transform Japan into a peaceful and pluralistic society that would no longer be capable of waging offensive war. The constitution specifically renounced war as a national policy, and Japan unilaterally agreed to maintain armed forces only sufficient for self-defense. Perhaps most important, the constitution established a parliamentary form of government based on a bicameral legislature, an independent judiciary, and a universal franchise; it also reduced the power of the emperor and guaranteed human rights.

MAP 9.1 Modern Japan. Shown here are the four main islands that comprise the contemporary state of Japan. ➤ *Which is the largest?*

But more than a written constitution was needed to demilitarize Japan and place it on a new course. Like the Meiji leaders in the late nineteenth century, occupation administrators wished to transform Japanese social institutions and hoped their policies would be accepted by the Japanese people as readily as those of the Meiji period had been. The Meiji reforms, however, had been crafted to reflect native traditions and had set Japan on a path quite different from that of the modern West. Some Japanese observers believed that a fundamental reversal of trends begun with the Meiji Restoration would be needed before Japan would be ready to adopt the Western capitalist, democratic model.

One of the sturdy pillars of Japanese militarism had been the giant business cartels, known as *zaibatsu*. Allied policy was designed to break up the *zaibatsu* into smaller units in the belief that corporate concentration, in Japan as in the United States, not only hindered competition but was inherently undemocratic and conducive to political authoritarianism. Occupation planners also intended to promote the formation of independent labor unions, to

# THE EMPEROR IS NOT DIVINE

*At the close of World War II, the United States agreed that Japan could retain the emperor, but only on the condition that he renounce his divinity. When the governments of Great Britain and the Soviet Union advocated that Hirohito be tried as a war criminal, General Douglas MacArthur, the supreme commander of Allied occupation forces in Japan, argued that the emperor had a greater grasp of democratic principles than most other Japanese and that his presence was vital to the success of Allied occupation policy. That recommendation was upheld. On New Year's Day, 1946, the emperor issued a rescript denying his divinity. To many Japanese of the era, however, he remained a divine figure.*

## HIROHITO, RESCRIPT ON DIVINITY

In greeting the New Year, we recall to mind that the Emperor Meiji proclaimed as the basis of our national policy the five clauses of the Charter at the beginning of the Meiji era. . . .

The proclamation is evident in its significance and high in its ideals. We wish to make this oath anew and restore the country to stand on its own feet again. We have to reaffirm the principles embodied in the Charter and proceed unflinchingly toward elimination of misguided practices of the past; and keeping in close touch with the desires of the people, we will construct a new Japan through thoroughly being pacific, the officials and the people alike obtaining rich culture and advancing the standard of living of the people.

The devastation of the war inflicted upon our cities, the miseries of the destitute, the stagnation of trade, shortage of food, and the great and growing number of unemployed are indeed heart-rending, but if the nation is firmly united in its resolve to face the present ordeal and to see civilization consistently in peace, a bright future will undoubtedly be ours, not only for our country but for the whole of humanity.

Love of the family and love of country are especially strong in this country. With more of this devotion should we now work toward love of mankind.

We feel deeply concerned to note that consequent upon the protracted war ending in our defeat our people are liable to grow restless and to fall into the slough of despond. Radical tendencies in excess are gradually spreading and the sense of morality tends to lose its hold on the people with the result that there are signs of confusion of thoughts.

We stand by the people and we wish always to share with them in their moment of joys and sorrows. The ties between us and our people have always stood upon mutual trust and affection. They do not depend upon mere legends and myths. They are not predicated on the false conception that the Emperor is divine and that the Japanese people are superior to other races and fated to rule the world.

Our Government should make every effort to alleviate their trials and tribulations. At the same time, we trust that the people will rise to the occasion and will strive courageously for the solution of their outstanding difficulties and for the development of industry and culture. Acting upon a consciousness of solidarity and of mutual aid and broad tolerance in their civil life, they will prove themselves worthy of their best tradition. By their supreme endeavors in that direction they will be able to render their substantial contribution to the welfare and advancement of mankind.

The resolution for the year should be made at the beginning of the year. We expect our people to join us in all exertions looking to accomplishment of this great undertaking with an indomitable spirit.

Source: John David Lu, *Sources of Japanese Tradition* (New York: McGraw-Hill, 1974), vol. 2, pp. 190–191; from *New York Times*, January 1, 1946.

---

lessen the power of the state over the economy, and to provide a mouthpiece for downtrodden Japanese workers. Economic inequality in rural areas was to be reduced by a comprehensive land reform program that would turn the land over to the people who farmed it. Finally, the educational system was to be remodeled along American lines so that it would turn out independent individuals rather than automatons subject to manipulation by the state.

The Allied program was an ambitious and even audacious plan to remake Japanese society and has been justly praised for its clear-sighted vision and altruistic motives. Parts of the program, such as the constitution, the land

reform program, and the educational system, succeeded brilliantly. But as other concerns began to intervene, changes or compromises were made that were not always successful. In particular, with the rise of Cold War sentiment in the United States in the late 1940s, the goal of decentralizing the Japanese economy gave way to the desire to make Japan a key partner in the effort to defend East Asia against international communism. Convinced of the need to promote economic recovery in Japan, U.S. policymakers began to show more tolerance for the *zaibatsu*. Concerned at growing radicalism within the new labor movement, where left-wing elements were gaining strength, U.S. occupation authorities placed less emphasis on the independence of the labor unions.

Cold War concerns also affected U.S. foreign relations with Japan. On September 8, 1951, the United States and other former belligerent nations signed a peace treaty restoring Japanese independence. In turn, Japan renounced any claim to such former colonies or territories as Taiwan (which had been returned to the Republic of China), Korea (which, after a period of joint Soviet and U.S. occupation, had become two independent states), and southern Sakhalin and the Kurile Islands (which had been ceded to the Soviet Union). The Soviet Union refused to sign the treaty on the grounds that it had not been permitted to play an active role in the occupation. On the same day, the Japanese and Americans signed a defensive alliance and agreed that the United States could maintain military bases on the Japanese islands. Japan was now formally independent, but in a new dependency relationship with the United States.

## The Transformation of Modern Japan: Politics and Government

By the early 1950s, then, Japan had regained at least partial control over its own destiny. Although it was linked closely to the United States through the new security treaty and the new U.S.-drafted constitution, Japan was now essentially free to move out on its own. As the world would soon discover, the Japanese adapted quickly to the new conditions. From a semifeudal society with autocratic leanings, Japan rapidly progressed into one of the most stable and advanced democracies in the world today.

The Allied occupation administrators started with the conviction that Japanese expansionism was directly linked to the institutional and ideological foundations of the Meiji Constitution. Accordingly, they set out to change Japanese politics into something closer to the pluralistic approach used in most Western nations. The concepts of universal suffrage, governmental accountability, and a balance of power among the executive, legislative, and judicial branches that were embodied in the constitution of 1947 have held firm, and Japan today is a stable and mature democratic society with a literate and politically active electorate and a government that usually seeks to meet the needs of its citizens.

Yet a number of characteristics of the current Japanese political system reflect the tenacity of the traditional political culture. Although postwar Japan had a multiparty system with two major parties, the Liberal Democrats and the Socialists, in practice there was a "government party" and a permanent opposition—the Liberal Democrats were not voted out of office for thirty years. The ruling Liberal Democratic Party included several factions, but disputes were usually based on personalities rather than substantive issues. Many of the leading Liberal Democrats controlled factions on a patron-client basis, and decisions on key issues, such as who should assume the prime ministership, were decided by a modern equivalent of the *genro* oligarchs.

That tradition changed suddenly in 1993 when the ruling Liberal Democrats, shaken by persistent reports of corruption and cronyism between politicians and business interests, failed to win a majority of seats in parliamentary elections. Mirohiro Hosokawa, the leader of one of several newly created parties in the Japanese political spectrum, was elected prime minister. He promised to launch a number of reforms to clean up the political system. The new coalition government, however, quickly split into feuding factions, and in 1995, the Liberal Democratic Party returned to power. Successive prime ministers failed to carry out promised reforms, and in 2001, Junichiro Koizumi (b. 1942), a former minister of health and welfare, was elected prime minister on a promise that he would initiate far-reaching reforms to fix the political system and make it more responsive to the needs of the Japanese people. His charisma raised expectations that he might be able to bring about significant changes; so far, however, he has had little success.

One of the problems plaguing the current system has been that it continues the centralizing tendencies of the Meiji period. The government is organized on a unitary rather than a federal basis; the local administrative units, called prefectures, have few of the powers of states in the United States. Moreover, the central government plays an active and sometimes intrusive role in various aspects of the economy, mediating management-labor disputes, establishing price and wage policies, and subsidizing vital industries and enterprises producing goods for export. This government intervention in the economy has traditionally been widely accepted and is often cited as a key reason for the efficiency of Japanese industry and the emergence of the country as an industrial giant.

In recent years, the tradition of active government involvement in the economy has increasingly come under fire. Japanese business, which previously sought government protection from imports, now argues that deregulation is needed to enable Japanese firms to innovate as a means of keeping up with the competition. Such reforms, however, have been resisted by powerful government ministries in Tokyo, which are accustomed to playing an active role in national affairs.

A third problem is related to the fact that the ruling Liberal Democratic Party has long been divided into factions that seek to protect their own interests and often resist changes that might benefit society as a whole. This tradition of factionalism has tended to insulate political figures from popular scrutiny and encouraged the susceptibility to secret dealing and official corruption. A number of senior politicians, including two recent prime ministers, have been forced to resign because of serious questions about improper financial dealings with business associates. Concern over political corruption was undoubtedly a major factor in the defeat suffered by the Liberal Democrats in the summer of 1993, and the issue continues to plague the political scene.

Last but certainly not least, minorities such as the *eta* (hereditary outcastes in traditional Japan, now known as the Burakumin) and Korean residents in Japan continue to be subjected to legal and social discrimination. For years, official sources were reluctant to divulge that thousands of Korean women were conscripted to serve as "comfort women" (prostitutes) for Japanese soldiers during the war, and many Koreans living in Japan contend that such condescending attitudes toward minorities continue to exist. Representatives of the "comfort women" have demanded both financial compensation and a formal letter of apology from the Japanese government for the treatment they received during the Pacific War. Negotiations over the issue are under way.

Japan's behavior during World War II has been an especially sensitive issue. During the early 1990s, critics at home and abroad charged that textbooks printed under the guidance of the Ministry of Education did not adequately discuss the atrocities committed by the Japanese government and armed forces during World War II. Other Asian governments were particularly incensed at Tokyo's failure to accept responsibility for such behavior and demanded a formal apology. The government expressed remorse, but only in the context of the aggressive actions of all colonial powers during the imperialist era. In the view of many Japanese, the actions of their government during the Pacific War were a form of self-defense. When new textbooks were published that openly discussed instances of Japanese wartime misconduct, including sex slavery, the use of slave labor, and the Nanjing Massacre (see the Prologue), many Japanese were outraged and initiated a campaign to delete or tone down references to atrocities committed by imperial troops during the Pacific War.

The issue is not simply an academic one, for fear of the potential revival of Japanese militarism is still strong elsewhere in the region. The United States has not shared this concern, however, and applauded a recent decision to enhance the role of Japanese self-defense forces in dealing with potential disturbances within the region.

This issue has provoked vigorous debate in Japan, where some observers have argued that their country must begin to adopt a more assertive stance toward the United States and play a larger role in Asian affairs. In the spring of 2000, a parliamentary commission was appointed to look into the matter.

## The Economy

Nowhere are the changes in postwar Japan so visible as in the economic sector, where the nation has developed into a major industrial and technological power in the space of a century, surpassing such advanced Western societies as Germany, France, and Great Britain. Here indeed is the Japanese miracle in its most concrete manifestation.

The process began a century ago in the single-minded determination of the Meiji modernizers to create a rich country and strong state. Their initial motive was to guarantee Japan's survival against Western imperialism, but this defensive urge evolved into a desire to excel and, during the years before World War II, to dominate. That desire led to the war in the Pacific and, in the eyes of some observers, still contributes to Japan's problems with its trading partners in the world today.

As we have seen, the officials of the Allied occupation identified the Meiji economic system with centralized power and the rise of Japanese militarism. Accordingly, MacArthur's planners set out to break up the *zaibatsu* and decentralize Japanese industry and commerce. But with the rise of Cold War tensions, the policy was scaled back in the late 1940s, and only the nineteen largest conglomerates were affected. In any event, the new antimonopoly law did not hinder the formation of looser ties between Japanese companies, and as a result, a new type of informal relationship, sometimes called the *keiretsu*, or "interlocking arrangement," began to take shape after World War II. Through such arrangements among suppliers, wholesalers, retailers, and financial institutions, the *zaibatsu* system was reconstituted under a new name.

The occupation administration had more success with its program to reform the agricultural system. Half of the population still lived on farms, and half of all farmers were still tenants. Under a stringent land reform program in the late 1940s, all lands owned by absentee landlords and all cultivated landholdings over an established maximum were sold on easy credit terms to the tenants. The maximum size of an individual farm was set at 7.5 acres, while an additional 2.5 acres could be leased to tenants. The reform program created a strong class of yeoman farmers, and tenants declined to about 10 percent of the rural population.

During the next fifty years, Japan re-created the stunning results of the Meiji era. At the end of the Allied occupation in 1950, the Japanese gross national product was about one-third that of Great Britain or France. Today, it is larger than both put together and well over half that of the United States. Japan is the greatest exporting nation in the world, and its per capita income equals or surpasses that of most advanced Western states. In terms of education, mortality rates, and health care, the quality of life in Japan is superior to that in the United States or the advanced nations of Western Europe.

By the mid-1980s, the economic challenge presented by Japan had begun to arouse increasing concern in both official and private circles in Europe and the United States. Explanations for the phenomenon tended to fall into two major categories. Some pointed to cultural factors: The Japanese are naturally group-oriented and find it easy to cooperate with one another. Traditionally hardworking and frugal, they are more inclined to save than to consume, a trait that boosts the savings rate and labor productivity. The Japanese are family-oriented and therefore spend less on welfare for the elderly, who normally live with their children. Like all Confucian societies, the Japanese value education, and consequently, the labor force is highly skilled. Finally, Japan is a homogeneous society in which people share common values and respond in similar ways to the challenges of the modern world.

Others cited more practical reasons for Japanese success. Paradoxically, Japan benefited from the total destruction of its industrial base during World War II because it did not face the problem of antiquated plants that plagued many industries in the United States. Under the terms of its constitution and the security treaty with the United States, Japan spends less than 1 percent of its gross national product on national defense, whereas the United States spends more than 5 percent. Labor productivity is high, not only because the Japanese are hard workers (according to statistics, Japanese workers spend substantially more time on the job than workers in other advanced societies) but also because corporations reward innovation and maintain good management-labor relations. Consequently, employee mobility and the number of days lost to labor stoppages are minimized (on an average day, according to one estimate, 603 Japanese workers are on strike compared to 11,956 Americans). Just as it did before World War II, the Japanese government promotes business interests rather than hindering them. Finally, some analysts charge that Japan uses unfair trade practices, subsidizing exports through the Ministry of International Trade and Industry (MITI), dumping goods at prices below cost to break into a foreign market, maintaining an artificially low standard of living at home to encourage exports, and unduly restricting imports from other countries.

There is some truth on both sides of the argument. Undoubtedly, Japan benefited from its privileged position beneath the U.S. nuclear umbrella as well as from its ability to operate in a free trade environment that provided both export markets and access to Western technology. The Japanese also took a number of practical steps to improve their competitive position in the world and the effectiveness of their economic system at home.

Yet many of these steps were possible precisely because of the cultural factors described here. The tradition of loyalty to the firm, for example, derives from the communal tradition in Japanese society. The concept of sacrificing one's personal interests to those of the state, though not necessarily rooted in the traditional period, was certainly fostered by the genro oligarchy during the Meiji era.

In recent years, the Japanese economy has run into serious difficulties, raising the question as to whether the vaunted Japanese model is as appealing as many observers earlier declared. A rise in the value of the yen hurt exports and burst the bubble of investment by Japanese banks that had taken place under the umbrella of government protection. Lacking a domestic market equivalent in size to the United States, the Japanese economy slipped into a long-term recession that continues today.

These economic difficulties have placed heavy pressure on some of the highly praised features of the Japanese economy. The tradition of lifetime employment created a bloated white-collar workforce and made downsizing difficult. Today, job security is on the decline as increasing numbers of workers are being laid off. Unfortunately, a disproportionate burden has fallen on women, who lack seniority and continue to suffer from various forms of discrimination in the workplace. A positive consequence is that job satisfaction is beginning to take precedence over security in the minds of many Japanese workers, and salary is beginning to reflect performance more than time on the job.

A final factor is that slowly but inexorably, the Japanese market is beginning to open up to international competition. Foreign automakers are winning a growing share of the domestic market, while the government—concerned at the prospect of food shortages—has committed itself to facilitating the importation of rice from abroad. This last move was especially sensitive, given the almost sacred role that rice farming holds in the Japanese mind-set.

At the same time, greater exposure to foreign economic competition may serve to improve the performance of Japanese manufacturers. In recent years, Japanese consumers have become increasingly concerned about the quality of some of their domestic products, provoking one cabinet minister to complain about "sloppiness and complacency" among Japanese firms (a scandal in the United States over defects in Firestone tires, produced by the Japanese tire manufacturer Bridgestone, was a case in point). One apparent reason for the country's quality problems is increasing competition from the United States, which has forced Japanese companies to adopt cost-cutting measures to meet the challenge from abroad.

## A Society in Transition

During the occupation, Allied planners set out to change social characteristics that they believed had contributed to Japanese aggressiveness before and during World War II. The new educational system removed all references to filial piety, patriotism, and loyalty to the emperor and emphasized the individualistic values of Western civilization. The new constitution and a revised civil code attempted to achieve true sexual equality by removing remaining legal restrictions on women's rights to obtain a divorce, hold a job, or change their domicile. Women were guaranteed the right to vote and were encouraged to enter politics.

Such efforts to remake Japanese behavior through legislation were only partly successful. Since the end of World War II, Japan has unquestionably become a more individualistic and egalitarian society. Freedom of choice in marriage and occupation is taken for granted, and social mobility, though not so extensive as in the United States, has increased considerably. Although Allied occupation policy established the legal framework for these developments, primary credit must be assigned to the evolution of the Japanese themselves into an urbanized and technologically advanced industrial society.

At the same time, many of the distinctive characteristics of traditional Japanese society have persisted, in somewhat altered form. The emphasis on loyalty to the group and community relationships, for example, known in Japanese as *amae*, is reflected in the strength of corporate loyalties in contemporary Japan. Even though competition among enterprises in a given industry is often quite vigorous, social cohesiveness among both management and labor personnel is exceptionally strong within each individual corporation, although, as we have seen, that attitude has eroded somewhat in recent years.

One possible product of this attitude may be the relatively egalitarian nature of Japanese society in terms of income. A chief executive officer in Japan receives, on average, seventeen times the salary of the average worker, compared with eighty-five times in the United States. The disparity between wealth and poverty is also generally less in Japan than in most European countries and certainly less than in the United States.

Emphasis on the work ethic also remains strong. The tradition of hard work is implanted at a young age within the educational system. The Japanese school year runs for 240 days, compared to 180 days in the United States, and work assignments outside class tend to be more extensive (according to one source, a Japanese student averages about five hours of homework per day). Competition for acceptance into universities is intense, and many young Japanese take cram courses to prepare for the "examination hell" that lies ahead. The results are impressive: the literacy rate in Japanese schools is almost 100 percent, and Japanese schoolchildren consistently earn higher scores on achievement tests than children in other advanced countries. At the same time, this devotion to success has often been accompanied by bullying by teachers and what Americans might consider an oppressive sense of conformity (see the box on p. 187).

Some young Japanese find suicide the only escape from the pressures emanating from society, school, and family. Parental pride often becomes a factor, with "education mothers" pressuring their children to work hard and succeed for the honor of the family. Ironically, once the student is accepted into college, the amount of work assigned tends to decrease because graduates of the best universities are virtually guaranteed lucrative employment offers. Nevertheless, the early training instills an attitude of deference to group interests that persists throughout life. Some outside observers, however, believe such attitudes can have a detrimental effect on individual initiative.

The tension between the Japanese way and the foreign approach is especially noticeable in Japanese baseball, where major league teams frequently hire U.S. players. One American noted the case of Tatsunori Hara, one of the best Japanese players in the league. "He had so many different people telling him what to do," remarked Warren Cromartie, a teammate, "it's a wonder he could still swing the bat. They turned him into a robot, instead of just letting him play naturally and expressing his natural talent." To his Japanese coach, however, conformity brought teamwork, and teamwork in Japan is the road to success.[1]

By all accounts, independent thinking is on the increase in Japan, and some schools are beginning to emphasize creativity over rote learning. In some cases, it leads to antisocial behavior, such as crime or membership in a teen gang. Usually, it is expressed in more indirect

# GROWING UP IN JAPAN

*Japanese schoolchildren are exposed to a much more regimented environment than U.S. children experience. Most Japanese schoolchildren, for example, wear black-and-white uniforms to school. These regulations are examples of rules adopted by middle school systems in various parts of Japan. The Ministry of Education in Tokyo concluded that these regulations were excessive, but they are probably typical.*

## SCHOOL REGULATIONS: JAPANESE STYLE

1. Boys' hair should not touch the eyebrows, the ears, or the top of the collar.
2. No one should have a permanent wave, or dye his or her hair. Girls should not wear ribbons or accessories in their hair. Hair dryers should not be used.
3. School uniform skirts should be ____ centimeters above the ground, no more and no less (differs by school and region).
4. Keep your uniform clean and pressed at all times. Girls' middy blouses should have two buttons on the back collar. Boys' pant cuffs should be of the prescribed width. No more than 12 eyelets should be on the shoes. The number of buttons on a shirt and tucks in a shirt are also prescribed.
5. Wear your school badge at all times. It should be positioned exactly.
6. Going to school in the morning, wear your book bag strap on the right shoulder; in the afternoon on the way home, wear it on the left shoulder. Your book case thickness, filled and unfilled, is also prescribed.
7. Girls should wear only regulation white underpants of 100% cotton.
8. When you raise your hand to be called on, your arm should extend forward and up at the angle prescribed in your handbook.
9. Your own route to and from school is marked in your student rule handbook; carefully observe which side of each street you are to use on the way to and from school.
10. After school you are to go directly home, unless your parent has written a note permitting you to go to another location. Permission will not be granted by the school unless the other location is a suitable one. You must not go to coffee shops. You must be home by ____ o'clock.
11. It is not permitted to drive or ride a motorcycle, or to have a license to drive one.
12. Before and after school, no matter where you are, you represent our school, so you should behave in ways we can all be proud of.

Source: Reprinted with permission of The Free Press, a division of Simon & Schuster Adult Publishing Group, from *The Material Child: Coming of Age in Japan and America* by Merry White. Copyright © 1993 by Merry White. All rights reserved.

ways, such as the recent fashion among young people of dyeing their hair brown (known in Japanese as "tea hair"). Because the practice is banned in many schools and generally frowned upon by the older generation (one police chief dumped a pitcher of beer on a student with brown hair whom he noticed in a bar), many young Japanese dye their hair as a gesture of independence and a means of gaining acceptance among their peers. When seeking employment or getting married, however, they return their hair to its natural color.

One of the more tenacious legacies of the past in Japanese society is sexual inequality. Although women are now legally protected against discrimination in employment, very few have reached senior levels in business, education, or politics, and in the words of one Western scholar, they remain "acutely disadvantaged"—though ironically, in a recent survey of business executives in Japan, a majority declared that women were smarter than men. Women now make up nearly 50 percent of the workforce, but most are in retail or service occupations, and their average salary is only about half that of men. There is a feminist movement in Japan, but it has none of the vigor and mass support of its counterpart in the United States.

Most women in Japan consider being a homemaker the ideal position; a poll taken during the 1980s found that only 15 percent of Japanese women wanted a full-time job.[2] In the home, a Japanese woman has considerable responsibility. She is expected to be a "good wife and wise mother" and has the primary responsibility for managing the family finances and raising the children. Japanese husbands carry little of the workload around the house, spending an average of nine minutes a day on housework, compared to twenty-six minutes for American husbands. At the same time, Japanese divorce rates are well below those of the United States.

Japan's welfare system also differs profoundly from its Western counterparts. Applicants are required to seek assistance first from their own families, and the physically able are ineligible for government aid. As a result, less than 1 percent of the population receives welfare benefits, compared with more than 10 percent who receive some form of assistance in the United States. Outside observers interpret the difference as the product of several factors, including low levels of drug addiction and illegitimacy, as well as the importance in Japan of the work ethic and family responsibility.

Traditionally, it was the responsibility of the eldest child in a Japanese family to care for aging parents, but that system, too, is beginning to break down because of limited housing space and the growing tendency of working-age women to seek jobs in the marketplace. The proportion of Japanese older than sixty-five years of age who live with their children has dropped from 80 percent in 1970 to about 50 percent today. At the same time, public and private pension plans are under increasing financial pressure, partly because of a low birthrate and a graying population. Japan today has the highest proportion of people older than sixty-five—17 percent of the country's total population of 130 million—of any industrialized country in the world.

Whether the unique character of modern Japan will endure is unclear. Confidence in the Japanese "economic miracle" has been shaken because of the recent downturn, and there are indications of a growing tendency toward hedonism and individualism among Japanese youth. Older Japanese frequently complain that the younger generation lacks their sense of loyalty and willingness to sacrifice. Some have also discerned signs that the concept of loyalty to one's employer may be beginning to erode among Japanese youth. Some observers have predicted that with increasing affluence, Japan will become more like the industrialized societies in the West. Nevertheless, Japan is unlikely to evolve into a photocopy of the United States. Not only is Japan a much more homogeneous society, but its small size and dearth of natural resources encourage a strong work ethic and a sense of togetherness that have dissipated in American society.

## Religion and Culture

The sense of racial and cultural pride that characterizes contemporary Japan is rather different from Japanese attitudes at the beginning of the Meiji era. When Japan was opened to the West in the nineteenth century, many Japanese became convinced of the superiority of foreign ideas and institutions and were especially interested in Western religion and culture. Although Christian converts were few, numbering less than 1 percent of the population, the influence of Christianity was out of proportion to the size of the community. Many intellectuals during the Meiji era were impressed by the emotional commitment shown by missionaries in Japan and viewed Christianity as a contemporary version of Confucianism.

Today, Japan includes almost 1.5 million Christians along with 93 million Buddhists. Many Japanese also follow Shinto, no longer identified with reverence for the emperor and the state. As in the West, increasing urbanization has led to a decline in the practice of organized religion, although evangelical sects have proliferated in recent years. In all likelihood, their members, like those belonging to similar sects elsewhere, are seeking spiritual underpinnings in an increasingly secular and complex world. The largest and best-known sect is the Soka Gakkai, a lay Buddhist organization that has attracted millions of followers and formed its own political party, the Komeito.

Western literature, art, and music also had a major impact on Japanese society. Western influence led to the rapid decline of traditional forms of drama and poetry and the growth in popularity of the prose novel. After the Japanese defeat in World War II, many of the writers who had been active before the war resurfaced, but now their writing reflected their demoralization, echoing the spiritual vacuum of the times. Labeled apure, from the first part of the French après-guerre (postwar), these disillusioned authors were attracted to existentialism, and some turned to hedonism and nihilism. This "lost generation" described its anguish with piercing despair; several of its luminaries committed suicide. For them, defeat was compounded by fear of the Americanization of postwar Japan.

One of the best examples of this attitude was novelist Yukio Mishima (1925–1970), who led a crusade to stem the tide of what he described as America's "universal and uniform 'Coca-Colonization'" of the world in general and Japan in particular.[3] In Confessions of a Mask, written in 1949, Mishima described the awakening of a young man to his own homosexuality. His later novels, The Thirst for Love and The Temple of the Golden Pavilion, are riveting narratives about disturbed characters. Mishima's ritual suicide in 1970 was the subject of widespread speculation and transformed him into a cult figure.

One of Japan's most serious-minded contemporary authors is Kenzaburo Oe (b. 1935). His work, which was rewarded with the Nobel Prize in Literature in 1994, presents Japan's ongoing quest for modern identity and purpose. His characters reflect the spiritual anguish precipitated by the collapse of the imperial Japanese tradition and the subsequent adoption of Western culture—a trend that, according to Oe, has culminated in unabashed materialism, cultural decline, and a moral void. Yet unlike Mishima, he does not seek to reinstill the imperial traditions of the past but rather wants to regain spiritual meaning by retrieving the sense of communality and innocence found in rural Japan.

In *Teach Us to Outgrow Our Madness*, a collection of four novellas, Oe describes the fascination of Japanese children when they first saw a black American soldier held in captivity at the end of World War II. Initially viewing him as an intimidating oddity, the children eventually accept him as a human being, admiring his powerful body and sense of joy in being alive.

Haruki Murakami (b. 1949), one of Japan's most popular authors today, was one of the first to discard the introspective and somber style of the earlier postwar period. Characters in his novels typically take the form of a detached antihero, reflecting the emptiness of corporate life in contemporary Japan. In *The Wind-Up Bird Chronicle* (1997), Murakami highlights the capacity for irrational violence in Japanese society and the failure of the nation to accept its guilt for the behavior of Japanese troops during World War II.

Since the 1970s, increasing affluence and a high literacy rate have contributed to a massive quantity of publications, ranging from popular potboilers to first-rate fiction. Much of this new literature deals with the common concerns of all affluent industrialized nations, including the effects of urbanization, advanced technology, and mass consumption. One recent phenomenon is the so-called industrial novel, which seeks to lay bare the vicious infighting and pressure tactics that characterize Japanese business today. A wildly popular genre is the "art-manga," or literary cartoon. Although most manga are meant as pure entertainment, author Michio Hisauchi presents serious subjects, such as Japanese soldiers marooned after the war on an island in the South Pacific, in *Japan's Junglest Day*, a full-length novel in comic book form with cartoon characters posing philosophical questions.

There were many women writers during early Japanese history, but they have labored under many disabilities in a male-dominated society. Japanese literary critics, who were invariably men, accepted "female" literature as long as it dealt exclusively with what they viewed as appropriately "female" subjects, such as the "mysteries" of the female psyche and motherhood. Even today, Japan has separate literary awards for men and women, and women are not considered capable of abstract or objective writing. Nevertheless, many contemporary women authors are daring to broach "male" subjects and are producing works of considerable merit.

Other aspects of Japanese culture have also been influenced by Western ideas, although without the intense preoccupation with synthesis that is evident in literature. Western music is popular in Japan, and scores of Japanese classical musicians have succeeded in the West. Even rap music has gained a foothold among Japanese youth, although without its association in the United

© Barry Cronin Newsmakers/Getty Images

**COOL OTAKU FASHION TEENS.** Fashion-conscious teenagers have become Japan's most dedicated consumers. With the economy in the doldrums and real estate costs soaring, many young people live with their families well into their twenties, using the money saved to purchase the latest styles in clothing. Avid readers of fashion magazines, these *otaku* ("obsessed") teenagers—heirs of Japan's long affluence—pay exorbitant prices for hip-hop outfits, platform shoes, and layered dresses.

States with sex, drugs, and violence. Although some of the lyrics betray an attitude of modest revolt against the uptight world of Japanese society, most lack any such connotations. An example is the rap song "Street Life":

*Now's the time to hip-hop,*
*Everybody's crazy about rap,*
*Hey, hey, you all, listen up,*
*Listen to my rap and cheer up.*

As one singer remarked, "We've been very fortunate, and we don't want to bother our moms and dads. So we don't sing songs that would disturb parents."[4]

No longer are Japanese authors and painters seeking to revive the old Japan of the tea ceremony and falling plum blossoms. Raised in the crowded cities of postwar Japan, soaking up movies and television, rock music and jeans, Coca-Cola and McDonald's, many contemporary Japanese speak the universal language of today's world. Yet even as the Japanese enter the global marketplace, they retain ties to their own traditions. Businesspeople sometimes use traditional Taoist forms of physical and mental training to reduce the stress inherent in their jobs, while others retreat to a Zen monastery to learn to focus their willpower as a means of besting a competitor.

There are some signs that under the surface, the tension between traditional and modern is exacting a price. As novelists such as Yukio Mishima and Kenzaburo Oe feared, the growing focus on material possessions and the decline of traditional religious beliefs have left a spiritual void that is undermining the sense of community and purpose that have motivated the country since the Meiji era. Some young people have reacted to the emptiness of their lives by joining religious cults such as Aum Shinri Kyo, which came to widespread world attention in 1995 when members of the organization, inspired by their leader Asahara Shoko, carried out a poison gas attack on the Tokyo subway that killed several people. Such incidents serve as a warning that Japan is not immune to the social ills that currently plague many Western countries.

## SOUTH KOREA: A PENINSULA DIVIDED

While the world was focused on the economic miracle occurring on the Japanese islands, another miracle of sorts was taking place across the Sea of Japan on the Asian mainland. In 1953, the Korean peninsula was exhausted from three years of bitter fraternal war, a conflict that took the lives of an estimated four million Koreans on both sides of the 38th parallel and turned as much as one-quarter of the population into refugees. Although a cease-fire was signed at Panmunjom in July 1953, it was a fragile peace that left two heavily armed and mutually hostile countries facing each other suspiciously.

North of the truce line was the People's Republic of Korea (PRK), a police state under the dictatorial rule of Communist leader Kim Il Sung (1912–1994). To the south was the Republic of Korea, under the equally autocratic President Syngman Rhee (1875–1965), a fierce anti-Communist who had led the resistance to the northern invasion and now placed his country under U.S. military protection. But U.S. troops could not protect Rhee from his own people, many of whom resented his reliance on the political power of the wealthy landlord class. After several years of harsh rule, marked by government corruption, fraudulent elections, and police brutality, demonstrations broke out in the capital city of Seoul in the spring of 1960 and forced him into retirement.

The Rhee era was followed by a brief period of multi-party democratic government, but in 1961, a coup d'état placed General Chung Hee Park (1917–1979) in power. The new regime promulgated a new constitution, and in 1963, Park was elected president of a civilian government. He set out to foster recovery of the economy from decades of foreign occupation and civil war. Adopting the nineteenth-century Japanese slogan "Rich Country and Strong State," Park built up a strong military while relying on U.S. and later Japanese assistance to help build a strong manufacturing base in what had been a predominantly agricultural society. Because the private sector had been relatively weak under Japanese rule, the government played an active role in the process by instituting a series of five-year plans that targeted specific industries for development, promoted exports, and funded infrastructure development. Under a land reform program, large landowners were required to sell all their farmland above 7.4 acres to their tenants at low prices.

The program was a solid success. Benefiting from the Confucian principles of thrift, respect for education, and hard work (during the 1960s and 1970s, South Korean workers spent an average of sixty hours a week at their jobs), as well as from Japanese capital and technology, Korea gradually emerged as a major industrial power in East Asia. The economic growth rate rose from less than 5 percent annually in the 1950s to an average of 9 percent under Park. The largest corporations—including Samsung, Daewoo, and Hyundai—were transformed into massive conglomerates called *chaebol*, the Korean equivalent of the *zaibatsu* of prewar Japan. Taking advantage of relatively low wages and a stunningly high rate of saving, Korean businesses began to compete actively with the Japanese for export markets in Asia and throughout the world.

The Japanese became concerned about their "hungry spirit" and began refusing to share technology with the South Koreans. Per capita income also increased dramatically, from less than $90 (in U.S. dollars) annually in 1960 to $1,560 (twice that of Communist North Korea) twenty years later.

But like many other countries in the region, South Korea was slow to develop democratic principles. Although his government functioned with the trappings of democracy, Park continued to rule by autocratic means and suppressed all forms of dissidence. In 1979, Park was assassinated, and after a brief interregnum of democratic rule, a new military government under General Chun Doo Hwan (b. 1931) seized power. The new regime was as authoritarian as its predecessors, but opposition to autocratic rule had now spread from the ranks of college and high school students, who had led the early resistance, to much of the urban population. Protest against government policies became increasingly frequent. In 1987, massive demonstrations drove government troops out of the southern city of Kwangju, but the troops returned in force and killed an estimated two thousand demonstrators.

With Chun under increasing pressure from the United States to moderate the oppressive character of his rule, national elections were finally held in 1989. The government nominee, Roh Tae Woo, won the election with less than 40 percent of the vote. New elections in 1992 brought Kim Young Sam to the presidency. Kim selected several women for his cabinet and promised to make South Korea "a freer and more mature democracy." He also attempted to crack down on the rising influence of the giant *chaebols*, accused of giving massive bribes in return for favors from government officials. In the meantime, representatives of South Korea had made tentative contacts with the Communist regime in North Korea on possible steps toward eventual reunification of the peninsula.

But the problems of South Korea were more serious than the endemic problem of corruption. A growing trade deficit, combined with a declining growth rate, led to a rising incidence of unemployment and bankruptcy. Ironically, a second problem resulted from the economic collapse of Seoul's bitter rival, the PRK. Under the rule of Kim Il Sung's son Kim Jong Il, the North Korean economy was in a state of free fall, raising the specter of an

## The Korean Peninsula Since 1953

------- Cease-fire line
++++ Major rail lines

CHINA

Korea Bay

Pyongyang

Sea of Japan

38th Parallel

Panmunjom
Inchon · Seoul

Yellow Sea

Kwangju · Pusan
JAPAN

Korea Strait

0  100  200  300 Kilometers
0      100    200 Miles

Courtesy of William J. Duiker

⇒ KOREAN BRIDAL COUPLE.
Young married couples all over the world enjoy having their wedding photos taken at historical sites. This young Korean bride in a traditional red gown is posing in front of the Polguksa Temple near Kyongju, the site of the ancient Silla kingdom.

outflow of refugees that could swamp neighboring countries. To relieve the immediate effects of a food shortage, the Communist government in Pyongyang relaxed its restrictions on private farming, while Seoul agreed to provide food aid to alleviate the famine.

In the fall of 1997, a sudden drop in the value of the Korean currency, the *won*, led to bank failures and a decision to seek assistance from the International Monetary Fund (IMF). In December, an angry electorate voted Kim Young Sam (whose administration was tarnished by reports of corruption) out of office and elected his rival Kim Dae Jung to the presidency. But although the new chief executive promised drastic reforms, his regime too was charged with corruption and incompetence, while relations with North Korea, now on the verge of becoming a nuclear power, remained tense.

# TAIWAN: THE OTHER CHINA

South Korea was not the only rising industrial power trying to imitate the success of the Japanese in East Asia. To the south on the island of Taiwan, the Republic of China began to do the same.

After retreating to Taiwan following their defeat by the Communists, Chiang Kai-shek and his followers established a new capital at Taipei and set out to build a strong and prosperous nation based on Chinese traditions and the principles of Sun Yat-sen. The government, which continued to refer to itself as the Republic of China (ROC), contended that it remained the legitimate representative of the Chinese people and that it would eventually return in triumph to the mainland.

The Nationalists had much more success on Taiwan than they had achieved on the mainland. In the relatively secure environment provided by a security treaty with the United States, signed in 1954, and the comforting presence of the U.S. Seventh Fleet in the Taiwan Strait, the ROC was able to concentrate on economic growth without worrying about a Communist invasion. The regime possessed a number of other advantages that it had not enjoyed in Nanjing. Fifty years of efficient Japanese rule had left be-

hind a relatively modern economic infrastructure and an educated populace, although the island had absorbed considerable damage during World War II and much of its agricultural produce had been exported to Japan at low prices. With only a small population to deal with (about seven million in 1945), the ROC could make good use of foreign assistance and the efforts of its own energetic people to build a modern industrialized society.

The government moved rapidly to create a solid agricultural base. A land reform program, more effectively designed and implemented than the one introduced in the early 1930s on the mainland, led to the reduction of rents, while landholdings over 3 acres were purchased by the government and resold to the tenants at reasonable prices. As in Meiji Japan, the previous owners were compensated by government bonds. The results were gratifying: food production doubled over the next generation and began to make up a substantial proportion of exports.

In the meantime, the government strongly encouraged the development of local manufacturing and commerce. By the 1970s, Taiwan was one of the most dynamic industrial economies in East Asia. The agricultural proportion of the gross national product declined from 36 percent in 1952 to only 9 percent thirty years later. At first, the industrial and commercial sector was composed of relatively small firms engaged in exporting textiles and food products, but the 1960s saw a shift to heavy industry, including shipbuilding, steel, petrochemicals, and machinery, and a growing emphasis on exports. The government played a major role in the process, targeting strategic industries for support and investing in infrastructure. At the same time, as in Japan, the government stressed the importance of private enterprise and encouraged foreign investment and a high rate of internal savings. By the mid-1980s, more than three-quarters of the population lived in urban areas.

In contrast to the People's Republic of China (PRC) on the mainland, the ROC actively maintained Chinese tradition, promoting respect for Confucius and the ethical principles of the past, such as hard work, frugality, and filial piety. Although there was some corruption in both the government and the private sector, income differentials between the wealthy and the poor were generally less than elsewhere in the region, and the overall standard of living increased substantially. Health and

Modern Taiwan

CHINA
Taiwan Strait
Keelung
Taipei · Chinkuashih
Hsinchu
Changhua Taichung
Lukang · Ts'aot'un
Yüanlin · Puli
Nant'ou
Pescadores Is. · Chiai
· Tainan
Kaohsiung · P'ingtung
Pacific Ocean
Hualien

0    50    100    150 Kilometers
0         50         100 Miles

sanitation improved, literacy rates were quite high, and an active family planning program reduced the rate of population growth. Nevertheless, the total population on the island increased to about twenty million in the mid-1980s.

In one respect, however, Chiang Kai-shek had not changed: increasing prosperity did not lead to the democratization of the political process. The Nationalists continued to rule by emergency decree and refused to permit the formation of opposition political parties on the grounds that the danger of invasion from the mainland had not subsided. Propaganda material from the PRC was rigorously prohibited, and dissident activities (promoting either rapprochement with the mainland or the establishment of an independent Republic of Taiwan) were ruthlessly suppressed. Although representatives to the provincial government of the province of Taiwan were chosen in local elections, the central government (technically representing the entire population of China) was dominated by mainlanders who had fled to the island with Chiang in 1949.

Some friction developed between the mainlanders (as the new arrivals were called), who numbered about two million, and the native Taiwanese; except for a few aboriginal peoples in the mountains, most of the natives were ethnic Chinese whose ancestors had emigrated to the island during the Qing dynasty. While the mainlanders were dominant in government and the professions, the native Taiwanese were prominent in commerce. Mainlanders tended to view the local population with a measure of condescension, and at least in the early years, intermarriage between members of the two groups was rare. Many Taiwanese remembered with anger the events of March 1947, when Nationalist troops had killed hundreds of Taiwanese demonstrators in Taipei. More than one thousand leading members of the local Taiwanese community were arrested and killed in the subsequent repression. By the 1980s, however, these fissures in Taiwanese society had begun to diminish; by that time, an ever-higher proportion of the population had been born on the island and identified themselves as Taiwanese.

During the 1980s, the ROC slowly began to evolve toward a more representative form of government—a process that was facilitated by the death of Chiang Kai-shek in 1975. Chiang Ching-kuo (1909–1988), his son and successor, was less concerned about the danger from the mainland and more tolerant of free expression. On his death, he was succeeded as president by Lee Teng-hui (b. 1923), a native Taiwanese. By the end of the 1980s, democratization was under way, including elections and the formation of legal opposition parties. A national election in 1992 resulted in a bare majority for the Nationalists

over strong opposition from the Democratic Progressive Party (DPP).

But political liberalization had its dangers; some leading Democratic Progressives began to agitate for an independent Republic of Taiwan, a possibility that aroused concern within the Nationalist government in Taipei and frenzied hostility in the PRC. In the spring of 2000, DPP candidate Chen Shui-bian (b. 1950) won election to the presidency, ending half a century of Nationalist Party rule on Taiwan. His elevation to the position angered Beijing, which noted that in the past he had called for an independent Taiwanese state. Chen backed away from that position and called for the resumption of talks with PRC, but Chinese leaders remain suspicious of his intentions and reacted with hostility to U.S. plans to provide advanced military equipment to the island.

Whether Taiwan will remain an independent state or be united with mainland is impossible to predict. Certainly, the outcome depends in good measure on developments in the PRC. During his visit to China in 1972, U.S. President Richard Nixon said that this was a question for the Chinese people to decide (see Chapter 1). In 1979, President Jimmy Carter abrogated the mutual security treaty between the United States and the ROC that had been in force since 1954 and switched U.S. diplomatic recognition from the Republic of China to the PRC. But the United States continues to provide defensive military assistance to the Taiwanese armed forces and has made it clear that it supports self-determination for the people of Taiwan and that it expects the final resolution of the Chinese civil war to be by peaceful means. In the meantime, economic and cultural contacts between Taiwan and the mainland are steadily increasing, thus making the costs of any future military confrontation increasingly expensive for both sides. However, the Taiwanese have shown no inclination to accept the PRC's offer of "one country, two systems," under which the ROC would accept the PRC as the legitimate government of China in return for autonomous control over the affairs of Taiwan.

# SINGAPORE AND HONG KONG: THE LITTLEST TIGERS

The smallest but by no means the least successful of the "Little Tigers" are Singapore and Hong Kong. Both are essentially city-states with large populations densely packed into small territories. Singapore, once a British crown colony and briefly a part of the state of Malaysia, is now an independent nation. Hong Kong was a British colony until it was returned to PRC control, but with autonomous status, in 1997. In recent years, both have emerged as industrial powerhouses with standards of living well above the level of their neighbors.

The success of Singapore must be ascribed in good measure to the will and energy of its political leaders. When it became independent in August 1965, Singapore was in a state of transition. Its longtime position as an entrepôt for trade between the Indian Ocean and the South China Sea was declining in importance. With only 618 square miles of territory, much of it marshland and tropical jungle, Singapore had little to offer but the frugality and industriousness of its predominantly overseas Chinese population. But a recent history of political radicalism, fostered by the rise of influential labor unions, had frightened away foreign investors.

Within a decade, Singapore's role and reputation had dramatically changed. Under the leadership of Prime Minister Lee Kuan-yew (b. 1923), once the firebrand leader of the radical People's Action Party, the government encouraged the growth of an attractive business climate while engaging in massive public works projects to feed, house, and educate the nation's two million citizens. The major components of success have been shipbuilding, oil refineries, tourism, electronics, and finance — the city-state has become the banking hub of the entire region.

Like the other Little Tigers, Singapore has relied on a combination of government planning, entrepreneurial spirit, export promotion, high productivity, and an exceptionally high rate of saving to achieve industrial growth rates of nearly 10 percent annually over the past quarter century. Unlike some other industrializing countries in the region, it has encouraged the presence of multinational corporations to provide much needed capital and technological input. Population growth has been controlled by a stringent family planning program, and literacy rates are among the highest in Asia.

As in the other Little Tigers, an authoritarian political system has guaranteed a stable environment for economic growth. Until his recent retirement, Lee Kuan-yew and his People's Action Party dominated Sin-

The Republic of Singapore

gaporean politics, and opposition elements were intimidated into silence or arrested. The prime minister openly declared that the Western model of pluralist democracy was not appropriate for Singapore and lauded the Meiji model of centralized development (see the box on p. 195). Confucian values of thrift, hard work, and obedience to authority have been promoted as the ideology of the state. The government has had a passion for cleanliness and at one time even undertook a campaign to persuade its citizens to flush the public urinals. In 1989, the local *Straits Times*, a mouthpiece of the government, published a photograph of a man walking sheepishly from a row of urinals. The caption read "Caught without a flush: Mr. Amar Mohamed leaving the Lucky Plaza toilet without flushing the urinal."[5]

But economic success is beginning to undermine the authoritarian foundations of the system as a more sophisticated citizenry begins to demand more political freedoms and an end to government paternalism. Lee Kuan-yew's successor, Goh Chok Tong (b. 1941), has promised a "kinder, gentler" Singapore, and political restrictions on individual behavior are gradually being relaxed. In the spring of 2000, the government announced the opening of a speaker's corner, where citizens would be permitted to express their views, provided they obtained a permit and did not break the law. While this was a small step, it provided a reason for optimism that a more pluralistic political system will gradually emerge.

The future of Hong Kong is not so clear-cut. As in Singapore, sensible government policies and the hard work of its people have enabled Hong Kong to thrive. At first, the prosperity of the colony depended on a plentiful supply of cheap labor. Inundated with refugees from the mainland during the 1950s and 1960s, the population of Hong Kong burgeoned to more than six million. Many of the newcomers were willing to work for starvation wages in sweatshops producing textiles, simple appliances, and toys for the export market. More recently, Hong Kong has benefited from increased tourism, manufacturing, and the growing economic prosperity of neighboring Guangdong Province, the most prosperous region of the PRC. In one respect, Hong Kong

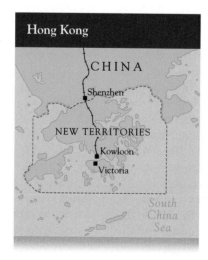

Hong Kong

# TO THOSE LIVING IN GLASS HOUSES

*Kishore Mahbubani is permanent secretary in the Ministry of Foreign Affairs in Singapore. Previously, he served as his country's ambassador to the United Nations. In this article, adapted from a piece in the Washington Quarterly, the author advises his audience to stop lecturing Asian societies on the issue of human rights and focus attention instead on problems in the United States. In his view, today the countries of the West have much to learn from their counterparts in East Asia. This viewpoint is shared by many other observers, political leaders, and foreign affairs specialists in the region.*

## KISHORE MAHBUBANI, "GO EAST, YOUNG MAN"

For the last century or more, in the passage of ideas across the Pacific, the flow has fundamentally been one way. Poverty-stricken and backward Asian societies have looked to the United States for leadership. Not surprisingly, a deeply ingrained belief has settled in the American mind that the U.S. mission in East Asia is to teach, not to learn. The time may have come for this mind-set to change.

In a major reversal of a pattern lasting centuries, many Western societies, including the U.S., are doing some major things fundamentally wrong, while a growing number of East Asian societies are doing the same things right. The results are most evident in the economic sphere. In purchasing power parity terms, East Asia's gross domestic product is already larger than that of either the U.S. or European community. Such economic prosperity, contrary to American belief, results not just from free-market arrangements but also from the right social and political choices. Although many East Asian societies have assumed some of the trappings of the West, they have also kept major social and cultural elements intact—elements that may explain their growing global competitiveness.

In most Asian eyes, the evidence of real social decay in the U.S. is clear and palpable. Since 1960, the U. S. population has grown by 41%. In the same period, there has been a 560% increase in violent crimes, a 419% increase in illegitimate births, a 400% increase in divorce rates, a 300% increase in children living in single-parent homes, a more than 200% increase in teenage suicide rates, and a drop of almost 80 points in Scholastic Aptitude Test scores. A clear American paradox is that a society that places such a high premium on freedom has effectively reduced the physical freedom of most Americans, especially those who live in large cities. They live in heavily fortified homes, think twice before taking an evening stroll around their neighborhoods, and feel increasingly threatened by random violence when they are outside.

To any Asian, it is obvious that the breakdown of the family and social order in the U.S. owes itself to a mindless ideology that maintains that the freedom of a small number of individuals who are known to pose a threat to society (criminals, terrorists, street gang members, drug dealers) should not be constrained (for example, through detention without trial), even if to do so would enhance the freedom of the majority. In short, principle takes precedence over people's well-being. This belief is purely and simply a gross violation of common sense. But it is the logical end product of a society that worships the notion of freedom as religiously as Hindus worship their sacred cows. Both must be kept absolutely unfettered, even when they obviously create great social discomfort. . . .

My hope is that Americans will come to visit East Asia in greater numbers. When they do, they will come to realize that their society has swung much too much in one direction: liberating the individual while imprisoning society. The relatively strong and stable family and social institutions of East Asia will appear more appealing. And as Americans experience the freedom of walking on city streets in Asia, they may begin to understand that freedom can also result from greater social order and discipline. Perhaps the best advice to give to a young American is: "Go East, Young Man."

Source: *Far Eastern Economic Review* (May 19, 1994), p. 32.

---

has differed from the other societies discussed in this chapter in that it has relied on an unbridled free market system rather than active state intervention in the economy. At the same time, by allocating substantial funds for transportation, sanitation, education, and public housing, the government has created favorable conditions for economic development.

Unlike the other Little Tigers, Hong Kong remained under colonial rule until very recently. British authorities did little to foster democratic institutions or practices, and most residents of the colony cared more about economic survival than political freedoms. In 1983, in talks between representatives of Great Britain and the PRC, the Chinese leaders made it clear they were determined to have Hong

# RETURN TO THE MOTHERLAND

*After lengthy negotiations in 1984, China and Great Britain agreed that on July 1, 1997, Hong Kong would return to Chinese sovereignty. Key sections of the agreement are included here. In succeeding years, authorities of the two countries held further negotiations. Some of the discussions raised questions in the minds of residents of Hong Kong as to whether their individual liberties would indeed be respected after the colony's return to China.*

## THE JOINT DECLARATION ON HONG KONG

The Hong Kong Special Administrative Region will be directly under the authority of the Central People's Government of the People's Republic of China. The Hong Kong Special Administrative Region will enjoy a high degree of autonomy, except in foreign and defense affairs, which are the responsibility of the Central People's Government.

The Hong Kong Special Administrative Region will be vested with executive, legislative, and independent judicial power, including that of final adjudication. The laws currently in force in Hong Kong will remain basically unchanged.

The Government of the Hong Kong Special Administrative Region will be composed of local inhabitants. The chief executive will be appointed by the Central People's Government on the basis of the results of elections or consultations by the chief executive of the Hong Kong Special Administrative Region for appointment by the Central People's Government. . . .

The current social and economic systems in Hong Kong will remain unchanged, and so will the lifestyle. Rights and freedoms, including those of the person, of speech, of the press, of assembly, of association, of travel, of movement, of correspondence, of strike, of choice of occupation, of academic research, and of religious belief will be ensured by law. . . . Private property, ownership of enterprises, legitimate right of inheritance, and foreign investment will be protected by law.

Source: Kevin Rafferty, *City on the Rocks* (New York: Penguin, 1991).

---

Kong return to mainland authority in 1997, when the British ninety-nine-year lease over the New Territories, the foodbasket of the colony of Hong Kong, ran out. The British agreed, on the condition that satisfactory arrangements could be made for the welfare of the population. The Chinese promised that for fifty years, the people of Hong Kong would live under a capitalist system and be essentially self-governing. Recent statements by Chinese leaders, however, have raised questions about the degree of autonomy Hong Kong will receive under Chinese rule, which began on July 1, 1997 (see the box above). A decision by the local government in 2003 to expand security restrictions aroused widespread public protests.

## ON THE MARGINS OF ASIA: POSTWAR AUSTRALIA AND NEW ZEALAND

Geographically, Australia and New Zealand are not part of Asia, and throughout their short history, both countries have identified themselves culturally and politically with the West rather than with their Asian neighbors. Their political institutions and values are derived from Europe, and the form and content of their economies resemble those of the advanced countries of the world rather than the preindustrial societies of much of Southeast Asia. Both are currently members of the British Commonwealth and of the U.S.-led ANZUS alliance (Australia, New Zealand, and the United States), which serves to shield them from political turmoil elsewhere in the region.

Yet trends in recent years have been drawing both states, especially Australia, closer to Asia. In the first place, immigration from East and Southeast Asia has increased rapidly. More than one-half of current immigrants into Australia come from East Asia, and about 7 percent of the population of about eighteen million people is now of Asian descent. In New Zealand, residents of Asian descent represent only about 3 percent of the population of 3.5 million, but about 12 percent of the population are Maoris, Polynesian peoples who settled on the islands about a thousand years ago. Second, trade relations with Asia are increasing rapidly. About 60 percent of Australia's export markets today are in East Asia, and the region is the source of about one-half of its imports. Asian trade with New Zealand is also on the increase.

At the same time, the links that bind both countries to Great Britain and the United States have been loosening. Ties with London became increasingly distant after Great

➤ **THE HONG KONG SKYLINE.** Hong Kong reverted to Chinese sovereignty in 1997 after a century of British rule. To commemorate the occasion, the imposing Conference Center, shown here in the foreground, was built on reclaimed shoreland in the Hong Kong harbor.

Britain decided to join the European Community in the early 1970s. There are moves under way in Australia and New Zealand to withdraw from the British Commonwealth, although the outcome is far from certain. Security ties with the United States remain important, but many Australians opposed their government's decision to cooperate with Washington during the Vietnam War, and the government today is seeking to establish closer political and military ties with the ASEAN alliance. Further removed from Asia both physically and psychologically, New Zealand assigns less importance to its security treaty with the United States and has been vocally critical of U.S. nuclear policies in the region.

Whether Australia and New Zealand will ever become an integral part of the Asia-Pacific region is uncertain. Cultural differences stemming from the European origins of the majority of the population in both countries hinder mutual understanding on both sides of the divide, and many ASEAN leaders (see Chapter 8) express reluctance to accept the two countries as full members of the

alliance. Both countries continue to face problems in bringing about the integration of indigenous peoples—the aborigines and the Maoris—into the general population. But economic and geographic realities act as a powerful force, and should the Pacific region continue on its current course toward economic prosperity and political stability, the role of Australia and New Zealand will assume greater significance.

## CONCLUSION

What explains the striking ability of Japan and the four Little Tigers to follow the Western example and transform themselves into export-oriented societies capable of competing with the advanced nations of Europe and the Western Hemisphere? Some analysts point to the traditional character traits of Confucian societies, such as thrift, a work ethic, respect for education, and obedience to authority. In a recent poll of Asian executives, more than 80 percent expressed the belief that Asian values differ from those of the West, and most add that these values have contributed significantly to the region's recent success. Others place more emphasis on deliberate steps taken by government and economic leaders to meet the political, economic, and social challenges their societies face.

There seems no reason to doubt that cultural factors connected to East Asian social traditions have contributed to the economic success of these societies. Certainly, habits such as frugality, industriousness, and subordination of individual desires have all played a role in their governments' ability to concentrate on the collective interest. Political elites in these countries have been highly conscious of these factors and willing to use them for national purposes. Prime Minister Lee Kuan-yew of Singapore deliberately fostered the inculcation of such ideals among the citizens of his small nation and lamented the decline of Confucian values among the young.

The importance of specifically Confucian values, however, should not be overemphasized as a factor in what authors Roy Hofheinz and Kent E. Calder call the "East Asia Edge." In the first place, until recently, mainland China did not share in the economic success of its neighbors despite a long tradition of espousing Confucian values. In fact, some historians in recent years have maintained that it was precisely those Confucian values that hindered China's early response to the challenge of the West.

As this and preceding chapters have shown, without active encouragement by political elites, such traditions cannot be effectively harnessed for the good of society as a whole. The creative talents of the Chinese people were not efficiently utilized under Mao Zedong or in the Little Tigers while they were under European or Japanese colonial rule (although Japanese colonialism did lead to the creation of an infrastructure more conducive to later development than was the case in European colonies). Only when a "modernizing elite" took charge and began to place a high priority on economic development were the stunning advances of recent decades achieved. Rural poverty was reduced, if not eliminated, by stringent land reform and population control programs. Profit incentives and foreign investment were encouraged, and the development of export markets received high priority.

There was, of course, another common factor in the successes achieved by Japan and its emulators. All the Little Tigers received substantial inputs of capital and technology from the advanced nations of the West— Taiwan and South Korea from the United States, Hong Kong and Singapore from Britain. Japan relied to a greater degree on its own efforts but received a significant advantage by being placed under the U.S. security umbrella and guaranteed access to markets and sources of raw materials in a region dominated by U.S. naval power.

To some observers, economic advancement in the region has sometimes been achieved at the cost of political freedom and individual human rights. Until recently, government repression of opposition has been common throughout East Asia except in Japan. In addition, the rights of national minorities and women are often still limited in comparison with the advanced countries of the West. Some commentators in the region take vigorous exception to such criticism, and argue that pluralistic political systems could be very dangerous and destabilizing in the heterogeneous societies that currently exist in the region (see the box on p. 195).

Recent developments such as the financial crisis of 1997 have somewhat tarnished the image of the "Asian miracle," and there is now widespread concern that some of the very factors that contributed to economic success in previous years are now making it difficult for governments in the region to develop increased openness and accountability in their financial systems. Still, it should be kept in mind that progress in political pluralism and human rights has not always been easy to achieve in Europe and North America and even now frequently fails to match expectations. A rising standard of living, increased social mobility, and a changing regional environment brought about by the end of the Cold War should go far to enhance political freedoms and promote social justice in the countries bordering the western Pacific.

| 1945 | 1955 | 1965 | 1975 | 1985 | 1995 | 2005 |
|---|---|---|---|---|---|---|

Korean War

Assassination of
Chung Hee Park

Student riots
in South
Korea

Economic recession
in Japan

End of
World War II
in Asia

Independence of
Republic of Singapore

First free
elections
in Taiwan

Financial crisis
throughout
the region

U.S. occupation
of Japan

Hong Kong
returns to China

##  INFOTRAC COLLEGE EDITION

Visit source collections at **http://infotrac.thomsonlearning.com**, and use the Search function with the following key terms:

Japan history
Japan women
Keiretsu
Korea

##  WORLD HISTORY RESOURCES

Visit the *The World Since World War II* Companion Web site for resources specific to this textbook:

**http://history.wadsworth.com/duiker_wwii/**

The Wadsworth World History Resource Center at **http://history.wadsworth.com/world/** offers a variety of tools to help you succeed in this course, including access to quizzes; images; documents; interactive simulations, maps, and timelines; movie explorations; and a wealth of other sources.

## CHAPTER NOTES

1. Robert Whiting, *You Gotta Have Wa* (New York, 1990), p. 69.
2. Janet Hunter, *The Emergence of Modern Japan: An Introductory History Since 1853* (London, 1989), p. 152.
3. Yukio Mishima and Geoffrey Bownas, eds., *New Writing in Japan* (Harmondsworth, England, 1972), p. 16.
4. *New York Times*, January 29, 1996.
5. Stan Seser, "A Reporter at Large," *New Yorker*, January 13, 1992, p. 44.

# Reflection

# PART II

The colonial peoples of Africa and Asia had modest reasons for hope as World War II came to a close. In the Atlantic Charter, issued after their meeting near the coast of Newfoundland in August 1941, Franklin Roosevelt and Winston Churchill had set forth a joint declaration of their peace aims calling for the self-determination of all peoples and self-government and sovereign rights for all nations that had been deprived of them. Although Churchill later disavowed the assumption that he had meant these conditions to apply to colonial areas, Roosevelt on frequent occasions during the war voiced his own intention to bring about the end of colonial domination throughout the world at the close of the conflict.

It took many years to complete the process, but the promise contained in the Atlantic Charter was eventually fulfilled. Although some powers were reluctant to divest themselves of their colonies, World War II had severely undermined the stability of the colonial order, and by the end of the 1940s, most colonies in Asia had received their independence. Africa followed a decade or two later. In a few instances—notably in Algeria, Indonesia, and Vietnam—the transition to independence was a violent one, but for the most part, it was realized by peaceful means.

In their own writings, public declarations, and statements, the leaders of these newly liberated countries set forth three broad goals at the outset of independence: to throw off the shackles of Western economic domination and ensure material prosperity for all their citizens, to introduce new political institutions that would enhance the right of self-determination of their peoples, and to develop a sense of nationhood and establish secure territorial boundaries. It was a measure of their own optimism and the intellectual and cultural influence of their colonial protectors that the governments of most of the newly liberated countries opted to follow a capitalist or moderately socialist path toward economic development. Only in a few cases—China, North Korea, and Vietnam were the most notable examples—did revolutionary leaders decide to pursue the Communist model of development.

Within a few years of the restoration of independence, reality had set in as most of the new governments in Asia and Africa fell short of their ambitious goals. Virtually all of them remained economically dependent on the advanced industrial nations or the Soviet Union. Several faced severe problems of urban and rural poverty. At the same time, fledgling democratic governments were gradually replaced by military dictatorships or one-party regimes that dis-mantled representative institutions and oppressed dissident elements and ethnic minorities within their borders.

What had happened to tarnish the bright dreams of affluence and political self-determination? During the 1950s and 1960s, one school of thought was dominant among scholars and government officials in the United States. Modernization theory adopted the view that the problems faced by the newly independent countries were a consequence of the difficult transition from a traditional agrarian to a modern industrial society. Modernization theorists were convinced that the countries of Asia, Africa, and Latin America were destined to follow the path of the West toward the creation of modern industrial societies but would need time as well as substantial amounts of economic and technological assistance to complete the journey. In their view, it was the duty of the United States and other advanced capitalist nations to provide such assistance while encouraging the leaders of these states to follow the path already adopted by the West. Some countries going through this difficult period were especially vulnerable to Communist-led insurgent movements. In such cases, it was in the interests of the United States and its allies to intervene, with military power if necessary, to hasten the transition and put the country on the path to self-sustaining growth.

Modernization theory soon began to come under attack from a generation of younger scholars, many of whom had reached maturity during the Vietnam War and who had growing doubts about the roots of the problem and the efficacy of the modernization approach. In their view, the responsibility for continued economic underdevelopment in the developing world lay not with the countries themselves but with their continued domination by the former colonial powers. In this view, known as dependency theory, the countries of Asia, Africa, and Latin America were the victims of the international marketplace, which charged high prices for the manufactured goods of the West while paying low prices for the raw material exports of preindustrial countries. Efforts by these countries to build up their own industrial sectors and move into the stage of self-sustaining growth were hampered by foreign control—through European- and American-owned corporations—over many of their resources. To end this "neocolonial" relationship, the dependency theory advocates argued, developing societies should reduce their economic ties with the West and practice a policy of economic self-reliance, thereby taking control of their own destinies. They should also ignore urgings that they adopt the Western model of capitalist democracy, which had little relevance to conditions in their parts of the world.

Both of these approaches, of course, were directly linked to the ideological divisions of the Cold War and reflected the political bias of their advocates. Although modernization theorists were certainly correct in pointing out some of the key factors involved in economic development and in suggesting that some traditional attitudes and practices were incompatible with economic change, they were too quick to see the Western model of development as the only relevant one and ignored the fact that traditional customs and practices were not necessarily incompatible with nation building. They also too readily identified economic development in the developing world with the interests of the United States and its allies.

By the same token, the advocates of dependency theory alluded correctly to the unfair and often disadvantageous relationship that continued to exist between the former colonies and the industrialized nations of the world and to the impact that this relationship had on the efforts of developing countries to overcome their economic difficulties. But they often rationalized many of the mistakes made by the leaders of developing countries while assigning all of the blame for their plight on the evil and self-serving practices of the industrialized world. At the same time, the recommendation by some dependency theorists of a policy of self-reliance was not only naive but sometimes disastrous, depriving the new nations of badly needed technology and capital resources.

In recent years, the differences between these two schools of thought have narrowed somewhat as their advocates have attempted to respond to criticism of the perceived weaknesses in their theories. Although the two approaches still have some methodological and ideological differences, there is a growing consensus that there are different roads to development and that the international marketplace can have both beneficial and harmful effects. At the same time, a new school of development theory, known as the world systems approach, has attempted to place recent developments within the broad context of world history. According to world systems theory, during the era of capitalism, the "core" countries of the industrializing West created a strong economic relationship with "peripheral" areas in the Third World to exploit their markets and sources of raw materials. That system is now beginning to develop serious internal contradictions and may be in the process of transformation, an issue that we will discuss in Chapter 10.

A second area of concern for the leaders of African and Asian countries after World War II was to create a new political culture responsive to the needs of their citizens. For the most part, they accepted the concept of democracy as the defining theme of that culture. Within a decade, however, democratic systems throughout the developing world were replaced by military dictatorships or one-party governments that redefined the concept of democracy to fit their own preferences. Some Western observers criticized the new leaders for their autocratic tendencies, and others attempted to explain the phenomenon by pointing out that after traditional forms of authority were replaced, it would take time to lay the basis for pluralistic political systems. In the interim, a strong government party under the leadership of a single charismatic individual could mobilize the population to seek common goals. Whatever the case, it was clear that many had underestimated the difficulties in building democratic political institutions in developing societies.

The problem of establishing a common national identity was in some ways the most daunting of all the challenges facing the new nations of Asia and Africa. Many of these new states were a composite of a wide variety of ethnic, religious, and linguistic groups that found it difficult to agree on common symbols of nationalism. Problems of establishing an official language and delineating territorial boundaries left over from the colonial era created difficulties in many countries. In some cases, these problems were exacerbated by political and economic changes. The introduction of the concept of democracy sharpened the desire of individual groups to have a separate identity within a larger nation, and economic development often favored some at the expense of others.

The introduction of Western ideas and customs has also had a destabilizing effect in many areas. Often such ideas are welcomed by some groups and resisted by others. Where Western influence has the effect of undermining traditional customs and religious beliefs—as, for example, in the Middle East—it provokes violent hostility and sparks tension and even conflict within individual societies. To some, Western customs and values represent the wave of the future and are welcomed as a sign of progress. To others, they are destructive of indigenous traditions and a barrier to the growth of a genuine national identity based on history and culture.

From the 1950s to the 1970s, the political and economic difficulties experienced by many developing nations in Asia, Africa, and Latin America led to chronic instability in a number of countries and transformed the developing world into a major theater of Cold War confrontation. During the 1980s, however, a number of new factors entered the equation and shifted the focus away from ideological competition. China's shift to a more accommodating policy toward the West removed fears of more wars of national liberation supported by Beijing. At the same time, the Communist victory in Vietnam led not to falling dominoes throughout Southeast Asia but to bitter conflict between erstwhile Communist allies, Vietnam and China, and Vietnam and

Cambodia. It was clear that national interests and historical rivalries took precedence over ideological agreement.

In the meantime, the growing success of the Little Tigers and the poor economic performance of socialist regimes led a number of developing countries to adopt a free market approach to economic development. As we have seen, some countries benefited from indigenous cultural and historical factors and others from a high level of foreign aid and investment. But the role of government leadership in hindering or promoting economic growth should not be ignored. The situation in China is an obvious case in point. While policies adopted in the early 1950s may have been beneficial in rectifying economic inequities and focusing attention on infrastructure development, the Great Leap Forward and the Cultural Revolution had disastrous economic effects. Since the late 1970s, China has realized massive progress with a combination of centralized party leadership and economic policies emphasizing innovation and the interplay of free market forces. By some measures, China today has the third largest economy in the world.

Similarly, there have been tantalizing signs in recent years of a revival of interest in the democratic model in various parts of Asia, Africa, and Latin America. The best examples have been the free elections in South Korea, Taiwan, and the Philippines, but similar developments have taken place in a number of African countries. Nevertheless, it is clear that in many areas, democratic institutions are quite fragile, and experiments in democratic pluralism have failed in a number of places. The recent financial crisis in Asia has placed great pressure on the tenuous stability of existing political systems and, as in the case of Indonesia, on the precarious unity of the state. Many political leaders in Asia and Africa are convinced that such democratic practices as free elections and freedom of the press can be destabilizing and destructive of other national objectives. Many still do not believe that democracy and economic development go hand in hand.

Future trends in the region, then, remain obscure as the impact of global interconnectedness provokes widespread resistance. Under the surface, however, the influence of the West continues unabated as changing economic circumstances have led to more secular attitudes, a decline in traditional hierarchical relationships, and a more open attitude toward sexual practices. In part, this change has been a consequence of the influence of Western music, movies, and television. But it is also a product of the growth of an affluent middle class in many societies of Asia and Africa. This middle class is often strongly influenced by Western ways, and its sons and daughters ape the behavior, dress, and lifestyles of their counterparts in Europe and North America. When Reebok sneakers are worn and coveted in Lagos and Nairobi, Bombay and Islamabad, Beijing and Hanoi, it is clear that the impact of modern Western civilization has been universalized.

# BEGINNING A
# NEW MILLENNIUM

# CONSTRUCTING
## A NEW
## WORLD ORDER

rom a historical perspective, World War II can be perceived as the culmination of the imperialist era. Competition among the European powers for markets and sources of raw materials began to accelerate during the early years of the nineteenth century and intensified as the effects of the Industrial Revolution made their way through western and central Europe. By 1900, virtually all of Asia and Africa had come under some degree of formal or informal colonial control. World War I weakened the European powers but did not bring the era of imperialism to an end, and the seeds of a second world confrontation were planted at the Versailles peace conference, which failed to resolve the problems that had led to the war in the first place. Those seeds began to sprout in the 1930s when Hitler's Germany sought to recoup its losses and Japan became an active participant in the race for spoils in the Pacific region.

As World War II came to a close, the leaders of the victorious Allied nations were presented with a second opportunity to fashion a lasting peace based on the principles of social justice and self-determination. There were several issues on their postwar agenda. Europe needed to be revived from the ashes of the war and restored to the level of political stability and economic achievement that it had seemingly attained at the beginning of the century. Beyond the continent of Europe, the colonial system had to be dismantled and the promise of self-determination enshrined in the Atlantic Charter applied on a global scale. The defeated nations of Germany, Italy, and Japan had to be reintegrated into the world community in order that the revanchist policies of the interwar era not be repeated. Finally, it was vital that the wartime alliance of the United States, Great Britain, and the Soviet Union be maintained into the postwar era so that bitter national rivalries among the powers did not once again threaten world peace.

In the decades following the war, the first three goals were essentially realized. During the 1950s and 1960s, the capitalist nations managed to recover from the extended economic depression that had contributed to the start of World War II and advanced to a level of economic prosperity never before seen. The bloody conflicts that had erupted among European nations during the first half of the twentieth century came to an end, and Germany and Japan were fully integrated into the world community. At the same time, the Western colonial empires in Asia and Africa were gradually dismantled, and the peoples of both continents once again recovered their independence.

But if the victorious nations of World War II had managed to resolve several of the key problems that had contributed to a half century of bloody conflict, the ultimate prerequisite for success—an end to the competitive balance-of-power system that had been a contributing factor in both world wars—was hampered by the emergence of a grueling and sometimes tense ideological struggle between the socialist and capitalist blocs, a competition headed by the only two remaining great powers, the Soviet Union and the United States. While the two superpowers managed to avoid an open confrontation, the postwar world was divided for fifty years into two heavily armed camps in a balance of terror that on one occasion—the Cuban Missile Crisis—brought the world briefly to the brink of a nuclear holocaust.

In retrospect, the failure of the victorious world leaders to perpetuate the Grand Alliance seems virtually inevitable. Although the debate over who started the Cold War has been raging among historians for decades, it seems clear that the underlying causes of the ideological conflict lie not within the complex personalities of world leaders such as Joseph Stalin and Harry Truman (although they may have contributed to the prob-

lem) but much deeper in the political, economic, and social conditions that existed in the world at midcentury. The rapid recovery of Western Europe had reduced the bitterness of class conflict and helped build strong foundations for the cooperative system of capitalist welfare states that emerged in the postwar era throughout the region, but much of the remainder of the world was just entering the early stages of the Industrial Revolution and was thus vulnerable to the bitter political, economic, and social turmoil that had marked the European experience in the twentieth century.

Under such circumstances, it is hardly surprising that the capitalist and the Communist nations would become entangled in a bitter competition over influence in the Third World. Representing dynamic and mutually contradictory ideologies, both the United States and the Soviet Union were convinced that they represented the wave of the future and were determined to shape postwar reality to reflect their own worldview. The particular form that the Cold War eventually took—with two heavily armed power blocs facing each other across a deep cultural and ideological divide—was not necessarily preordained, but given the volatility of postwar conditions and the vast gap in mutual understanding and cultural experience, it is difficult to see how the intense rivalry that characterized the East-West relationship could have been avoided. •

## AFTER THE COLD WAR: THE END OF HISTORY?

The decline of communism in the final decades of the century brought an end to an era, not only in the Soviet Union but in much of the rest of the world as well. For more than a generation, thousands of intellectuals and political elites in Asia, Africa, and Latin America had looked to Marxism-Leninism as an appealing developmental ideology that could rush preindustrial societies through the modernization process without the painful economic and social inequities associated with capitalism. Communism, many thought, could make more effective use of scarce capital and resources while carrying through the reforms needed to bring an end to centuries of inequality in the political and social arenas.

The results, however, were much less than advertised. Although such diverse societies as China, Vietnam, and Cuba got off to an impressive start under Communist regimes, after a generation of party rule all were increasingly characterized by economic stagnation, low productivity, and underemployment. Even before the collapse of the Soviet Union, prominent Communist states such as China and Vietnam had begun to adopt reforms that broke with ideological orthodoxy and borrowed liberally from the capitalist model.

To many historians, the disintegration of the Soviet Union signaled the end of communism as a competitive force in the global environment. In some parts of the world, however, it has survived in the form of Communist parties presiding over a mixed economy combining components of both socialism and capitalism. Why have Communist political systems survived in some areas while the Marxist-Leninist economic model in its classic form has not? In the first place, it is obvious that one of the consequences of long-term Communist rule was the suffocation of alternative political forces and ideas. As the situation in Eastern Europe has demonstrated, even after the passing of communism itself, Communist parties often appeared to be the only political force with the experience, discipline, and self-confidence to govern complex and changing societies.

That monopoly of political experience, of course, is no accident. In its Leninist incarnation, modern communism is preeminently a strategy for seizing and retaining power. The first duty of a Communist Party on seizing control is to determine "who defeats whom" and to establish a dictatorship of the proletariat. As a result, even when perceptive party leaders recognize the failure of the Marxist model to promote the creation of a technologically advanced industrial society, they view the Leninist paradigm as a useful means of maintaining political stability while undergoing the difficult transition through the early stages of the Industrial Revolution. In such countries as China and Vietnam today, Marxism-Leninism has thus become primarily a political technique—a Marxist variant of the single-party or military regimes that arose in the Third World during the immediate postwar era. It is still too early to predict how successful such regimes will ultimately be or what kind of political culture will succeed them, but there is modest reason to hope that as their economic reform programs begin to succeed, they will eventually evolve into pluralistic societies such as are now taking shape elsewhere around the world.

The wave of optimism that accompanied the end of the Cold War was all too brief. After a short period of euphoria—some observers speculated that the world had reached the "end of history," when the liberal democratic system had demonstrated its clear superiority and the major problems in the future would be strictly economic—it soon became clear that forces were now being released that had long been held in check by the ideological rigidities of the Cold War. The era of conflict that had long characterized the twentieth century was not at an end; it was simply in the process of taking a different form (see the box on p. 207).

Nowhere was this trend more immediately apparent than in Southeast Asia, where even before the end of the Cold War, erstwhile allies in China, Vietnam, and Cambodia turned on each other in a fratricidal conflict that combined territorial ambitions with geopolitical concerns and deep-seated historical suspicions based on the memory of past conflicts. Ideology, it was clear, was no barrier to historical and cultural rivalries. The pattern was repeated elsewhere: in Africa, where several nations erupted into civil war during the late 1980s and 1990s; in the Balkans, where the Yugoslavian Federation broke apart in a bitter conflict that has yet to be fully resolved; and of course in the Middle East, where the historical disputes in Palestine and the Persian Gulf have grown in intensity and erupted repeatedly into open war. The irony of this explosion of national, ethnic, and religious sentiment is that it has taken place at a time when it is becoming increasingly evident that the main problems in today's society—such as environmental pollution, overpopulation, and unequal distribution of resources—are shared to one degree or another by all humanity. In a world that is increasingly characterized by global interdependence, how can it be that the world is increasingly being pulled apart?

## PROBLEMS OF CAPITALISM

These problems are by no means limited to the developing world. After a generation of rapid growth, most of the capitalist states in Europe and North America began in the late 1980s to suffer through a general slowdown in economic performance. This slowdown has in turn given rise to a number of related problems, several with serious social and political implications. These problems include an increase in the level of unemployment; government belt-tightening policies to reduce social services and welfare and retirement benefits; and in many countries, an accompanying growth in popular resentment against mi-

# CONTEMPORARY CIVILIZATION AND ITS DISCONTENTS

*With the end of superpower rivalry and the collapse of the Soviet Union in 1991, the attention of the world shifted to the new post–Cold War era. For many observers, the prognosis was excellent. U.S. President George H. W. Bush looked forward to a new era of peace and international cooperation, while pundits predicted the advent of a new "American century," marked by the victory of liberal democratic values and free enterprise capitalism. Some, however, held a more somber view. In a speech at Westminster College in Fulton, Missouri (the site of Winston Churchill's famous Iron Curtain speech in 1946), past Soviet president Mikhail Gorbachev pointed to ominous clouds on the horizon. One danger, he warned, was that of an "exaggerated nationalism," the product of centrifugal forces that had been frozen by the Cold War. Another was the growing inequality in the distribution of wealth between rich and poor nations.*

With the passage of time, it seems fair to say that Gorbachev had the more accurate vision of the immediate future. Although superpower conflict based on a fragile balance of nuclear terror had come to an end, sources of conflict still abound throughout the world, and the gap between rich and poor nations has grown ever wider. Strong forces—rapid transportation, mass entertainment, the Internet—are in the process of creating a single global civilization. But equally powerful impulses, sometimes armed with modern technology, violently resist the new global society and assert the primacy of traditional values and identities. In the face of such pressures, international organizations appear paralyzed by deep divisions over potential solutions while, as recent events in the Middle East demonstrate, the New World Order is still characterized primarily by the use or threat of force to achieve national goals.

How can nations and peoples bring an end to this spiraling cycle of violence in a world beset by bitter national, ethnic, and religious rivalries? For Mikhail Gorbachev, it is essential to develop new ways of thinking: to reject the traditional reliance on force in world politics, to increase mutual understanding and communication, and "to base international politics on moral and ethical norms that are common to all mankind." Vaclav Havel, the onetime playwright who became the first president of a post–Cold War Czechoslovakia, agreed. In a speech before the U.S. Houses of Congress in 1990, he called for a new human consciousness that would transcend family, community, and national interests in a broader commitment to the "family of man." In an address at Harvard University five years later, he noted that the clashing interests of globalism and tradition could only be transcended by a new spirit of tolerance, and by recognizing the reality of a multicultural and multipolar world civilization.

As both statesman were quick to concede, these were revolutionary goals and would not be easy to achieve. Yet the alternative was unthinkable. Without a new sense of human morality and responsibility, Havel warned the members of Congress, "the catastrophe toward which this world is headed—be it ecological, social, demographic or a general breakdown of civilization—will be unavoidable."

Sources: Speech by Mikhail Gorbachev at Fulton, Missouri, in the *New York Times*, May 7, 1992; Mikhail Gorbachev, *Perestroika* (New York: HarperCollins, 1997); Vaclav Havel, *The Art of the Impossible: Politics as Morality in Practice* (New York: Fromm, 1998); Speech by Vaclav Havel to the U. S. Congress, quoted in the *Washington Post*, February 22, 1990).

---

nority groups or recent immigrants, who are seen as responsible for deteriorating economic prospects.

## Europe: Unity or Disunity?

The problem of economic stagnation has been especially prevalent in Western Europe, where unemployment is at its highest level since the 1930s and economic growth in recent years has averaged less than 1 percent annually. Conditions have been exacerbated in recent years by the need for individual governments to set their financial houses in order so as to comply with the requirements for unification as called for by the Maastricht Treaty of 1991 (see Chapter 3). For an individual nation to take part in the process, government deficits must not greatly exceed 3 percent of gross domestic product, nor must the national debt greatly exceed 60 percent of total output. Inflation rates must also be cut to minimal levels.

The problem is that many countries are encountering difficulties in adopting the severe economic measures that are needed to qualify for the transition to economic unity. France, concerned at the potential impact on its own fragile economy, has threatened not to carry out the necessary reforms. In Italy, the refusal of the Communist Party to agree to belt-tightening measures almost led to the fall of the coalition government. Even in Germany, long the healthiest of all major Western European states, reductions in social benefits sharpened tensions between the eastern and western zones and undermined public support for the government of Gerhard Schröder.

But perhaps the most ominous consequence of the new economic austerity has been a rise in antiforeign sentiment. In Germany, attacks against foreign residents—mainly Turks, many of whom have lived in the country for years—have increased substantially. Conservative forces have turned to the idea of preserving "German culture" as a rallying cry to win the support of Germans concerned over the rapid process of change. In France, hostility to immigrants from North Africa has led to rising support for Jean-Marie Le Pen's National Front, which advocates strict limits on immigration and the ejection of many foreigners currently living in the country. It seems clear that the ethnic animosities that so often fueled conflict in Europe before World War II have not entirely abated.

By no means do all Europeans fear the costs of economic unity. Official sources argue that it will increase the region's ability to compete with economic powerhouses such as the United States and Japan. But fear of change and a strong legacy of nationalist sentiment have promoted public fears that economic unification could have disastrous consequences. This is especially true in Great Britain and also in Germany, where many see little benefit and much risk from joining a larger Europe.

At the same time, some of the smaller states within the European Union (EU) are afraid that their concerns will be ignored by the larger powers. Such concerns have also emerged in Eastern Europe, where several governments are seeking membership in the EU to improve their own economic conditions.

## The United States: Capitalism Ascendant

In some respects, the United States fared better than other capitalist states as the economic revival that took place in the 1990s enabled the Clinton administration to reduce budget deficits without having to engage in substantial tax increases or a massive reduction in welfare spending. Even there, however, continued increases in social spending provoked the passage of new legislation to reduce welfare and health care benefits. Nor has the steady growth in the gross domestic product led to increased prosperity for all Americans. Although the rich have been getting richer, the poorest 20 percent of the population has so far seen little benefit. The lack of sustained growth in consumer demand may be a major reason for the economic slowdown that began to appear early in the new century and has brought unemployment levels to the highest rate in recent years.

The United States has not yet witnessed the emergence of significant antiforeign sentiment on the scale of some countries in Europe, perhaps partly because of the salutary effect of a steadily growing economy. Recent history suggests that tolerance toward immigrants tends to decrease during periods of economic malaise, and vice versa. But there are indications that anger against the growing presence of foreign-born residents—especially those who have arrived illegally—is growing. Legislation to limit social benefits to noncitizens and to expel illegal aliens has been proposed at the state level and has been debated in Congress. Many American workers, with the support of labor unions, have vocally opposed the enactment of trade agreements such as the North American Free Trade Association (NAFTA) that would allegedly lead to a flight of jobs overseas as U.S. corporations seek to reduce production costs by hiring cheaper labor. Opponents of globalization have become increasingly vocal, leading to violent protest demonstrations at meetings of the World Trade Organization, the World Bank, and the International Monetary Fund.

Yet as in the case of European unity, there is solid economic logic in pursuing the goal of increasing globalization of trade. The U.S. industrial machine is increasingly dependent on the importation of raw materials from abroad, and corporate profits are to a rising degree a consequence of sales of U.S. goods in overseas markets. Although foreign competition can sometimes lead to a loss of jobs— or entire industries—in the United States, the overall effect is likely to be a growing market for U.S. goods in the international marketplace. Moreover, as the case of the automobile industry has demonstrated, increased competition is crucial for maintaining and enhancing the quality of American products. President George W. Bush, who came into office in January 2001, has voiced his support for the creation of a global free trade zone incorporating all the nations of the Western Hemisphere.

It is hardly surprising that the main proponent of the global economic marketplace is the United States, a country well placed to take full advantage of the technological revolution and turn it to its own advantage. Its large market relatively unfettered by onerous government regulations, generous amounts of capital, a tradition of political stability, and an outstanding system of higher education all combine to give the United States an edge over most of its rivals in the relentless drive to achieve a dominant position in the world economy. As Washington applies pressure on other governments to open up their economies to the competition of the international marketplace and to adopt concepts of human rights that accord with those in the United States, resentment of the U.S. behemoth and fears of U.S. global domination are once again on the rise, as they were during the immediate postwar era.

## Asian Miracle or Asian Myth?

Until quite recently, it was common to observe that the one area in the capitalist world that was in a strong position to advance rapidly in the economic sphere without suffering the social and political strains experienced in the West was East Asia, where Japan and the so-called Little Tigers appeared able to combine rapid economic growth with a minimum of social problems and a considerable degree of political stability. Pundits in the region and abroad opined that the "East Asian miracle" was a product of the amalgamation of capitalist economic techniques and a value system inherited from Confucius that stressed hard work, frugality, and the subordination of the individual to the community—all reminiscent of the "Puritan ethic" of the early capitalist era in the West.

There is indeed some similarity between the recent performance of many East Asian societies and early capitalism in the West. Some commentators in East Asia have pointed with pride to their traditional values and remarked that in the West such values as hard work and a habit of saving have been replaced by a certain hedonism that values individual over community interests and prizes gratification over future needs. Some observers in the West have agreed with this assessment and lamented the complacency and rampant materialism of Western culture.

As the twentieth century neared its end, however, the argument suddenly became academic, as evidence accumulated that the East Asian miracle itself may be a myth or at least an overstatement of a more complex reality. The financial crisis of 1997 demonstrated that the Pacific nations were not immune to the vicissitudes of capitalism and that overconfidence and lack of attention to fundamentals could be as destructive on one side of the ocean as the other. Mesmerized by the rhetorical vision of the Confucian work ethic and less experienced in riding the choppy waves of the capitalist business cycle, Asian governments and entrepreneurs alike became too complacent in their view that the bull market in the region would never end. Banks extended loans on shaky projects, and governments invested heavily in expensive infrastructure improvements that exploded budget deficits while promising few financial returns until the distant future. When foreign investors grew wary and began withdrawing their funds, the bubble burst. It has been a sobering experience. As one commentator put it, "It was all too Disneyland; so much glass that was too shiny. Now they are going through a cultural crisis triggered by the economic crisis. These countries have to become more pragmatic."[1]

It would be premature to conclude that the recent vision of a "Pacific century" will fade as surely as Khrushchev's famous boast to Eisenhower four decades ago that "we will bury you." The economic fundamentals in many East Asian countries are essentially sound, and the region will undoubtedly recover from the current crisis and resume the pace of steady growth that characterized its performance during the last quarter of the twentieth century. But the fiscal crisis of the late 1990s serves as a warning signal that success—in East Asia as in the West—is the product of hard work and can never be assumed.

# FROM THE INDUSTRIAL TO THE TECHNOLOGICAL REVOLUTION

As many observers have noted, a key aspect of the problem is that the world economy as a whole is in the process of transition to what has been called a "postindustrial age," characterized by the emergence of a system that is not only increasingly global in scope but also increasingly technology-intensive. This process, which futurologist Alvin Toffler has dubbed the Third Wave (the first two being the Agricultural and Industrial Revolutions), has caused difficulties for people in many walks of life—for blue-collar workers, whose high wages price them out of the market as firms begin to move their factories abroad; for the poor and uneducated, who lack the technical skills to handle complex tasks in the contemporary economy; and even for members of the middle class, who have been fired or forced into retirement as their employers seek to slim down to compete in the global marketplace.[2]

It is now increasingly clear that the Technological Revolution, like the Industrial Revolution that preceded it, will entail enormous consequences and may ultimately give birth to a level of social and political instability that has not been seen in the developed world since the Great Depression of the 1930s. The success of advanced capitalist states in the second half of the twentieth century was built on the foundations of a broad consensus on the importance of several propositions: (1) the importance of limiting income inequities to reduce the threat of political instability while maximizing domestic consumer demand; (2) the need for high levels of government investment in infrastructure projects such as education, communications, and transportation as a means of meeting the challenges of continued economic growth and technological innovation; and (3) the desirability of cooperative efforts in the international arena as a means of maintaining open markets for the free exchange of goods.

As the twenty-first century gains momentum, all of these assumptions are increasingly coming under attack. Citizens are reacting with growing hostility to the high tax rates needed to maintain the welfare state, refusing to support education and infrastructure development, and opposing the formation of trading alliances to promote the free movement of goods and labor across national borders. Such attitudes are being expressed by individuals and groups on all sides of the political spectrum, making the traditional designations of left-wing and right-wing politics increasingly meaningless. Although most governments and political elites have continued to support most of the programs that underpin the welfare state and the global marketplace, they are increasingly attacked by groups in society that feel they have been victimized by the system. The breakdown of the public consensus that brought modern capitalism to a pinnacle of achievement raises serious questions about the likelihood that the coming challenge of the Third Wave can be successfully met without a growing measure of political and social tension in both the domestic and international arenas.

# A TRANSVALUATION OF VALUES

Of course, not all the problems facing the advanced human societies around the world can be ascribed directly to economic factors. It is one of the paradoxes of the modern world that at a time of almost unsurpassed political stability and economic prosperity for the majority of the population in the advanced capitalist states, public cynicism about the system is increasingly widespread. Alienation and drug use among young people in many Western societies are at dangerously high levels, and although crime rates have dropped slightly in some areas, the rate of criminal activities remains much higher than in the immediate postwar era.

## The Family

The reasons advanced to explain this paradox vary widely. Some observers place the responsibility for many contemporary social problems on the decline of the traditional family system. The statistics are indeed disquieting. There has been a steady rise in the percentage of illegitimate births and single-parent families in countries throughout the Western world. In the United States, approximately half of all marriages will end in divorce. Even

CHINA CALLING. As the new century dawns, the entire world is becoming wired, as developing nations realize that economic success depends on informational technology. Shown here is a young Chinese reporting to his family on a visit to the Great Wall. By 2007 it is estimated that China will be the world's largest user of the internet, with 300 million individuals on line. By then, an equal number of Chinese will possess cellphones.

in two-parent families, more and more parents work full time, thus leaving the children to fend for themselves on their return from school.

Observers point to several factors as an explanation for these conditions: the growing emphasis in advanced capitalist states on an individualistic lifestyle devoted to instant gratification—a phenomenon that is promoted vigorously by the advertising media; the rise of the feminist movement, which has freed women from the servitude imposed on their predecessors, but at the expense of removing them from full-time responsibility for the care and nurturing of the next generation; and the increasing mobility of contemporary life, which disrupts traditional family ties and creates a sense of rootlessness and impersonality in the individual's relationship to the surrounding environment.

What is worth noting here is that to one degree or another, the traditional nuclear family is under attack in societies around the world, not just in the West. Even in East Asia, where the Confucian tradition of filial piety and family solidarity has been endlessly touted as a major factor in the region's economic success, the incidence of divorce and illegitimate births is on the rise, as is the percentage of women in the workforce. Older citizens frequently complain that the Asian youth of today are too materialistic, faddish, and steeped in the individualistic values of the West. Such criticisms are now voiced in mainland China as well as in the capitalist societies around its perimeter. Public opinion surveys suggest that some of the generational differences in Asian societies are only skin deep. When queried about their views, most young Asians express support for the same conservative values of family, hard work, and care for the elderly as their parents. Still, the evidence suggests that the trend away from the traditional family is a worldwide phenomenon.

## Religion

While some analysts cite the reduced role of the traditional family as a major factor in the widespread sense of malaise in the contemporary world, others point to the decline in religion and the increasing secularization of Western society. It seems indisputable that one of the causes of the widespread feeling of alienation in many societies is the absence of any sense of underlying meaning and purpose in life, which religious faith often provides. Historical experience suggests, however, that while intensity of religious fervor may serve to enhance the sense of community among believers, it can sometimes have a highly divisive impact on society as a whole, as the examples of Northern Ireland, Yugoslavia, and the Middle East vividly attest. Religion, by itself, cannot serve as a panacea for the problems of the contemporary world.

In any event, the issue of religion and its implications for social policy is complicated. Although the percentage of people attending church on a regular basis or professing firm religious convictions has been dropping steadily in many Western countries, the intensity of religious belief appears to be growing in many communities. This phenomenon is especially apparent in the United States, where the evangelical movement has become a significant force in politics and an influential factor in defining many social issues. But it has also occurred in Latin America, where a drop in membership in the Roman Catholic Church has been offset by significant increases in the popularity of evangelical Protestant sects. There are significant differences between the two cases, however. Whereas the evangelical movement in the United States tends to adopt conservative positions on social issues such as abortion rights, divorce, and sexual freedom, in Brazil one of the reasons advanced for the popularity of evangelical sects is the stand taken by the Vatican on issues such as divorce and abortion. In Brazil, even the vast majority of Catholics surveyed support the right to abortion in cases of rape or danger to the mother and believe in the importance of birth control to limit population growth and achieve smaller families.

For many evangelical Christians in the United States, the revival of religious convictions and the adoption of a Christian lifestyle are viewed as necessary prerequisites for resolving the problems of crime, drugs, and social alienation. Some evidence does suggest that children who attend church in the United States are less likely to be involved in crime and that they perform better in their schoolwork. Some in the evangelical movement, however, not only support a conservative social agenda but also express a growing suspicion of the role of technology and science in the contemporary world. Some Christian groups have opposed the teaching of evolutionary theory in the classroom or have demanded that public schools present the biblical interpretation of the creation of the earth. Although fear over the impact of science on contemporary life is widespread and understandable, efforts to turn the clock back to a mythical golden age are not likely to succeed in the face of powerful forces for change set in motion by advances in scientific knowledge.

## Technology

Concern about the impact of technology on contemporary life is by no means limited to evangelicals. Voices across the political and social spectrum have begun to suggest that scientific advances are at least partly responsible for the psychological malaise now so prevalent in much of the modern world. The criticism dates back at least to the advent of television. Television, in the eyes of its critics, has contributed to a decline in human communication and turned viewers from active participants in the experience of life into passive observers. With the advent of the computer, the process has accelerated as recent generations of young people raised on video games and surfing the World Wide Web find less and less time for personal relationships or creative activities. At the same time, however, the Internet provides an avenue for lonely individuals to communicate with the outside world and seek out others with common interests. The most that can be said at the present time is that such innovations provide both an opportunity and a danger—an opportunity to explore new avenues of communication and a danger that in the process, the nature of the human experience will be irrevocably changed.

## Capitalism

Some theorists argue that the party most responsible for the hedonism and materialism of contemporary life is the capitalist system, which has raised narcissism and conspicuous consumerism to the height of the modern consciousness. It is no doubt true that by promoting material consumption as perhaps the supreme good, modern capitalism has encouraged the acquisitive side of human nature and undermined the traditional virtues of frugality and self-denial and the life of the spirit. As Karl Marx perceptively noted more than a century ago, under capitalism money is "the universal self-constituted value of all things. It has therefore robbed the whole world, human as well as natural, of its own values."[3]

Perhaps, however, it is more accurate to state that capitalism simply recognizes the acquisitive side of human nature and sets out to make a profit from it. Recent events around the world suggest that efforts to suppress the acquisitive instinct are ultimately doomed to fail, no matter how stringently they are applied. It is thus left to individual human beings, families, and communities to decide how to supplement material aspirations with the higher values traditionally associated with the human experience. Perhaps it is worth observing that more than once, capitalism has demonstrated the ability to rectify its shortcomings when they threaten the survival of the system. It remains to be seen whether it can successfully deal with the corrosive effects of contemporary materialism on the traditional spiritual longings of humankind.

## ONE WORLD, ONE ENVIRONMENT

Another crucial factor that is affecting the evolution of society and the global economy is growing concern over the impact of industrialization on the earth's environment. There is nothing new about human beings causing damage to their natural surroundings. It may first have occurred when Neolithic peoples began to practice slash-and-burn agriculture or when excessive hunting thinned out the herds of bison and caribou in the Western Hemisphere. It almost certainly played a major role in the decline of the ancient civilizations in the Persian Gulf region and later of the Roman Empire.

Never before, however, has the danger of significant ecological damage been as extensive as during the past century. The effects of chemicals introduced into the atmosphere or into rivers, lakes, and oceans have increasingly threatened the health and well-being of all living species. For many years, the main focus of environmental concern was in the developed countries of the West, where industrial effluents, automobile exhaust, and the use of artificial fertilizers and insecticides led to urban smog, extensive damage to crops and wildlife, and a major reduction of the ozone layer in the upper atmosphere. In recent decades, however, it has become clear that the problem is now global in scope and demands vigorous action in the international arena.

The opening of Eastern Europe after the revolutions of 1989 brought to the world's attention the incredible environmental destruction in that region caused by unfettered industrial pollution. Communist governments had obviously operated under the assumption that production quotas were much more important than environmental protection. The nuclear power disaster at Chernobyl in the Ukraine in 1986 made Europeans acutely aware of potential environmental hazards, and 1987 was touted as the "year of the environment." Many European states now felt compelled to advocate new regulations to protect the environment, and many of them established government ministries to oversee environmental issues.

For some, such official actions were insufficient, and beginning in the 1980s, a number of new political parties were established to focus exclusively on environmental issues. Although these so-called Green movements and parties have played an important role in making people aware of ecological problems, they have by no means been able to control the debate. Too often, environmental issues come out second in clashes with economic issues. Still, during the 1990s, more and more European governments were beginning to sponsor projects to safeguard the environment and clean up the worst sources of pollution.

In recent years, the problem has spread elsewhere. China's headlong rush to industrialization has resulted in major ecological damage in that country. Industrial smog has created almost unlivable conditions in many cities, and hillsides denuded of their forests have caused severe problems of erosion and destruction of farmlands. Some environmentalists believe that levels of pollution in China are already higher than in the fully developed industrial societies of the West, a reality that raises serious questions about Beijing's ability to re-create the automotive culture of the modern West in China.

Destruction of the rain forest is a growing problem in many parts of the world, notably in Brazil and in the Indonesian archipelago. With the forest cover throughout the earth rapidly declining, there is less plant life to perform the crucial process of reducing carbon dioxide levels in the atmosphere. In 1997, forest fires on the Indonesian islands of Sumatra and Borneo created a blanket of smoke over the entire region, forcing schools and offices to close and causing thousands of respiratory ailments. Some of the damage could be attributed to the traditional slash-and-burn techniques used by subsistence farmers to clear forest cover for their farmlands, but the primary cause was the clearing of forestland to create or expand palm oil plantations, one of the region's major sources of export revenue.

One of the few salutary consequences of such incidents has been a growing international consensus that environmental concerns have taken on a truly global character. Although the danger of global warming—allegedly caused by the release, as a result of industrialization, of certain gases into the atmosphere—has not yet been definitively proved, it had become a source of sufficient concern to bring about an international conference on the subject in Kyoto in December 1997. If, as many scientists predict, worldwide temperatures should increase, the rise in sea levels could pose a significant threat to low-lying islands and coastal areas throughout the world, while climatic change could lead to severe droughts or excessive rainfall in cultivated areas.

It is one thing to recognize a problem, however, and quite another to resolve it. So far, cooperative efforts among nations to alleviate environmental problems have all too often been hindered by economic forces or by political, ethnic, and religious disputes. The 1997 conference on global warming, for example, was marked by bitter disagreement over the degree to which developing countries should share the burden of cleaning up the environment. As a result, it achieved few concrete results.

The fact is that few nations have been willing to take unilateral action that might pose an obstacle to economic development plans or lead to a rise in unemployment. India, Pakistan, and Bangladesh have squabbled over the use of the waters of the Ganges and Indus Rivers, as have Israel and its neighbors over the scarce water resources of the Middle East. Pollution of the Rhine River by factories along its banks provokes angry disputes among European nations, and the United States and Canada have argued about the effects of acid rain on Canadian forests.

Today, such disputes represent a major obstacle to the challenge of meeting the threat of global warming. Measures to reduce the release of harmful gases into the atmosphere will be costly and could have significant negative effects on economic growth. Politicians who embrace such measures, then, are risking political suicide. As President Bill Clinton remarked about a proposal to reduce the danger of global warming by raising energy prices, such a measure "either won't pass the Senate or it won't pass muster with the American people." In any event, what is most needed is a degree of international cooperation that would bring about major efforts to reduce pollution levels throughout the world. So far, there is little indication that advanced and developing nations are close to agreement on how the sacrifice is to be divided. International meetings convened to discuss how to implement the agreement hammered out at the Kyoto conference have been mired in dispute, and in 2001, President George W. Bush declared that the United States would not sign the treaty as it stands.

## THE POPULATION DEBATE

At the root of much of the concern about the environment is the worry that global population growth could eventually outstrip the capacity of the world to feed itself. Concern over excessive population growth, of course, dates back to the fears expressed in the early nineteenth century by the British economist Thomas Malthus, who worried that population growth would increase more rapidly than food supply. It peaked in the decades immediately following World War II, when a rise in world birthrates and a decline in infant mortality combined to fuel a dramatic increase in population in much of the Third World. The concern was set aside for a period after the 1970s, when the Green Revolution improved crop yields and statistical evidence appeared to suggest that the rate of population growth was declining in many countries of Asia and Latin America.

Yet some experts question whether increases in food production through technological innovation (in recent years, the Green Revolution has been supplemented by a "Blue Revolution" to increase food yields from the world's oceans, seas, and rivers) can keep up indefinitely with world population growth, which continues today, though at a slightly reduced rate from earlier levels. From a total of 2.5 billion people in 1950, world population rose to 5.7 billion in 1995 and is predicted to reach ten billion in the middle of this century. Today, many eyes are focused on India, where the population recently surpassed one billion, and on China, where family planning programs have lost effectiveness in recent years and where precious rice lands have been turned to industrial or commercial use.

# GLOBAL VILLAGE OR CLASH OF CIVILIZATIONS?

For four decades, such global challenges were all too frequently submerged in the public consciousness as the two major power blocs competed for advantage. The collapse of the Soviet Union brought an end to the Cold War but left world leaders almost totally unprepared to face the consequences. Statesmen, scholars, and political pundits began to forecast the emergence of a "new world order." Few, however, had any real idea of what it would entail. With the division of the world into two squabbling ideological power blocs suddenly at an end, there was little certainty, and much speculation, about what was going to take its place.

One hypothesis that won support in some quarters was that the decline of communism signaled that the industrial capitalist democracies of the West had triumphed in the war of ideas and would now proceed to remake the rest of the world in their own image. Some people cited as evidence a widely discussed book, *The End of History and the Last Man*, in which the American scholar Francis Fukuyama argued that capitalism and the Western concept of liberal democracy, while hardly ideal in their capacity to satisfy all human aspirations, are at least more effective than rival doctrines in achieving those longings and therefore deserve consideration as the best available ideology to be applied universally throughout the globe.[4]

Fukuyama's thesis provoked a firestorm of debate. Many critics pointed out the absence of any religious component in the liberal democratic model and argued the need for a return to religious faith, with its emphasis on the life of the spirit and traditional moral values. Others, noting that greater human freedom and increasing material prosperity have not led to a heightened sense of human achievement and emotional satisfaction but rather to increasing alienation and a crass pursuit of hedonistic pleasures, argued that a new and perhaps "postmodernist" paradigm for the human experience must be found.

Whether or not Fukuyama's proposition is true, it is much too early to assume (as he would no doubt admit) that the liberal democratic model has in fact triumphed in the clash of ideas that dominated the twentieth century. Although it is no doubt true that much of the world is now linked together in the economic marketplace created by the Western industrial nations, it seems clear from the discussion of contemporary issues in this chapter that the future hegemony of Western political ideas and institutions is by no means assured, despite their current dominating position as a result of the decline of communism.

For one thing, in much of the world today, Western values are threatened or are under direct attack. In Africa, even the facade of democratic institutions has been discarded as autocratic leaders rely on the power of the gun as sole justification for their actions. In India, the decline of the once dominant Congress Party has led to the emergence of fragile governments, religious strife, and spreading official corruption, leaving the future of the world's largest democracy in doubt. Even in East Asia, where pluralistic societies have begun to appear in a number of industrializing countries, leading political figures have expressed serious reservations about Western concepts of democracy and individualism and openly questioned their relevance to their societies. The issue was raised at a meeting of the ASEAN states in July 1997, when feisty Malaysian Prime Minister Mahathir Mohamad declared that the Universal Declaration of Human Rights, passed after World War II at the behest of the victorious Western nations, was not appropriate to the needs of poorer non-Western countries and should be reviewed. The reaction was immediate. One U.S. official attending the conference retorted that the sentiments contained in the Universal Declaration were "shared by all peoples and all cultures" and had not been imposed by the West. Nevertheless, a number of political leaders in the region echoed Mahathir's views and insisted on the need for a review. Their comments were quickly seconded by Chinese President Jiang Zemin, who declared during a visit to the United States later in the year that human rights were not a matter that could be dictated by the powerful nations of the world but rather an issue to be determined by individual societies on the basis of their own traditions and course of development.

Although one factor involved in the debate is undoubtedly the rising frustration of Asian leaders at continuing Western domination of the global economy, in fact political elites in much of the world today do not accept the Western assumption that individual rights must take precedence over community interests, asserting instead the more traditional view that community concerns must ultimately be given priority. Some argue that in defining human rights almost exclusively in terms of individual freedom, Western commentators ignore the importance of providing adequate food and shelter for all members of society.

It is possible, of course, that the liberal democratic model will become more acceptable in parts of Africa and Asia to the degree that societies in those regions proceed successfully through the advanced stages of the industrial and technological revolutions, thus giving birth to the middle-class values that underlie modern civilization in the West. There is no guarantee, however, that current conditions, which have been relatively favorable to that process, will continue indefinitely, or that all peoples and all societies will share equally in the benefits. The fact is that just as the Industrial Revolution exacerbated existing tensions in and among the nations of Europe, globalization and the Technological Revolution are imposing their own strains on human societies today. Should such strains become increasingly intense, they could trigger political and social conflict.

In *The Clash of Civilizations and the Remaking of the World Order,* Samuel P. Huntington has responded to these concerns by suggesting that the post–Cold War era, far from marking the triumph of the Western idea, will be characterized by increased global fragmentation and a "clash of civilizations" based on ethnic, cultural, or religious differences. According to Huntington, cultural identity has replaced shared ideology as the dominant force in world affairs. As a result, he argues, the coming decades may see an emerging world dominated by disputing cultural blocs in East Asia, Western Europe and the United States, Eurasia, and the Middle East, with the societies in each region coalescing around common cultural features against perceived threats from rival forces elsewhere around the globe. The dream of a universal order dominated by Western values, he concludes, is a fantasy.[5]

Events in recent years have appeared to bear out Huntington's hypothesis. The collapse of the Soviet Union led to the emergence of several squabbling new nations and a general atmosphere of conflict and tension in the Balkans and at other points along the perimeter of the old Soviet Empire. Even more dramatically, the terrorist attack in September 2001 appeared to have set the advanced nations of the West and the Muslim world on a collision course.

In fact, the phenomenon is worldwide in scope and growing in importance. Even as the world becomes more global in culture and interdependent in its mutual relations, forces have been at work attempting to redefine the political, cultural, and ethnic ways in which it is divided. This process is taking place not only in developing countries but also in the West, where fear of the Technological Revolution and public anger at the impact of globalization and foreign competition have reached disturbing levels. Such views are often dismissed by sophisticated commentators as atavistic attempts by uninformed people seeking to return to a mythical past. But perhaps they should more accurately be interpreted as an inevitable consequence of the rising thirst for self-protection and group identity in an impersonal and rapidly changing world. Shared culture is one defense against the impersonal world around us.

Huntington's thesis serves as a useful corrective to the complacent tendency of many observers in Europe and the United States to see Western civilization as the zenith and the final destination of human achievement. In the promotion by Western leaders of the concepts of universal human rights and a global marketplace, there is a recognizable element of the cultural arrogance that was reflected in the doctrine of social Darwinism at the end of the nineteenth century. Both views take as their starting point the assumption that the Western conceptualization of the human experience is universal in scope and will ultimately, inexorably spread to the rest of the world. Neither gives much credence to the view that other civilizations might have seized on a corner of the truth and thus have something to offer.

That is not to say, however, that Huntington's vision of clashing civilizations is necessarily the most persuasive characterization of the probable state of the world in the twenty-first century. In dividing the world into competing cultural blocs, Huntington has probably underestimated the centrifugal forces at work in the various regions of the world. As many critics have noted, deep-rooted cultural and historical rivalries exist among the various nations in southern and eastern Asia and in the Middle East, as well as in Africa, preventing any meaningful degree of mutual cooperation against allegedly hostile forces in the outside world. Differences between the United States and leading European nations over the decision to invade Iraq demonstrate that fissures are growing even within the Western alliance.

Huntington also tends to ignore the transformative effect of the Industrial Revolution and the emerging global informational network. As the Industrial and Technological Revolutions spread across the face of the earth, their impact is measurably stronger in some societies than in others, thus intensifying political, economic, and cultural distinctions in a given region while establishing links between individual societies in that region and their counterparts undergoing similar experiences in other parts of the world. Although the parallel drive to global industrial hegemony in Japan and the United States, for example, has served to divide the two countries on a variety of issues, it has intensified tensions between Japan and its competitor South Korea and weakened the political and cultural ties that have historically existed between Japan and China.

The most likely scenario for the next few decades, then, is more complex than either the global village hypothesis or its conceptual rival, the clash of civilizations. The world of the twenty-first century will be characterized by simultaneous trends toward globalization and fragmentation, as the inexorable thrust of technology and information transforms societies and gives rise to counterreactions among individuals and communities seeking to preserve a group identity and a sense of meaning and purpose in a confusing world.

Under such conditions, how can world leaders hope to resolve localized conflicts and prevent them from spreading into neighboring regions, with consequences that could bring an end to the current period of economic expansion and usher in a new era of global impoverishment? To some analysts, the answer lies in strengthening the capacity of the United Nations and various regional security organizations to deal effectively with local conflicts. In recent years, the UN has dispatched peacekeeping missions to nearly twenty different nations on five continents, with a total troop commitment of more than 40,000 military personnel. Nearly 100,000 NATO troops are currently attempting to preserve a fragile cease-fire in the Balkans. The challenge is not only to bring about an end to a particular conflict but also to resolve the problems that gave rise to the dispute in the first place.

Some observers argue that the UN and similar multinational organizations are not the answer. The second Bush administration in the United States, for example, prefers to place its faith in unilateral strategies such as the construction of an antimissile defense system (a successor of the "Star Wars" project of the 1980s), combined with the adoption of a policy of disengagement from conflicts that take place in areas deemed not vital to U.S. national security. One drawback to such an approach is that conflicts in isolated parts of the world often have the potential to spread, thus affecting issues of vital concern such as the oil supply in the Middle East or the safety of trade routes in Southeast Asia.

The U.S. decision in 2003 to launch a preemptive invasion of Iraq has also sparked controversy, arousing mis-

givings among its allies in Europe, who fear that unilateral actions not sanctioned by the UN could undermine global stability and spark a wave of anti-U.S. sentiment in various parts of the world.

# THE ARTS: MIRROR OF THE AGE

If, as the Spanish tenor Placido Domingo once observed, the arts are the signature of their age, what has been happening in literature, art, music, and architecture in recent decades is a reflection of the evolving global response to the rapid changes taking place in human society today. This reaction has sometimes been described as postmodernism, although today's developments are much too diverse to be placed under a single label. Some of the arts are still experimenting with the modernist quest for the new and the radical. Others have begun to return to more traditional styles as a reaction against globalization and a response to the search for national and cultural identity in a bewildering world (see the box on p. 217).

The most appropriate label for the contemporary cultural scene, in fact, is probably pluralism. The arts today are an eclectic hybrid, combining different movements, genres, and media, as well as incorporating different ethnic or national characteristics. There is no doubt that Western culture has strongly influenced the development of the arts throughout the world in recent decades. In fact, the process has gone in both directions as art forms from Africa and Asia have profoundly enriched the cultural scene in the West. One ironic illustration is that some of the best literature in the English and French languages today is being written in the nations that were once under British or French colonial rule. Today, global interchange in the arts is playing the same creative role that the exchange of technology between different regions played in stimulating the Industrial Revolution. As one Japanese composer declared not long ago, "I would like to develop in two directions at once: as a Japanese with respect to tradition, and as a Westerner with respect to innovation. . . . In that way I can avoid isolation from the tradition and yet also push toward the future in each new work."[6]

Such a globalization of culture, however, has its price. Because of the popularity of Western culture throughout the Third World, local cultural forms are being eroded and destroyed as a result of contamination by Western music, mass television, and commercial hype. Although what has been called the "McWorld culture" of Coca-Cola, jeans, and rock is considered merely cosmetic by some, others see it as cultural neoimperialism and a real

# AN AGE OF POSTMODERNISM

*Postmodernism is the name that has often been applied to the development of the arts in the latter part of the twentieth century. Appearing first in philosophy, linguistics, and literary criticism in the 1960s, it soon spread to architecture, music, the visual arts, and literature. At its most elemental level, postmodernism is a critique and departure from modernism, the avant-garde culture of the first half of the twentieth century, and a return to selected aspects of traditional Western culture. At the same time, it has continued the twentieth-century countertradition of artistic experimentation, distorting and reordering traditional culture through the prism of modernity.*

The term *postmodernism* was first used in architecture in 1977 when it became apparent that traditional architectural styles were beginning to alter or erode the modernist international style. Of all the arts, it seems logical that architecture would be the most inclined to return to traditional elements, because it interacts most directly with people's daily lives. Architecture thus began to free itself from the repetitiveness and impersonality of the international style. In reaction to the forests of identical glass and steel boxes, and perhaps accelerated by a new enthusiasm for historic preservation and urban renewal, American architects began to reincorporate traditional materials, shapes, and decorative elements into their buildings. Anyone sighting an American city today cannot fail to observe its postmodern skyline of pyramidal and cupolaed skyscrapers of blue-green glass and brick. Even modernist rectangular malls have tacked on Greek columns and Egyptian pyramid-shaped entryways.

As we have previously observed, twentieth-century composers experimented radically with the basic components of Western music, from tonality and melody to rhythm and form. But like architecture, music relies on the financial support of a broad segment of the public. Audiences must support orchestras to perform a composer's work. Yet much of twentieth-century music has antagonized concertgoers to the extent that to survive, orchestras have performed mainly premodern music. During the 1970s, composers began to respond, abandoning radical experimentation in favor of a return to more conventional forms. Some use the "quotation" technique, refracting traditional music through a modernist prism, while others strive for more accessibility through a simpler and more romantic style in an effort to bring about a postmodern reconciliation with the past.

In discussing art and literature, it is more difficult to pin down postmodernism, emerging as it does from the philosophical skepticism of the age, which rejects the existence of universally valid truths. Most simply, postmodernism can be viewed as a methodology for distinguishing what is real from

the unreal in our age, which is being controlled and altered by the onslaught of mass media, "high-tech," and global consumerism.

Gradually artists and writers became engaged in politics, channeling their theoretical inquiries toward the rectification of social injustices. Seeking to reverse the traditional interpretation of history by heterosexual white males, some postmodernists championed the rights of feminists, ethnic and racial minorities, gays and lesbians, and invited them to recount their own individual stories. Advocates of postmodernism also expressed anger at the control exercised by the mass media over the individual consciousness, as well as the corporate ownership of public space. The individual mind, they argue, has been transformed into a simple screen reflecting an ever-changing series of images from the media culture.

Postmodern literature and art share several identifying characteristics. First and foremost is a common sense of irreverence, resulting from the perception of an indeterminate world. Couched in an attitude of detached irony, postmodern works enjoy laughing in the face of convention, absolutist theories, and the seriousness of modernism. Although such attitudes first appeared at the beginning of the twentieth century with Marcel Duchamp, the Dadaists, and the Surrealists, postmodernism has raised the pose of irreverence to an even higher level. As American author Kurt Vonnnegut (b. 1922) remarked in 1973, he had been "programmed . . . to insult" as a means of shocking his readers into demanding social reforms.

One popular form of postmodern fiction is the "rewriting" of a previous novel from the point of view of one of the championed minorities. John Barth's retelling of *The Arabian Nights*, for example, was written from the feminist perspective of Scheherazade's younger sister. A more recent novel recounts the familiar tale of Margaret Mitchell's *Gone With the Wind* from the vantage point of the black slaves at Tara during the Civil War. Postmodern artists use this same convention by superimposing ethnic, feminist, or homosexual images on familiar works of art. But perhaps the most successful vehicle for the postmodern novel is found in science fiction, which has traditionally focused on the relationship between man and machine. In the hands of postmodernist authors, modern human beings, increasingly deprived of human contact, communicate with one another through electronic chat rooms and experience computer sex, all the while wired to the world on a cell phone.

Source: Paula Geyh et al. (eds.), *Postmodern American Fiction: A Norton Anthology* (New York: W. W. Norton, 1998).

cause for alarm. How does a society preserve its traditional culture when the young prefer to spend their evenings at a Hard Rock Café rather than attend a traditional folk opera or *wayang* puppet theater? World conferences have been convened to safeguard traditional cultures from extinction, but is there sufficient time, money, or inclination to reverse the tide?

What do contemporary trends in the art world have to say about the changes that have occurred between the beginning and the end of the twentieth century? One reply is that the euphoric optimism of artists during the age of Picasso and Stravinsky has been seriously tempered a century later. Naiveté has been replaced by cynicism or irony as protection against the underlying pessimism of the current age.

One dominant characteristic of the new art is its reticence—its reserve in expressing the dissonance and disillusioning events of the past century. It would appear that we entered the twentieth century with too many expectations, hopes that had been fueled by the promise of revolution and scientific discoveries. Yet however extraordinary the recent advances in medicine, genetics, telecommunications, computer technology, and space exploration have been, humankind seems to remain as befuddled as ever. It is no wonder that despite the impressive recent advances in science, human beings entered the new millennium a little worn and subdued.

What, then, are the prospects for the coming years? One critic has complained that postmodernism, "with its sad air of the parades gone by,"[7] is spent and exhausted. Others suggest that there is nothing new left to say that has not been expressed previously and more effectively. The public itself appears satiated and desensitized after a century of "shocking" art and, as in the case of world events, almost incapable of being shocked any further. Human sensibilities have been irrevocably altered by the media, by technology, and especially by the cataclysmic events that have taken place in our times. Perhaps the twentieth century was the age of revolt, representing "freedom from," while the next hundred years will be an era seeking "freedom for."

What is comforting is that no matter how pessimistic and disillusioned people claim to be, hope springs eternal as young writers, artists, and composers continue to grapple with their craft, searching for new ways to express the human condition. How can one not be astonished by architect Frank Gehry's new Guggenheim Museum in Bilbao, Spain (see the photo on p. 203), with its thrusting turrets and billowing sails of titanium? Such exuberance can only testify to humanity's indomitable spirit and ceaseless imagination—characteristics that are badly needed as the world embarks on its next century.

**DOWNTOWN BEIJING TODAY**
Deng Xiaoping's policy of four modernizations has had a dramatic visual effect on the capitol city of Beijing, as evidenced by this photo of skyscrapers thrusting up beyond the walls of the fifteenth-century Imperial City.

# WORLD HISTORY RESOURCES

Visit the *The World Since World War II* Companion Web site for resources specific to this textbook:

**http://history.wadsworth.com/duiker_wwii/**

The Wadsworth World History Resource Center at **http://history.wadsworth.com/world/** offers a variety of tools to help you succeed in this course, including access to quizzes; images; documents; interactive simulations, maps, and timelines; movie explorations; and a wealth of other sources.

# CHAPTER NOTES

1. Henny Sender, "Now for the Hard Part," *Far Eastern Economic Review*, September 25, 1997.
2. Alvin Toffler and Heidi Toffler, *Creating a New Civilization: The Politics of the Third Wave* (Atlanta, 1995).
3. Quoted in John Cassidy, "The Return of Karl Marx," *New Yorker*, October 20, 1997, p. 250.
4. Fukuyama's original thesis was expressed in "The End of History," *National Interest*, Summer 1989. He has defended his views in Timothy Burns, ed., *After History? Francis Fukuyama and His Critics* (Lanham, Md., 1994). Fukuyama contends—rightly in my view—that his concept of the "end of history" has been widely misinterpreted. I hope I have not done so in these comments.
5. Samuel P. Huntington, *The Clash of Civilizations and the Remaking of the World Order* (New York, 1996). An earlier version was published under the title "The Clash of Civilizations?" in *Foreign Affairs*, Summer 1993.
6. The composer was Toru Takemitsu. See Robert P. Moran, *Twentieth-Century Music* (New York, 1991), p. 422.
7. Herbert Muschamp, "The Miracle in Bilbao," *New York Times Magazine*, September 7, 1997, p. 72.

# SUGGESTED READING

## Prologue. The Outbreak of World War II

For a general study of fascism, see S. G. Payne, *A History of Fascism* (Madison, Wis., 1996). The best biography of Mussolini is D. Mack Smith, *Mussolini* (New York, 1982). Two brief but sound surveys of Nazi Germany are J. Spielvogel, *Hitler and Nazi Germany: A History,* 3d ed. (Englewood Cliffs, N.J., 1996), and J. Bendersky, *A History of Nazi Germany* (Chicago, 1985). On Hitler, see A. Bullock, *Hitler: A Study in Tyranny* (New York, 1964), and Bullock's recent *Hitler, 1889–1936: Hubris* (New York, 1999). For an analysis of how Hitler changed Germany, see J. Lucas, *The Hitler of History* (New York, 1997).

General works on World War II include M. K. Dziewanowski, *War at Any Price: World War II in Europe, 1939–1945,* 2d ed. (Englewood Cliffs, N.J., 1991), and G. Weinberg, *A World at Arms: A Global History of World War II* (Cambridge, 1994). On the Holocaust, see R. Hilberg, *The Destruction of the European Jews,* rev. ed., 3 vols. (New York, 1985), and L. Yahil, *The Holocaust* (New York, 1990). On the war in the Pacific, see R. Spector, *The Eagle Against the Sun: The American War With Japan* (New York, 1991), and H. Cook and T. Cook, *Japan at War: An Oral History* (New York, 1992).

## Chapter 1. In the Grip of the Cold War: The Breakdown of the Yalta System

There is a substantial literature on the Cold War. Two general accounts are R. B. Levering, *The Cold War, 1945–1972* (Arlington Heights, Ill., 1982), and B. A. Weisberger, *Cold War, Cold Peace: The United States and Russia Since 1945* (New York, 1984). Assigning blame for the Cold War to the Soviet Union are H. Feis, *From Trust to Terror: The Onset of the Cold War, 1945–1950* (New York, 1970), and A. Ulam, *The Rivals: America and Russia Since World War II* (New York, 1971). Revisionist studies include J. Kolko and G. Kolko, *The Limits of Power: The World and United States Foreign Policy, 1945–1954* (New York, 1972), and W. La Feber, *America, Russia, and the Cold War, 1945–1966,* 2d ed. (New York, 1972). On the end of the Cold War, see W. G. Hyland, *The Cold War Is Over* (New York, 1990), and B. Denitch, *The End of the Cold War* (Minneapolis, 1990).

Recent studies on the Cold War in Asia include O. A. Westad, *Cold War and Revolution: Soviet-American Rivalry and the Origins of the Chinese Civil War* (New York, 1993), D. A. Mayers, *Cracking the Monolith: U.S. Policy Against the Sino-Soviet Alliance, 1949–1955* (Baton Rouge, La., 1986), and S. Goncharov, J. W. Lewis, and Xue Litai, *Uncertain Partners: Stalin, Mao, and the Korean War* (Stanford, Calif., 1993). For a retrospective account, see J. L. Gaddis, *We Now Know: Rethinking Cold War History* (Oxford, 1997). On the role of Vietnam in the Cold War, see F. Logevall, *Choosing War: The Lost Chance for Peace and the Escalation of the War in Vietnam* (Berkeley, Calif., 1999), W. J. Duiker, *U.S. Containment Policy and the Conflict in Indochina* (Stanford, Calif., 1995), and M. Lind, *Vietnam: The Necessary War* (New York, 1999).

## Chapter 2. Brave New World: The Rise and Fall of Communism in the Soviet Union and Eastern Europe

For a general overview of Soviet society, see D. K. Shipler, *Russia: Broken Idols, Solemn Dreams* (New York, 1983). On the Khrushchev years, see E. Crankshaw, *Khrushchev: A Career* (New York, 1966). Also see S. F. Cohen, *Rethinking the Soviet Experience* (New York, 1985). For an internal view, see V. Zubok and K. Pleshakov, *Inside the Kremlin's Cold War: From Stalin to Khrushchev* (Cambridge, 1996). For an inquiry into the reasons for the Soviet collapse, see R. Strayer, *Why Did the Soviet Union Collapse? Understanding Historical Change* (New York, 1998).

A number of books have appeared on the post-Soviet era in Russia. See, for example, W. Laqueur, *Soviet Union 2000: Reform or Revolution?* (New York, 1990), and C. Freeland, *Sale of the Century: Russia's Wild Ride from Communism to Capitalism* (New York, 2000).

For a general study of the Soviet satellites in Eastern Europe, see A. Brown and J. Gary, *Culture and Political Changes in Communist States* (London, 1977), and S. Fischer-Galati, *Eastern Europe in the 1980s* (London, 1981). On Yugoslavia, see L. J. Cohen and P. Warwick, *Political Cohesion in a Fragile Mosaic* (Boulder, Colo., 1983). For an account of the collapse of the satellite system, see

T. G. Ash, *The Magic Lantern: The Revolution of '89 Witnessed in Warsaw, Budapest, Berlin, and Prague* (New York, 1990).

## Chapter 3. Postwar Europe: On the Path to Unity?

For a general survey of postwar European history, see W. Laqueur, *Europe in Our Time* (New York, 1990). The rebuilding of Europe after World War II is examined in A. Milward, *The Reconstruction of Western Europe, 1945–1951* (Berkeley, Calif., 1984), and M. Hogan, *The Marshall Plan: America, Britain, and the Reconstruction of Western Europe, 1947–1952* (New York, 1987). On the building of common institutions in Western Europe, see S. Henig, *The Uniting of Europe: From Discord to Concord* (London, 1997).

For a survey of West Germany, see H. A. Turner, *Germany from Partition to Reunification* (New Haven, Conn., 1992). France under de Gaulle is examined in A. Shennan, *De Gaulle* (New York, 1993). On Britain, see K. O. Morgan, *The People's Peace: British History, 1945–1990* (Oxford, 1992). On the recent history of Europe, see E. J. Evans, *Thatcher and Thatcherism* (New York, 1997); S. Baumann-Reynolds, *François Mitterrand* (Westport, Conn., 1995), and K. Jarausch, *The Rush to German Unity* (New York, 1994).

On social conditions in Europe, see A. Sampson, *The New Europeans* (New York, 1968), and T. G. Ash, *A History of the Present: Essays, Sketches, and Dispatches from Europe in the 1990s* (New York, 1999). The problems of guest workers and immigrants are examined in J. Miller, *Foreign Workers in Western Europe* (London, 1981). On the development of the environmental movement, see M. O'Neill, *Green Parties and Political Change in Contemporary Europe* (Aldershot, England, 1997).

On the changing role of women in European society, see D. Meyer, *Sex and Power: The Rise of Women in America, Russia, Sweden and Italy* (Middletown, Conn., 1987), and C. Duchen, *Women's Rights and Women's Lives in France, 1944–1968* (New York, 1994). A broader historical view is presented in B. G. Smith, *Changing Lives: Women in European History Since 1700* (Lexington, Mass., 1989). Also see T. Keefe, *Simone de Beauvoir* (New York, 1998).

For a general view of postwar thought, see R. N. Stromberg, *European Intellectual History Since 1789*, 5th ed. (Englewood Cliffs, N.J., 1990). On contemporary art, consult R. Lambert, *Cambridge Introduction to the History of Art: The Twentieth Century* (Cambridge, 1981). Also see the bibliography in Chapter 1.

## Chapter 4. The United States, Canada, and Latin America

For a general survey of American history, see S. Thernstrom, *A History of the American People*, 2d ed. (San Diego, Calif., 1989). The Truman administration is covered in R. J. Donovan, *Tumultuous Years: The Presidency of Harry S Truman* (New York, 1997). Also see David McCullough's prize-winning biography, *Truman* (New York, 1992). On Eisenhower, see S. Ambrose, *Eisenhower: The President* (New York, 1984). For an insider's account of Camelot, see A. Schlesinger Jr., *A Thousand Days: John F. Kennedy in the White House* (Boston, 1965). On the turbulent decade of the 1960s, consult W. O'Neill, *Coming Apart: An Informal History of America in the 1960s* (Chicago, 1971). On Nixon and Watergate, see J. A. Lukas, *Nightmare: The Underside of the Nixon Years* (New York, 1976). Other insightful works include B. Glad, *Jimmy Carter: From Plains to the White House* (New York, 1980), and G. Wills, *Reagan's America: Innocents at Home* (New York, 1987). On postwar Canadian history, see R. Bothwell, I. Drummond, and J. English, *Canada Since 1945* (Toronto, 1981).

On social issues, see W. Nugent, *The Structure of American Social History* (Bloomington, Ind., 1981). Popular culture is treated in R. Maltby (ed.), *Passing Parade: A History of Popular Culture in the Twentieth Century* (New York, 1989). On the women's liberation movement, see D. Bouchier, *The Feminist Challenge: The Movement for Women's Liberation in Britain and the United States* (New York, 1983), and A. Cherlin, *Marriage, Divorce, Remarriage* (Cambridge, Mass., 1981). D. J. Garrow, *Martin Luther King Jr. and the Southern Christian Leadership Conference* (New York, 1986), discusses the emergence of the civil rights movement. For the most accessible introduction to American literature, consult *The Norton Anthology of American Literature*, shorter 4th ed. (New York, 1995). For an overview of American art since the 1960s, see I. Sandler's fascinating *Art of the Postmodern Era* (New York, 1996).

For general surveys of Latin American history, see E. B. Burns, *Latin America: A Concise Interpretive Survey*, 4th ed. (Englewood Cliffs, N.J., 1986), and E. Williamson, *The Penguin History of Latin America* (London, 1992). Also see T. E. Skidmore and P. H. Smith, *Modern Latin America*, 3d ed. (New York, 1992). On the role of the military, see A. Rouquié, *The Military and the State in Latin America* (Berkeley, Calif., 1987). U.S.-Latin American relations are examined in B. Wood, *The Dismantling of the Good Neighbor Policy* (Austin, Tex., 1985). For individual countries examined in this chapter, see L. A. Pérez, *Cuba: Between Reform and Revolution* (New York, 1988),

B. Loveman, *Chile: The Legacy of Hispanic Capitalism*, 2d ed. (New York, 1988); J. A. Booth, *The End and the Beginning: The Nicaraguan Revolution* (Boulder, Colo., 1985); J. A. Page, *Perón: A Biography* (New York, 1983); D. Rock, *Argentina, 1516–1987: From Spanish Colonization to Alfonsín*, 2d ed. (New York, 1987); R. Da Matta, *Carnivals, Rogues, and Heroes: An Interpretation of the Brazilian Dilemma* (Notre Dame, Ind., 1991); and M. C. Meyer and W. L. Sherman, *The Course of Mexican History*, 4th ed. (New York, 1991). On Latin American literature, see N. Lindstrom, *Twentieth-Century Spanish American Fiction* (Austin, Tex., 1994).

## Chapter 5. The East Is Red: China Under Communism

There are a large number of useful studies on postwar China. The most comprehensive treatment of the Communist period is M. Meisner, *Mao's China, and After: A History of the People's Republic* (New York, 1986). For documents, see M. Selden, *The People's Republic of China: A Documentary History of Revolutionary Change* (New York, 1978).

There are many studies on various aspects of the Communist period in China. For a detailed analysis of economic and social issues, see F. Schurmann, *Ideology and Organization in Communist China* (Berkeley, Calif., 1968). The Cultural Revolution is treated dramatically in S. Karnow, *Mao and China: Inside China's Cultural Revolution* (New York, 1972). For an individual account, see the celebrated book by Nien Cheng, *Life and Death in Shanghai* (New York, 1986), and also Liang Heng and J. Shapiro, *After the Revolution* (New York, 1986). For the early post-Mao period, see O. Schell, *To Get Rich Is Glorious* (New York, 1986). On the Tiananmen incident, see L. Feigon's eyewitness account, *China Rising: The Meaning of Tiananmen* (Chicago, 1990). On China's dissident movement, see Liu Binyan, *China's Crisis, China's Hope* (Cambridge, 1990), and A. Nathan, *China's Transition* (New York, 1999).

On economic and political conditions in post-Mao China, see H. Harding, *China's Second Revolution: Reform After Mao* (Washington, D.C., 1987), K. Lieberthal, *Governing China: From Revolution Through Reform* (New York, 1995), and R. MacFarquahar (ed.), *The Politics of China: The Eras of Mao and Deng*, 2d ed. (Cambridge, 1993). Also see Bruce Gilley, *Tiger on the Brink: Jiang Zemin and China's New Elite* (Berkeley, Calif., 1998). Social conditions are considered in G. Barmée, *In the Red: On Contemporary Chinese Culture* (New York, 2000). On the controversial issue of Tibet, see T. Shakya, *The Dragon in the Land of Snows: The History of Modern Tibet Since 1947* (New York, 1999). China's changing relationship with the United States is dealt with provocatively in R. Bernstein and R. Munro, *The Coming Conflict with China* (New York, 1997).

For the most comprehensive introduction to twentieth-century Chinese art, consult M. Sullivan, *Arts and Artists of Twentieth-Century China* (Berkeley, Calif., 1996). On literature, see the chapters on Ding Ling and her contemporaries in J. Spence, *The Gate of Heavenly Peace* (New York, 1981). Also see E. Widmer and D. D. Wang (eds.), *From May Fourth to June Fourth: Fiction and Film in Twentieth-Century China* (Cambridge, 1993), and J. Lou and H. Goldblatt, *The Columbia Anthology of Modern Chinese Literature* (New York, 1995).

## Chapter 6. Emerging Africa

For a general survey of African history, see J. Reader, *Africa: A Biography of the Continent* (New York, 1998), R. Oliver, *The African Experience* (New York, 1992), which contains interesting essays on a variety of themes, and K. Shillington, *History of Africa* (New York, 1989), which takes a chronological and geographical approach and includes excellent maps and illustrations. Two worthy treatments are B. Davidson, *Africa in History: Themes and Outlines*, rev. ed. (New York, 1991), and P. Curtin et al., *African History* (London, 1995).

On nationalist movements, see P. Gifford and W. R. Louis (eds.), *The Transfer of Power in Africa* (New Haven, Conn., 1982). For a poignant analysis of the hidden costs of nation building, see N. F. Mostert, *The Epic of South Africa's Creation and the Tragedy of the Xhosa People* (London, 1992). For a survey of economic conditions, see *Sub-Saharan Africa: From Crisis to Sustainable Growth* (Washington, D.C., 1989), issued by the World Bank. Also see J. Illiffe, *The African Poor* (Cambridge, England, 1983). On political events, see S. Decalo, *Coups and Army Rule in Africa* (New Haven, Conn., 1990).

On African literature, see D. Wright, *New Directions in African Fiction* (New York, 1997), L. S. Klein (ed.), *African Literatures in the Twentieth Century: A Guide* (New York, 1986), and C. H. Bruner (ed.), *African Women's Writing* (Oxford, 1993).

## Chapter 7. Ferment in the Middle East

Good general surveys of the modern Middle East include A. Goldschmidt Jr., *A Concise History of the Middle East* (Boulder, Colo., 2001), and G. E. Perry, *The Middle East: Fourteen Islamic Centuries* (Elizabeth, N.J., 1992).

On Israel and the Palestinian question, see B. Reich, *Israel: Land of Tradition and Conflict* (Boulder, Colo., 1985), and B. Wasserstein, *Divided Jerusalem: The Struggle for the Holy City* (New Haven, Conn., 2000). On U.S.-Israeli relations, see S. Green, *Living by the Sword: America and Israel in the Middle East, 1968–1997* (London, 1998). The issue of oil is examined in G. Luciani, *The Oil Companies and the Arab World* (New York, 1984). For expert analysis on the current situation in the region, see B. Lewis, *What Went Wrong? Western Impact and Middle Eastern Response* (Oxford, 2001), and P. L. Bergen, *Holy War, Inc.: Inside the Secret World of Osama bin Laden* (New York, 2001).

On the Iranian Revolution, see S. Bakash, *The Reign of the Ayatollahs* (New York, 1984), and B. Rubin, *Iran Since the Revolution* (Boulder, Colo., 1985). On politics, see R. R. Anderson, R. F. Seibert, and J. G. Wagner, *Politics and Change in the Middle East: Sources of Conflict and Accommodation* (Englewood Cliffs, N.J., 1993). For a general anthology of literature in the Middle East, see J. Kritzeck, *Modern Islamic Literature from 1800 to the Present* (New York, 1970). For a scholarly but accessible overview, also see M. M. Abdawi, *A Short History of Modern Arab Literature* (Oxford, 1993). For an introduction to women's issues, see F. Mernissi, *Beyond the Veil: Male-Female Dynamics in a Modern Muslim Society* (Bloomington, Ind., 1987), and L. Ahmed, *Women and Gender in Islam* (New Haven, Conn., 1992).

## Chapter 8. Nationalism Triumphant: The Emergence of Independent States in South and Southeast Asia

For a recent survey of contemporary Indian history, see S. Wolpert, *A New History of India*, rev. ed. (New York, 1989). For two interesting accounts written for nonspecialists, see B. Crossette, *India: Facing the Twenty-First Century* (Bloomington, Ind., 1993), and S. Tharoor, *India: From Midnight to the Millennium* (New York, 1997). Also see P. Brass, *The New Cambridge History of India: The Politics of India Since Independence* (Cambridge, England, 1990), Ishrat Husain, *Pakistan: The Economy of an Elitist State* (Oxford, 1999), and C. Baxter, *Bangladesh: From a Nation to a State* (Boulder, Colo., 1997). A recent overview, packed with interesting ideas, is S. Khilnani, *The Idea of India* (New York, 1998).

On the period surrounding independence, see the dramatic account by L. Collins and D. Lapierre, *Freedom at Midnight* (New York, 1975). On Indira Gandhi, see K. Bhatia, *Indira: A Biography of Prime Minister Gandhi* (New York, 1974).

For a useful anthology of Indian fiction since independence, see S. Rushdie and E. West (eds.), *Mirror Work* (New York, 1997), and S. Tharu and K. Lalita (eds.), *Women Writing in India*, vol. 2 (New York, 1993).

For an introductory survey of modern Southeast Asia with a strong emphasis on recent events, see D. R. SarDesai, *Southeast Asia: Past and Present*, 2d ed. (Boulder, Colo., 1989). For a more scholarly approach, see D. J. Steinberg (ed.), *In Search of Southeast Asia*, 2d ed. (New York, 1985). On Thailand, see P. Phongpaichit and C. Baker, *Thailand's Crisis* (Singapore, 2001). The best overall survey of the Philippines is D. J. Steinberg, *The Philippines: A Singular and a Plural Place* (Boulder, Colo., 1994). For a recent treatment of politics in Singapore, see R. Vasil, *Governing Singapore: A History of National Development and Democracy* (Singapore, 2000). For insight into the problem of racial divisions in Malaysia, see M. bin Mohamad, *The Malay Dilemma* (Kuala Lumpur, 1970).

There is a rich selection of materials on modern Indonesia. On the Sukarno era, see J. Legge, *Sukarno* (New York, 1972). On the Suharto era and its origins, see M. Vatikiotis, *Indonesian Politics Under Suharto* (London, 1993). The most up-to-date treatment of Indonesia in its present state of crisis is G. Lloyd and S. Smith (eds.), *Indonesia Today: Challenges of History* (Singapore, 2001). Most of the literature on Indochina in recent decades has dealt with the Vietnam War and related conflicts in Laos and Cambodia. On conditions in Vietnam since the end of the war, see R. Shaplen, *Bitter Victory* (New York, 1986), a study by a veteran journalist, and W. J. Duiker, *Vietnam: Revolution in Transition*, 2d ed. (Boulder, Colo., 1995). For an excellent anthology of contemporary Vietnamese fiction, see *Vietnam: A Traveler's Literary Companion* (San Francisco, 1996).

## Chapter 9. Toward the Pacific Century?

The number of books in English on modern Japan has increased in direct proportion to Japan's rise as a major industrial power. The immediate postwar era is dealt with in J. W. Dower, *Embracing Defeat: Japan in the Wake of World War II* (New York, 1999). For a topical approach with a strong emphasis on social matters, J. E. Hunter, *The Emergence of Modern Japan: An Introductory History Since 1853* (London, 1989), is excellent.

Relatively little has been written on Japanese politics and government. A good treatment, if somewhat outdated, is J. A. A. Stockwin, *Japan: Divided Politics in a Growth Economy* (London, 1982). Political dissent and its consequences are dealt with in N. Fields, *In the Realm of the Dying Emperor* (New York, 1991). For a contemporary treatment of economic conditions in Japan, see D. Flath, *The Japanese Economy* (Oxford, 2000). Japanese social issues are treated in R. J. Hendry, *Understanding Japanese Society* (London, 1987), and T. C. Bestor, *Neighborhood Tokyo* (Stanford, Calif., 1989). On the role of women in modern Japan, see S. Buckley, *Broken Silence: Voices of Japanese Feminism* (Berkeley, Calif., 1996), N. Bornoff, *Pink Samurai: Love, Marriage, and Sex in Contemporary Japan* (New York, 1991), and K. Fujimura-Fanselow and A. Kameda (eds.), *Japanese Women* (New York, 1995).

Books attempting to explain Japanese economic issues have become a growth industry. The classic account of the Japanese miracle is E. F. Vogel, *Japan as Number One: Lessons for America* (Cambridge, Mass., 1979). For a provocative response providing insight into Japan's current economic weakness, see J. Woronoff, *Japan as—Anything but—Number One* (Armonk, N.Y., 1991). On the role of government in promoting business in Japan, see C. Johnson, *MITI and the Japanese Miracle* (Stanford, Calif., 1982). For the impact of economics on society, see R. J. Smith, *Kurusu: The Price of Progress in a Japanese Village* (Stanford, Calif., 1978).

On Japanese literature after World War II, see D. Keene, *Dawn to the West: Japanese Literature in the Modern Era* (New York, 1984), and A. Birnbaum, *Monkey Brain Sushi: New Tastes in Japanese Fiction* (Tokyo, 1991). For Japanese fiction, see K. Oe, *Teach Us to Outgrow Our Madness* (New York, 1977) and *The Silent Cry* (Tokyo, 1974). See also H. Murakami, *The Wind-Up Bird Chronicle* (New York, 1997).

On the four Little Tigers and their economic development, see E. F. Vogel, *The Four Little Dragons: The Spread of Industrialization in East Asia* (Cambridge, Mass., 1991), J. W. Morley (ed.), *Driven by Growth: Political Change in the Asia-Pacific Region* (Armonk, N.Y., 1992), and J. Woronoff, *Asia's Miracle Economies* (New York, 1986). For individual treatments of the Little Tigers, see

H. Sohn, *Authoritarianism and Opposition in South Korea* (London, 1989), D. F. Simon, *Taiwan: Beyond the Economic Miracle* (Armonk, N.Y., 1992), Lee Kuan-yew, *From Third World to First: The Singapore Story, 1965–2000* (New York, 2000), and K. Rafferty, *City on the Rocks: Hong Kong's Uncertain Future* (London, 1991).

## Chapter 10. Constructing a New World Order

For divergent visions of the future world order (or disorder), see S. P. Huntington, *The Clash of Civilizations and the Remaking of World Order* (New York, 1996), and F. Fukuyama, *The End of History and the Last Man* (New York, 1992). Also of interest is J. Scott, *Seeing like a State: How Certain Schemes to Improve the Human Condition Have Failed* (New Haven, Conn., 1998). An account of the impact of the fall of communism is contained in R. Skidelsky, *The Road from Serfdom: The Economic and Political Consequences of the End of Communism* (New York, 1996). Also see F. Furet, *The Passing of an Illusion: The Idea of Communism in the Twentieth Century* (Chicago, 1999).

On the Technological Revolution and its impact, see A. Toffler and H. Toffler, *Creating a New Civilization: The Politics of the Third Wave* (Atlanta, 1997). On the dangers of globalization, see J. E. Stiglitz, *Globalism and Its Discontents* (New York, 2002). For a fascinating analysis of the contrasting pulls of globalization and diversification in the world today, see B. R. Barber, *Jihad vs. McWorld* (New York, 1995).

On current trends in the cultural field, see B. Nettl et al., *Excursions in World Music*, 2d ed. (Upper Saddle River, N.J., 1997), P. Geyh et al. (eds.), *Postmodern American Fiction: A Norton Anthology* (New York, 1998), and D. Damrosch, *What Is World Literature?* (Princeton, N.J., 2003).

# PHOTO CREDITS

# INDEX

A page number followed by *p* indicates a photograph; a page number followed by *m* indicates a map.

## D

*The Dark Child* (Lay), 138
Dayton Accords (1995), 72
Deconstruction doctrine, 79
Dei-Anang, Michael Francis, 124–125
De Klerk, F. W., 133
Democracy
    China's New Democracy model of, 103–104
    Indonesia's Guided Democracy model of, 172
    Israeli practice of, 152
    Japanese experiment (1920s) with, 7
    recent trends in Asian, 174, 197–198, 201–202, 214–215
    rise of dictatorial regimes retreating from, 200–201, 214
Democracy Wall of 1979 (People's Republic of China), 108
Democratic Republic of the Congo, 127, 133–134
Deng Xiaoping, 106–109, 112–113
Dependency theory, 200–201
Desai, Anita, 170
*Détente* (U.S.-Soviet), 38–39
Devi, Phoolan ("bandit queen"), 169
*Devil on the Cross* (Ngugi Wa Thiong'o), 138
Dictatorial regimes
    Latin American move toward, 92–94
    rise of European, 5
Diefenbaker, John, 88
Ding Ling, 116
*Disgrace* (Coetzee), 138
*Doctor Zhivago* (Pasternak), 55
Domingo, Placido, 217
Dongo, Margaret, 137
Don Segundo Sombra (Guiraldes), 138
Drug culture, 210–211
Dubcek, Alexander, 54
Dubois, W.E.B., 129
Duchamp, Marcel, 96
Duong Thu Huong, 177
Dutch colonialism, 12, 15, 19
Dutch East Indies, 12, 15, 19

## E

Eastern European states
    adoption/rejection of communism by, 51–54, 64, 66, 71
    authoritarian governments of pre-W.W. II, 5
    Brezhnev Doctrine on, 53–54
    cultural/social developments in, 54–58
    map of former Soviet Union and, 59m
    map of Soviet Union and, 52m
    NATO membership by, 75–76
    NATO plans to expand into, 75–76
    from Soviet satellites to sovereign, 71
    territorial changes after W.W. II in, 21–22
    Truman Doctrine and containment of, 28–32
East Germany. *See* GDR (German Democratic Republic) [East Germany]
East Pakistan (Bangladesh), 162–163
East Timor, 175
EC (European Community), 71, 72, 75
Echeverría, Luis, 94
Economic development
    China's collectivization land reform and, 104–106
    under Deng leadership in China, 108
    economics of oil and Middle Eastern, 152–154
    failure of China's Great Leap Forward, 202
    Great British postwar, 66, 69–70
    Great Depression (1930s) and, 4
    under Japanese *zaibatsu* system, 7
    of Latin America during interwar years, 90
    of Latin America (1960s), 88–95
    "little tigers" and Asian, 193–198
    Nazi Germany, 4–5
    by new African states, 129–134
    postwar European, 65, 71, 75–76
    of postwar India, 165–167
    of postwar Japan, 184–186
    of South Korea, 190–192
    Soviet Five-Year Plans for, 6–7, 46–48
    Soviet NEP program and, 6
    of Soviet Union during Brezhnev years, 48–49
    U.S. New Deal programs for, 83–84
    of U.S. during 1950s/1960s, 208–209
ECSC (European Coal and Steel Community), 70
Educational system
    changes in postwar European, 76–77
    in Eastern European communist states, 56–57
    postwar Japanese, 186–187
    student protest movement of postwar, 94
    in U.S., 84, 86, 101
EEC (European Economic Community), 70–71
Egypt
    colonial rule of, 126, 144
    nationalism of Suez Canal by, 145
    status of women in modern, 155–157
    struggle for independence by, 127
Eisenhower, Dwight D., 16, 38, 40, 82, 91
Ekwenzi, Cyprian, 130
Elam tigers, 164
El Salvador, 43
Emecheta, Buchi, 140
*The End of History and the Last Man* (Fukuyama), 214

Enlightenment (18th century), 3
Environmentalism movement, 78, 96, 167, 212–213
Erbakan, Necmettin, 155
Eritrea, 132
Estrada, Joseph, 174
Ethiopia, 42, 130, 132
EU (European Union), 72, 74–75, 77, 155, 208
EURATOM (European Atomic Energy Community), 70, 74–75
Eurocommunism movement (1970s), 66
European Recovery Program (Marshall Plan), 65–66
European states
    cultural/social developments of postwar, 66, 76–80
    environmental and Green movements of, 212–213
    events leading to World War II and, 2–12
    Great Depression and, 4
    map of postwar, 31m
    Marshall Plan (1947) and, 65–66
    post-Cold War economic unity of, 206–208
    postwar economic recovery/renewal of, 70–71, 75–76, 207–208
    *See also* Eastern European states; International relations; World War II (1939–1945)
Existentialism philosophy/expression, 78–79

## F

Falklands War (1982), 93
Fa Lun Gong religious movement (People's Republic of China), 111
Family, transvaluation of values and, 210–211
    *See also* Cultural/social developments; Population growth
Family planning program (People's Republic of China), 214
Farah, Nuruddin, 138
Far Eastern Commission (Japanese occupation regime), 181
Farouk, King (Egypt), 127, 145
Fascism, birth of, 2–3
Faulkner, William, 99
*The Feminine Mystique* (Friedan), 95
Ford, Gerald, 85–86
*For Whom the Bell Tolls* (Hemingway), 99
"Four Modernizations" (People's Republic of China), 108
Fox, Vicente, 95
France
    Brazzaville Declaration (1944) on colonies of, 126
    colonialism policy of, 126

Mahathir Mohamad, 214
Mahbubani, Kishore, 195
Mahfouz, Naguib, 155, 157–158
Major, John, 74
Makoto Saito, 8
Malaya, 12, 15, 19, 172
Malaysia, 172, 176
Malcolm X, 84
Malenkov, Georgy, 37, 46
Mali, 130
Malthus, Thomas, 213
Manchuria
    returned to Chinese control, 32
    Soviet occupation of, 32–33
Mandela, Nelson, 133, 140
Mao Zedong
    China under rule by, 36, 103–108
    and Chinese Civil War, 32–35
    split between Soviet Union and, 39–40
Maozedong Thought, 106, 108
Maps
    of China today, 111m
    of Eastern Europe and the Soviet Union, 52m
    of Eastern European states and former Soviet Union, 59m
    European/North Africa W.W. II battles, 14m
    Europe today, 72m
    of Israel and surrounding area, 147m
    of modern Africa, 128m
    of modern Japan, 181m
    of modern Middle East, 150m
    of modern South Asia, 164m
    of modern Southeast Asia, 173m
    South American political trends (1960s), 89m
    territorial changes in Europe after W.W. II, 31m
    World War II Asian and Pacific battles, 16m
Marcos, Ferdinand, 174
Marshall, George C., 29, 34–35, 65
Marshall Plan (1947), 27–29, 65–66
Marx, Karl
    on capitalism exploitation, 45, 54
    on creating/producing activities, 212
    regarding socialism, 45, 54, 56
    Russian Marxism and, 75
Marxism
    application in revolutionary China, 104–108
    on classless society, 56
    Eastern European "little Stalins" (1950s) and, 51–54
    See also Communism
Mau Mau movement (Kenya), 127
Mbeki, Thabo, 133
Mboya, Tom, 132

Meiji Constitution (1889) [Japan], 181, 183
Mein Kampf (Hitler), 4, 14
Meir, Golda, 155
Menem, Carlos Saúl, 93
Mexico
    NAFTA agreement between U.S. and, 94–95
    postwar history of, 94–95
Michel, Samora, 131
Middle class, in India, 167
Middle East
    contemporary literature and art in the, 154, 156–158
    economics of oil in, 152–154
    Iranian revolution and, 148–150
    Islamic revival in, 154–155
    map of modern, 150m
    Palestine question and, 144–148
    politics in contemporary, 152–154
    status of modern women in, 149, 155–156
Midnight's Children (Rushdie), 171
Milosevic, Slobodan, 71–73
Minimalism music, 98
Minsuito (Japan), 7
Mishima Yukio, 157, 188
Mistral, Gabriela, 149
MITI (Ministry of International Trade and Industry) [Japan], 185
Mitterrand, François, 68, 73, 80
Mobutu Sese Seko, 129, 134
Modernist architecture, 98
Modernization theory, 200–201
Moi, Daniel arap, 138, 140
Molotov, Vyacheslav, 32, 46
The Moor's Last Sigh (Rushdie), 171
Morocco, 127, 132
Mo Yan, 117–118
Mozambique, 127, 131
Mubarak, Hosni, 152
Mugabe, Robert, 137
Muhammad V (Morocco), 127
"Mukden incident" (1931), 1
Mulroney, Brian, 88
Munich Conference (1938), 9–10, 43
Murakami Haruki, 189
Musharaff, Pervaiz, 165
Music
    Japan and influence of Western, 189–190
    of modern Africa, 140
    of modern Middle East, 158
    under People's Republic of China, 117
    popular culture, 98–100
    recent trends in, 97, 216
    in Soviet Union, 54
    trends in Southeast Asian, 178
Muslim Brotherhood, 154–155
Muslim League (India), 162
Muslims
    Iranian revolution leadership by, 148–150

Palestine question and, 144–145
South Asian conflicts between Hindus and, 164
spread of Nigerian conflict of Christians and, 132–134, 137
See also Islam
Mussolini, Benito, 2–3, 8
Myanmar (Burma), 172, 174–175
My Dream (Xu Mangyao), 117

# N

NAFTA (North American Free Trade Association), 94–95, 208
Nagasaki bombing (1945), 17
Nagy, Imre, 53
Naipaul, V. S., 171
Nanjing massacre (1937), 184
Nasrin, Taslima, 171
Nasser, Gamal Abdul, 132, 145–146, 152–153, 156, 158
Nationalism
    end of Cold War and emergence of "exaggerated," 207
    Pan-Africanism and, 129–130
Nationalist party (Guomindang) [China]
    rule of Taiwan by, 192–193
National Socialists (Nazi Germany), 4–5
NATO (North Atlantic Treaty Organization)
    creation of, 29–30, 70, 74–75
    European unity and expansion of, 61, 75–76
    France pulled out of, 68
    peace-keeping duties of, 216
    plans to expand into Eastern Europe, 75–76
Nazi Germany
    Blitzkrieg (Lightning war) strategy used by, 12
    events leading to World War II and, 8–12
    Hitler and, 2–5, 8–10, 12–15
    rise to power by, 2–4
    See also Germany; World War II (1939–1945)
Nazi-Soviet Nonaggression Pact (1939), 10, 12
Nehru, Jawaharlal, 162–163, 165, 166
Neo-Nazi groups, 75
NEP (New Economic Policy) [Soviet Union], 6, 104
Netanyahu, Benjamin, 147
Netherlands, the, 13
New Deal (U.S.), 83–84
New Democracy (People's Republic of China), 104–106
New World Order
    George Bush on, 62, 207
    global or clash of civilizations in, 207
    post-Cold War and, 207
    postwar progress toward, 82

Religion
  breakup of East and West Pakistan and, 163
  in contemporary life, 211–216
  as element of India-Pakistan conflict, 160
  incompatibility of science and Western, 211
  People's Republic of China and tolerance of, 111
  of postwar Japan, 188–189
Religious conflicts
  East Timor Muslim-Christian, 175
  Indonesian Muslims demands for Islamic state, 173, 175
  Northern Ireland, 70
  persecution of Bosnian Muslims, 71–72
  South Asia Hindu-Islam, 166
  spread of Nigerian, 133
  See also Anti-Semitism; Palestine
The Republic of Wine (Mo Yan), 117
Rhee Syngman, 190
Robbe-Grillet, Alain, 79
ROC (Republic of China). See Taiwan
Roh Tae Woo, 191
Romania, 9, 15
Rommel, Erwin, 15, 144
Roosevelt, Franklin Delano, 12, 15, 17, 22, 26, 27, 32, 200
Rushdie, Salman, 171
Russia (post-Soviet)
  developments following creation of, 60–61
  events leading to, 58–60
  map of Eastern Europe and, 59m
  See also Soviet Union
Rwanda, 133

# S

Sakharov, Andrei, 48
Salcedo, Doris, 97
Salina, Carlos, 94
SALT II (1979), 42
SALT I treaty (1972), 42
Sandinista National Liberation Front (Nicaragua), 43, 92
Sandinista regime (Nicaragua), 43, 92
Saramago, José, 79–80
Saro-Wiwa, Ken, 133
Sarraute, Nathalie, 79
Sartre, Jean-Paul, 78–79
The Satanic Verses (Rushdie), 171
Sati, 170
Saudi Arabia, 113, 145, 148, 152
Savimbi, Julius, 132
Schlesinger, Arthur F., Jr., 85
Schmidt, Helmut, 69
Scientific developments
  incompatibility of Western religion and, 211

postwar alliance of technology and, 100–101
  See also Technology
SDI (Strategic Defense Initiative) [U.S.], 43
Second Class Citizen (Emecheta), 140
Second Sex, the (Beauvior), 78
Seiyukai (Japan), 7
Senegal, 126, 129
Senghor, Leopold, 129, 132
Serbia, independence from Yugoslavia (1991) by, 71
Serbian "ethnic cleansing," 72–73
Sexual revolution (1960s), 77, 211
Shame, A Novel (Nastin), 171
Shamir, Itzhak, 147
Sharon, Ariel, 148, 158
Shidehara diplomacy (Japan), 7
Shoko Asahara, 190
Shostakovich, Dmitri, 54
"Shuttle diplomacy" (U.S.), 147
Sierra Leone, 134
Sikh separatism issue (India), 164, 165–166
Silent Spring (Carson), 96
Singapore, 98, 193–195
Sino-Soviet dispute, 39–40
Slavery, in Africa, 135
SLORC (Myanmar), 175
Slovakia, 75
Slovenia, 71
Social change. See Cultural/social developments
Social classes, growth of Indian middle, 167
Social Darwinism
  applied to colonialism, 129
  Western values as application of, 215
Socialism
  Ba'ath Party (Syria) promotion of, 145
  in India, 162–163, 167
  Italian fascism born within, 2
  postwar French, 68, 73–74
  postwar Great British, 69
  transition by China to, 104–107
Social Security program (U.S.), 83
Society. See Cultural/social developments
Soka Gakkai, 188
Solzhenitsyn, Alexander, 48, 55
Somalia, 42, 130, 132
Somoza, Anastasio, 92
Song of Lawino (p'Bitek Okot), 137
The Sotweed Factor (Barth), 99
The Sound and the Fury (Faulkner), 99
South Africa
  end of apartheid in, 133
  impact of colonialism in, 126
  new constitution (1996) of, 133
  political changes in modern, 132–133
  struggle for independence, 127, 132–133
  white domination of political scene in, 126
South American political trends (1960s), 89m

  See also Latin America
South Asia
  Indian art and literature of, 170–171
  Islam-Hindu conflict in, 162, 164–166
  map of, 164m
  politics of communalism in, 165–166
  poverty and pluralism problems in, 166–168
  See also India; Pakistan
Southeast Asia
  ASEAN and conflict/cooperation in, 175–176
  cultural trends in, 177–178
  daily life in contemporary, 176–177
  dismantling of colonialism in, 172
  economic achievements of modern, 175
  era of independent states in, 171–175
  map of modern, 173m
  recent trends in democracy in, 174–175
  See also Asia; Vietnam
Southern Rhodesia, 126, 132
South Korea, 190–192
South Vietnam
  division of North and, 36, 40
  invaded by North Vietnam, 40–41
  See also Vietnam War
Soviet Union
  Afghanistan invasion by, 43, 59
  Brezhnev Doctrine on Eastern Europe, 53–56
  Brezhnev years (1964–1982) of, 48–51
  Cold War and, 27–44
  Cuban Missile Crisis (1962) and, 38–39
  cultural/social developments in, 54–58
  "de-Stalinization" policy of (1950s), 47–48
  détente between U.S. and, 38–39
  disintegration of, 58–60
  dispute between China and, 39–40
  end of the Cold War and, 215
  glasnost policy of, 59
  Lyubyanka Prison in, 49p
  Manchurian occupation by, 32–33
  map of Eastern Europe and, 52m
  peaceful coexistence policy under Khrushchev, 37–38
  perestroika reform program of, 58–59
  postwar, 27–32, 45–51
  promotion of athletics in, 55, 57
  Reagan's "evil empire" policy on, 43, 45
  reflections on postwar, 62
  replaced by Commonwealth of Independent States (1991), 59–60
  space race (1960s) and, 100
  sphere of influence over Eastern Europe by, 51–54
  Stalinism of, 6–7, 9
  during World War II, 12, 14–17, 18, 20–21
  See also Russia (post-Soviet)
Soyinka, Wole, 133, 134, 138